Sinews of Empire

Michael Craton was born in England and educated at the ancient "bluecoat school" Christ's Hospital, and the University of London. For eight years he was a high school teacher, mainly in Nassau where he wrote the popular *History of the Bahamas*. In 1963 he migrated to Canada, gained a doctorate at McMaster University and began teaching Imperial and West Indian History at the University of Waterloo. Dividing his time equally between teaching, research and writing, Professor Craton is fortunately able to visit the West Indies and Europe frequently. In 1970 he wrote, with James Walvin, the first history of a single sugar estate, *A Jamaican Plantation; The History of Worthy Park, 1670–1970*. This led to the writing of *Sinews of Empire* and work on a larger study of slave society and individual slaves called *Discovering the Invisible Man*.

Sinews of Empire

A SHORT HISTORY OF BRITISH SLAVERY

By Michael Craton

ANCHOR BOOKS
ANCHOR PRESS/DOUBLEDAY
GARDEN CITY, NEW YORK
1974

The Anchor Press edition is the first publication of *Sinews of Empire: A Short History of British Slavery*.

Anchor Books edition: 1974

Library of Congress Cataloging in Publication Data

Craton, Michael.
  Sinews of empire.

  Bibliography: p. 385
  1. Slavery in Great Britain—History. 2. Slave-trade—Great
Britain—History. I. Title.
HT1161.C64 1974   301.44'93'09171242
ISBN: 0-385-06339-3
Library of Congress Catalog Card Number 73–16502

ACKNOWLEDGMENTS

The author gratefully acknowledges permission from the following to quote or otherwise use in this book certain copyrighted material:

Cambridge University Press for figures taken from sundry tables in *An Abstract of British Historical Statistics* by P. Deane and B. R. Mitchell.

Philip D. Curtin and the University of Wisconsin Press for data on slave exports and imports in tables on pages 26, 140, 150, and 199 of *The Atlantic Slave Trade: A Census.*

Faber & Faber Ltd. for statistics on the slave trade and East Indian immigration from Appendices I and VI of *British Imperial Trusteeship, 1783–1850* by G. R. Mellor.

Kenneth G. Davies for the analysis of slave-trading cargoes on pages 165–79 and 310–17 of *The Royal African Company.*

Douglas G. Hall for figures of land redistribution in Jamaica on pages 161–62 of *Free Jamaica, 1838–1865.*

Christopher Lloyd for data on the Anti-slavery Squadron in Appendices A, B, C, and F of *The Royal Navy and the Slave Trade.*

Bobby Moore of the University of Guyana for a quotation from an unpublished conference paper on slave rebellions given at Georgetown, Guyana, in March 1971.

Rt. Hon. Dr. Eric E. Williams for data from Chapter Three of *Capitalism and Slavery* and a quotation from pages 502–4 of *From Columbus to Castro: The History of the Caribbean, 1492–1969.*

Peter H. Wood for figures on South Carolina slave imports in a conference paper given at Rochester, New York, in March 1972.

Yale University Press for material from Appendix 14 of *Members of Parliament, 1734–1832* by Gerrit P. Judd.

Maps by John Morris.

CONTENTS

PREFACE

Since *Sinews of Empire* is something of a pastiche of other persons' ideas cemented and varnished by the author's idiosyncrasies, it is especially just that credit should be distributed widely while blame is retained. In a sense every scholar ever met and every book read has contributed; but particular inspiration has been drawn from the work of Elizabeth Donnan, Richard Pares, Eric Williams, Elsa Goveia, Philip Curtin, and Edward Brathwaite. More directly, the generous give-and-take of the slavery conferences held at Georgetown, Guyana, in March 1971 and at Rochester, New York, in March 1972 have proved invaluable. Beyond this, certain closer friends deserve special acknowledgment. The interest, advice, and criticism of Jim Walvin, Arnie Sio, Dick Sheridan, Roger Anstey and Stan Engerman have been constantly invigorating, as in a more generalized way have been the encouragement and stimulus provided by my colleagues at Waterloo, John New and David Wright, and by Bert McCready at McMaster University.

The book was begun in Jamaica, the bulk written in England and Canada, and the first draft finished in the Bahamas—all within the compass of the eight months "on," four months "off" of an academic year. A research grant from the Canada Council made much fruitful journeying possible, but the unremitting generosity and tolerance—the love—of others were even more sustaining. Especial thanks must go to George and Beryl Clarke of Worthy Park, Jamaica, to Terry and Julia Smith and Patrick Bethel of Nassau, Bahamas, to my mother, and to my brother David and Sherry, his wife. But fittingly it is to my department and university whom I dedicate this book. *Sinews of Empire* is the end product for which my colleagues in the Department of History were endlessly tolerant of bad manners and forgetfulness, not to mention absences in sunny climes whenever (it must have seemed) the Canadian ice was thickest. Many of the book's ideas were aired or even generated in the permanent informal seminar conducted in the departmental work room, a somewhat spartan refuge greatly preferred to a luxurious lounge on another floor because of the presence of an inextinguishable Cona coffee pot. Equally valued contributors were my senior students, for whom the developing book stood in lieu of a formal course of lectures and whose discussions and researches were extremely useful in shaping and polishing it. Garry Greenland, Eric Pickering, and Barry Wood contributed materially to the book. Not least of all were Heather McLeod and Debbie Lee Brown, who uncomplainingly became experts in translating the hieroglyphics that serve me as script and kept mail, Xerography, and typescript flowing promptly.

INTRODUCTION

The British slavery with which *Sinews of Empire* deals includes both Britain's involvement in the Atlantic slave trade and the institution of plantation slavery within the British Empire. Yet this is not a history of the Atlantic slave trade in general, or a study of slavery in the United States and those parts of the New World that were never British. Now that the British Empire is as dead as chattel slavery and formal imperialism of the old kind is also part of the past, such a study may seem unduly partial. The writer who detaches the topic of British slavery from the over-all pattern of European Atlantic slavery and from the study of imperialism in general may reasonably be expected to furnish some explanation.

One advantage of concentrating on one nation's involvement in slavery is, paradoxically, to widen the subject's normal scope. Most previous studies, even when claiming to be comprehensive, have in fact been severely limited. Because of the dictates of space they have generally concentrated on one aspect: the scandalous details of the slave trade, the lives of slaves on plantations, the movements to end the trade and free the slaves, or even on the vital but restricted topic of the relationship of slavery—in inception, development and decline—to European capitalism.

A truly comprehensive history of European Atlantic slavery would be a multivolume work consuming a scholar's lifetime. Yet within the compass of one hundred thousand words this book concentrates equally on all aspects of British slavery. Its base, framework, and core are treatments of British slavery's origins and organization, nature, and historical morphology. It also considers not only the attitudes and arguments of those literate men who profited from and defended slavery, or who attacked it, but also the actions and attitudes of the almost anonymous victims of the system. Its most original aspect is its concern with the legacies of slavery: in the fate of the free Negro, in the lingering social traces where plantations survived, and in the attitudes of the legatees, particularly the social historians of the ex-colonial world.

In considering the detachment of British from other varieties of slavery, other justifications besides comprehensiveness occur. British slavery, while for long dominant in the most powerful European empire, was ended earlier than elsewhere; yet a general history of Atlantic slavery would tend both to minimize the scale of British slavery and to describe it in anachronistic terms. This book, by concentrating on British slavery, aims to place it more correctly in perspective.

Certain facts are inescapable. Slavery was the basis of the most valued part of that British mercantilist empire which, in a later era and under a different covenant, came to cover 30 percent of the world's land area. British slavery by any account has had a decided, if indirect, influence on a large portion of the modern world. The slave colonies were never more than a proportion of the British Empire; the British slave trade nominally ended in 1808 and British slavery in 1838. Yet in the two preceding centuries of the British Empire's emergence, Britain's share of the Atlantic trade amounted to about 50 percent of the total, involving the forcible transference and brutal acculturation of probably two million African blacks. The value of this selective study, if not the guilt of slavery's British proponents, should be judged at least in like proportion.

Because, like most mercantilist empires, the "first" British Empire was based very largely on plantations that were themselves dependent on slavery, the participation of Britain in the slave trade was geared to the size and importance of the British plantation colonies. The eventual predominance of Britons in the European slave trade at the end of the eighteenth century was a natural corollary of the dominance of British imperialism at the very end of the period when plantations were commonly regarded as the most profitable type of colony. At the very moment of British plantation slavery's apogee, however, India, the independence of the United States and Latin America, and the Industrial Revolution encouraged a new type of "free trade" empire. Largely as a result, slavery declined toward extinction.

Yet in other parts of the world such as the United States, Cuba, and Brazil, plantations continued to grow in importance. Consequently, the institution of slavery—and even the slave trade—actually expanded and were intensified, in the case of the United States for thirty years after the emancipation of British slaves in 1834, and in Brazil for more than fifty years. Slavery in the southern United States continued deep into the English Victorian age and the period of industrialization in the northern United States. By the time that slavery was outlawed in Cuba and Brazil, England's proletariat had general free education, the penny press, and universal male suffrage, Italy and Germany had emerged as major powers, and Europe herself had already embarked on the dangerous course of a third "new imperialism" only to find the United States a manufacturing and trading rival.

Slavery between 1838 and 1888 was clearly very different in its nature as in its causes from that which had characterized the age of European mercantilism.

Indeed, slave-grown cotton, sugar, tobacco, and coffee —produced in areas that in no case were colonies in the strict mercantilist sense—helped to speed the progress of the unenslaved "Western" world. Yet these facts have not prevented commentators from extrapolating from examples in Brazil, Cuba, and the United States toward the earlier slavery of the European empires. United States writers in particular—demonstrating perhaps an imperialism of scholarship—have tended to generalize from a form of slavery that developed only after American independence and the introduction of Eli Whitney's cotton gin. This was in innumerable ways distinct from that found in their own areas when they were British colonies. In comparing and contrasting slavery in all British colonies before 1775 this book may serve to point up distinctions in American slavery that have hitherto been missed or glossed over. It cannot, however, serve in any sense as a substitute for the swelling output of scholarship on slavery in the United States or in other non-British areas, such as Brazil and Cuba, nor contribute more than a sidelight on the discussion of comparative systems into which slavery studies are increasingly being channeled.

British slavery was certainly in many ways distinct. The recent phase of comparative studies has emphasized differences as much as common ground. For example, the earlier generalizations of Eugene Genovese on United States slavery, while brilliantly suggestive, have had to be revised when tested against other systems. Genovese's Marxist model of a pre-industrial, pre-bourgeois society or "civilisation," paternalistically closed, in which profitability was less important than social reciprocation, was extremely plausible in the nineteenth-century American context. But it could not be traced equally in the earlier "slave societies" of the British West Indies, with their practical absence of a recognizable indigenous master culture, their absentee owners and exploitative managers both exceedingly interested in profitability and uninterested in the slaves as human beings, their indubitably alienated blacks. Similarly, the study of all Latin American systems—or even of those of the Dutch and Danes—with their different laws, customs, and economic needs, allows for contrasts at least as often as comparisons.

One of the great advantages of concentrating on British slavery is the wealth of primary and secondary materials available. While this plenitude has lured many historians into the pitfall of regarding the best-known as generally true, the comparative dearth of material on non-British systems, particularly in English, has also allowed for rich speculative generalization in those areas. A study of British slavery has thus the best of both worlds: a host of illuminating hypotheses from other areas, and an almost inexhaustible fund of information against which to test them. In this book then, what came before the initiation of British slavery toward the end of the sixteenth century and what came after 1838 will be treated to the degree necessary in order to establish origins and legacies; to place British slavery in context. What went on in other imperial systems will only be treated where tangential, or where comparisons are invaluable.

Attempting an overview of European Atlantic slavery in this narrow space is dangerous; but an equal or greater danger lies in failing to reconcile "imperialist" and "colonial" (or ex-colonial) interpretations. Each side has its array of myths, and even if these cannot be fully recognized and treated in themselves as historical facts, some sort of respectable balance must be sought. Proponents of the former school, those who maintain that imperial and colonial history, even when viewed critically, can only be interpreted from the metropolis outward, have had their day. To maintain today that British or even European influences were determinant in slave society seems hopelessly to distort the facts. But should a scholar go over entirely to the revisionists? These maintain that European involvement was but a transitory phase in the history of imperialistic capitalism, that the determinant in "slave society" (which includes whites as well as blacks) was the black slave, and that the crucial poles that slavery bridged were the culture of pre-Europeanized Africa and the creation of a modern black West Indian society.

Certainly—to paraphrase the impeccable formula put forward by Philip D. Curtin in *The Atlantic Slave Trade: A Census*—this book will contain little if any moralizing on the evils of slavery and will not apportion retrospective blame to the individuals or groups responsible. Slavery's evils—even when not inferred from the simple description—"can be taken for granted as a point long since proven beyond dispute." This does not in any way imply that slavery was morally equivocal or even that there should necessarily be a law of limitations for historical crimes, but rather represents a point of view that the historian works best when attempting to be neutral. Deleting the conventional references to morality and guilt will certainly save time and space; it should also help to see the past more plainly.

Rather, in dealing with the development of slave and postslave society in the British Empire-Commonwealth, the following study is informed by two notions that call for introductory definitions: syncretization and symbiosis.

Those who look for the origins of a national or regional culture entirely outside the area are likely to distort the facts. Societies, institutions, and cultures develop syncretically—that is, by adapting their original and dominant influences to the environment. In the slave plantation colonies and the modern nations that have evolved from them this syncretic process is to be termed creolization.

In his recent book, *The Development of Creole Society in Jamaica,* the Barbadian poet-historian Edward Brathwaite defines the concept of creolization in a way that is entirely convincing. By common consent, the West Indies have been shaped by two "great traditions," based on Africa and Europe. To most modern commentators, following the beguilingly brilliant analysis of M. G. Smith (1965), this has meant that the West Indies have therefore been polarized into a plural society permanently subject to tensions and alienation, and therefore unlikely to produce a truly indigenous culture. To Brathwaite, however, this conclusion is unduly pessimistic. By his analysis neither "great tradition" can be entirely dominant, distinct, or even relevant, since both are external or "nonresident" influences. On the contrary, the marriage of both "great traditions," or rather their syncretization within the creole context, has gradually produced an authentic "residential" culture that may in due course be recognized as an indigenous "great tradition" in its own right.

Related to the process of creolization, and perhaps the most intriguing of the characteristics of plantation slavery and its legacies apparent to the objective outsider, is the artificial symbiosis that occurred, in the sense of a reciprocal relationship, often paradoxical, between apparent opposites, as between persecutors and victims, cat and mouse. Symbiosis developed in an obvious form in the practically closed societies of the West Indian plantations, between masters and slaves. It has persisted to a degree between employers and employed wherever traces of the plantation economy are still found, without the absolutely rigid racial and color division that slave society embodied. The old love-hate relationship between imperial metropolis and colony is likewise continued in many guises in a world of nominal independence; and it is probably for these uncomfortable reasons that many nationalists in the ex-colonial world castigate nearly every undesirable feature in their present-day society as evidence either of "slave mentality" or "neocolonialism," failing to recognize that the past cannot be exorcised by sloganeering alone. An objective writer is no more able to assert with certainty whether it was race or class or function that determined slave society than he is to decide whether economics was the dominant or determinant factor in West African, West Indian, or any history. Such historiographic problems quickly resolve to the difficult question at the base of most historical inquiries: phenomenology or determinism?

These dangerous shoals must be skirted here, but the present writer still feels bound to acknowledge from the beginning the degree to which economic determinism informs his general method. In one sense at least the slave trade—like empire itself—was motivated by the conscious economic interest of individuals or groups, even when this was raised to the comparative abstraction of state monopoly. Concurrently, another human attribute was manifested: the tendency of needs to be rationalized as theories. These characteristics were evident throughout the history of British involvement in Atlantic slavery, though the question of whether they shaped or were conditioned by historical occurrences must be left to psychologists of human motivation or philosophers of cause and effect.

As early as 1562 it was apparent that profit might be made from shipping African slaves. But for almost a century the English made but modest progress, trading in West Africa almost as much for other commodities as for slaves, and in the West Indies torn between serving the needs of Iberian planters and salvaging their trade in cooperation with the Dutch and French. Gradually, however, it became apparent that the plantations and slave trade were capable of far greater extension than the Iberians dreamed. In rivalry with their former buccaneering allies, the English first moved into plantations and then began to grow sugar in large quantities, thereby multiplying the need for black slaves—though the problem of where precisely the capital came from that sparked or fueled the whole process remains open for debate. In 1700, the European trade in West African slaves was probably no more than 10,000 a year, but by the third quarter of the eighteenth century the West African trade rose to as many as 75,000 slaves a year. Of this total, English traders carried some 38,000, and English planters were responsible for a like proportion of the 150,000 tons of sugar produced annually in the West Indies.

From the first the English plantations and slave trade required and enjoyed the support of the Crown in the granting of monopoly privileges; but so potent was the motive force generated that planters, merchants, and slave traders themselves were able to impose their will upon the imperial government during the mid-eighteenth century. Though the planters jealously guarded the independence of their corrupt colonial legislatures, planters and West Indian merchants enjoyed unparalleled influence at Westminster, which brought them protection in a double sense (warships and protective sugar duties). Meanwhile the independent traders to West Africa and the manufacturers who provided them with trade goods, though they had fully overthrown the monopoly of the chartered Royal African Company by 1752, could yet persuade the government to provide £10,000 a year for the upkeep of the West African forts.

To the minds of the "imperial" and institutional schools of British Empire history, the slave-sugar empire was acquired in a haphazard or "absent-minded" way, in the sense that imperial policy followed rather than led. Yet the determinant—far from ill-directed or absent-minded—was from the beginning conscious economic interest; and the attitudes of traders and planters were conditioned by their economic needs. Commercial success—as readers, for example, of *Robinson Crusoe* can readily see—was its own morality.

Guilt was a later invention. Slaves were first valuable and then invaluable commodities; they were therefore depersonalized or even dehumanized. Captain Canot (c. 1800) was not using irony when he wrote of West African slavery:

> A man, therefore, becomes the standard of prices. A slave is a note of hand that may be discounted or pawned; he is a bill of exchange that carries himself to his destination and pays a debt bodily; he is a tax that walks corporately into the chieftain's treasure.

It is not at all surprising that blacks continued to be regarded as inferior in quality—among such extremists as the planter Edward Long even as a separate species of humankind—as long as it was necessary for them to be inferior in status.

The fourth quarter of the eighteenth century, however, saw two parallel movements, contrapuntally related to each other: the decline of the supremacy of the sugar plantations and the growth of philanthropic sentiment. An important function of this book is to reassess their relative effect: to see whether or not abolition destroyed the slave plantations, was a "nail in their coffin," or even was but a symptom of a decline that had already occurred. The early traders and planters were cheerfully—dissolutely—amoral; they were thrown on the defensive by the apostles of the Age of Enlightenment, who combined moral with economic liberalism. Opponents of slavery on religious grounds could be easily countered, at least until they won over a segment of the Established Church, for they were mostly sectaries. The defensive task became more difficult, however, as the notion gained ground after 1783 that the sugar colonies were the pampered darlings of an Empire that should properly expand into other areas, and employ a less formal type of imperialism.

The pious expansionism of the British Empire in the nineteenth century—the study of which so often serves these days as British imperial history—has hitherto conditioned attitudes toward the earlier, more ingenuously materialistic, Empire. As late as 1788 a witness before the imperial Parliament could honestly state:

> An immediate Abolition of slavery is incoherent with the Interest and Policy of Great Britain, that from the Silence of the Planters it may be concluded, they place such Confidence in the Wisdom of the British Senate as renders any serious Opposition unnecessary.

Even the arguments against slavery annexed as Further Evidence to the 1789 report were compelled to maintain that slavery was inefficient, and therefore economically as well as morally wrong. Thus the growing movement for the regulation, then abolition, of the slave trade, and for the betterment of the lot and final freeing of the slaves, while it was increasingly urged on moralistic grounds, owed its success (as slavery itself had owed it origins and extension) to material and economic factors that hardly entered the debate —a fact that explains to a certain extent the fate of the black after emancipation. In this modified economic determinism indebtedness must be acknowledged to the pioneer work of Dr. Eric Williams, though it will be clear that there are many points of divergence or disagreement.

This book is not mainly concerned with what people want, or need, to feel about history, but with what actually happened, and why. Yet even if this honestly inspired purpose is regarded as immodest or impractical, the book can claim practical value on other grounds. Although the area it covers is immense, with a length of no more than a hundred thousand words it can be no more than an essay. But it is the first book to comprehend so many aspects of British slavery, and should therefore have some value as a handy synthesis. Moreover, the subject of slavery is one constantly subject to scholarly research and re-examination, the piecemeal findings of which are often hidden away in journals or diffused in specialist studies. By attempting to bring together these latest researches and revisions, this moderate-sized work, while disclaiming great originality, can perhaps serve not only to give the interested general reader an over-all view of British slavery but also bring him up to date—at least with the questions if not with all the answers.

Let us begin then with one of the most difficult but intriguing of conundrums: Did West African slavery develop merely because of the labor needs of plantations in the Americas, or were American plantations developed because of the availability of West African slaves?

Sinews of Empire

Chapter 1

ORIGINS

The Need

British slavery beguilingly seems to begin with a single clearcut event: the first slaving voyage of John Hawkins of Plymouth in 1562. The great chronicler Richard Hakluyt, writing twenty years later, described the venture in his terse and tantalizing style:

> MASTER JOHN HAUKINS having made divers voyages to the Iles of the Canaries, and there by his good and upright dealing being growen in love and favour with the people, informed himselfe amongst them by diligent inquisition, of the state of the West India, whereof hee had received some knowledge by the instructions of his father, but increased the same by the advertisements and reports of that people. And being amongst other particulars assured, that Negros were very good marchandise in Hispaniola, and that store of Negros might easily bee had upon the coast of Guinea, resolved with himselfe to make triall thereof, and communicated that devise with his worshipfull friendes of London.[1]

Immediately it appears that Hawkins' voyage was by no means fortuitous. The Devonian came cannily to a trade already long in being. By 1562 clearly there existed a need for slave labor in the foreign plantations of the West Indies, blacks suitable for enslavement were available in West Africa, and the machinery of ships and capital had already developed in England to enable enterprising Englishmen to engage in what was regarded as but another potentially profitable trade. Need, supply, machinery: Hawkins was merely the first Englishman to realize the connection. Obviously, the British involvement cannot be understood without looking closely at its context.

Probably no one will ever certainly know the very origins, but the European market for cane sugar and the connection between sugar plantations and slavery —even African slavery—were anciently established. It is perhaps not fanciful to suggest that the sugar cane merely followed the westward trail of migration and adaptation blazed by more basic staples in a more ingenuous epoch, once societies had become sophisticated enough to organize the labor and skills necessary for its growth and processing. Scholars of agricultural origins and dispersals suggest that the sugar cane, like certain grain crops thousands of years before, originated in Southeast Asia and arrived in southern Europe in the Middle Ages by way of India, Arabia, and Syria on its way to Africa and America.[2]

The secrets of sugar production, like so many European "discoveries," were almost certainly acquired from the Arabs who, incidentally, enslaved indifferently both whites and blacks.[3] Arabs carried the sugar cane as far west as Sicily and Malaga, but its cultivation and processing by Europeans dates from the time of the First Crusade. Enterprising Venetians established irrigated plantations, mills, and boiling houses around Tyre as early as the 1120s, and other Christians extended the industry throughout Palestine and Syria over the following century. After the expulsion of the Christians from the Near East, the Venetians grew large quantities of sugar in Cyprus, even employing "Ethiopian" slaves, and the migration of the system farther westward may well have been sped by the decline of Venice in the face of Ottoman expansion. Christian control of Cyprus survived into the sixteenth century but, being vulnerable, its mines and plantations languished after the fall of Constantinople, and well before 1453 Italian capital had migrated to develop the sugar industry in Sicily, Valencia, Andalusia, and the Algarve, complete with systems of cane husbandry and sugar technology that were to remain essentially unaltered for 350 years. For example, the vertical three-roller mill, which was not improved on greatly in British plantations until the 1790s, was said to have been invented in Sicily by Pietro Speciale of Palermo in 1449.[4]

The renewal of conflict between Cross and Crescent that characterized the fifteenth century probably produced fresh supplies of Moorish Moslem captives to work Spanish and Portuguese plantations and mines, even as Turkish conquests deprived Europe of sugar from the eastern Mediterranean and black slaves from the Upper Nile. At the same time conflict with the Barbary Moors reduced the flow of gold dust and slaves from the western Sudan to the North African ports to an expensive trickle, even as the general European demand for gold to make into coinage multiplied.[5] Spaniards and Portuguese alike engaged in conflict with the Moslem paynim, but their religious motives, however sincerely felt, were tinged with material greed: the Portuguese chiefly for trade, the Spaniards mainly for land, and both for gold.

For many reasons the Portuguese were the pioneers, combining the visionary project of linking up with Prester John with the more practical aim of achieving direct access to the West Africa of which they had heard from Catalan mapmakers and Jewish entrepreneurs. As the result of Prince Henry's enterprises, the West African coast below Morocco was successfully discovered and explored and its trade first tapped. More important in the eyes of European Christians, a series of three papal bulls between 1452 and 1456 awarded the Portuguese Crown the monopoly of the African coast, significantly specifying the rights to trade even with the "Saracens," to capture lands and place in perpetual bondage all "pagans and unbelievers inimical to Christ."[6] To the Spaniards was left only the prospect of land and mines to the west.

It was the Portuguese who acquired Madeira (1419), the Azores (1439), and the Cape Verde Islands (1456) by virtue of prior discovery and effective occupation; but these were all deserted when they found and settled them. The Spaniards began their overseas expansion modestly with the acquisition by Castilians and Andalusians around 1475 of the Canary Islands (called by the ancients the Fortunate Isles), which turned out to be strategically placed on the latitude where the southeasterly winds for America began. In the Canaries the Spaniards found a primitive Berber people, the Guanches, who could conveniently be enslaved. Sugar plantations were soon established, and it was Canary canes that Columbus first carried to Hispaniola in 1493. The Canary Island plantations thus provided a model for those in the New World as they themselves had been anticipated in southern Spain, Sicily, and Cyprus. The chief difference was merely the greater distances involved.

It was also in the islands called Fortunate that the unfortunate problems of enslaving an indigenous people were first encountered by Europeans. The Guanches proved intractable and soon almost died out through abuse and disease. Yet replacements were fairly easily obtained from the Portuguese, who had first carried a heterogeneous party of African captives to Lisbon in 1441 and had a small trade in Guinea slaves well established by 1475.[7] Indeed, on the equatorial island of São Tomé in the Bight of Biafra, Portuguese settlers had developed a flourishing sugar industry based upon large plantations and the almost illimitable supply of black slaves from the nearby coast, long before Columbus first landed in the West

Indies.[8] It is chiefly because of the importance of the discovery of this huge supply of labor that Dr. Eric Williams has recently asserted that "the decisive landmark in the fifteenth century, representing the transition from the Middle Ages to the modern era, was the Portuguese exploration and conquest of the West African coastline,"[9] devaluing the famous statement of Adam Smith that the most important occurrences in the history of the world were the discovery of America by Christopher Columbus (1492) and the successful voyage around the Cape of Good Hope by Vasco da Gama (1498).[10]

From the time of Columbus' first commission from the Catholic sovereigns, the Spaniards in the New World were interested in precious metals, lands, subject peoples (if possible, converts), and trade—in that order. The quest for mines and the preference for that type of quasifeudal agriculture with which they were chiefly familiar in Old Spain led the Spaniards in time to focus on the American mainland, but plantations were established even earlier in the island and lowland regions where gold and silver were rare and hacienda agriculture impractical. In Brazil the Portuguese also developed plantations, though later, after a period when that giant province was simply regarded as a stopping place on the route to Asia or the source of a moderately lucrative trade in hides and dyewood. It was the non-Iberian powers that were destined to expand hugely the sugar-slave nexus of Africa and America, but long before any other European nations appeared in the Western Hemisphere the nature of the plantation economy had been fixed by the Iberians and most of its problems had already become apparent.

Having introduced the first canes into Hispaniola, Columbus wrote with typical enthusiasm to Ferdinand and Isabella in January 1494 concerning the future of sugar production in the West Indies, comparing conditions favorably with those he had observed in Andalusia and Sicily.[11] Soil and climate were indeed ideal and market conditions were better than for the other plantation crops that Columbus advocated or the Spaniards developed later, such as cotton, indigo, pimento, cocoa, and ginger. So insatiable was the European demand for sugar that prices remained level or actually rose for two hundred years[12]; but as in many of his assessments of the potential of the Caribbean, Columbus exaggerated the prospects for sugar under a Spanish regime. Sugar was produced as early as 1503, but it was simply cane syrup for local consumption; it was not until the first *trapiche,* or animal-powered mill, was introduced in 1516 that cargoes of sugar were shipped abroad. In 1535 the publicist Oviedo stated that there were twenty *ingenios* (factories) in Hispaniola, and four *trapiches* besides; but he went on to say that the potential was far from being realized. The wastage through poor technology or lack of shipping, he claimed, "would make another great province rich."[13]

Despite the fortunate combination of currents and winds, pioneered by Columbus, which made Spanish traffic with the West Indies one of the easiest long ocean two-way voyages, Spain never developed the large and efficient merchant marine necessary to exploit adequately colonial staples such as sugar. Related to this was the fundamental deficiency of Spanish capital, without which expensive plantations, in common with shipping, could not be developed or supplied with sufficient imported laborers, even if such were readily available. Oviedo wrote:

> Each of the important and well-equipped *ingenios,* in addition to the great expense and value of the building or factory where the sugar is made, and another large building in which it is refined and stored, often requires an investment of ten or twelve thousand gold ducats before it is complete and ready for operation. And if I should say fifteen thousand ducats, I should not be exaggerating, for they require at least eighty or one hun-

dred Negroes working all the time, and even one hundred and twenty or more to be well supplied; and close by a good herd or two of a thousand or two or three thousand head of cattle to feed the workers; aside from the expense of trained workers and foremen for making the sugar, and carts to haul the cane to the mill and bring in wood, and people to make bread and cultivate and irrigate the canefields, and other things that must be done and continual expenditure of money.[14]

Although the Spanish Crown at the time of Charles V made efforts to encourage plantations, by aiding the emigration of experts, granting protection in suits for debt and even issuing licenses for investment by non-Spanish subjects of the Hapsburg Empire,[15] the general policy of monopoly and exclusion followed by Spain served to inhibit the growth of plantations as of all overseas commerce. Yet probably the worst problems faced by plantations in the New World, Spanish and non-Spanish alike, were those of labor. Earlier it was discovered that, whereas most crops could be grown with work forces of a moderate size, sugar plantations, chiefly because of the need to harvest, carry, and process the canes rapidly, needed almost as many workers as there were acres in canes. Obviously, this large work force could only be efficient if obtained as cheaply and retained as long as possible, being forced to work under some form of constraint. These requirements demanded a type of slavery, though it was by no means certain at first whether the constrained workers should be Amerindians under the *encomienda* system, indentured whites, or imported African slaves.

The inevitability of the preference for black slaves can best be illustrated arithmetically. Amerindians were least suitable of all, not so much because they were unwilling workers, as because on plantations—as in mines and fisheries—they died out in horrifying numbers, largely through disease, at a rate that may

have been as high as 25 percent per year. Clearly
some form of imported labor was necessary, and of
the alternatives white indentured servants generally
worked best. But since servants' indentures were from
five to ten years in duration, this represented a "dropout" rate of from 10 to 20 percent per year, even
without the losses through death (most severe in these
early years of acclimatization) and escapes from the
system by the ambitious or hopelessly alienated. Slaves
had no term fixed by man on their service, so mortality
alone (probably never higher than 10 percent per year
once on plantations and generally much less) decreed
their dropout rate. Moreover, once the Atlantic slave
trade was fully in operation, the supply of fresh black
slaves was easier to obtain than that of Amerindians
or whites, and keeping up numbers was but a matter
of economics.

Traditionally, the first blacks in the New World
were free men in Columbus' crews, and the first slaves
were the domestics of some of the very first settlers.
The first slave cargo, consisting of seventeen blacks
and mining equipment, sailed from Seville to Hispaniola in 1505, and by 1510 the demand of the mines
and plantations was sufficient for the beginning of
shipments from Africa by way of the Portuguese.[16]
The Jeronimite friars of Santo Domingo forwarded
a telling plea to Charles V as early as 1516:

> especially that leave be given to them [the planters] to
> bring in *bozales* [heathen blacks] of the kind of which
> we already have experience. Wherefore here it is
> agreed that Your Highness should command us to
> grant licences to send armed ships from this island to
> fetch them from the Cape Verde Islands or Guinea, or
> that it may be done by some other persons to bring
> them here. Your Highness may believe that if this is
> permitted it will be very advantageous for the future
> of the settlers of these islands, and for the royal reve-
> nue; as also for the Indians your vassals, who will be
> cared for and eased in their work, and can better
> cultivate their souls' welfare, and will increase in num-
> bers.[17]

The subsequent influx of slaves was probably a fairly accurate index of the expansion of plantations. Oviedo wrote in 1535 that there were so many blacks in Hispaniola "as a result of the sugar factories, that the land seems an effigy or an image of Ethiopia itself."[18] Yet it is unlikely that the planters would have echoed his opinion, for though runaways and rebellions were already a problem, their own petitions to the Crown constantly reiterated the need for a larger supply of cheaper blacks. "We are dying of hunger through lack of Negroes and laborers to till the soil," wrote the Council of Santo Domingo in 1555,

> as a result of the fact that ships come only in fleets, provisions arrive from Spain at intervals of years, and we are without bread, wine, soup, oil, cloth, linens. When they arrive, the prices are exorbitant, and if we attempt to have them valued [or ask for credit] the merchandise is hidden.[19]

Official policy led directly to the Spanish planters being starved of slaves at prices which they could afford, as well as indirectly contributing to the lack of shipping and credit. From the very beginning the Crown had regulated the shipment and control of slaves, charging a duty that was originally two ducats per slave; but from 1518 the slave trade was a royal monopoly, granted not to all Spaniards even under license, but to individuals, companies or, ultimately, countries, in the form of *asientos*, or monopoly treaties.[20] Clearly, the control exercised by the Portuguese over the African coast was a severe embarrassment to the Spaniards until the uniting of the Crowns of Spain and Portugal between 1580 and 1640. Moreover, the large premiums paid by the *asientistos* for their privileges were added to the high cost of trading indirectly with West Africa and the duty levied by the Crown (eventually 7½ percent *ad valorem*) in raising the price of Spanish slaves.[21]

Catholic and legalistic sensibilities also hampered

the trade in slaves to Spanish colonies, producing different objections to the importation of all types of
African. First of all, Moslems and Jews (finally expelled from Spain at the time of Columbus' first voyage) were by reasons of infidelity fittest for capture
and enslavement; but their deeply ingrained religious
beliefs made them insidious influences in a nominally
Christian society, and their importation was expressly
forbidden. Yet Christian and educated slaves, despite
the value placed on them by some colonials, were likewise deemed unsuitable by the Crown; for, besides
the serious doubts as to whether Christians could be
enslaved, there were ample social reasons for discouraging the import of blacks who might develop
ideas above their station "debauching the ignorant,
stirring them up to be mutinous and disobedient to
their masters."[22] Obviously, the most suitable of all
were the unassimilated *bozales* of Guinea, unless
they came from tribes like the Jaloffs, who lived by
war. Yet even with *bozales,* official doubts eventually
arose, stirred by Canon lawyers and humanitarians
close to the Spanish Court. Bishop Las Casas, for
example, although he preferred Christians to *bozales,*
had originally encouraged the importation of Africans,
ignorant of the means by which the Portuguese acquired them and of the opinion that since they were
particularly suited to servile labor in hot climates they
would not die off like Amerindians. "Formerly" he
wrote in retrospect,

> before there were any sugar mills in Hispaniola, it was
> the consensus of opinion that if a Negro was not
> hanged, he would never die, because we had never
> seen a Negro die of disease. For it is a fact that the
> Negroes, like oranges, found this land more natural to
> them than their native Guinea.[23]

Events proved Las Casas wrong, and in his *History of
the Indies* (1559) he recanted, although by that time
black slavery had become so vital that his original

views had become entrenched among the planters as an article of faith. "As the number of sugar mills increased," explained the Bishop of Chiapa,

> (the water mills needing at least eighty slaves and the animal-drawn mills about thirty or forty), the need to import Negroes to work them also increased and so did the profits from the King's duties. The consequence was that the Portuguese who had long been carrying on their man-stealing in Guinea and unjustly enslaving the Negroes, seeing that we had such need of slaves and paid a good price for them redoubled their efforts to steal and capture them in all possible ways, bad and wicked. In like manner the Negroes, seeing in their turn how desperately they are sought and wanted, fight unjust wars among themselves and in other illicit ways steal and sell their neighbours to the Portuguese. Thus, we ourselves are responsible for all the sins committed by the Negroes, besides those we commit in buying them.[24]

Besides this, the morality of enslaving even heathen Africans captured in authentic wars gradually came into doubt in Spain. In 1573 Albornoz denied that the law of Christ "authorized the liberty of the soul at the price of the slavery of the body,"[25] and although his book was placed on the Index his ideas gained ground, widening that rift between metropolitan idealists and practical colonists that became a characteristic not only of the Spanish but of all European empires. A prescient reader might have anticipated this outcome even in the accounts given by Columbus in 1500 of the first white settlers in Hispaniola. "There are few who are not vagabonds," he wrote,

> and not one with a wife and children . . . such an abandoned race, who neither fear God, the King, nor the Queen, and are wholly given up to wickedness and violence . . . there are not six among them who are not on the lookout to gather what they can and depart speedily.[26]

It was the perennial shortage of black slaves and other supplies that gave clandestine foreign traders their first opportunities to break into the Europe–West Africa–West Indies triangle of trade; but this was aided by the alienation that had grown up between an impractical legalistic government and selfishly pragmatic colonial planters.

The Portuguese plantations in Brazil suffered from some but not all of the problems faced by the settlers of New Spain. The predilection for Asian trade, the lack of capital and shipping, and the greater difficulties of making return voyages with plantation crops, decreed that Brazilian plantations would begin later and develop more slowly. By the time of the amalgamation of the Iberian Crowns, however, Brazil had over 100 sugar plantations, producing 750,000 *arrobas* of sugar a year with a work force of 10,000 slaves, compared with perhaps 150 plantations worked by 15,000 slaves in the Spanish Caribbean, with an output (though not all for export to Europe) of some 600,000 *arrobas* a year.[27] By 1600 a Brazilian planter was able to brag that the sugar of Brazil was more profitable to the dual monarchy "than all the pepper, spices, jewels and luxury goods imported in the Indiamen from Golden Goa."[28]

At the time of the union Brazilian plantations were expanding rapidly while the Spanish remained almost static. This development was aided by the less rigid nature of Portuguese mercantilist controls, which permitted in practice a greater degree of foreign commerce and investment, by the lack of rigid discrimination against Jews, and also perhaps by that easygoing attitude toward miscegenation of which Gilberto Freyre makes so much.[29] Easily the most important asset in the development of Brazilian plantations, however, was the Portuguese control of the African slave trade down to at least 1580, when it probably amounted to 2,500 *peças da India* (or about 4,000 individual slaves) a year.[30]

Willem Bosman, one of the best of the early narrators of the Guinea trade, called the Portuguese "setting dogs," whose function was "to spring the game, which as soon as they had done, was seized by others."[31] The very success of Portuguese slave trading and Brazilian sugar (as well as the Eastern trade) motivated the Dutch to attack Portugal from 1598 onward, using the union with Spain as a convenient excuse—just as the English under Elizabeth I had used the failure of Hawkins' attempts at legitimate trade as an excuse to attack the Caribbean and Spanish Main. The Dutch seized the Gold Coast, São Tomé, Angola, and northern Brazil at much the same time as the English were settling Barbados and the Leewards and seizing Jamaica from the Spaniards. Although the Dutch were expelled from all but the forts of the Gold Coast, their involvement in the slave trade and the sugar plantations was a vital development. Expelled from Pernambuco, they carried their newly won expertise, their shipping, and their capital to Guyana, and from there to Barbados, where the introduction of sugar plantations and the concomitant surge in the slave trade amounted to a revolution. This was well described in the papers of Sir Robert Harley:

> It happen'd that the Duch loosing Brasille, many Duch and Jews repairing to Barbadoes began the planting and making of sugar, which caused the Duch with shipping often to releive them and Credit when they were ready to perish. Likewise the Duch being ingaged on the coast of Giney in Affrick for negros slaves having lost Brasille not knowing where to vent them they trusted them to Barbadoes, this was the first rise of the plantacion that made it able to subsiste and trafficke.[32]

From the time of the emergence of rival maritime powers in the period of the Protestant Reformation, it was rapidly evident that the Portuguese monopoly of the slave trade, like the Spanish monopoly of Caribbean plantations, was doomed. The Dutch, the English, and, to a certain extent, the French brought to both enterprises far greater resources of capital and shipping. They also brought greater insensitivity—a capitalistic pragmatism without Canon Law either to define and justify slavery, or to dignify it by protecting the rights of the slaves. Yet all else was inherited. As the Spanish had set the pattern of the sugar plantations in the New World, so the Portuguese had established the pattern of the slave trade in West Africa long before the English and other Europeans appeared on the scene.

THE SUPPLY

Despite the prior claims of Egyptians, Greeks, Phoenicians, Genoese, and Dieppois,[33] the Portuguese were the first maritime strangers systematically to visit the West African coast south of Cape Bojador, if only for the reason that they were the first who felt a pressing need to do so. The waves, rocks, and fogs that were thought to guard a "Green Sea of Darkness" were bypassed by 1434, and by 1475 the Portuguese were familiar with the entire coast and islands as far south as São Tomé and the River Congo. Because of this activity by Europeans a century before the English appeared on the coast (not to mention the tenuous overland contacts from an earlier period), it is extremely difficult now to estimate accurately the effects upon West Africa of European penetration and of the Atlantic slave trade that the English came to dominate. What is most surprising is not the European ignorance of Africa during the Middle Ages but the degree to which ignorance about the interior persisted after the "opening up" of the coast. The authenticity of Sir John Mandeville was not fully tested until the age of Sir Henry Rider Haggard. This legendizing ignorance, coupled with the eurocentricity of most of the writers on West Africa from the fifteenth century almost to the present day, has allowed the perpetuation of the contradictory myths that whereas the

Europeans did not introduce slavery—merely adapting what they found—it was the European contact that gave West Africa a history at all.

Greater knowledge and wisdom have now placed the contact between Europe and West Africa in better perspective—delineating, for example, the ways in which the Atlantic slave trade debased the indigenous African forms of serfdom. This more balanced viewpoint allows us to realize that it may not even have been the European contact that determined the turning of the inward-looking kingdoms of the savanna toward the western sea, so much as demographic pressures brought about by such factors as technical developments, migration, population growth, the evolution of states, and the gradual loss of water resources which has extended the Sahara Desert since ancient times.

The reasons then for the long-preserved isolation and integrity of the West African interior were threefold: geographical, political, and commercial. The European traders and their commentators, reluctant in any case to admit that Europeans were merely tolerated at the outlets and did not control the sources of their trades, always made much of the geographical and climatic factors that prevented them from penetrating easily into West Africa. They were much slower to acknowledge that an equal determinant was the sheer power and sophistication of the African kingdoms, which made them at least the equal of the political and military units of medieval Europe, and not vulnerable to outsiders until long after the changes brought about by the European Renaissance and industrialization. In such conditions a reciprocal trade was not only the best but the only possible form, and in this reciprocity even the commercial dominance of Europe was not established until long after the Portuguese period.

Rumor spoke of huge kingdoms deep in the interior of West Africa, little inferior to those of Europe, a re-

port that subsequent knowledge has confirmed was
largely true. Cadamosto (c. 1457) and Pacheco (c.
1505) were able to piece together scraps of information about Jenni, Mali, and Timbuktu from the West
African coast that seemed to corroborate what they
had read in the Arab geographies. João de Barros
(1555) recounted how the very first sailors heard of a
great king called Mandimansa, who may have been
the ruler of the Empire of Mali, then just past its
peak.[34] Beyond this, direct information remained
tantalizingly scarce. This was not chiefly due to the
official Portuguese policy of protective secrecy but to
the lack of actual progress inland. In contrast to the
ways in which they were able to penetrate into the interior as far as they wished south of the equator, in
the Congo, Angola, and Mozambique, the Portuguese,
like their successors, found penetration blocked in
West Africa. Even scientific explorations were only
possible from the end of the eighteenth century, when
the power of the kingdoms of the savanna was on the
wane and European analysis was clouded by controversies over the nature, effects, and morality of the
Atlantic slave trade, then at its height. It was not until modern times that European scholars were able
to sketch in the outlines of West African history with
any accuracy or estimate its determinant forces with
objectivity.

These forces were geographical as much as evolutionary. West Africa, like most of the African continent, has a generally narrow coastal belt and an interior plateau irregularly broken by higher lands, in
this case the Futa Jalon and Guinea highlands and
the mountains of the Cameroons. But these characteristics were far less important than the climatic conditions that determine the amount of rainfall and the
seasons when it falls most commonly. Highly distinctive climatic belts exist in West Africa, running
roughly along lines of latitude, and therefore at right
angles to the western coast but parallel to the coast

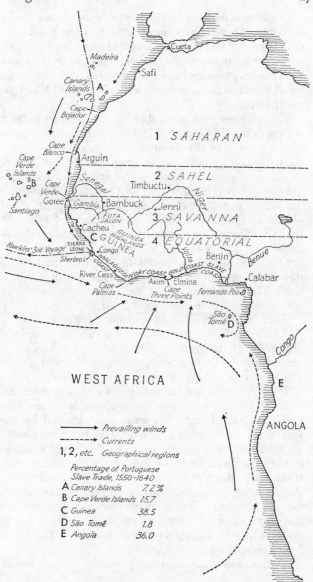

Madeira

Cueta

Safi

Canary
Islands A
D

Cape
Bojador

1 *SAHARAN*

Cape
Blanco Arguin

Cape
Verde
Islands
B

2 *SAHEL*

Cape
Verde

Senegal

Timbuctu

Niger

Goree
Santiago

Gambia Bambuck

Jenni

FUTA
JALON

3 *SAVANNA*

Cacheu

GUINEA
HIGHLANDS

SIERRA
LEONE

4 *EQUATORIAL*

C GUINEA

Hawkins' 3rd Voyage

Benin

Benue

Sherbro I.

MALAGUETA
COAST

Congo

Volta

SLAVE
COAST

River Cess IVORY COAST GOLD COAST

Calabar

Cape
Palmas

Axim Elmina
Cape
Three Points

Fernando Poo

São
Tomé D

Congo

WEST AFRICA

E

ANGOLA

→ *Prevailing winds*

---→ *Currents*

1, 2, *etc.* *Geographical regions*

Percentage of Portuguese
Slave Trade, 1550-1640
A *Canary Islands* *7.2%*
B *Cape Verde Islands 15.7*
C *Guinea* *38.5*
D *São Tomé* *1.8*
E *Angola* *36.0*

where it runs eastward from Sierra Leone to the Bight of Benin. These shade imperceptibly from the bone-dry wastes of the Sahara Desert in the north through a wide region of scrub (Sahel) and grassy savanna with summer seasonal rains, to the area of dense equatorial forest in the south, with heavy rainfall throughout the year.

The savanna was undoubtedly the most important region in the development of West Africa, at least until the coming of the Europeans by sea. Indeed, even then the areas where the savanna lands come closest to the coast were those where the first important trading contacts were made, in Senegambia and—through the occurrence of a stretch receiving less than 35 inches of rain a year—on the Gold Coast. An area of sufficient rainfall or irrigation (such as provided by the Tigris-Euphrates, the Nile, or the "inland delta" of the Niger) with seasonal variations in climate seems to be that most favorable to the development of civilizations. The interposition of a belt of savanna extending across the width of subtropical Africa north of the equator between two areas less suitable for habitation and more difficult for communications also explains why most of the formative influences in West Africa came from the eastern Sudan in successive but almost constant waves of migration.

The first great formative influence was agriculture, brought by black peoples somewhere between 4000 and 5000 B.C., though this was overshadowed by the spread of iron-working around the time of Christ. Agriculture developed far more readily in the savanna than in the forest belt, the more intensive system possible with shorter fallow periods and—eventually—deep hoeing, ridge cultivation, and irrigation providing the surpluses that allowed trade to develop and the enjoyment of the leisure that could lead to crafts, rituals, and government expertise. They also led to expanding population.[35]

At the same time, iron weapons, the greater mobility brought by the introduction of the camel and the horse, the benefits of trading contacts—made with the peoples of the Mediterranean to the north as well as those to the east—and finally the dynamic effects of the spread of Islam aided the creation and cyclical development of empires half the size of Europe, centered on the upper Niger and based upon a monarchy exercising divine right and a militaristic "feudal" system. The most notable were the empires of ancient Ghana, Mali, and Songhay.[36]

The pressure of an expanding population and the natural aggressiveness of developing cultures, exacerbated by the inexorable southward spread of the Sahara, determined that iron-age black kingdoms of the savanna kind (though without mounted troops) progressively conquered and colonized the aboriginal peoples of the forest belt. The deeper the forest was penetrated and tamed, the smaller the political units tended to be. Once the coast was reached, the distinctive type was a chieftainate only a few square miles in extent, though still based on systems of divine kingship imposed or introduced alongside improved technology in agriculture, warfare, and creative art. In some regions, such as the Nok plateau of mid-Nigeria (where iron was found in abundance) and at Benin in the Niger Delta with its spiritual center, Ife, these cultures had reached a remarkable level of development before the European period. Powers fluctuated constantly and the general process was continuous, only slowing to a halt with the imposition of modern political boundaries and alien systems of rule after the Congress of Berlin in 1884. What the precolonial European contacts did do was simply to introduce new forms of trade and new weapons, so that patterns —though not necessarily types—of rule were changed more rapidly than ever before. Paradoxically, this increased African resistance to European penetration rather than the reverse. Recently and rapidly developed forest nations such as Dahomey and Ashanti

proved to the end even more fiercely independent
than the kingdoms of the savanna.

There were obviously significant parallels between
the formative and reactive influences of the Europeans
on West Africa down to the partition era and those of
North African peoples such as the Berbers during an
earlier era. The introduction of the blunderbuss into
the coastal regions by European traders, providing
fortunate chieftains with corps of elite gunmen, was
similar in effect to the more gradual introduction of
the horse into the western Sudan, which brought
about the creation of a class of military knights in
"medieval" Mali. Yet while scholars are mostly agreed
on the general influences of trade and war, there remains considerable controversy over the details of the
ways in which the European contact shaped West
African societies as a whole, particularly in relation to
the exacerbation of domestic forms of slavery.

These controversies have recently been very well
summarized by J. D. Fage, who reduces them to two
counterposed arguments before putting forward a
personal assessment.[37] One common interpretation
(now almost completely *passé*) is, in Fage's words,
"that the institution of slavery was endemic in, and a
natural feature of, indigenous West African society, so
that when foreigners arrived in West Africa with a demand for slaves, West Africans were able immediately
to organize an export trade in slaves on an ever-in-
creasing scale." This viewpoint is most easily dismissed by pointing out that the examples chosen for
illustration almost invariably date from the European
period, so that it is difficult to ascribe purely African
causes; and also by the fact that the types of slavery
described were essentially different from those imposed
by the Atlantic trade. Archibald Dalzel's horrific descriptions of Dahomey (1793), for example, even if
not exaggerated for partisan reasons, picture a brutal
political regime of recent origin in which, as he admitted himself, *all* inhabitants were in a sense as

slaves to the King. Even Rattray's classic reconstruction of Ashanti society (first published in 1929), while listing a wide range of types of slave, provides little positive evidence as to how the system developed or which of its elements antedated the European period. Moreover, even the least free of the five main types of Ashanti slave, the *odonko* and the *domum*, had more practical rights than any slave on American plantations, just as the freest commoners in Ashanti society had less freedom of operation than their contemporary European counterparts outside the dominions of the Tsar.

The contrary view to that which exaggerates the rigor of indigenous West African slavery maintains, again in Fage's words, "that it was the external demands for labour which led to a great growth in the institution of slavery in West Africa, and so corrupted its indigenous society." The most distinguished proponent of this argument is Walter Rodney, whose recent work on the Upper Guinea coast carries a great deal of plausibility.[38] He not only shows by examples how the European slave trade debased societies in the region even beyond the fringes of direct contact, but also argues that slavery within normal definitions did not exist before the coming of the Portuguese. Unfortunately, the obscurity of the African sources and the variety and fluctuation in political and social organization leave Rodney's conclusions open to debate even in his chosen region. Besides, what may be true of the Upper Guinea coast was almost certainly not true for the rest of West Africa in general.

A less controvertible example of the ways in which the European slave trade changed an indigenous African society occurred in an area where the English trade was never dominant, the Kingdom of the Congo. There, a genuine effort by the Portuguese Crown to assimilate the people and open up trade on a footing of equality was followed eventually by the complete breakdown of the society under the pressures of the slave trade. Domestic slavery was well established in the Congo when the first Portuguese arrived in 1483, for the normal African reason that the kingdom had been established through conquest and absorption. But the only slaves whose export was permitted by the King (save for a few servant-slaves sent as presents) were those recently captured in war. Later, however, the demand for slaves in Brazil, coupled with a serious decline in the authority exercised by the Portuguese Crown, led to the sale of increasing numbers of Congolese, the King being unable to resist the blandishments and trickeries of the slave traders and the missionaries who were often their willing accomplices. The final stage was reached when the Congo itself was destroyed as a political entity and reduced to a tributary area by the Angolans, who had been armed and encouraged in their predatory incursions by Portuguese slave traders at Luanda. By that time the prestige of rulers like the King of Ngola was based not only on the power they gained by access to Portuguese guns but also on the numbers of slaves held as chattels as by the Europeans that they possessed, as by-products of their involvement.[39]

J. D. Fage does not deny the effects of European trade on indigenous forms of slavery, but rather maintains that the creation of a trade in slaves and the consequent extension of the institution of slavery were not functions uniquely of European but of all types of trade. Trade made slaves a valuable commodity, produced a leisured class that perceived the advantages of domestic bondsmen, and led to wars that accelerated the common African process by which nations and their peoples were constantly being subjected to and subsumed by others. Upper Guinea and the Congo were atypical in the sense that they had not developed the type of political unit based on trade before the Europeans came. Yet in areas that had done so—such as the kingdoms of the Niger bend and delta—there was, according to Fage, ample evidence of

> a close correlation . . . between economic development (and political development, because indigenous commercial activity was largely king- or state-directed) and the growth of the institution of slavery . . . [in the sense] that a slave was a man or woman who was owned by some other person, whose labour was regarded as having economic value, and whose person had a commercial value.[40]

Fage's implication that we should not blame the European contact but the influences of trade and state-building in general is ingenious; but it does depend upon the dubious notion that West African slavery was anywhere at any time before 1441 comparable to what it became under European influence. Basil Davidson, probably the best European summarizer of the West African situation, comes to different conclusions, though he does strongly develop the argument that West African society was akin to that of early medieval Europe and that many of the aspects and effects of slavery as it developed were common to both continents at different periods of time.[41] In both areas, the freedom of the individual tended to be jeopardized whenever the economic needs determined.

While warning against the dangers of generalization, Davidson draws a parallel between the situation in West Africa—where constant migration and successive state-building produced societies in which one segment of the population were the subjugated vassals of the other—with the emergent period of fedualism in Europe. In both areas there was a steady progress away from complete servitude among the vassal people, even if this process was accompanied by the equalization of the status of all commoners and an opening up of the caste distinction between the rulers and the ruled. In Europe there tended to be an evolution from slave to serf to peasant landholder who was practically free, or rather, a steady homogenization of all types within the laboring class. In areas specifically conquered, such as England at the time of the Normans, the process was particularly evident, with the indigenous people subjugated as a whole. The Saxons, however, resisted the tendency toward depressing them as a race toward the lowest level of pre-Conquest society, and tended as a whole to evolve legally toward the degree of freedom enjoyed by the freest of the "lower orders" before 1066. This process can doubtless be observed elsewhere in Europe, and in Africa the descendants of enslaved captives or subjugated peoples could become (as in the Empire of Songhay) "blacksmiths, boatbuilders, stablemen, makers of songs, bodyguards of their sovereign lord. Along with the 'free peasants'—whose social condition was really little different—these 'vassal peasants' and 'vassal artisans' formed the great bulk of the population."[42]

Bosman, writing in 1700, described slave caravans placed under the command of men who were themselves technically slaves but who possessed, in fact, more power than their nominal lords. And as late as 1861, the American black traveler Martin Delany went so far as to assert of southern Nigeria:

> It is simply preposterous to talk about slavery, as the term is understood, either legalized or existing in this part of Africa. It is nonsense. The system is a patriarchal one, there being no actual difference, socially, between the slave (called by their protector son or daughter) and the children of the person with whom they live.[43]

This compares intriguingly with the more contemporary remarks of the converted slave trader John Newton (1788), which ascribed the differences in slavery largely to differences in the intensity of agricultural needs:

> The state of slavery among these wild barbarous people, as we esteem them, is much milder than in our colonies. For as, on the one hand, they have no land

in high cultivation like our West India plantations, and
therefore no call for that excessive unintermitted labour
which exhausts our slaves; so, on the other hand, no
man is permitted to draw blood even from a slave.[44]

Strong rulers traded in slaves, but generally only with
people captured in warfare. Pacheco in 1505 described how the Benin traders were quite willing to
provide such captives, but regarded it as highly im-
proper to trade people who had come under the official protection of the *oba*, or King. This inhibition,
sadly, did not last. When the demand for slaves outran the supply of genuine captives so that their prices
became more attractive, the traders of Benin, like
most African middlemen, quite willingly traded their
own compatriots despite the strictures of their law. An
instructive parallel is noted by Basil Davidson to the
ineffectual bans of excommunication placed by Popes
Clement V and Martin V on the Venetians and Genoese in the fourteenth century, for persistently trading
in Christian whites as well as pagan blacks whenever
the price was right.[45] The *Communitas Christiana*
could not believe that these whites were bona fide
war captives, or even criminals, though it was far
more gullible when it came to the enslavement of African blacks. In later years the Europeans connived in
and even encouraged wars for which the chief motive
was the rounding up of captives, though it is hardly
likely that this sad phenomenon was new to West Africa. Wars with slaves as the most valuable booty were
at least as old as the ancient Egyptian excursions into
Nubia or those Roman campaigns after which thousands of slaves of all complexions were herded in
chains in triumphal processions.

The conclusion is inescapable that just as there was
much common social, economic, and political ground
between the Europe of Emperor and Pope and the
West Africa of priestly Kings, European rulers and
traders can be fully blamed no more than Africans for

initiating West African slavery. If there is a villain it is
trade itself; or rather, the complex situation whereby
a "need" arises for the placing of some human beings
in bondage to others. Even where slavery had not developed at all, the potential for enslavement existed
throughout West Africa long before the Europeans
came by sea. The need for huge quantities of chattel
laborers arose eventually from the American plantations, though not until the Portuguese had been on the
West African coast for more than half a century.

Once they had rounded Cape Bojador in their lateen-
rigged caravels, the Portuguese found the south-flow-
ing Canary Current and northeast trade winds excel-
lently suited for return voyages as far as the region of
Senegambia. By the time of the death of Prince Henry
in 1460 they had doubled the equally daunting Cape
Verde and reached Sierra Leone, but it took another
decade to brave the strongly eastward-flowing currents and onshore winds of the Gulf of Guinea and
discover that in the latitude of the equator south of
the Bight of Biafra these conditions changed, and a
west-flowing current carried vessels easily out into the
Atlantic and so back to Europe.

Currents and winds thus aided the European vessels venturing to West Africa once navigational aids
and provisioning were adequate for long voyages, and
these conditions were found to extend to transatlantic
voyages later. Conditions on the West African coast
itself, however, were less conducive to easy trade.
Only the value of West African goods and the expectation of their increase persuaded the Portuguese to
overcome the lack of harbors and navigable rivers, the
uncomfortable and often fatal climate, and the inimical attitudes of peoples such as the fierce Jaloffs of
Senegambia, whom Portuguese and Spaniards found
almost as untamable as true Moors. Indeed, these difficulties explain why the Portuguese preferred where
they could to work from island bases such as Arguin,

Santiago, and the other Cape Verde Islands, São Tomé and Fernando Po.

The first Portuguese *feitoria*—or combined fort and trading post—was established just south of Cape Blanco at Arguin in 1443; but the coast there was hopelessly arid and the Berber inhabitants, the Azenegues, few. Farther south, in Senegambia and on the Upper Guinea coast, the land was more fertile and populous as the rainfall increased. Adequate anchorages were more common, especially among the islands and "drowned valleys" of Sierra Leone and what is still Portuguese Guinea, where the tidal range is as much as twenty-three feet. But the rains here proved to be monsoonal, leading the Europeans to shun the coast during the torrential summer season. Moreover, as the people shaded in complexion and features toward the purer black and away from the cultural influences of Islam, their political fragmentation made trading relations difficult to establish and maintain. This was particularly so because the indigenous peoples, whom the first Europeans called Sapes, appear to have been in a process of disruption through the migratory incursions of other tribes given the generic name of Manes.[46]

Beyond Sierra Leone the Portuguese found areas more richly rewarding in trade and named successively, in due course, after their chief commodities: malagueta pepper, ivory, gold, and slaves. Yet this coastal stretch of over fifteen hundred miles, being equatorial in climate, was for the most part oppressively humid and extremely unhealthy for unseasoned Europeans, and with few harbors on a lee shore, trade goods, then as for centuries afterward, had generally to be shipped out to waiting vessels in small boats thrust through breaking surf. Here the Portuguese established their two most important early stations on the mainland at El Mina (1482), situated on that part of the coast of the present Ghana, which is freakishly dry, and Axim (1503), on what was then

the Ivory Coast. The importance attached to the
gold trade is attested by the very name of the former;
the difficulty of obtaining the gold dust and ivory
peacefully, by the fact that both settlements consisted
almost solely of formidable castles.

Until the sixteenth century the trade in slaves
(then, of course, only to Europe) was secondary—
and often incidental—to that in other commodities,
of which gold was easily the most important. The
Portuguese settlements at Arguin, on the Senegal and
Gambia rivers, and at Elmina, were obviously designed to tap the interior gold fields, the exact sites
of which were then unknown but which are now
thought to have been centered around Jenni on the
upper Niger, Bambuck on the upper Senegal, and
near the headwaters of the River Volta.[47] Beyond
Elmina, however, the Portuguese opened up trading
relations with native kingdoms in the Niger Delta
(particularly the powerful city-state of Benin) and
on the River Congo, which had little to offer in return for European goods but black slaves.[48] Indeed,
there is sure evidence that in the early years the
Portuguese purchased slaves at Benin for disposal to
local chieftains at São Jorge de Mina (Elmina) in
return for the gold that they craved far more than
slaves. At first the Portuguese discovered that a copper pan delivered at Gato, the port of Benin, would
be paid for in gold worth thirty times the cost of
the original copper at the mines of Extramadura, and
the internal trafficking in slaves was probably an attempt to maintain something like this level of profit.
Yet the traders with whom the Portuguese dealt soon
established the high relative value placed upon gold
in Europe, and bargaining became sharper. The sporadic attempts of the Portuguese to penetrate inland
were largely concerned with efforts either to control
the sources of the gold trade or at least to obtain
more favorable terms, much as embassies were later
sent inland from the Portuguese and English factories

on the upper west coast of India to the Mogul's court at Delhi.

By 1550 a beginning had been made in the Atlantic slave trade, but other commodities were still regarded as more important, particularly gold. After 1498 and before the plantations in the West Indies and Brazil were properly under way, Portuguese energies were mainly directed toward the East, and the West African trade was casually and often indirectly organized. The Portuguese "presence" in West Africa was not enough to discourage other Europeans, any more than it was able to overawe West African societies. Except for the half-dozen *feitorias* strung out along three thousand miles of coastline between Arguin and Loanga, it consisted largely of *lançados* (i.e., those who had thrown in their lot with the natives, sometimes called *tangomaos*, "tattooed men"), ill-organized middlemen who ventured a few miles up rivers like the Gambia and Cacheu and lived in parlous amity with the Africans. Desperate half-castes for the most part —hardly Portuguese any more—they were almost impossible to control from Lisbon and, like the Spanish planters on the coasts of America, they were often as eager to deal with foreign traders as with their own countrymen.[49]

FORERUNNERS

These then were the conditions that John Hawkins found when he first arrived on the West African coast in December 1562. As far as we know, he was the first Englishman to trade in slaves, but he had been preceded by several of his countrymen engaged in other ventures in Africa and America, the details of those not given by Richard Hakluyt having been pieced together by James A. Williamson, Irene Wright, and G. C. Smith.[50] John Hawkins' own father, William, had pioneered a triangular trade involving

England, Upper Guinea, and Brazil in three voyages between 1530 and 1532, and the English merchants resident at San Lucar de Barrameda near Seville may have traded with the Caribbean some years before. The Calendar of (Venetian) State Papers records that Edward IV made a request of the Pope for English merchants to be allowed to trade with Africa, corroborating Hakluyt's account that as early as 1481 it was necessary for John II of Portugal to send an embassy in order to forestall two English merchants called Tintam and Fabian, who were outfitting for a Guinea voyage.[51]

Serious English involvement in West Africa and America, however, dates from the period after the death of Henry VIII, first during the interval of good relations with Spain that followed the marriage of Queen Mary to Philip II, and then during the reign of Elizabeth I, as the Protestant English mariners increasingly saw the advantage of invading the monopolies claimed by Catholic Portugal and Spain. "So woorthie attempts," wrote Richard Eden in 1553,

> so much the greatlier to be esteemed, as before never enterprised by Englishmen . . . [are] to the great commoditie of our merchants, if the same be not hindered by the ambition of such, as for the conquering of fortie or fiftie miles here and there and erecting of certaine fortresses, thinke to be Lordes of halfe the world, envying that other should enjoy the commodities, which they themselves cannot wholy possesse. And although such as have been at charges in the discovering and conquering of such landes ought by good reason to have certaine privileges, preheminences, and tributes for the same, yet (to speak under correction) it may seeme somewhat rigorous, and agaynst good reason and conscience, or rather agaynst the Charitie that ought to be among Christian men, that such as invade the dominions of other should not permit other friendly to use the trade or marchandise in places neerer, or seldome frequented of them.[52]

In the decade before 1562 English ships had become a familiar sight around the Portuguese islands of Madeira and the Spanish Canaries, many of them sailing on to experiment with the varieties of West African trade. In 1551 and 1552 Thomas Wyndham traded with the "Barbary Moores" at Safi, returning to England from the Canary Islands with a cargo of sugar, dates, and almonds; but in the following year, with the aid of a renegade Portuguese Jew called Pinteado, he rounded Cape Blanco and entered the region of the "Blacke Moores of Ginney." A fine cargo of malagueta pepper was obtained at the River Sestos in what is now Liberia, and Wyndham sailed on to Benin. There opening up trade proved difficult, and the unhealthiness of the coast in that season led to the death of Wyndham himself and three quarters of his crews, including the pilot Pinteado. In 1554 John Lok of London was much more successful, setting out later in the year and sailing no farther than Elmina on the Gold Coast. Lok's voyage was as much for exploration as for trade, its journal combining the usual picturesque speculations about the interior (such as a disquisition upon the "oliphant"), with extremely precise details concerning navigation and trade.[53] Equally valuable for later voyagers were the accounts brought back by William Towerson of successive ventures to the River Sestos in 1555, Elmina in 1556, and Benin in 1557.[54] Both Lok and Towerson wrote of the profits to be made by trading basins, bracelets, and bells of copper, tin, pewter, and brass, ingots of iron, cutlery and cloth in return for pepper, ivory, and gold; but also of the difficulties posed by official Portuguese opposition, increasing competition for the available commodities, and the sharp bargaining of many African traders. These conditions applied particularly to Benin and the Gold Coast, but even on the less frequented coasts the natives were coming to suspect the motives of the Europeans because of the increase in the trade in slaves. For example, on his first voyage William Tow-

erson found that certain blacks on the Ivory Coast
would not come aboard his flagship until he had sworn
a solemn oath "by the water of the Sea" not to carry
them away.[55]

The nervousness of the ivory traders was well
founded. In the previous year one of John Lok's officers had seized and carried away four blacks, probably the first such slaves ever seen in England.[56] At
Shamma, Towerson found,

> the Negroes bent against us, because that the last
> yeere M. Gainsh did take away the Captaines sonne
> and three others from this place with their golde, and
> all that they had about them: which was the cause that
> they became friends with the Portugales, whom before
> they hated, as did appear the last yeere by the courte-
> ous intertainement which the Trinitie had there, when
> the Capitaine came aboord the ship, and brought them
> to his towne, and offered them ground to build a
> Castle in, and there they had good sales.[57]

On his second voyage, in 1556, William Towerson
took back two of the blacks abducted in 1554—one
of them now called George—as guides and interpreters, and also to reestablish English credit on the
Ivory Coast, a precaution that was extremely successful. Reaching Shamma again, Towerson sent the
two blacks ahead; the crew followed and

> were very well received, and the people were very
> glad . . . specially one of the brothers wives, and one of
> their aunts, which received them with much joy, and
> so did all the rest of the people, as if they had been
> their naturall brethren: we comforted the captaine and
> told him that hee should not feare the Portugals, for
> wee would defend him from them: whereupon we
> caused our boats to shoote off their bases and harque-
> busses, and caused our men to come on shore with
> their long bowes, and they shot before the captaine,
> which he, with all the rest of the people, wondred
> much at, specially to see them shoot so far as they did,
> and assaied to draw their bowes but could not.[58]

These pioneer voyages, as well as the arrival of the four black slaves brought by Gainsh, evidently had a strong impact in London. In 1561 the first company of "Marchants adventurers for Guinie" was projected by five grandees, who included Benjamin Gonson, Treasurer of the Navy; William Winter, Surveyor of the Navy and Master of the Ordnance; and three prominent merchants. They drew up articles to be carried out by John Lok, which included the building of a fort "upon the coast of Mina in the king of Habaan's country?"[59] Lok refused to return to Africa, "not for feare of the Portugals, which there we shall meet (and yet alone without ayde) . . . nor raging of the seas (whose rage God is above to rule)," but because of the unseaworthiness of the ships provided.[60] Instead, a voyage was led by one William Rutter, which encountered strong opposition and much disease, and brought home trade goods of but moderate value. The English fort on the Gold Coast was not built for another century.

In preparing for his three great voyages, John Hawkins learned well from all his predecessors and from his own experience of Atlantic trade as far south as the Canary Islands, as well as benefiting from his excellent connections in the City of London and the Court. The direct trade with Africa was obviously inferior to the project he now had in mind: a triangular trade that would bring back to England the most valuable commodities that Africa and America had to offer (or their profits) if at the price of engaging in a trade in black slaves. In the unlikely event that there were any qualms on the latter score, they were doubtless erased by reports of the prices that slaves were said to fetch in the Spanish colonies: 400 gold pesos (£135) apiece for *bozales,* 500 to 600 pesos for those with some knowledge of Spanish, and up to 900 pesos (£300) for those carried across to the "mayne land of Peru."[61] For ease of sailing and the procuring of blacks, Upper Guinea was clearly preferable to the coast of Lower Guinea beyond Cape Palmas. All that was needed then was money, ships, and—ideally—the agreement not only of Hawkins' own sovereign, but also those of Portugal and Spain. Elizabeth I was known to be well disposed, but if the Iberian monarchs were opposed Hawkins was prepared to stand on the wording of the Treaty of Cateau-Cambrésis between Spain and France (1559) that there was "No Peace beyond the Line"—which in fact meant the lines of the Tropic of Cancer and the meridian passing through Hierro in the Canary Islands.

John Hawkins had moved from Plymouth to London around 1559, where he married the daughter of Benjamin Gonson, whose lucrative office Hawkins was to fill only a few years later. With his father-in-law he formed a syndicate that included William Winter and two London magnates, Sir Thomas Lodge and Sir Lionel Duckett, two of that class of "merchant adventurers" who were providing the risk capital that was helping England to enter her most expansive commercial period. Most of Hawkins' partners had already ventured in the Guinea trade, and a third merchant associate, Edward Castellin, was a member of an Anglo-Spanish family whose connections might prove valuable. Together these adventurers represented financial resources sufficient to charter, man, arm, victual, and provide with suitable trade goods three smallish vessels totaling perhaps four-hundred tons, the *Salomon*, *Swallow*, and *Jonas*. After the success of the first voyage, Hawkins was able to obtain far greater financial and moral support, including the involvement of William Cecil and three other privy councilors and substantial though discreet investment by Queen Elizabeth herself.[62]

The royal discretion was occasioned far more by the diplomatic dangers of obviously encouraging the invasion of the Iberian monopolies than by a tender conscience concerning the morality of a trade in slaves. It is true that the royal commissions to Hawkins played down the slave trade, just as commentators from Hakluyt onward thought it politic to concentrate on other types of enterprise; but this was disingenuousness. The details of discussions in the Privy Council show without doubt that Elizabeth was well aware of the nature of the trade in which she connived. In trade she was simply the *primus inter pares*, far more concerned about reasons of state than her merchant subjects but with no more qualms over the morality of enslavement than, say, the morality of the question of disposing of the "sturdy beggars" who flocked the English countryside. Elizabeth I never found it necessary to proclaim a justification for the English slave trade (perhaps it was never important enough during her reign); but the official attitude toward slavery—and the contemporary contempt for blacks—can best be inferred from a proclamation made toward the end of Elizabeth's reign, in 1601. This ordered the rounding up of all "Negroes and blackamoors" in England, both for "the relief which these people consume, as also for that most of them are infidels having no understanding of Christ or his Gospel," so that they could be "avoided and discharged out of her majesty's realm" by the Lübeck merchant who had been granted the monopoly.[63]

The account of John Hawkins' three slave-trading voyages is too well known to need detailed retelling here.[64] To understand much of what occurred it is necessary, however, to penetrate beyond Hakluyt's apologetic heroics to the complaints and instructions to be traced in the Spanish and Portuguese archives, and then to read between the lines. Just as Elizabeth I dissimulated over her involvement, so the pleading of the Portuguese traders and the Spanish planters should be largely discounted. The success of Hawkins' first voyage, for example, would have been severely limited without the connivance of the Portuguese *lançados* and the slave-starved Spanish planters of Hispaniola, as well as without the contributions made by Hawkins' Spanish associate in the Canary Islands, Pedro de Ponte, and the pilot from Cadiz familiar with the West Indies, Juan Martinez, who joined the first expedition at Teneriffe.

Arriving on the coast of Sierra Leone, Hawkins, as laconically described in Hakluyt, took "300 negroes at the least besides other merchandises which that country yieldeth . . . partly by the sword, and partly by other means."[65] J. A. Williamson argued that Hawkins hardly engaged in rounding up blacks for himself, but seized—or, more likely, bought at his own prices—the slaves, merchandise, and two vessels from the Portuguese, who thereupon complained lustily to Lisbon. Likewise, having sailed quite rapidly over to northern Hispaniola, Hawkins found most planters quite ready to be "persuaded" to trade, and even an official, one Lorenzo Bernaldez (a converted Jew), willing to act collusively.

Yet success magnified the risks involved. The very size of the fleet needed to carry the slaves and return cargoes, and to defend against attack by other Europeans beyond the Lines, was bound to excite the concern of the Iberians about their monopoly, as well as to make the Africans clear about the Englishmen's intentions. Hawkins had been careful to pay the Spanish King's slave duties in Hispaniola on his first voyage and had sent his two least valuable cargoes of sugar and hides to San Lucar. But these ships were impounded and firm instructions sent out to the Spanish colonies to have no traffic with the English. Once again, most of the blacks carried across the Atlantic—this time some 600, cramped for the most part in the hold of the huge but leaky *Jesus of Lübeck* of 700 tons—were obtained from the Portuguese, but less willingly than before. Moreover, in order to augment his store, Hawkins found it necessary to take Africans by force of arms. This was probably resented by the *lançados* almost as much as by the Africans themselves, because it was a regression to a form of trade they had abandoned years before. In skirmishes with the Africans, Hawkins lost seven men killed, with 27 wounded, by spears and poisoned darts; besides, when he reached the Spanish Main he had to accompany his trading with a show of force. Yet all in all, with only two months spent on the African coast and six weeks on the Middle Passage, the second voyage was a commercial success, returning the investors a profit of 60 percent for the loss of 20 English lives.

Investment was even more readily available in 1567 and enough was subscribed for equipping six ships, totaling 1,333 tons and manned by 408 men. Since all the ships were armed and two were known to belong to the Queen, the flotilla had more the appearance of a war fleet than a trading venture. Besides, Spaniards, Portuguese, and West Africans were amply forewarned. As a result, opposition and ill-fortune, coupled with the arrogant confidence of John Hawkins, turned this third voyage into a succession of disasters. Fights with Spanish ships almost broke out in Plymouth Sound before the fleet set sail, and again at Teneriffe; and once on the African coast Hawkins' men were involved in battles with Portuguese as well as Africans in order to round up slaves. In these savage encounters, the superiority of English weapons and tactics was by no means apparent. At Cape Verde, for example, wrote Hakluyt's narrator,

> we landed 150 men, hoping to obtain some Negros, where we got but fewe, and those with great hurt and damage to our men which chiefly proceded from their envenomed arrowes: and although in the beginning they seemed to be but small hurts, yet there hardly escaped any that had blood drawen of them, but died in strange sort, with their mouthes shut some tenne dayes before they died, and after their wounds were whole.[66]

Having tarried longer on the coast than he deemed
healthy, Hawkins had only garnered about 150 slaves
and was about to change his plans and risk a descent
on Elmina, when his original venture was saved by
an offer from the King of Sierra Leone to take part
in an attack upon the city of Conga and share in
the captives made. In this first recorded instance of
Englishmen participating in the "African" method of
enslavement, Hawkins obtained 260 slaves, compared
with the King's estimated haul of 600, at the cost
of six English dead and 40 wounded. Later, such
partnerships were to be less expensive in English
blood, and more efficient too, since Hawkins' random
captives included both the very young and the aged.
Yet the setbacks of Hawkins' "third troublesome voyage" had hardly begun. After spending longer in
Africa and on the Middle Passage than before, Hawkins had great difficulty "making vent of his Negros"
and found that in most places his "trade" consisted of
pitched battles followed by plunder. The climax was
what English Protestant writers always called "the
Massacre of San Juan de Uloa," when the English fleet
was destroyed at the Mexican port of Vera Cruz by
a superior Spanish force, only two vessels and perhaps 40 men escaping to England to tell their one-
sided tale.

The incident at San Juan has obscured the subsequent phase in the English Guinea trade, particularly since Richard Hakluyt and his successor Samuel
Purchas—with their predilection for pioneer voyages,
picturesque discoveries, and the deeds of derring-
do—remain the most popular contemporary sources.
The period from 1568 to 1585 was one of Anglo-
Spanish confrontation involving almost as much fighting as the war that lasted officially from 1585 to 1603.
Yet this thirty-five-years war was in itself an expres-
sion mainly of commercial rivalry. It was fought by
the English seadogs over the very right to be allowed
to trade in Africa and the New World, and ended only

when they had shown the Iberians by their rapacious exploits that peace without monopoly was preferable to war.

Nominally, Portugal and Spain made common cause between 1580 and 1640, but if this strengthened their combined power it stimulated rather than quelled the jealous rivalry of other nations. For a time the union of the Iberians led to a trade equally from Seville and Lisbon to Guinea by vessels with licenses (or "registers") for certain numbers of slaves, which may have reached a peak of three thousand a year from Upper Guinea alone between 1585 and 1590.[67] Portuguese control over the Cape Verde Islands was not seriously threatened, yet either increased resistance by the natives to the stepped-up slave trade (as Rodney claims), or rivalry with the other Europeans, led to the need to fortify both Cacheu and Guinola on the Upper Guinea coast around 1590.[68] Besides this, many of the *lançados* fell even farther away from the control of the imperial government, in which they were emulating the Portuguese emigrés, particularly Jews, who flocked to other countries to escape the hated Castilians.

So seriously compromised did the Portuguese slave trade in Upper Guinea become that the premium that the holder of the monopoly of the registers was prepared to pay fell from 27,000 *cruzados* in 1607 to 9,400 *cruzados* in 1637.[69] Indeed, over the whole expanse of the Guinea coast, the English, Dutch, and French interlopers progressively loosened the Portuguese hold. Hakluyt himself recounted many direct voyages to Lower Guinea before the end of the reign of Elizabeth I, including the granting of trade monopolies as early as 1588. Through the very secrecy that was necessary, details are lacking. But there were probably at least as many surreptitious ventures on the triangular routes to Brazil and the Caribbean, such as that in 1591 by Christopher Newport, of which we hear mainly because he failed to dispose of his cargo of 300 slaves in Puerto Rico. Altogether, a fair share of the average of 2,800 slaves a year whom Curtin estimates left Africa for America between 1570 and 1600 may have gone in English ships. Thereafter, of course, the rate of the general trade rose rapidly: to 7,000 a year after the signing of peace in 1603, almost 15,000 after the Treaty of Munster in 1648 (by which Spain formally renounced her Caribbean monopoly), and 24,000 after the signing of the Anglo-Spanish Treaty of Madrid in 1670, at which time the English share of the trade was at least 30 percent.[70] Before 1600 the advantages of the triangular trade had been manifested, and to percipient men even the gold of Nombre de Dios and the plunder of Spanish galleons appeared inferior in the long run. As Basil Davidson pointed out, by the England–Africa–America trade,

> three separate profits were taken and all in Europe: the first profit was that of selling consumer goods to the slavers; the second derived from selling slaves to the planters and mineowners of the Americas; while the third (and biggest) was realized in the sale of American and West Indian cargoes in Europe.[71]

Unrealistically, John Hawkins had planned to inveigle or force his way into a trade which through royal monopoly was denied to most of the Spaniards themselves. With his failure, a clandestine trade was bound to continue. Yet whether official or unofficial, both these forms of trade were concerned with supplying the colonies of foreigners, an enterprise that the English came to regard as fit for Dutchmen. Peace and the expansion of plantations meant a considerable increase in the English slave trade between 1603 and 1640; but this was as nothing compared with the increase once the English developed plantations for themselves. Then the West African and West Indian trades reached a volume and a degree of steady profit beyond the grandest dreams of John Hawkins and his contemporaries.

For almost two hundred years the supply of African slaves expanded to match the needs of the American plantations. As a careful reader will probably complain, this statement clumsily hedges the conundrum originally posed. Perhaps it was insoluble in the first place, if not irrelevant—with the need of the plantations taking the role of the chicken and the supply of slaves in West Africa that of the egg in a more famous riddle. Certainly, the origins of the British slave trade do illustrate one fact that dominated the whole history of British involvement in slave trading and slavery itself: the power of the profit motive. For it was the triple profit of the triangular trade that provided motive and motive force for that sociopolitical nexus of planters, merchants, and manufacturers which, in the emergent capitalism of the mercantilist age, came to regard itself not only as "those with a stake in the country" but as the country itself. This was what the "first" British Empire was all about.

Chapter 2

ORGANIZATION

Over-all Pattern of the Slave Trade

"If you go to Barbados," wrote the rascally George Downing to his cousin John Winthrop Jr. in 1645,

> you shall see a flourishing Island, many able men, I believe they have bought this year no less than a thousand Negroes, and the more they buy the better able they are to buy, for in a year and a half they will earn (with God's blessing) as much as they cost. . . .[1]

The man who was later to be the speculative builder of Whitehall saw and described the Barbados sugar revolution plain: the profits from sugar once slaves were obtained to grow it, the availability of West African blacks once capital was found, the fortunate tendency of capital in the sugar and slave enterprises to generate itself. He advised that even if a West Indian planter began like his fellows in more northerly English colonies, his fortune would quickly become far more splendid:

> A man that will settle there must look to procure servants, which if you can get out of England, for 6, or 8, or 9 years time, only paying their passages . . . it would do very well, for so thereby you should be able to do something upon a plantation, and in short time be able, with good husbandry, to procure Negroes (the

life of this place) out of the increase of your plantation.[2]

These predictions were uncannily fulfilled. Two years
before George Downing had descended on Barbados
(the second graduate of Harvard College, he had
gone to preach, but with his eyes open for the main
chance, like any good Puritan), the island's population
had consisted of some 25,000 whites, of whom no
less than 8,600 were styled proprietors and 10,000,
servants. There were only 6,400 slaves, of whom a few
were Amerindians. Within 40 years, as sugar production rose to 8,000 tons a year, the slave population
soared to 37,000, virtually all being blacks from West
Africa. At the same time, the total of whites actually
declined to 17,000 and, as a result of the consolidation of holdings toward the 250 acres of sugar land
regarded as optimal for efficient production, the number of those reckoned as "considerable proprietors"
fell to less than 500. The number of whites in Barbados remained more or less static after 1680, and
in sugar production the island had also reached a
plateau about this time. It had become, in fact, a
"saturated" colony, though as the slave trade (if not
sugar production) became more efficient, the slave
population increased steadily until it had doubled
once more to 75,000 by 1780.[3]

In 1680 there were barely 2,000 white indentured
servants left in Barbados, many of the remaining
whites having deserted the island. One commentator
in 1667 even computed them as "12,000 good men
at least formerly proprietors . . . and tradesmen,
wormed out of their small settlements by greedy
neighbours."[4] Barbadian planters and poor whites
parted with mutual recriminations, the planters be-
moaning their lost laborers, the servants blaming the
consolidating planters for depriving them of their
chances of modest proprietorship. Yet, as a result of
the exodus, Barbados helped to seed other plantation

colonies while creating the slave-oriented plantation society that provided a pattern to be followed in the colonies seeded.

St. Kitts, Nevis, Antigua, and Montserrat were well established by 1667, and eventually they were to produce altogether about as much sugar with roughly as many slaves as Barbados; but owing to the difficulties of developing scattered and mainly mountainous islands over which English control was by no means assured, there was a significant time lag of 40 to 50 years in their development. As late as 1672 there were only 4,200 slaves in the 4 main islands of the English Leewards, and the Barbadian total for 1680 was not exceeded until 1720. As in Barbados, the rapid increase peaked, though around 1740 rather than 1690, the subsequent average increase in both areas being remarkably similar, at 0.4 percent per year.[5]

Jamaica, captured from the Spaniards by Cromwell's "Western Design" in 1655 with the help of 5,000 white troops recruited in Barbados and the Leewards, was destined to overshadow the other English islands and to become the standard by which all others were judged. But progress was slow as long as Barbados and the Leewards had first call upon the available capital and slaves. Jamaica was additionally retarded by the difficulties of penetrating the interior, taming the Maroons, and solving the problems of the island's vulnerability, coupled with the privileged, speculative pre-emption of much of the most plantable land by the original patentees and their descendants.

The hundreds of small holdings hopefully begun by the private soldiers of Cromwell's tattered army disappeared even more completely from Jamaica than those in Barbados, as the poorer whites died off or were bought out and drifted into the ranks of managers, bookkeepers, and senior craftsmen on larger estates. Those with greater resources did rather better. Carey Helyar, for example, who founded Bybrook in

St. Thomas-ye-Vale in 1669 (one of the three oldest sugar estates still active in Jamaica), enjoyed the benefits of friendship with the slave-trading Governor Thomas Modyford and mercantile connections in London, which provided capital for a sugar factory, 55 blacks, and even 14 indentured servants. Yet when Carey Helyar died suddenly in 1672, Bybrook languished, only recovering once the Jamaican sugar boom began in earnest in the 1730s.[6]

Unlike Barbados and the Leewards, where all the land suitable for sugar cane was soon taken up and overproduction exhausted the soil, Jamaica was never quite fully exploited before sugar and slavery declined. Consequently, for at least 75 years expanding sugar production and slave population kept approximate pace. In 1670 there were only some 9,000 slaves in Jamaica, a total barely in excess of the number of whites. The white population of Jamaica, after an actual decline between 1690 and 1700, rose gradually, but only to 18,000 a century later. This was the same number as in Barbados, an island one-thirtieth the size. The slave population, however, increased rapidly and steadily at about 2.5 percent per year. As early as 1690 blacks outnumbered whites in Jamaica by 4 to 1, as high a proportion as was ever reached in Barbados in slavery days. Yet in Jamaica the ratio climbed to 6 to 1 by 1710, 10 to 1 by 1740, and 12 to 1, the level approximately maintained, by 1780. At that time there were about 200,000 black slaves in Jamaica, or more than a fifth of the total for the entire British Empire, and Jamaica was producing 50,000 tons of sugar a year, or roughly half of all British production. When the slave trade ended in 1808, Jamaica had more than 300,000 slaves, and the per capita production of sugar had actually risen from a fifth to a third of a ton per year.[7]

Jamaica, Barbados, and the Leewards were always before 1808 the chief British sugar colonies, and as such remained the focus of the British slave trade.

Their combined influx reached a peak of 13,000 slaves a year between 1780 and 1808, or 82 percent of the total for all British colonies, having never fallen below an average of 7,500 a year, or 67 percent, for any decade since 1700.[8] Indeed, the spread of slavery was as much due to the dynamic generated by these islands as to the intrinsic requirements of other colonies, even those subsequently developed as plantation colonies. In the seventeenth century sugar bred slavery, but in the eighteenth century slavery bred more slavery.

Besides the basic sugar colonies, three other major types of British slave colony can therefore be distinguished. A second type consisted of those colonies acquired later where some degree of planting with slave labor was already carried on, but which greatly expanded under the influence of an efficient imperial slave trade: Grenada, Dominica, St. Vincent, Tobago, St. Lucia, and finally the Guyanas and Trinidad.[9] In each an initial surge of population was followed by a more moderate increase or actual leveling off as capital ran out, as the initial enthusiasm was blunted by local difficulties, or as the plateau of economic production was reached. Because these colonies were acquired piecemeal as the result of successive wars, however, their combined population increase was much more gradual, rising from a total of 12,000 blacks in 1750 and 30,000 in 1763, to 80,000 in 1783 and 160,000 in 1808.[10] To these colonies were added the Cape of Good Hope and Mauritius, with a combined slave population of 100,000, by the terms of the peace treaties of 1815. Their slaves, however, could not legally be augmented from outside because of the ending of the British slave trade in 1808.[11]

A third type of British slave colony was that in which the development of a slave plantation economy definitely postdated the initial settlement and was positively encouraged by the existence of a vigorous West African trade already organized to serve other areas. In this category must be placed the plantation colonies of the North American mainland, to which the slave migration was slight before 1700, but which developed rapidly between then and the achievement of American independence, particularly as the Americans themselves joined heavily in the West African trade once it was freed from monopolistic metropolitan controls.

There had been a few slaves in Virginia almost from the earliest days, but the tobacco plantations were first developed mainly as small holdings worked by white labor. Later, slaves enabled planter grandees to extend their tobacco plantations and to move into the production of other plantation staples. Aided by the relative healthiness of the climate, the black population of Virginia and neighboring Maryland, no more than 22,000 in 1700, had risen to 245,000 by 1775, though the proportion of the two colonies' total population represented by black slaves merely rose from 20 to 35 percent.[12]

Moreover, despite some consolidation in the last years of the colonial period, slave holdings remained small. In Lancaster County, Virginia, for example, one of the areas most densely populated with blacks, seven out of ten white farmers owned slaves, but 63 percent owned five or less in 1775. This compared with the average holding of about 240 for the 1,500 to 1,800 sugar plantations of the British West Indies at about that time.[13]

The Carolinas, founded many decades later, owed their economic expansion much more to the black than did the colonies to the north. Indeed, slavery was inherent in their foundation, for John Locke (more commonly remembered as a theoretical opponent of slavery) had found it politic to incorporate slavery into their "Fundamental Constitutions" in 1669. Moreover, many of the first settlers, being from Barbados, brought their slaves with them. At first the Carolinas devoted themselves to the production of ships' stores (sugar proving unsuitable), but within 25 years plantations growing rice and indigo were well rooted, especially in the coastal lowlands in the hinterland of Charleston. By 1700 the population of South Carolina was 60 percent black, possibly rising to 70 percent by 1725.[14] Although this fell to 50 percent by 1775 as large numbers of whites not involved in the plantation economy migrated to the colony, South Carolina remained more densely populated with slaves than any colony farther north except Virginia, and the nearest approximation on the American mainland to a West Indian plantation colony. By 1775, besides, large slave populations were present in the adjacent colonies of North Carolina (30 percent of the total population) and Georgia (36 percent), in the latter of which slavery—legalized in 1747—had helped to destroy the egalitarian idealism of its foundation in 1735 and had even led to a direct trade with Africa by 1766.

To these mainland plantation colonies perhaps should be added Bermuda and the Bahamas. The former was a colony that never developed important slave plantations but acquired a slave population largely because of its connections with Virginia. The latter was a territorially larger colony that might have developed plantations and acquired a larger slave population but for the paucity of the soil. In both Bermuda and the Bahamas, however, the slave populations multiplied suddenly after 1783 with the migration of Loyalist planters from the Carolinas, and more steadily thereafter as the lightly worked slaves flourished and increased naturally.[15]

A final type of British slave colony includes all the remainder: those without significant plantations and therefore no overriding need of slaves, but which acquired slave populations almost accidentally—because the slave trade was *there*. In much the same fashion England itself acquired as many as 20,000 blacks by 1772 as flotsam and jetsam of the trade it organized to serve the plantation colonies. From the beginnings, when John Pym encouraged the Providence Islanders to gather blacks and grace where they could, and John Winthrop, Sr., recorded the first cargo of "negars" arriving in New England in 1636 without moralizing comment,[16] the Puritan colonists were quite ready to engage in slave trading without qualm, and their example was avidly followed by the inheritors of the mercantile Dutch in New York and New Jersey. By 1740, when Rhode Island was merely the most active of several areas engaged in a flourishing African trade, considerable numbers of black slaves were settled in close proximity to the ports of New England and the middle colonies, just as the English blacks were most numerous in and around London, Bristol, Liverpool, and Lancaster.[17]

The Quakers were exceptional in their opposition to slavery, but they hardly counted. Even in "Quaker" Pennsylvania, black slavery was not eradicated until after American independence. Yet in none of the New England or middle colonies was there ever such a large proportion of black slaves that the institution of slavery became entrenched by repressive "police" laws quite as in the plantation colonies. In the New England colonies as a whole, the black population never represented more than 3.5 percent of the total, Rhode Island being individually highest with between 5.5 and 6.5 percent. Although the proportion in the middle colonies was about three times as high (Delaware with about 20 percent being highest), there were only about 50,000 slaves in the middle and New England colonies combined in 1775 out of a total population of well over a million. This compared with a slave population in the five southern colonies of approximately 500,000 out of 1,500,000.[18]

All in all, the colonies of the American mainland on the eve of independence contained a slave population larger in total than that of the British sugar colonies of the Caribbean. Yet this huge population should not lead to an assumption, made by some writers, that the slave trade of both areas was at anything like a similar level. So far it is mainly the growth of slave populations that has been considered here, rather than the pattern of the supplying trade. There was little correlation between the two because of very great variations in the rate of slave mortality and fertility from colony to colony and time to time. Clearly, a colony in which slaves reproduced themselves at a healthy rate and did not suffer from high death rates would need a far smaller trade in fresh slaves in order to expand than a colony less fortunate in both respects. For a variety of sad reasons to be considered later, black slaves did not normally achieve an excess of births over deaths in the West Indian plantations, and importations were necessary just to keep numbers up. Conditions were much better on the American mainland even in the plantation colonies, though it was only in those colonies without plantations, where slave populations were small and work generally less onerous, that demographic conditions were positively healthy.

As will be shown in Chapter 4, the rate of slave mortality gradually decreased even in purely plantation colonies, and tended in any case to improve as a colony approached economic and demographic saturation. The rate of "natural decrease" (excess of deaths over births) was thus worst in the early years of fastest development, when a rate of general expansion of 2 percent a year might only be bought at the cost of an importation amounting to 8 percent or even more of the total slave population per year. As a rough rule of thumb, however, it may be taken that the annual rate of natural decrease among the slaves in a sugar plantation colony was about 3 percent per year while the colony was halfway toward economic saturation, falling as low as 1 percent or less once the plantation economy had ceased to expand.

In the colonies of the American mainland it appears that the slaves increased naturally even in the plantation colonies during the early years of development. Noel Deerr, the sugar historian, presuming that mortality/fertility factors were the same in all slave colonies, predicated from the fact that the total slave population in the Thirteen Colonies in 1775 was approximately the same as that of the British West Indies a total of slave imports into British North America similar to that measured for the British Caribbean—that is, about 1,500,000 between 1650 and 1775. In fact, recent computations, made mainly by Stetson and Curtin from other sources, point to a total importation into British North America of no more than 275,000, or roughly one sixth of the total for the British West Indies. This must be explained entirely by the differences in the mortality/fertility rates. The figures for the total populations and trade of the Thirteen Colonies do indeed seem to indicate rates of "natural increase" (excess of births over deaths) that rise steadily from about 9 per thousand around 1720 to about 18 per thousand in 1775.

Appreciation of the above factors will aid an understanding of the disparities between population growth and slave importations in the following tables. Comparing them enables us to arrive at figures for natural increase or decrease, and relating all three to figures of plantation produce would help to show the way in which slave demography and the plantation economy were indissolubly interrelated. Yet even when we have differentiated the colonies and gained an accurate picture of the quantitative pattern of population, trade, and production (not forgetting to take into account the slave trade to foreign colonies), we have still only looked at one side of the slave trade: its destinations. For Africa, in a sense, the destination of the slaves was immaterial, and from this undifferentiated picture of the demands laid upon Africa between 1600 and 1808, perhaps we can turn to consider the organization of the British trade in Africa itself.

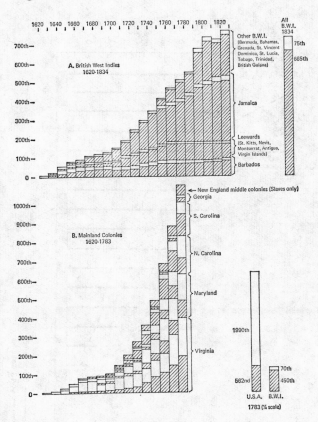

British Slave Colonies: Population, 1620–1834. (Shaded area=Slaves)

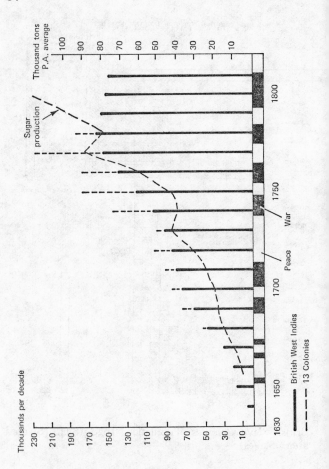

British America: Slave Trade, 1630–1807.

MONOPOLY VS. FREE TRADE

Broadly speaking, the British slave trade began with private enterprise, survived its emergent years with the aid of state-granted monopolies and, during its eighteenth-century heyday, gradually reverted to completely free trade. In this process the history of the British slave trade between 1600 and 1800 accurately prefigured the commercial history of the British Empire as a whole over a far longer period, providing the earliest illustration of the dicta that a policy of protection was expediential and flexible, and that free trade was always more efficient wherever it was possible.

Yet from beginning to end, the state was never entirely dissociated from the British slave trade, even in that period before the "bourgeois revolution" increasingly identified state and commerce. Although Tudor seamen were notable individualists, some notions of monopoly were coeval with British expansionism, the value of exclusive trading privileges and state support being self-evident. It has already been shown how, in confronting Portuguese and Spanish exclusiveness on difficult coasts and in strange and distant seas, the earliest venturers sought backers close to the Court. John Hawkins even obtained investment—though little overt support—from the monarch herself.

Rather more formal was the "regulated" partnership of eight merchants of London and Exeter granted a fine-sounding patent of monopoly of all English trade to Senegambia for ten years, in 1588, though it was not until thirty years later that the first incorporated joint stock company for trade with Africa was chartered by James I.[19] This Company of Adventurers of London, which enjoyed a monopoly nominally extending from south of "Barbary" to the Cape of Good Hope, was dominated by Sir Robert Rich (later Earl of Warwick), who significantly combined commercial aspiration on an imperial scale with puritanism and the support of Parliament against the pretensions of the Stuarts.

The pioneer African Company enjoyed only intermittent success. At first it was chiefly interested in the River Gambia, which had the advantages of being within as little as three weeks' sailing from England. It also suffered a minimum of interference from foreign rivals, and offered navigation deep into an interior where gold was said to abound. Originally it was this gold and other trade goods, not slaves, that lured the company, and in 1620 Richard Jobson, the third captain sent out to the Gambia, even went so far as to abjure slave trading in an often-quoted passage.[20] Yet the idealistic distaste voiced by Jobson for trading in "any that had our own shapes"—if indeed it were ever a general sentiment—did not survive the discovery that slaves were the most profitable West African commodity. Reorganized in 1624 and 1631, the company extended its operations to Sierra Leone, the Gold Coast, and the Bight of Benin, building the first permanent English post in Africa at Coromantine in the Gold Coast in 1631. Now popularly known as the "Gynney and Bynney Company," its transatlantic trade in slaves increased greatly with the creation of English sugar plantations in the West Indies after 1640, though the direct trade in gold, ivory, and hides remained important.

The period of the English civil wars and interregnum brought confusion and finally disaster to the Gynney and Bynney Company. During the wars ships and settlements were plundered first by Royalists and then by the Dutch. The company's monopoly was broken by interlopers, and yet company and interlopers combined were unable to satisfy the West Indian demand for slaves. With the Restoration—which saw so many imperial and commercial enterprises already initiated or extended by Parliament enthusiastically endorsed by the Crown—it was inevitable that the West African enterprise would be reformed. In December 1660 a Company of Royal Adventurers into Africa was chartered, with shareholders who eventually included the King and Queen, a prince, four dukes, eight earls, and seven barons, as well as forty-nine wealthy men without titles. The second charter of the company, issued in January 1663, was the first specifically to mention the trade in slaves, though both the 1660 and 1663 charters appeared worded to challenge the supremacy in the West African trade then enjoyed by the Dutch, much as the Navigation Acts passed in the same years obviously threatened Holland's general commercial sway.[21]

A leading force in the new company was Prince Rupert who, besides having once been a governor of the prewar company, had led his Royalist squadron to West Africa and the West Indies in 1652. It may well have been Rupert's notorious impetuosity that precipitated conflict with the Dutch and the consequent financial ruin of the Royal Adventurers, much as his headlong cavalry charges had lost at least two battles for the Royalists during the civil wars. However, some sort of collision was inevitable, given the convergent imperial and commercial courses being steered by England and Holland. In 1661 Captain Robert Holmes, a roistering veteran of Rupert's fleet, seized the fort at the mouth of the Gambia owned by the Courlanders, whom the Dutch regarded as under their protection. Two years later, in response to the detention of six merchant ships, Holmes temporarily captured all the Dutch posts in West Africa save Elmina.[22] Retribution was almost immediate, for late in 1664 de Ruyter even more easily seized or recaptured every one of the posts held by the English except the strongest, Cape Coast Castle, an action that "became the Occasion, at least the Popular Pretence of the war with Holland."[23]

The Company of Royal Adventurers suffered from the dilemma that while it needed both posts in West Africa and peace for success, the acquisition of posts was bound to provoke a war that would be financially insupportable. Besides, even during peacetime there were serious organizational flaws. Top-heavy yet undercapitalized, the company could neither supply the West Indian planters with sufficient slaves nor adequately collect the debts the planters incurred. Consequently, interlopers flourished. When it was disbanded, the Company of Adventurers claimed to have established forts, factories, or "lodges" at James Island in the Gambia, Coromantine, Commenda, Takoradi, Anti, Antasham, Wyamba, and 11 other places, and in the last year before the second Dutch war to have sent 40 ships to West Africa with goods worth £160,-000 and no less than 6,000 slaves to the British West Indies. Yet by 1669 it had almost ceased to trade on its own account, instead selling licenses to private traders and even leasing to Gambia trade to a separate set of Adventurers for seven years. With debts totaling £57,000 and its stock at 10 percent of its original value, the Company of Royal Adventurers was moribund. But the principle of monopoly was too valuable to let die, and on September 27, 1672 a charter was issued to a new body called the Royal African Company, pledged to avoid earlier mistakes.[24]

Besides being more tightly governed, the Royal African Company drew its support from a much broader and more practical base of shareholders than its predecessor. Nobility and courtiers remained, but the proportion of stock held by them was never high and gradually diminished. At least two thirds of the shares were owned by businessmen, mainly those with overseas interests already.[25] Although the predominance of the tightly knit community of established entrepreneurs based in London was to prove a check on future expansion, these men would at least be more likely to look to questions of profit than to reasons of state and matters of imperial policy. One result was that, with the tacit agreement of the Dutch and most of the other African trading powers, West Africa became practically a neutral ground in the commercial wars of the subsequent period. A serious exception was the rivalry between England and France down to the English capture of Goree and Senegal in the Seven Years' War; though this was the doing of the statesmen and naval captains, not the merchants. On the Gold Coast alone over 35 trading places belonging to seven European powers coexisted without military conflict, exhibiting that same commercial freemasonry that allowed West Indian planters so often to behave as if European regulations and even wars were irrelevant, and merchants normally to order their captains not to fight at the risk of their cargo if detained.

In at least one respect, however, the Royal African Company was more of a state enterprise than its predecessors. Besides retaining a two-thirds interest in all gold discovered, the King assumed the ultimate suzerainty over all areas actually held by the company in West Africa, in return for the nominal payment of two elephants "whenever we, our heirs and successors, or any of them, shall arrive, land or come into the Dominions." The royal charter was the legal origin of the territorial claims to those areas that eventually became the four British colonies of West Africa, but it held little but moral value for the Royal African Company in 1672. The success of the company was to be determined by practical criteria, particularly whether it could supply the demand for slaves at a reasonable price yet still make a profit, and thus justify the retention of a legal monopoly and the suppression of private traders.

In a valiant attempt to cover at least the lucrative areas of its five-thousand-mile monopoly and to fulfill the demand that one early commentator placed as high as twenty-five thousand slaves a year,[26] the Royal African Company pursued three basic forms of trade: based on factories, on shallow-draft vessels, and on oceangoing ships. West Africa was also divided into seven main trading regions: the Gambia (not taken over by the company until 1676), Sierra Leone, the Windward and Gold coasts, the Bights of Benin and Biafra, and "Angola." The factory or "Castle" trade was that based upon a fortified barrack, storehouse and slave barracoon (sometimes called a "trunk"). The chief large factories were at James Island in the Gambia, Bence Island at Sierra Leone, York Island in the River Sherbro a hundred miles to the southeast, and Cape Coast Castle on the comparatively healthy Gold Coast, where the company's agent-general resided. These large factories, with territorial rights established by treaties of varied validity with native chieftains, served as defensible entrepôts either for chains of smaller factories (such as the three minor posts on the River Gambia or the dozen subsidiary posts on the Gold Coast) or as the bases for sloops or large canoes to trade directly with native settlements at points up to hundreds of miles along the coasts or up the navigable rivers.

Although there were never more than a few hundred Englishmen resident in West Africa—Cape Coast Castle's garrison of 100 at most and James Island's 70 being the largest concentrations—the areas of factory trading were naturally those most acculturated—or corrupted—by English contact. Considerable townships grew up outside the walls, inhabited by the agents of native traders, by interpreters, traders' servants, petty tradesmen, craftsmen, harlots, and similar hangers-on. The inhabitants tended to speak a crudely effective *lingua franca* or pidgin, made up of sailors' English mixed with Portuguese and African words. Some of the words most commonly used included "palaver" (a trade negotiation), "panyar" (to kidnap), "caboceer" (a native official or slave agent), and the inevitable "dash" (tax or bribe).[27]

The grander their establishment, the more the Eng-

lish officials attempted to stand aloof. At Cape Coast
Castle buglers blew the curfew at sundown and caboceers invited inside at any time were expected to
drink at the door. Yet at Commendar, the local chief's
agents supped with the company's factor, and in even
less important posts on the Sherbro or Gambia a single
Englishman might live in complete intimacy with the
Africans by the grace, or greed, of the local ruler,
much like his predecessors, the Portuguese *lançados*.
As Richard Jobson had pointed out, the farther the
European penetrated inland, the less sophisticated the
native traders became, the smaller were the dashes
demanded, and the cheaper the trade goods.[28]

In some areas trading was carried on directly from
ships, with a few agents the only Englishmen in
residence. These areas included those where there
were less trade or few obvious trading places, such
as the Windward Coast from Cape Mount to Cape
Three Points, notoriously unhealthy regions such as
the Cameroons or Congo, or areas like Benin or Calabar, where the native kingdoms were strong and
forbade the establishment of fortified European settlements. Only at Whydaw on the Slave Coast of the
Bight of Benin (which after 1737 became the chief
outlet for the aggressive Dahomey kingdom) did the
English boast a more substantial settlement related
to the "ship" trade, and that was chiefly to keep up
with the Dutch, French, and Portuguese, who were
also settled there. Not that this concentration of Europeans weakened the native authority, for the king of
Whydaw was usually the arbiter in the frequent commercial disputes between the factors. Elsewhere Kings
required salutes as well as presents in return for trading privileges, and in the cases of Ashanti and Dahomey behaved with quite splendid condescension.

On less frequented parts of the coast the ship trade
would include "smoking" and "boating"—that is, either
making smoke signals for the natives to come out over
the surf in canoes for trade, or sending the ship's crew

out in longboats to find trade goods or make the occasional panyaring foray. South of the Bight of Biafra,
in the regions still dominated by the Portuguese and
called indiscriminately Angola by the English, the
Royal African Company had no settlements and carried on little permanent trade, though as the slave
trade expanded, this area became increasingly important. Besides slaves the company continued considerable trade in gold (minting in all a quarter-million
sovereigns), ivory, hides, and beeswax with Senegambia, Upper Guinea, and the Gold Coast; from the
River Sherbro it even developed a new trade in dyewood. But the ship trade beyond the River Volta was
almost exclusively in slaves and their provisions for the
Atlantic crossing.[29]

Despite its advantages the Royal African Company
did not come close to justifying its monopoly, never
raising anything like the £100,000 a year average for
trade goods regarded as the minimum for steady profits, and in only one year (1686–87) carrying even
10,000 slaves. Almost from the beginning, the company's legal privileges therefore became grievances
to those deprived of trade or slaves, and from 1680 a
virulent pamphlet warfare developed in which hired
writers stumbled into arguments over the merits and
demerits of chartered companies, protection, free
trade, and *laissez faire,* which were to be revived a
century later.[30] Basically, the company argued that
its monopoly was a well-deserved return for the upkeep of the West African forts and the maintenance
of an English "presence" in West Africa at little cost
to the government. The forts and armed vessels patrolling the coasts were held to be necessary for a successful trade in the face of European rivalry and possible
African unfriendliness. Yet the company found it impossible to maintain them adequately without a fair
margin of profit, particularly since they were strung
out over such a huge expanse of difficult coast. Un-

fortunately, profitability fell far below its potential because the company was undercut by interlopers whom it was almost powerless to prosecute in either West Africa or the West Indies. Moreover, to add to the problem of the capital tied up in the West African shore establishments and the cost of pursuing interlopers on the seas and through the Admiralty courts, there was the lack of liquidity caused by the unwillingness—or inability—of the West Indian planters to pay cash or pay promptly for the slaves they bought. The demand made by the Council of Trade and Plantations on several occasions that the Royal African Company provide the English colonies with a minimum supply of slaves at predetermined prices, was particularly onerous to an organization attempting to operate on rational business principles and provide its shareholders with a fair return.

Naturally, the opposite side in the controversy argued that the Royal African Company was trying to enjoy the benefits of monopoly without its wider responsibilities. The antimonopolists agreed with the company that the slave trade was of great benefit to the commerce, "navigation" and general prosperity of England, as well as being vital to the plantation colonies, but maintained strongly that the monopoly was curtailing the benefits by limiting them to a privileged few. Interlopers, it was plausibly maintained, were able to undercut the Royal African Company because they were more efficient. They managed quite well outside the monopoly, and since the company had clearly failed to fulfill the purposes for which a monopoly had been given it, neither defending West Africa nor supplying the English plantations adequately, the monopoly seemed totally unnecessary. It was claimed that both the value of the West African forts and the company's expenditure on them had been greatly exaggerated, and that as a defensive factor or even as a symbol of power they were mostly ludicrous. Moreover, it was held that the company's profits had been consistently understated and that the prices charged for slaves were exorbitant.[31] The Royal African Company's chief failing, however, was said to be its preference for the profitable Spanish market in slaves, to the detriment of the English colonies. Jamaican planters in particular were galled to find most of the healthiest slaves shipped to their island re-exported to Spanish colonies, leaving only "refuse" slaves, for whom they had to pay prices inflated by Spanish bullion. Such a profitable "free trade" as that with the Spanish colonies was all very well, argued the Jamaicans, but it should not be protected by a monopoly designed to nurture the British, not the Spanish, Empire.

Besides the broadsides from Grub Street, Parliament was peppered by petitions against the Royal African Company's monopoly. These came from the agents of West Indian colonies, which wanted more and cheaper slaves; from North American colonies, which wished to engage in the trade; from English merchants and shipowners outside London; and from manufacturers who felt that free trade would increase their exports. In 1698 an "Act to Settle the Trade to Africa" was passed,[32] whereby the slave trade was thrown open to all on payment of a 10 percent duty to the company for the upkeep of the forts. Henceforward any merchant wishing to trade legitimately had simply to clear for West Africa at a customs house and pay 10 percent of the value of all trade goods carried, though an unknown number of slavers continued to trade illicitly. Within a couple of years it was said that most, if not all, licit West African trade was being carried on by the "10 percent men," among whom, paradoxically, were quite a few shareholders of the Royal African Company acting in a private capacity.

When the "Ten Per Cent" Act was allowed to run out in 1712 and the slave trade was made completely free, the Royal African Company might well have disappeared entirely. That it lingered on until 1752 and even enjoyed two periods of modest revival was due to two occurrences: the granting of the *Spanish asiento* in 1713 and the surge of new capital generated at the time of the South Sea Bubble.

The official right to supply the Spanish Empire with its slaves had always been a snare to English traders.[33] The foolhardy agreement to supply the Genoese *asientistas* Grillo and Lomelin with 3,500 slaves a year in Jamaica had contributed to the downfall of the Royal Adventurers in the 1660s; yet this did not deter the Royal African Company from making an equally chimerical arrangement with the Spaniard Santiago Castillo in 1689. During the War of the Spanish Succession negotiations for the complete English takeover of the *asiento* were begun as early as 1707,[34] and the sole right to supply 4,800 *piezas de India* a year was one of the spoils of victory at Utrecht in 1713. The business of supply was delegated to a new organization, the South Sea Company, but the Royal African Company served as a subcontractor and enthusiastically sent out 40 ships within the first 2 years. All hopes of sustained profits from slave trading by chartered companies, however, had long faded. After a slump in 1715 the Royal African Company managed to raise £300,000 for trade goods between 1720 and 1723, sending out 2,284 slaves in the last of these years, without coming close to an over-all profit.[35] A considerable re-export trade in slaves to the Spanish colonies did continue, averaging 2,000 a year from Jamaica alone from 1700 to 1800, but this was soon entirely managed by private traders. In addition there was an increasing direct trade in English vessels to Brazil and even the French islands as well as the Spanish colonies, which is much harder to quantify but may have totaled as many as 10,000 in some years during the 1780s.[36] This apparently anti-mercantilist behavior was a result of the pragmatic flexibility that had triumphed in the English slave trade between 1698 and 1752.

Another result, probably less pleasing to "patriotic" Englishmen, was the arrival in large numbers on the African coast after 1700 of American slavers. By 1750 Newport, the chief port of Rhode Island, was said to have 170—or half its merchant fleet—engaged in slave trading; and in 1768 American mainland vessels were said to be carrying over 6,000 slaves a year.[37] Little is known of the relations between old English and New Englanders in West Africa, but the facts that the Americans were very soon supplying a large proportion of the trade of the mainland plantation colonies, and were serious rivals for the West Indies trade long before 1775, may very well have been important contributory causes of the great divergence of like from like in the War of American Independence. At first, however, the trade was expanding fast enough to satisfy all.

After 1730 the sole function of the once-monopolistic Royal African Company was the administration of the West African forts, with the aid of a parliamentary subsidy of £10,000 a year, paid from 1730 to 1745.[38] With the withdrawal of the subsidy, the company slid rapidly into extinction, leaving behind only the loosely regulated Company of African Merchants entrusted with the nominal management of trade and forts, created by an Act of 1750.[39] The English slave trade, now at the threshold of its greatest expansion and success, was essentially in private hands and operating under principles of practically free trade and even *laissez faire*, a trend that was not reversed until the first regulatory legislation was passed in 1788.

Yet in a sense, the support of the state for the West African trade was not withdrawn at this juncture, at least potentially. As during the nineteenth century, the very existence of "free trade" implied that overt protection was no longer necessary, for the position of metropolitan economic strength that was the end of "mercantilism" had already been achieved. As time went on, the American slave traders were among the first to discover this fact, and claim that what was called free trade was merely a delusionary tactic. To them the Company of African Merchants was little but a union of metropolitan capitalists designed to provide rules for self-protection and machinery for lobbying Parliament. The West African forts apparently were no longer necessary, but a Parliament and Privy Council that were quite prepared to legislate minute modifications of the acts of trade for the benefit of metropolitan lobbyists would be quite ready to send out a naval squadron to protect English interests in West Africa, or even reactivate the forts if called upon—as indeed happened between 1775 and 1783. Henry Laurens, the South Carolina slave factor and revolutionary leader, came to write, with perhaps exaggerated force, in 1776:

> Acts of parliament have established the slave trade in favour of the home-residing English, and almost totally prohibited the Americans from reaping any share of it. Men-of-war, forts, castles, governors, companies and committees are employed and authorized by the English parliament to protect, regulate, and extend the slave trade. Negroes are brought by Englishmen and sold as slaves to Americans. Bristol, Liverpool, Manchester and Birmingham etc., live upon the slave trade. The British parliament now employ their men-of-war to steal these negroes from the Americans to whom they had sold them, pretending to set the poor wretches free, but basely trepan and sell them into tenfold worse slavery in the West Indies, where probably they will become the property of Englishmen again, and of some who sit in parliament.[40]

These bitter sentiments were, however, probably unthinkable as early as 1748, when Henry Laurens first engaged in the trade. For the demand for slaves then appeared almost insatiable, and the removal of the last vestiges of the Royal African Company's monopoly must have seemed even more of a boon to American than to English traders, in the sense that it completely legitimized a trade they would probably have engaged in anyway because of its obvious profitability.

WEST AFRICA

Three results of "free trade" and an open-ended demand for slaves were the steady rise in slave prices, the systematic scouring of the coast for recruits, and the increase in the brutal efficiency of the trade. The disappearance of the Royal African Company and the decline of the forts led to a relative as well as absolute increase in the ship trade and this, coupled with the increased demand, placed more rather than less power in the hands of African rulers and middlemen. The trade corrupted the best of men, for only the callous survived and maximum power was reserved for the most cynical of all. Demographically, the effect of the Atlantic trade on West Africa may have been less serious than was at one time thought, and over the entire period the forcible transference of some eleven million Africans may have done little more than slow the over-all natural rate of increase almost to a stop.[41] However, the eighteenth-century trade, which transferred as many slaves as the previous and subsequent centuries combined, must have had a more deleterious effect in general, and in particular regions the depletion was demographically disastrous. Certainly, as nearly all travelers reported, the eighteenth century saw the ramification of the Atlantic slave trade deeper into the African interior, an increased tendency to go to war for captives and the consequent acceleration in the shift of political patterns.[42]

Yet, if the trade intensified, if the areas of concentration changed or fluctuated, and if trading became sharper, the actual organization of the slave trade changed remarkably little from 1600 to 1800. As the answers given by the expert witnesses to the inquiries of 1788–89 showed, there was more variety on different parts of the coast at any one time than there was from period to period in any given part. The detailed accounts of trade given in 1830 by Captain Hugh Crow, the last of the legitimate Liverpool slavers, and by Governor J. B. Weuves and Captain John Matthews in 1789, largely echoed those retailed by William Snelgrave and John Atkins in the 1730s or by such traders as Thomas Phillips (1693–94) in Churchill and Astley's magnificent collections of voyages; just as these details can be found anticipated in the voluminous records of the Royal African Company, or even in such ingenuous accounts as that given by Captain John Blake of the Guinea Company's pink *Supply* in 1652.[43] The main problems to be solved in West Africa were well known long before the slave trade reached its peak, and probably no one ever expressed these constants more succinctly than Atkins in 1735:

> The Success of a Voyage depends first, on the well sorting, and on the well timing of a Cargo. Secondly, in a knowledge of the places of Trade, what, and how much may be expected every where. Thirdly, in dramming well with English Spirits, and conforming to the Humours of the Negroes. Fourthly, in timely furnishing proper Food for the Slaves. Fifthly, in Dispatch; and Lastly, the good Order and Management of slaves when on board.[44]

Nothing remained so constant in general but required so nice a calculation from place to place and time to time as the goods carried out to West Africa in payment for slaves. Although the variety contained in each cargo or even exchanged for a single slave was staggering, they comprised basically either items regarded as currency in West Africa or manufactures, many African traders requiring half of each. Gold by ounce weight remained a standard method of evaluating trade goods for Europeans, but was not often used in payment for slaves, chiefly because its export from Europe was regarded as anathema in orthodox economic theory. More commonly used as currency was iron, which had symbolic as well as practical value in West Africa, where the blacksmith had always been an important figure in society. In the early years the "manella," or split ring of iron used as an ornament, was an important item of trade; but gradually it was superseded by plain bars of iron, easy to weigh and to convert in the blacksmiths' forges. More durable metals and alloys such as copper, lead, brass, and pewter were also imported in large quantities and were sometimes used as currency and as raw materials for native manufactures. More often, however, their value was assessed in iron bars, and the fact that they were usually shipped in the form of basins and other utensils indicates that metalworking in West Africa was either not general or was a declining industry.

The strangest West African currency consisted of cowrie shells, particularly prized in the Bight of Benin, where the natives strung them together into necklaces of forty called "foggies" and bunches of five foggies called "gallinas." Not indigenous to West Africa, cowries were shipped in huge quantities from East Africa and the islands of the Indian Ocean, being sold to traders by the East India Company in 1700 for £4 per hundred pounds weight, approximately the price of a slave at Whydaw. The European slave traders were never entirely happy with cowrie shells as currency, for though the African traders insisted on payment by weight, the ordinary people regarded each shell as equally valuable regardless of size, and this double standard was thought to devalue other European trade goods. Much the same also applied to the glass and coral beads strung on necklaces occasionally used as currency in the trade.

The analysis made by K. G. Davies of the value of

the trade goods sent out by the Royal African Company at the height of its operations (1681–85) shows that metals and metalware accounted for 19 percent, and cowries, beads, and coral for 14 percent of the total. Of the manufactures exported, textiles made up no less than 60 percent of the over-all total by value; the remaining 7 percent consisted chiefly of cutlery, firearms, and gunpowder. The largest group of textiles were British woolens, particularly "perpetuanos," "says" and other types of serge, and "Welsh plains"— all cloths chosen for being reasonably hard-wearing, not too unbearably hot for the African climate, and cheap. Not far behind in total value was a bewildering array of East India textiles, mainly patterned cottons with names as colorful as the cloths themselves: "allejaes," "baftees," "brawles," "Guinea stuffs," "long cloths," "longees," "nicconees," "pautkees," "tapseels." Miscellaneous textiles made up a substantial third group, consisting of carpets, linen sheets, and cloths imported from Europe, such as the "sletias" from Silesia and the cheap "annabasses" and dearer "boysados" brought from Holland. The cutlery exported included swords and cutlasses as well as knives, all of which were beginning to be produced in vast quantity in the English Midlands around Birmingham. The same region produced muskets specially designed for the West African trade: short-barreled shotguns more like blunderbusses than rifles and said to be at least as dangerous to the firer as to those fired at.[45]

Examination of ships' manifests shows that goods exported to West Africa throughout the eighteenth century differed essentially little from those sent out by the Royal Africa Company. There was a general attempt to export a higher proportion of English goods, which cut into the re-export of European, East Indian, and even Irish textiles; and the proportion of firearms and cutlery rose with the West African demand. The only trade commodity that became greatly

more important during the eighteenth century was
liquor. French brandy and Dutch gin had always been
welcome in West Africa, but with the development of
sugar plantations, a determined attempt was made to
promote the export of rum, for obvious reasons. This
was especially true of the slavers who traded directly
from the West Indies to West Africa, and of the North
Americans, who developed the distilling of rum from
West Indies molasses very largely as a profitable component of their version of the triangular trade. Americans also shipped large quantities of tobacco (and
pipes), not only because smoking had become extremely popular in West Africa, but because agricultural products like tobacco were among the few
exports allowed them by the Old Colonial System.
Conversely, the difficulties experienced by colonials in
freighting with cheap manufactures as a result of imperial economic policy was one reason why so much
of the slave trade remained firmly under metropolitan
control.[46]

Yet, as John Atkins said in 1735, whatever advantages a trader enjoyed, however skilled he was in
"well sorting" and "well timing" his cargoes, and however carefully he applied himself to the important
task of assuaging the "fanciful and various humours"
of the Africans with firearms and firewater, the slave
trade was never certain. The chief problem was that
the supply of slaves in West Africa was rarely regular.
One reason was, rather paradoxically, the very prevalence of native wars. Although most English writers
believed that the majority of slaves were captives in
the wars that were endemic to West Africa (and were
even saved by the slave trade from the death that
would otherwise follow defeat),[47] there was some
controversy as to whether a period of actual war was
an encouragement to trade or a brake upon it. Probably petty wars or predatory campaigns brought large
supplies of slaves, but full-scale wars of retaliation, or

of empire-building such as accompanied the expansion of Ashanti from 1700 onward and of Dahomey in the 1730s, were disruptive over a wide area.[48] Yet in latter cases, although the control of subject peoples who could be enslaved and of trade routes to the coast may not have been the initial motives, the results of expansionism were undoubtedly a strengthening and more callous organizing of the slave trade. It is also perhaps significant evidence of the influence of European trade upon the most important examples of West African state-building during the Atlantic slavery period that the Dahomey and Ashanti came to control those coastal areas from which were exported the Africans most in demand for the European colonies.[49]

Preferences certainly played an important part in the pattern of exploitation of the West African coast, at least down to the mid-eighteenth century. Although they were almost totally ignorant of Africa and tribal society, the planters had well-established prejudices about the characters of Africans according to the port or part of the coast from which they were shipped. "Mandingoes" from Senegambia, for example, were not regarded as good laboring slaves, being (as John Barbot claimed in 1682) "genteel and courteous . . . but lewd and lazy to excess." They were, however, regarded as intelligent and cleanly, and thus thought to be especially suitable as craftsmen and house servants. In contrast, at the other end of the slave-trading region, the blacks from the Bight of Biafra, generically called "Iboes," though they included Ibibio and Efik as well as Ibo, were thought to make indifferent slaves. This was because, though tractable, they were despondent to the point of suicide and so unhealthy that it was said that "whosoever carries slaves from New Calabar over the West Indies, had need to pray for a quick passage."[50] "Angolans" were considered even worse in point of health and morale, and since they seemed to have no skills and to be incapable of learning, were regarded as fit only for the lowliest and dullest tasks.

Spanish and French planters considered that the Yoruba peoples shipped from the Bight of Benin made the best slaves, but the English generally preferred Gold Coast blacks, especially those shipped from Coromantine, for whom they paid the highest prices of all. Indeed, for the "Fantin, Akin and Ashanti Negroes, and all others called Kormantees"[51] was reserved that exaggerated praise (granted in India, for example, to the Sikhs) that English colonials gave to those proud people who made the best subjects because they were most difficult to assimilate. "They are not only the best and most faithful of our slaves," rhapsodized Christopher Codrington of Barbados in 1701,

> but are really all born Heroes. . . . There never was a raskal or coward of the nation, intrepid to the last degree, not a man of them but will stand to be cut to pieces without a sigh or groan, greatful and obedient to a kind master, but implacably revengeful when ill-treated. My Father, who had studied the genius and temper of all kinds of negroes 45 years with a very nice observation, would say, Noe man deserved a Corramante that would not treat him like a Friend rather than a Slave.[52]

The only planters who had doubts about the value of Coromantine slaves were those Jamaicans who having attributed the 1760 rebellion to Coromantines tried, in vain, to have the Assembly restrict their importation by a surtax. Doubtless the traders would have circumvented this prohibition easily enough, either by shipping their Coromantines elsewhere, or simply by labeling them differently. For even within the narrow bounds of the Gold Coast, slaves were said to vary so much that one begins to doubt whether the stereotypes bore any relation to race at all. Captain Phillips in 1694, for example, categorized the slaves from An-namoboe—less than ten miles from Coromantine—as "very bold and stout fellows, but the most desperate trecherous villains, and greatest cheats upon the whole coast," and said that those from Alampo, not far away, were regarded as worse than Angolans; "the worst and most washy of any that are brought to the West-Indies." Why, he could not guess,

> for they seem as well limb'd and lusty as any other negroes, and the only difference I perceiv'd in them, was, that they are not so black as the others, and are all circumcis'd, which no negroes else upon the whole coast (as I observ'd) are.[53]

Perhaps labels like Coromantine, Annamoboe, and Alampo were reserved for certain qualities rather than true racial differences, and tell us at least as much about the labelers as those labeled.

Moreover, by the mid-eighteenth century, when demand had far outstripped supply, choice was a luxury that few planters could afford. As the following table shows, the sources of supply altered significantly as the century progressed. Senegambia almost faded away as a slaving area, and although considerable numbers continued to be shipped from Sierra Leone, the Windward and Gold Coasts, the proportion of the total demand from those regions fell drastically. Probably because of European competition the Bight of Benin also declined as an English slaving area after 1740; but huge increases occurred in the numbers of slaves taken from the rich hinterland served by the Bight of Biafra, with its ports of Bonny, Old and New Calabar, and from the huge region south of São Tomé called Angola. By 1798 no less than 69 of the 150 Liverpool slave ships trading in that year cleared from the West Indies by way of Angola, with 34 from Bonny, 11 from the Gold Coast, and none at all from points to windward and farther north, though many may have called in there en route.

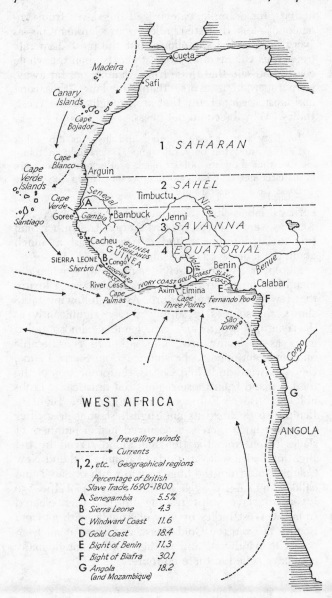

WEST AFRICA

→ *Prevailing winds*

--→ *Currents*

1, 2, *etc.* *Geographical regions*

Percentage of British
Slave Trade, 1690-1800

A	*Senegambia*	5.5%
B	*Sierra Leone*	4.3
C	*Windward Coast*	11.6
D	*Gold Coast*	18.4
E	*Bight of Benin*	11.3
F	*Bight of Biafra*	30.1
G	*Angola*	18.2
	(and Mozambique)	

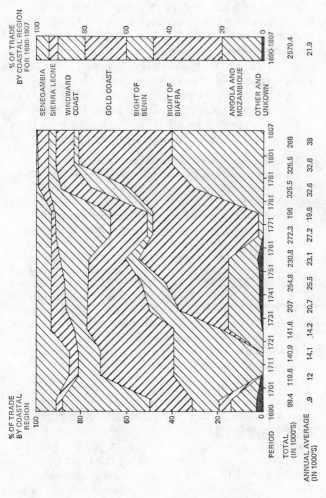

West African Origins of New World Slaves, 1690–1807.
Adapted by Barry Wood from P. D. Curtin, *Atlantic Slave Trade*, 150.

For even at the peak of efficiency of the Liverpool trade, slave cargoes were rarely made up rapidly or at a single African port. The difficulties experienced in avoiding delays on the coast and the horrifying decline in health that inevitably followed were constantly reiterated themes throughout the history of the European slave trade. "Since our Coming Into this River," wrote Captain John Blake from the Gambia in February 1652, in a heartfelt cry that might have been made in 1752 or 1789 but for the quaint spelling,

> It hath pleased the Lord aflickt us with much Sickness that we have bured three and twenty men. My Chefe and my Second maites and botswaine are three of them; both my Guneres maites and botswaines mait, three more, Mr. Dobes one of your factores foure, the rest of them being the lustiest men wee had In our Shipe. . . . It Is a very unhoulsom place that wee are burnt up for want of Are and breses, here Is noe but what Comes from the shore and they are so hot that they doe allmost Stifell us that It were beter to have none at all. . . . If our Companyes wyfes Comes to Inquire for newes to put them in as good Comfort as you may, becase they may not discomfort my wyfe. . . . I never See men dye So soudainely In my Life . . . for we have beuried all thes men In a months tyme, Sum tymes three or four In a day.[54]

The chief reasons for delay were difficulties in obtaining sufficient slaves, the time taken in palavers, and then too often further delays in obtaining provisions for the crossing. During the voyage of the Royal African Company's ship *James* in 1675–76, for example, eight months were spent patrolling the Gold Coast for a lading, and this was by no means abnormal, even though in this case confused orders from the company's agent-general, the unreliability of local chiefs, and the activities of interlopers added to the delay.[55] A more typical voyage was that of Thomas Phillips' *Hannibal* to Whydaw in 1693–94, which also spent eight busy months upon the African coast.[56] Setting

off from the Downs on October 5, 1693 in company
with the *East India Merchant* and at the same time as
two ships destined for Angola and one each for the
Bight of Biafra and the Gambia, the *Hannibal* arrived
off Cape Mesurado just before the New Year. Coasting
slowly toward the Gold Coast while vainly seeking
easy trade, Phillips arrived at Cape Coast Castle on
February 27, 1694 to find that the supply of gold and
slaves in that region was greatly depleted because
"the country was all in wars." So, after watering and
lading with 700 chests of corn for the slaves he sailed
for Whydaw, arriving there on May 1.

Having left the *Hannibal* with the *East India Merchant* in the road, Phillips went ashore to the company's factory, which he found three miles inland in
such a pestilential swampy area that he was not surprised so few of the company's servants posted there
ever lived long enough to return to England. "'Tis
compass'd round with a mud-wall about six feet high,"
he recounted,

> and on the south-side is the gate; within is a large
> yard, a mud thatch'd house, where the factor lives,
> with the white men; also a store-house, a trunk for
> slaves, and a place where they bury their dead white
> men, call'd, very improperly, the hog-yard; there is also
> a good forge, and some other small houses.

The factor, a Mr. Peirson, proved "a brisk man, and
had good interest with the king, and credit with the
subjects," possessing "good skill in treating them both
civil and rough, as occasion requir'd." He also maintained a bodyguard of stalwart slaves from the Gold
Coast who were said to be "bold, brave and sensible"
as well as loyal, and quite capable of beating "the best
forty men the king of Whydaw had in his kingdom."
Yet the initiative for trade lay definitely with the King
and his caboceers. "As soon as the king understood of
our landing," Phillips went on,

> he sent two of his cappasheirs, or noblemen, to complement us at our factory where we design'd to con-

tinue that night and pay our devoirs to his majesty
next day, which we signify'd to them, and they, by a
foot-express, to their monarch; whereupon he sent two
more of his grandees to invite us there that night, saying he waited for us . . . whereupon being unwilling
to infringe the custom, or give his majesty any offence,
we took our hamocks, and Mr. Peirson, myself, Capt.
Clay [of the *East India Merchant*], our surgeons, purs-
ers, and about 12 men, arm'd for our guard, were
carry'd to the king's town, which contains about 50
houses.

The Englishmen were immediately conducted by the
caboceers, with great ceremony, into an audience with
the King. After a few conventional politenesses, the
King turned straight to business, inquiring closely as
to the ships' cargoes and putting on a great show
of anger when he heard that they did not include
presents of silks, muskets, and pictures promised by
an earlier trader. The next day the "palavera," or
bargaining over slaves prices, took place, with the
King and the caboceers forcing what the traders
considered pretty stiff terms. Only when agreement
had been reached did the King assign the traders
lodgings and a warehouse (even then without doors
or locks) and order the "town crier" to ring the bell
that told those with slaves to sell to bring them down
to the King's trunk for trade.

Phillips and Clay were compelled to take the
King's personal trade slaves first, at steep prices despite their poor quality, and then the caboceers'. But
after the first day they alternated at the trunk so that
the native traders could not play one Englishman off
against the other. When they were first presented, the
slaves were carefully inspected by the ship's surgeons,

to see that they were sound in wind and limb, making
them jump, stretch out their arms swiftly, looking into
their mouths to judge of their age; for the cappasheirs
are so cunning, that they shave them all close before
we see them, so that let them be never so old we can
see no grey hairs in their heads or beards; and then

having liquor'd them well and sleek with palm oil 'tis
no easy matter to know an old one from a middle-age
one, but by the teeths decay; but our greatest care of
all is to buy none that are pox'd, lest they should infect
the rest aboard.

As each slave was purchased, he or she was branded
by one of the sailors,

on the breast or shoulder with a hot iron, having the
letter of the ship's name on it, the place being before
anointed with a little palm oil, which caus'd but little
pain, the mark being usually well in four or five days,
appearing very plain and white after.

Each seller was then given a note, specifying the type
of slave and the amount of merchandise agreed to at
the palaver as the price of sale for that type. This note
was redeemed the following day at the company's
temporary warehouse.

Some indication of the need for good accountancy
and mutual trust can be deduced from the following typical parcel of trade goods agreed to for each
healthy male slave in a palaver at Quashie's Town
near Dixcove, Gold Coast, in August 1789: four
Dane guns, two half barrels of powder, two pieces
fine chintz, two of patna, four "bajudepants," two nicconees, six romauls, three half cotton, the "two blues,"
one half taffeta, four lead bars, two small brass pans—
combined value about fourteen ounces of gold.[57]
An even more heterogeneous selection, derived from
trade at Bonny in 1803 when prices were at their
highest, is often quoted: one piece (of fourteen to
eighteen yards) each of chintz, baft, chelloe, ban-
danna, nicconee, and "photae," three pieces romauls
(equivalent to forty-five handkerchiefs), one large
brass pan, two muskets, 25 kegs of powder, 100 flints,
two bags of shot, 20 knives, four iron pots, four hats,
four caps, four cutlasses, six bunches of beads, 14
gallons of brandy—combined value, about £25.[58]
The slaves bought at Whydaw in 1694 were not

given over into the traders' custody until they reached the factory or perhaps the ships. When 50 or 60 had been purchased, they were conveyed to the seashore by a caboceer entitled Captain of the Slaves, who handed them over to a Captain of the Sand. Finally they were carried out in canoes or longboats to the ships, where they were shackled two-and-two "to prevent their mutiny or swimming ashore." Besides the price paid for the slaves bought, the traders were expected to pay to the King the value of six slaves as his dash,[59] to the caboceers the value of two for their role in the palaver, to the Captain of the Slaves two for conveying the trade goods safely up to the King's town and the bought slaves safely back, the Captain of the Sand two for guarding the goods and slaves on the beach, one each for the interpreter and the man in charge of watering the ship, and the value of half a slave "or as many cowries as the bell could contain" to the bellman or crier, who had the easiest job of all. All this was in addition to the cost of "factory charges, victualling the negroes after bought till they get aboard, and hire of porters to bring up the goods from the sea-side; which is seven miles at least. . . ." Later it was estimated that the costs, or "custom" at Whydaw amounted to no less than £400 per cargo.

Buying slaves in a parcel or all of one tribe and language was obviously the most efficient way to trade, but this was (with justification) always regarded as more dangerous to security than when a cargo was made up piecemeal. In cases like that of the *Hannibal*, captains tended to employ semi-assimilated Africans to train and divide the newcomers. Until the *Hannibal* was ready to sail, the new slaves were largely under the control of 30 or 40 "tame" slaves from the Gold Coast called by the old Iberian name "gromettas," who slept among them. Their duties were to prevent quarreling, give early warning of plots being hatched, teach the few words of English necessary for obedience, and instruct the newcomers in the crude elements of hygiene, such as scraping the excrement off the decks in the morning "to eschew any distempers that may engender from filth and nastiness." The chiefs of these gromettas, also called "guardians," were even given a cat-o'-nine-tails as a symbol of authority, which they exercised with relish, introducing the new slaves to the type of black overseer with whom they were to become all too familiar in the New World. At long last Captain Phillips made up his cargo of 700 slaves, consisting of 480 men and 220 women and, taking aboard as provisions more corn, yams, sweet potatoes, "figolas" (kidney beans), dried plantains, coconuts, and citrus fruits, set sail for Barbados by way of São Tomé on July 27, 1694. Captain Clay and the *East India Merchant* with 650 slaves were several days behind.

MIDDLE PASSAGE

An Atlantic crossing in a slaver was always an unpleasant business, but in conditions of exceptional delay, bad weather, shortage of provisions, epidemic, slave mutiny, or sadistic captaincy, such a voyage could become a nightmare as hideous as any in history. Even without the effects of guilt and blame, the normal reader's taste for horror and outrage has ensured that exceptional cases have always been given prominence. This was particularly true during the abolition campaign, though at the same time the defenders of the trade, in compensation, stretched credulity to paint the Middle Passage in a more favorable light. Captain Hugh Crow, looking back before the end of slavery but long after the ending of the trade, went so far as to claim that he was feted as hero and savior by certain blacks in Jamaica, who wrote a song in his honor after he had fought his way clear of three French privateers.[60] Like most ostentatiously brave men, Crow was a romantic. Most of his slaving colleagues were as unlikely to romanticize their business as to engage an enemy more heavily armed than themselves. Indeed, the most demoralizing aspect of the slave trade, as of slave owning in general, was that by regarding slaves as chattels, commodities, cargo, and not as human beings, traders and owners (sustained by the law) became even more inured to the sufferings of the slaves than to those of their seamen and white servants. As Lord Mansfield said during the infamous *Zong* insurance case (1783): "The matter left to the jury, was, whether it was from necessity; for they had no doubt (though it shocks one very much) that the case of the slaves was the same as if horses had been thrown overboard."[61] Even kindness was not humanity but good business. Perhaps the insensitivity of the traders was unconsciously demonstrated by Hugh Crow himself in echoing the common argument:

> Could anyone in his senses suppose, that after paying perhaps £25 for a negro, their owners would not take especial care of them, and give them the comforts which would conduce to their health?

Unfortunately, however, survival on the Middle Passage was not even a case of good management so much as of good luck. With the immediate shipping of a healthy cargo, a rapid transatlantic voyage, good food, and vigilant supervision, there were cases where not a single slave was lost; and yet there were others where under the same conditions half the slaves died. In contrast, there were voyages in which under the most brutally inauspicious circumstances, undeserving captains were able to collect handsome bonuses for cargoes delivered almost intact,[62] even if, as was often the case, the losses among the crew were proportionately greater than among the slaves. When life was such a lottery, fatalism—if not cynicism—was inevitable. While there were a dozen ways in which a hugely profitable voyage could be turned into disaster, there was no sure way to prevent misfortune; and some afflictions such as epidemics seemed, in the slavers' ignorance of causes, merely the operation of malignant chance. "What the small-pox spar'd," lamented Captain Phillips,

> the flux swept off to our great regret, after all our pains and care to give their messes in due order and season, keeping their lodgings as clean and sweet as possible, and enduring so much misery and stench so long among a parcel of creatures nastier than swine; and after all our expectations to be defeated by their mortality.[63]

Between the loading of the first slaves and sailing for America was a time of constant vigilance by the crew, for as Captain Phillips pointed out, it was then while they lay "in sight of their own country" that the slaves were most likely to make their escape or rebel. "To prevent which," said the *Hannibal's* captain,

> we always keep centinels upon the hatchways, and have a chest full of small arms, ready loaded and prim'd constantly lying at hand upon the quarter-deck, together with some granada shells; and two of our quarter-deck guns, pointing on the deck thence, and two more out of the steerage, the door at which is always kept shut, and well barr'd; they are fed twice a day, at 10 in the morning, and 4 in the evening, which is the time they are aptest to mutiny, being all upon deck; therefore all that time, what of our men are not employ'd in distributing their victals to them, and settling them, stand to their arms; and some with lighted matches at the great guns that yaun upon them, loaden with partridge, till they have done and gone down to their kennels between decks.[64]

As the day for departure came closer, signified by the flying of a special flag, the daily firing of a signal gun, or the sending ashore of the gromettas, tension mounted. Most captains liked to set sail at night, though on the northern coasts it was a matter of using the tide and elsewhere the offshore breeze, which came only in the early morning. Once out of sight of land, supervision was somewhat relaxed, though few captains shared Thomas Phillips' reasoning that shackles could then be removed, since the slaves, being ignorant of seamanship, were no longer likely to rebel. "When we have completed our purchase of them," said William Littleton in 1789,

> we take the chain off their necks, and put a pair of shackles on their legs—which shackles have generally a ring upon them between their legs—through which we reeve a chain, by which chain we keep them to secure them whilst they are on deck.[65]

Except during rough weather, in most ships as many slaves as possible were kept on deck throughout the hours of daylight, with the men in the fore part of the ship separated from the women, girls and infants by the boys herded around the main hatchway. The very bows of the ship, the "airiest part" and conveniently close to the "heads," was usually reserved as a "hospital" for sick slaves.[66] A similar method of separation was employed in the holds, as can be seen in the famous engraving commissioned by Thomas Clarkson in 1789, of the *Brookes* of Liverpool. On some ships the children, the sick, and even some of the trustier adults were allowed to remain on deck all night, though this was less from humanity than from the impossible overcrowding below. Before regulations were introduced in 1788, it was usual to carry at least two slaves for each ton of a ship's displacement. This was bad enough with large vessels, but most slavers were small, probably averaging under 100 tons displacement in 1700 and scarcely 200 by 1800.[67] It was quite normal for a ship displacing 100 tons to carry 250 slaves, or one of 50 tons over 100. In

1789, John Knox testified that in one voyage he had
carried 450 slaves in a vessel of 108 tons, proudly
adding that only 18 lives had been lost on the Middle Passage.[68] There is evidence of some small vessels with less than 4 feet depth in the holds, though
most slave ships were constructed comparatively high
between decks.[69] This space, however, was generally
no more than 5½ feet, so that a tall slave might only
stand upright under the hatchway, which might give
an extra foot of headroom. Most of the space in the
hold, however, was divided by shelves, into which the
slaves were crammed with so little space that they
could not sit upright or even lie on their backs fully
stretched out all at the same time. Although "wind
sails" were often fitted to deflect whatever breeze
there was through the gratings, the slave hold in the
doldrums became like a furnace, and the stench, even
when the slaves were not sick from dysentery, was
notorious.

In a well-regulated slave ship in fine weather the
holds were daily scraped and sprinkled with vinegar,
and occasionally "fumigated" by the simple expedient
of dipping a red-hot iron in a pannikin of vinegar.
Considerable care was also taken that the slaves were
given enough to eat of food to which they were accustomed, and sufficient water. "Early in the morning,
soon after daylight," said William Littleton,

> they have some biscuit distributed to every man and
> woman and person on board, and a glass of inferior
> brandy or rum, diluted with water half and half; when
> their first general meal is ready, that is generally served
> to them, and they have generally more than they can
> eat—some is left—in the evening again, about Four or
> Five o'clock, they have a second meal of another kind
> of food—we seldom serve them with the same sort of
> food twice in the same day—we vary it as often as we
> can, and give them all regularly their allowance as
> often as we find it necessary—this depends on the heat
> of the weather.[70]

"Their chief diet is called dabbadab," wrote Captain Phillips of the Whydaw blacks,

> being Indian corn ground as small as oat-meal, in iron mills, which we carry for that purpose; and after mix'd with water, and boil'd well in a large copper furnace, till 'tis thick as a pudding, about a peckful of which in vessels, call'd crews, is allow'd to 10 men, with a little salt, malagetta, and palm oil, to relish.[71]

At other meals a mess of yams, sweet potatoes, or dried plantains was served, with perhaps some fish caught from the ship, salt "stock" fish, or even a slice or two of salt beef added. Citrus fruits were sometimes boiled into the morning grog as a specific against scurvy, though this seems to have been a disease that affected the crew more often than the slaves.[72] Yet for the slaves protein foods were sadly deficient, and African provisions were rarely plentiful enough for an entire crossing. At least half the time the slaves were expected to subsist on boiled "horse beans," huge quantities of which were shipped out from England throughout the history of the slave trade. Opinion as to their popularity and food value varied. Phillips claimed that the slaves found them delectable, "beating their breast, eating them, and crying Pram! Pram! which is Very good! They are indeed the best diet for them," he added, "having a binding quality, and consequently good to prevent the flux."[73] Later commentators, however, pointed out that horse beans were regarded in England as being unfit for human consumption and cited cases of slaves being persuaded to eat them only by being threatened with burning coals as an alternative.

A wise captain did his utmost to give his slaves at least some exercise and to keep them distracted if he could not actually make them happy. A common feature was the evening dances, which some writers painted in glamorous colors with the slaves gaily cavorting either to their own drums and lutes, or to the "bagpipes, harp and fiddle" of the crew. Others more realistically described the pathetic spectacle of slaves, sick, lethargic, and in chains, compelled to jig for an hour or more at the threat of the lash, for the good of their health or souls. "The utmost Attention is paid to the keeping up their Spirits, and to indulge them in all their little Humours," said James Penny in 1789. After dinner

> they are . . . supplied with Pipes and Tobacco; both Sexes sometimes will smoak—they are amused with instruments of music peculiar to their own Country, with which we provided them; and when tired of Music and Dancing, they go on to Games of Chance—The Women are supplied with Beads, which they make into Ornaments.[74]

James Penny even claimed that as the voyage went on he had found the slaves with good treatment "perfectly reconciled to their condition, and in Appearance as happy as any of his Crew" (a rather dubious comparison in the light of the notorious disaffection of some white crewmen), and that in his opinion similar kind treatment and favorable responses were the rule rather than the exception in the trade.

Yet so much—good feeding and treatment, the relative contentment of the slaves and their health—could hinge upon a smooth and rapid crossing, and this in turn was largely dependent upon the season of the year and the part of Africa cleared from. The autumn season of West Atlantic hurricanes was clearly to be shunned, but with delays in Africa and on the voyage itself this was not always possible. Moreover, localized "tornadoes" were likely to occur in the equatorial belt in any month of the year. The swiftest and least troublesome voyage was likely to begin from Senegambia or Upper Guinea, not far south of the region of northeast tradewinds, and four-week crossings were not unknown. Most English slavers, however, traded much farther south and southeast, and had first to sail westward about a thousand miles along the Equator to clear the Bight and then beat laboriously northward to the latitude of the Canaries before they could find easterly winds to carry them across the Atlantic. Ships from the bights of Benin and Biafra, and even from the Gold Coast and Angola to north and south, often called at the Portuguese islands of Fernado Po or São Tomé for water, wood, and fresh provisions; but some were forced to make a farther landfall in West Africa, or even Brazil, if winds were unfavorable or negligible. Even less fortunate vessels found themselves becalmed in midocean for months at a stretch, with horrifying results.

The worst and most common affliction of the Middle Passage was disease. At the best of times, dislocation, migration, and trade are prime causes of epidemic, when localized immunities to disease break down with mutual contact. The triangular trade of Atlantic slavery peculiarly focused the disease-causing viruses, bacteria, and parasites of three continents, with results made even more spectacular on the Middle Passage because of overcrowding and debility.[75]

Of the chief scourges of slavery, smallpox, serious enough in Europe, was devastating on the Middle Passage. "The negroes are so incident to the smallpox," wrote James Phillips, "that few ships that carry them escape without it, and sometimes it makes vast havock and destruction among them." Though without knowing it they had carried the disease, the white crewmen were usually immune. "I have several white men and boys aboard that had never had that distemper," related the *Hannibal*'s captain,

> and were constantly among the blacks that were sick of it, yet none of them in the least catch'd it, tho' it be the very same malady in its effects, as well as symptoms, among the blacks, as among us in England, beginning with the pain in the head, back, shivering, vomiting, fever, etc.

As least as general a gift from Europe—though less obvious in their depredations—were the varieties of the common cold, which could strike the Africans with vicious force and, with pulmonary complications, often kill. In return, the West African "climate" infected Europeans on the coast with disease to which Africans were comparatively immune, such as *falciparum* malaria, yellow fever, blackwater fever, and sleeping sickness, killing off as many as two thirds of all new residents within a year and leaving perhaps one in a hundred to make his permanent residence in West Africa, "the white man's grave."[76]

The most notorious disease to travel from tropical America to tropical Africa and the slave ships was syphilis—though opportunities for infection on board ship were severely limited—and refined strains of malaria and yellow fever to which Africans had limited resistance. Yet, many of the diseases that swept the crowded holds of the slave ships and later infected the "creole" slaves on plantations, were African in origin, made epidemic not only by close contact but by the intermingling of people from various parts of Africa where lack of communication had reduced the size of disease environments. Some diseases, such as the disfiguring elephantiasis, leprosy,[77] and yaws (a nonvenereal cousin of syphilis) or the blinding ophthalmia, appeared peculiar to Africans; but others were regarded with more consternation and horror because they attacked white men as well as blacks, particularly landsmen on their first slaving voyage. Most dreaded of all were the varieties of bacillary and amoebic dysentery, especially the descriptively entitled "bloody flux" and "white flux," for which there seemed neither prevention nor cure. "The distemper which my men as well as the blacks mostly die of," wrote Phillips,

> was the white flux, which was so violent and inveterate, that no medicine would in the least check it; so that when any of our men were seiz'd with it, we esteem'd

him a dead man, as he generally proved. I cannot imagine what should cause it in them so suddenly, they
being free from it till about a week after we left the
island of St. Thomas [São Tomé]. And next to the
malignity of the climate, I can attribute it to nothing
else but the unpurg'd black sugar, and raw unwhole-
some rum they bought there, of which they drank in
punch to great excess, and which it was not in my
power to hinder, having chastis'd several of them, and
flung overboard what rum and sugar I could find.

The medical treatment provided on the slave ships
was as rudimentary as one would expect from the
general ignorance of the day, the scanty qualifications
of the ships' "surgeons," and the cheese-paring of
the traders (who pragmatically considered a bonus
to the surgeons of a shilling a head for all slaves
safely delivered a better investment than expensive
medicines). In 1789, when asked whether in case of
sickness the slaves were supplied with medicines and
taken care of, William Littleton replied: "They are—
We take out medicines for that purpose, and the
Surgeon every morning visits them below, to know if
any of them have any complaints; and frequently
administers medicines to them below, as well as
upon deck."[78] On closer inquiry, however, it tran-
spired that the "medicines" administered were little
more than sago, cornflower, wine, and "spices," which
amount to herbal remedies.[79] Surgeons a century
later had not much improved on James Phillips' treatments, which included a diet of costive vegetables for
the flux, or giving to those in the agonies of smallpox "as much water as they desir'd to drink, and
some palm-oil to anoint their sores." Prayer would
have been no more effective, for bitter experience
showed that only "seasoning"—the slow building-up
of immunities among the survivors—could reverse or
slow the epidemiological effects of the Atlantic trade.
This, of course, applied at least as much to the
hardened white crewmen of the slavers and the few
veteran soldiers and factors in West Africa, as to the

new slaves dispersed among the creoles on American plantations.

If they knew next to nothing of the physiological causes of slave mortality, the traders knew even less of the psychological effects of the slave trade. These could also kill: indirectly through lowering resistance to disease, directly through suicide or "mutiny." Some captains came close to treating the symptoms by keeping the slaves distracted or under rigorous control; the deeper causes they could only attribute—with superb rationalization—to African "humours" or lack of moral fiber. Ignorant themselves, all captains were conditioned to believe that African attitudes stemmed from natural stupidity. Many told tales of the curious beliefs held by Africans that they were being transported to be eaten by transatlantic anthropophagi and that even their spirits would not return if their bodies were dismembered. Few traders had Captain Snelgrave's sense to tell the captives plainly the real fate in store for them; though Snelgrave himself was not above threatening those who rebelled with instant dismemberment.[80]

The attitudes of West Africans to their immediate dislocation and an unknown and potentially worse ultimate fate differed in ways that were usually characterized as "Ibo" despondency or "Coromantine" resistance. "The negroes are so wilful and loth to leave their own country," admitted Captain Phillips (though talking of Whydaw slaves)

> that they often leap'd out of the canoes, boat and ship, and kept under water till they were drowned to avoid being taken up and saved by our boats, which pursued them; they having more dreadful apprehension of Barbadoes than we can have of hell.

On the voyage of the *Hannibal* no less than 12 slaves drowned themselves, and others were deterred only by the sight of their fellows torn asunder by the scavenging sharks, which habitually trailed the slave ships

just as seagulls shadow fishing boats. Instead, some
"starv'd themselves to death; for 'tis their belief," asserted Phillips, "that when they die they return home
to their own country and friends again." Yet Ibo slaves
were said to be even more troublesome, lapsing *en
masse* into an irreversible state of "fixed melancholy,"
refusing to eat and constantly looking for other ways,
such as hanging themselves or cutting their throats,
to end their misery.

Fiercer spirits preferred rebellion, though this too
was tantamount to suicide.[81] "I have been several
voyages when there has been no attempt made by
our Negroes to mutiny," wrote Snelgrave in 1734,

> which, I believe, was owing chiefly to their being kindly
> used, and to my officers care in keeping a good watch.
> But sometimes we meet with stout stubborn people
> amongst them, who are never to be made easy; and
> these are generally some of the Cormantines.[82]

Snelgrave went on to describe the voyage of the
Henry and *Elizabeth* of London to the Gold Coast
in 1721 when Coromantines were bought whom the
traders "were obliged to secure . . . very well in irons,
and watch them narrowly: Yet they nevertheless
mutinied, tho' they had little prospect of succeeding."
The first outbreak was quelled, but Snelgrave heard
from the "linguists" (interpreters and agents) aboard
that the slaves continued to plot. A short while later,
a slave aboard the *Elizabeth* broke from his chains
and killed the cooper with an ax, and Snelgrave
determined to make a salutary example of him. In full
view of the slaves brought up on decks of the eight
ships then anchored in the roads, the culprit was
hoisted up to the fore yardarm and shot to death by
ten white crewmen with muskets. "This struck a sudden Damp upon our Negroe-Men," claimed Snelgrave,

> who thought that, on account of my Profit, I would not
> have executed him. The body being cut down upon the

Deck, the head was cut off and thrown overboard. This last part was done, to let our Negroes see, that all who offended thus, should be served in the same manner. For many of the Blacks believe that if they are put to death and not dismembered, they shall return again to their own Country, after they are thrown overboard. But neither the Person that was executed, nor his Country men of Corramantee (as I understood afterwords) were so weak as to believe any such thing; tho' many I had on board from other Countries had that Opinion.[83]

Captain Snelgrave, like an old-fashioned army officer, believed that "kindness" was not incompatible with constant vigilance and the threat of violent punishment, just as even less enlightened traders believed that slaves—like soldiers—might best be cowed by being kept mystified about their fate. Nearly all agreed that the worst fault was being too familiar with the blacks. This opinion Snelgrave drove home with his anecdote of Captain Masservy of the *Ferrers* galley, who was wont to wonder among his slaves while they were being fed, on the principle of the old proverb, "The Master's Eye makes the horse fat," "Being on the Forecastle of the ship, amongst the Men-Negroes when they were eating their Vitals," wrote Snelgrave,

they laid hold on him, and beat out his Brains with the little tubs, out of which they eat their boiled Rice. This Mutiny having been plotted amongst all the grown Negroes on board, they run to the forepart of the Ship in a body and endeavoured to force the Barricado on the Quarter-Deck, not regarding the Musquets or half Pikes, that were presented to their Breasts by the white Men, through the Loop-holes. So that at last the chief Mate was obliged to order one of the Quarter-deck Guns laden with Partridge-Shot, to be fired amongst them; which occasioned a terrible Distruction: For there were near eighty Negroes kill'd and downed, many jumping overboard when the Gun was fired. This indeed put an end to the Mutiny, but most of the

Slaves that remained alive grew so sullen, that several of them were starved to death, obstinately refusing to take any Sustanance: And after the Ship was arrived at Jamaica, they attempted twice to mutiny, before the Sale of them began. This with their former Misbehaviour coming to be publickly known, none of the Planters cared to buy them, tho' offered at a low Price. So that this proved a very unsuccessful Voyage, for the Ship was detained many Months at Jamaica on that account, and at last was lost there in a huricane.[84]

Slave voyages differed so widely that it is almost as misleading to talk of "average mortalities" on the Middle Passage as of the "average" slave. James Phillips described two voyages, on one of which he lost 14 and on the other 320 of 700 slaves, and in the inquiries of 1788–92 different witnesses could argue to averages of under 5 percent and over 35 percent per crossing, depending on which side of the controversy they were supporting.[85] Even today, estimates by reputable scholars vary from Basil Davidson's 13 percent to Robert Rotberg's 33 percent.[86] All in all, the evidence seems to point toward a steady decrease in average mortality on the Middle Passage from at least 20 percent at the beginning of the eighteenth century to well under 15 percent at the end of the English trade. The improvement was probably due more to greater efficiency—cutting down the chances of mortality so far as was humanly possible—than to the introduction of regulations after 1788. It has been calculated that the Royal African Company between 1680 and 1688 lost 23.4 percent of the slaves between purchase in West Africa and delivery in the West Indies, though this included losses both while making up cargoes on the African coast and while waiting for sales in the Caribbean.[87] Toward the other end of the period the merchants of Liverpool, in estimating their profits and losses in 1788, calculated mortality of slaves in transit at only 5 percent, whatever the ratio per ton. Though it was then in their interest to argue for the greatest possible expenses, the Liverpool merchants probably deluded themselves or were disingenuous, for T. F. Buxton, analyzing ships carrying 47,308 slaves in 1791 and 1792, calculated an average mortality of 14.3 percent.[88] This figure is convincingly close to the famous compilations of returns made by Gaston Martin (1931) and Dieudonné Rinchon (1938) of slave ships sailing from Nantes from 1715 to 1792. Contrary to most contemporary witnesses, who attributed the highest mortality to cargoes sailing from Angola, Rinchon calculated losses of 10.4 percent from Senegambia, 12.5 percent from Angola, 17.2 percent from Upper and Lower Guinea, and 22.3 percent from distant Mozambique, over the period 1748 to 1792. Relating mortality to the length of the voyage is aided by figures derived from the early nineteenth-century Brazilian trade, when average losses had been reduced to 9.7 percent, which show that the mortality on voyages of less than a month's duration averaged 5.1 percent, but for those of six weeks about eight percent and for those of eight weeks or more, a disastrous 26 percent.[89]

It is also worth pointing out here that the losses among white crew men were proportionately far higher than those for the slaves. In 1788 Thomas Clarkson (after one of the earliest pieces of such research) testified that of the 3,170 seamen sailing on the 88 slavers that set out from Liverpool in 1786, at least 20.3 percent died, with 34.7 percent more deserting or discharged in West Africa and the West Indies. The comparable figures for Bristol in 1784–85 were 23.7 percent dead and 26.3 percent deserted or discharged. These rates were five times as high as those in the East Indies trade, ten times as high as those on ships sailing only between Great Britain and the West Indies, and 20 times as high as in the Russian, Newfoundland, and Greenland trades.[90] If it is true to say that the slave trade brutalized the traders even while it degraded the slaves, one of the

chief reasons can be seen to have been the horrifying mortality that devalued life for the whites at least
as much as for the blacks they traded in.

DESTINATIONS

Because of the prevailing winds and currents, a remarkable proportion of English slavers continued to
call successively at Barbados, the Leeward Islands,
and Jamaica, with some going on to mainland North
America—thus retracing in each voyage the sequence
of development of the chief slave plantation colonies.
Even after Barbados and the Leewards became comparatively saturated with slaves, slave ships destined
for Jamaica were practically bound to make their first
landfall to windward at one of the lesser Antilles;
and despite the takeover of much of the mainland
trade by New Englanders, a majority of the ships
carrying slaves for Virginia and the Middle Colonies
passed through the Caribbean first, with only South
Carolina receiving nearly all its slaves direct from
Africa. The plantation trade was further shaped by
the natural desire of the transatlantic slavers to cur-
tail their voyages as much as possible and achieve a
quick turnaround. There was thus a tendency for certain colonial ports, notably Bridgetown (Barbados),
Basseterre (St. Kitts), St. John (Antigua), Kingston
(Jamaica), and Charleston (South Carolina) to become major entrepôts from which slaves were transshipped. Altogether, these patterns of distribution had
important effects on the mortality and consequent
prices of slaves, as on the mechanics of purchase,
payment, and capitalization (which also influenced
slave prices), if not also on the quality of the slaves
destined for each colony and thus its subsequent
demographic character.

The retail price of slaves was, of course, governed
by their quality, the laws of supply and demand, and

the ability of planters to pay. Yet it was clearly in the traders' interest—and thus, indirectly, the planters' too—to dispose of their cargoes at a single market, in large groups, as soon as an adequate price was agreed upon. It was usual for owners to give their captains great powers of discretion in making sales (as well as generous bonuses), and in the earlier years of the trade it was common for captains to wait longish periods while market conditions were being ascertained, to shop around between islands and to bargain at great length with planters, sometimes for individual slaves. In these respects the Royal African Company theoretically enjoyed advantages, both through its monopoly in an insatiable market and through the work of its local agents in arranging sales before the ships arrived. The free traders after 1712 had greater flexibility, but were generally without the services of a network of agents to instruct them in the most certain and lucrative markets, or to arrange for sales in advance. As the trade expanded, however, and as credit conditions became more uniform and communications more efficient, it became increasingly common for individual planters or small syndicates to purchase whole cargoes, and for the management of sales in each colony to fall under the control of agents working on a 10 or 15 percent commission. Enterprising planters even outfitted ships in the direct African trade, though the more usual form of slave trading organized from the colonies rather than the metropolis was for commission agents (such as Henry Laurens of South Carolina) to involve themselves in the entire business of slave trading. This included the hiring of vessels and crews, obtaining cargoes of trade goods, negotiating insurance, and sending out captains with detailed orders for each section of the triangular trade.

In most respects slave trading thus became rather more sophisticated at the point of delivery than in West Africa, though at least in the earlier years there

were many parallels between the methods used by
traders to sell planters and those used by Africans
to sell to Europeans on the African coast. The colonial
commission agents unconsciously copied the roles of
the African caboceers or "linguists," ever present and
all-important throughout the trading process—ascer-
taining from the buyers the extent of their need,
arranging for supply, fixing a schedule of prices by
negotiating with sellers what they would accept and
with buyers what they would pay, and finally organizing sales and accepting their commission. Similarly,
the trading sea captains were equivalent to the African "captains" who brought the slaves originally down
to the coast for sale; treating the slaves at least as
callously most of the time yet copying "African" methods in making them attractive for sale—just as wise
planters were as wary in buying as vigilant traders
on the African coast. Besides this, the psychological
trauma of dislocation and mystification affecting the
slaves themselves must have been remarkably similar in colonial harbors and vendue houses to those
brought about by sales on the African coast.

A typical early process was that by which Captain
Peter Blake disposed of the cargo of the Royal African Company's ship *James* in 1676.[91] The ship arrived at "Kerley" (Carlisle) Bay, Barbados, on Sunday, May 21, after a 74-day voyage in which 30 of
the 403 slaves aboard had died.[92] On Monday morning Edwyn Stede, one of the company's Barbados
factors, came out to the *James* to look over the slaves,
giving orders to prepare them for sale on the following Thursday. This entailed shaving the slaves and
giving them fresh water for washing, palm oil to im-
part a shine of spurious health to their limbs, and
pipes and tobacco to raise their spirits. If more ingenious and horrible means to disguise sickness were
used as were described later—such as smearing a mixture of rust and oil on skins to hide the smallpox, or
stuffing oakum in rectums to arrest the effects of the

flux—Captain Blake, quite naturally, did not record them.[93] Nor did he mention whether, like some captains, he landed the slaves to parade them through the streets, or even whether they were on public display before sale at all. Almost certainly, however, Edwyn Stede was busy advertising the cargo, both by posters and handbills distributed throughout Bridgetown and by advertisements in the Barbadian newspapers.

On the first day of the *James*'s sale 163 slaves were sold, with 70 and 118 on subsequent days. Presumably the method used was auctioning, either in the modern style or "by inch of candle," in which the last bidder before the candle sputtered out became the successful buyer. Another form of sale commonly used in the Lesser Antilles was the "scramble." In this method purchasers opted for types of slave at a pre-bargained price and were given tickets accordingly. Then the slaves were jumbled together in a kind of darkened tent of sailcloth on the ship's deck and, at a signal, were descended upon by the buyers, frantically grabbing the most likely-looking candidates. Although popular with traders as a means of disposing of indifferent slaves and enjoyed as a spectacle by provincial boors, this undignified performance was not universal, both because of the terror it inspired among the slaves (numbers of whom were known to have leaped overboard and been devoured by sharks, or to have run through the streets to escape their future owners) and because of the very real chance of infection at such close contact. Sometimes new slaves were not sold on board ship but on shore in the vendue house, where they would mingle for the first time with the creole slaves brought down for re-sale.[94] This was, in any case, the only method possible with those slaves refused in the shipboard sales when the ships had to sail on without them. For example, after the 351 healthier slaves in the cargo of the *James* had been sold, there were still 22 "refuse" slaves remaining. Five were sold to a planter 2 days later, but 7 men and 10 women had to be left behind with Edwyn Stede when the *James* set sail for Nevis on Saturday, June 10.

On this leg of its voyage the *James* carried a second cargo of blacks: 224 "Bight" slaves from New Calabar, transshipped from the *John Alexander*, the captain of which had declined to take them farther because the Nevis planters would not guarantee onward freighting of sugar. Before he even reached Charles Town, Peter Blake was summoned aboard the frigate H.M.S. *Phoenix* by Sir William Stapleton, governor of the Leewards, who angrily asked him why he had not brought his own cargo of Gold Coast slaves. Stapleton accused Blake of carrying "the refuse of the Shipps that were at Barbados" and was not mollified when told that they were a whole cargo, since Bight slaves were commonly regarded as second-rate. Prospects of sales in Nevis seemed even dimmer when the company's agent told Blake that he had instructions that if sales could not be made at £19 per head, the ship must be sent on to Jamaica. This last the captain was unwilling to accept, because the slaves were already sickly and the Jamaican planters would certainly label them the refuse of both Barbados and the Leewards. Furthermore, his crew, who he had promised would be on their way back to England within a fortnight, were close to mutiny. Luckily, the Nevis planters were starved for slaves and Blake was able to sell his whole cargo within a week, though for an average of less than 3,500 pounds of sugar each (about £18). This included 20 refuse slaves at 1,700 pounds of sugar apiece, and even "19 which being very bad were carryed ashoar 18 of them were sold for a Thousand pound of Sugar per head and one which was a mad Meuth [Mute?] was sould for 1400 li of Sugar"[95] Almost as important as his sales, Peter Blake was able to make up his homeward cargo with sugar freighted at £3 10s. per ton. He set sail from Nevis on July 8 1676 and anchored in the Downs on October 12, just over 18 months after setting out.

By 1750 the system of company agents tenuously holding onto their privileged position (which brought them personal fortunes but satisfied few others) had long been superseded by a myriad of competing slave factorage houses, all striving to keep an efficient intelligence service and provide the most attractive credit terms. Indeed, a predictable process of Darwinian consolidation was already far advanced. Small firms were squeezed out by those with greater resources, just as small islands became satellites of larger entrepôts, and—at least according to American complaints—the mainland traders suffered from the advantages unfairly enjoyed by the West Indians. Above all, in a trade dominated even more than most by the metropolis, it was only those colonial firms with good commercial connections with England that were consistently successful, and in course of time this meant that successful local factors were scarcely colonials at all.

Although from at least 1740 Rhode Island was the chief American mainland center for slave trading, the letter books of Henry Laurens of South Carolina, amply represented in Elizabeth Donnan's splendid collection of documents, are probably the finest source for the organization of the slave trade in the colonies as a whole. They are also invaluable for the more parochial concerns of South Carolina and for the commercial grievances that alienated many American merchants from England in the third quarter of the eighteenth century.[96] Henry Laurens was in the business of slave trading for at least 27 years before the American Revolution, and his durability was largely due to the excellent connections he made with the metropolis, beginning with a visit to England in 1748, the year that he and George Austin went into partnership to form the firm of Austin and Laurens. Yet much was also due to Laurens' general

business acumen, for there was a great deal of plausibility in his constant complaints that the mainland
trader had to be exceptionally ingenious to stay solvent under the old colonial system.

The first drawback to the business of slave trading
in the mainland plantation colonies was that too often
traders and planters simply had to accept the slaves
they could get. Of the 614 vessels carrying slaves to
Virginia between 1727 and 1769, for example, 410 had
come directly from West Indian ports, 65 from other
North American colonies, and eight from England;
only 128 were listed as having sailed directly from
Africa, with a further 28 reported as being from both
Africa and England. These figures are somewhat misleading since the largest cargoes came in the direct
African trade, and most of those vessels carrying
slaves to British North America from the British West
Indies carried other cargoes as well. In 1750–51, for
example, the 29 vessels listed as arriving in Virginia
from the West Indies with slaves carried a total of
only 368 slaves, with 13 slaves arriving in one other
vessel from another mainland colony; compared with
no fewer than 1,017 slaves brought in four vessels
from Africa and 713 in three ships listed as from
Bristol via Africa. For New Jersey (the middle colony
with the smallest importation of slaves) between 1718
and 1757, 28 vessels arrived with 611 slaves: seven
with 206 slaves from the Leewards, seven with 107
from Barbados, six with 68 from Jamaica, and three
with 204 from Africa.[97] The slaves obtained by way
of the West Indies were rarely of high quality because of the length of the voyage, and were often
refuse because of the preemptive advantages enjoyed
by first ports of call. "As good a Sale as ever I made
considering the assortment," claimed Henry Laurens
in reporting a mediocre return for 20 slaves in November 1764:

> one Man was maim'd by a shot in his ancle and not a
> little peppered with the Venereal disease, one of the

Girls very meagre and in a dangerous way and most of the females small and ordinary, nevertheless had there been 8 or 10 likely Men amongst them the average would have been Five or Seven Pounds sterling more, as I have sold them for Credit which commonly affects a Sale 10 per Ct. only for two or three Months.[98]

In a similar transaction from the same year Laurens wrote to his correspondents, Messrs. Smith and Baillie of St. Kitts, to explain in detail how he had disposed of 50 "new negroes" sent from the West Indies in the sloop *Mary Ann*. All the slaves had reached Charleston alive, but "extreamly meagre and thin," and when Laurens and his partner looked them over they were at a loss to know what to do. At first they planned to send them on to Georgetown in the Wynyaw district of South Carolina as a speculation, but the winds proved contrary. Then George Austin suggested Port Royal, but Laurens considered the project too chancy, since he did not "so well like the payments in the quarter." At length Mr. Francis Stuart, a planter of Beaumont, offered £ 11,200 currency for the parcel (that is, about £ 1,400 sterling, or £ 28 each), which Laurens countered with a minimum price of £ 12,135. This Stuart could only manage with extended credit, and Laurens was forced to accept payment in bills at nine months' sight, credit as long as he ever liked to give, presenting the following account:

5 Men not extraordinary	£ 300– £ 1500
10 Inferior 3 of them very ordinary	£ 280– £ 2800
15 Women chiefly small and very thin	£ 245– £ 3675
16 Girls very thin and slender	£ 200– £ 3200
4 Boys small	£ 240– £ 960
	£ 12,135

Henry Laurens considered these prices the best possible, especially in view of the impending arrival of ships from Africa, including one from the Windward Coast with 410 slaves "which would have

knocked the Sale . . . on the head." He apologized
for the extended credit, but pointed out that he too
suffered since he had already paid the South Carolina
duty on the blacks and certain advances on the whole
transaction. In rendering account Laurens informed
Smith and Baillie that he had credited them with
£10,905 (the proceeds of the sale less 10 percent
commission), though this was subsequently debited
£3,536 1s.7d. for the *Mary Ann's* return cargo of 244
barrels and 62½ half barrels of rice, and 5,000 roof
shingles.[99]

Henry Laurens and his fellow South Carolina
traders saw that a surer supply of slaves and an easier
profit could be obtained in trading directly with
Africa, and although slaves continued to arrive in
small numbers in ships trading in general cargoes
between islands and mainland, the direct trade had
become the norm for South Carolina by 1750. Yet the
African trade also had its peculiar problems. With
comparatively few voyages but large cargoes there
were the dangers of dearth being followed by glut,
of traders having to charge high prices for slaves at
times when planters were waiting for crop time or
returns, and of the consequent attenuation of local
credit facilities. Much more than the West Indians,
the mainlanders were dependent upon a steady supply of slaves at the right times of year. "I have ob-
serv'd," noted Laurens to the famous London firm of
Richard Oswald and Co. in 1762, "that 1500 Negroes
droping in by 4 or 5 Importations at a little distance
of time from each other have always yielded a greater
average than half the number arriv'd at the same
juncture,"[100] though he might have added that even
the latter case was greatly preferable to the same
number of slaves arriving haphazardly in 20 vessels
from the West Indies. "The Market in this Country
does not continue as in the West Indies long at a
medium price," summed up Laurens six years later:

our prices are (almost without exception) either high or too low to make tolerable profits by. In the West Indies terms of payment and prices do not greatly vary, you have a chance of going easily from one Island to another and the Merchant undertakes to turn out the Cargo at so much per head at least upon such terms of remittance, whence the objections that I make to such remittances from this place is no objection in the Islands, nor any where else where a stated price for the Cargo is found.[101]

Henry Laurens went to England again in 1771–72 and was extremely well received by the merchants of Bristol and Liverpool, who pressed him to act as their sole agent for South Carolina business. Yet the colonial factor could not be the dominant force in any trade, and even if an American became more independent, he had small hope of competing on equal terms with the metropolitans either in Africa or the West Indies. Laurens, who was to become President of the Continental Congress in 1777–78, became increasingly embittered with British imperialism and often threatened to forsake the trade in slaves. He is therefore seen by American patriots as a spokesman for liberal republicanism, with laudatory writers even discovering abolitionist sentiments in his expressions of tenderness for those "poor wretches," the slaves. Yet Laurens' motives were without doubt basically commercial and realistic. In his disaffection from slave trading in the 1760s and 1770s he was merely expressing the ambivalent opposition of American merchants to the Old Colonial System, as well as setting the tone for those English traders 40 years later who, while not actually converted to abolitionism, were no longer so adamant in their opposition to abolition because slave trading was not such a profitable business as it once had been, or had promised to be.

Chapter 3

SLAVES IN THE ECONOMY

SLAVE-TRADING PROFITS

As regards profits, the business of slave trading, like sugar itself, seems to have enjoyed a "golden age" when costs were low and prices relatively high, followed by a "silver age" when declining margins were offset by greater volume and efficiency, and a final period when—at least according to the traders—slave trading was scarcely profitable at all. Yet even this simplified pattern is not certain, for no aspect of slavery has been so clouded by the obscurantism of the traders and the exaggerations of anti-slavery writers as the question of profitability. Perhaps the most misleading of all "authorities" was Gomer Williams (1897), who confidently described "profits" of between 100 and 300 percent simply by deducting the cost of trade goods from the gross returns on the sale of slaves in the plantations without accounting for any overheads. Some of Gomer Williams' figures even find their way into his illustrious namesake's *Capitalism and Slavery*, though Eric Williams and most of his imitators generally give more credence to the figure of 30 percent profit more carefully calculated by J. Wallace of Liverpool in 1797.[1] Wallace's figures, however, derive from the years 1783 to 1793, a period of peace and prosperity; and Eric Williams himself cites Clarkson's statements that over the period of the American and maritime war, Liverpool slave traders actually lost £700,000, and the London merchants declined to engage in slave trading between 1763 and 1778 because of its unprofitability.[2] If, as at least one prominent abolitionist inferred, war did seriously inhibit slave trading's profitability, it should be pointed out that England was engaged in wars—of varying degrees of extra-European involvement—for some 75 of the 157 years between 1650 and 1807. It might also be argued that the switch in slave trading's focus from London first to Bristol and then to Liverpool is evidence not of increased profits but of the search for greater efficiency in the face of declining profitability.

Perhaps the most satisfactory way to estimate the extent and pattern of profits in the English slave trade is to examine critically one of the rare balance sheets published by the slave traders themselves, such as the one produced at the time of the great inquiry of 1788–89. Although this estimate was hypothetical and was designed chiefly to argue for an allowance of five slaves for each two tons of the slave ships' displacement in the forthcoming legislation, it does at least include all the relevant overheads.

Close examination of these figures shows that certain of the expenses, relating to insurance, wages and officers' commissions, "disbursements," and agents' fees, were fairly standard and could only minimally be "squeezed" for greater profits. Other factors, however, were obviously open to large variations, and these were the key to profit and loss in the slave-trading business: the cost of vessels, the ratio between cost of "outfit" and the price of slaves, the number of slaves carried, and the effect of fortuitous conditions such as wars, delays, and slave mortality. Another important though complex factor not considered adequately in the 1788 computation was the whole structure of credit, particularly the ways in which profits could be varied according to the terms by which the planters paid the traders for their slaves.

That the Liverpool slave traders after 1783 generally

	£	s.	d.	£	s.	d.
A Ship of 100 tons first cost building at £7	700					
Expence of Outfit including all her Furniture	700					
Extra Do fitting for the African Trade	350					
Amount of Cargo for 200 Negroes, including Insurance on the Ship and Cargo at £17.17.	3570					
Insurance on the Ship from the West Indies Valued at £1500 — at 2½ per Ct.	37	17	6	5357	17	6
Deduct for the common average of Mortality 5 per Ct. makes 190 each Av'g £34 Stg.				6460		
Agents Commissions at 10 per Ct. on £6460	646					
Captain's Do. . . . 6 per Ct. on Do.	402					
Mates privelege 1 Slave on the Neat proceeds	30	12				
Surgeons Do.	30	12				
Surgeons head Money 1s. per head on each Slave sold	9	10				
Ship's Disbursements in the West Indies	100					
Wages for 20 Men, Officers and Seamen included at 50/per Month for 12 Mo's is	600					
Interest on the Amo't of Cargo and Outfit for 12 Mo's	267	18		2086	12	
Add Total Amo't of Ships Cargo and Outfit				5357	17	6
				7444	9	6
Gross Sales of 190 Negroes at £34	6460					
Value of the Ship on her Return 1/3d. less	1166	14				
	7624	14				
	7444	9	6			
Neat Profit on the Voyage				181	4	6

". . . Estimate of an African Voyage upon the principle of limiting the Number of Negroes to be carried in each Vessel to 2 per ton."[3]

operated ships they owned themselves that had been specially designed, rather than hiring more or less suitable vessels, was one of the chief reasons for their supremacy. Before this, slave ships were usually not only small but also hired at a rate based on returning the cost of construction within three voyages of 12 months each. Analysis of Vice Admiralty Court returns and *Lloyd's Register of Shipping* shows that as the eighteenth century progressed there was a steady and remarkable increase in the life expectancy of oceangoing vessels from something like three to ten years on average. Even if the average round-trip voyage for a slaver was not reduced below a year by greater efficiency, the proslavery lobby itself reckoned that "only one ship in five miscarried." This would argue for a depreciation more like 20 percent than the 33⅓ percent used in the 1788 calculations, which alone would have increased the profit from £181 to £414 (or from 3 to 7 percent on the outlay) in the example cited. Storms, wrecks, and wartime captures would have cut drastically into these profits, though all such risks were insurable.

In 1797 J. Wallace calculated the profits of the slave trade at 30 percent by adding the cost of feeding and freighting each black (10s. and £3.5s.3¾d. respectively) to the price paid in West Africa (£27.-5s.10d.), and then deducting this total from the net price received in the plantations (£40.9s.6¾d.). This method could be sound enough if the component figures could be accurately arrived at. Wallace, however, used guesswork, for example arbitrarily taking exactly £50 as the gross price of each of the 31,690 slaves shipped by Liverpool traders between 1783 and 1793. Even if his figures hold some plausibility as an over-all average for the period treated, they must disguise large variations in individual slave-trading ventures, and are worthless in assessing long-term trends. As long as freighting costs (with obvious exceptions) are regarded as proportionately constant, an accurate index of relative profitability can be achieved by simply working out the ratio between the cost of slaves in West Africa and the prices received in the colonies. This method has the additional advantage of discounting the steady inflation of prices on both sides of the Atlantic throughout the period of the trade.

Altogether, there seems to have been a steady drop in the margin of profit on each slave carried from the time that free trade took over from monopoly until the end of the trade in 1807. Before 1700 the Royal African Company normally expected to sell its slaves for four times what it had paid for them in the value of trade goods, though, as has been shown, this did not prevent the company's bankruptcy because of overheads and costly mismanagement. The interlopers and later free traders fared much better, and may have achieved gross profit ratios as high as 6 to 1.

Slave Prices in West Africa and West Indies, 1676–1803, with Gross Profit Ratio.[4]

DATES	AFRICAN PRICE	PLANTATION PRICE (stg)		RATIO
1676-9	£3	Barbados	£15	
		Leewards	£16	5-6:1
		Jamaica	£17	
1679-88	£3	Jamaica (R.A.C.)	£13[6]	4.3:1
		Other islands	£13-16	4.3-5.3:1
1698-1707	£8-12		£23-41	circa 3:1
1744-60	£10-14	Jamaica (£50 curr.)	£36	circa 3:1
	e.g., 420 lbs. cowries at £3½ cwt. 6-11 oz. gold at 30-s			
1763	£12-15		£28-35	2.3:1
1787-8	£8-22	(av.)	£35-46	circa 1.5-3:1
	(Senegambia-Sierra Leone 15-18			
	Windward Coast and Bight of Benin £14-16			
	Gold Coast £18-22			
	Bonny, Calabar £12-18			
	Cameroons-Angola £8-10			
1795[5]	£27		£50	1.8:1
1803[7]	£25 (Bonny)		£50	2:1

Early in the eighteenth century, the cost of slaves in
Africa rose quite suddenly to £10 or more, but the
colonial price rose almost in proportion, so that a ratio
of 3 to 1 was normal throughout the years of the
plantations' greatest expansion. Traders who could
attract Africans with particularly cheap trade goods
did even better. Americans, for example, were able to
buy slaves in Africa as late as 1763 for 80 to 110
gallons of rum worth 1s.6d. a gallon, who could then
be sold in the colonies for up to £35 sterling per
head.

Between 1783 and the 1788 inquiry, however, the
prices of the best slaves in West Africa rose as high
as £22 in English trade goods, while the majority of
West Indian planters were unwilling or unable to
pay more than £50 Jamaican currency or £35 sterling. A gross profit ratio of less than 2 to 1 (such as
that predicated in the 1788 balance sheet tabulated
above and even in Wallace's unsympathetic estimates
for 1783–93) was scarcely a viable commercial prop-
osition at the best of times. The one relief was that,
until at least 1790, indifferent slaves could still be
purchased in West Africa for considerably less than
£22. In 1788 a witness testified that only Gold Coast
slaves commanded the top prices, that those from
the Bight of Biafra could still be obtained for from
£12 to £18, and that blacks from the Cameroons
and Angola could be had for as little as £8 to £10
apiece. The need for traders to maintain a gross profit
ratio approaching 3 to 1 while planters were unable
for financial reasons to insist on slaves of their choice,
alone may account for the great flood of blacks from
Bonny, Old and New Calabar, and Angola into the
English colonies toward the end of the trade. After
1800, however, even the slaves from Bonny began to
cost as much as £25 in trade goods, and the slim
prospects of persuading the English planters to pay

for raw, unseasoned slaves from an unpopular area prices they were used to paying only for healthy creoles with craft skills, discouraged an increasing number of English traders.

As always, there remained the magnet of higher prices in foreign markets, and there is strong evidence that the 1780s saw a surge in re-exports from Jamaica, Grenada, Dominica, and St. Vincent, as Spanish and even French mercantilist controls were somewhat relaxed. As the Royal African Company had found long before, however, this merely exacerbated problems; the difficulties of obtaining payment offset the benefit of higher prices, while the inflation brought about by apparent competition further stifled the trade upon which the English traders basically depended. The outbreak of revolution in Haiti in 1791 and war with France in 1793, moreover, seemed to close even this avenue of potential profit, though a profitable re-export trade to Cuba did reopen temporarily between 1801 and 1807, when prices as high as £100 sterling per slave were reported.[8]

With a steadily declining margin of gross profit on individual slaves, it became all the more important to cut down freighting overheads by increased efficiency. This could theoretically be achieved by carrying as many slaves as quickly and with as little loss of life as possible. On exceptional voyages when all conditions were favorable, handsome profits were made even toward the end of the trade, though the figures of £92,288 net profit on 2,136 slaves carried on six selected voyages between 1784 and 1805, given by Gomer Williams, are ludicrously exaggerated.[9] Always at least as common were voyages in which nothing went right, when actual losses were incurred. These unpublicized failures may well have predominated after regulations, from 1789 onward, reduced the size of cargoes so that large firms became less and less likely to make an over-all profit. Indeed, as early as 1788 it was claimed that 12 of the 30 principal Liverpool slave-trading firms had gone out of business since 1773.[10]

Like all traders, slavers complained of the difficulties of trading during wartime, yet it seems unlikely that wars did seriously affect profits or even have a major effect in retarding the general flow of slaves. Maritime conflict was in any case almost endemic during the slavery period. Slave traders learned to live with the threat of capture and showed great resilience and ingenuity. In the plantations serious local shortage of slaves—as of provisions and other supplies—occurred quite often; but the deficiencies were quickly made up when conditions eased, and the higher prices occasioned by short supply quite adequately compensated for higher wartime costs of acquisition and carriage. Besides this, insurance of cargoes was so well organized that the traders rarely suffered; increased premiums covered the risks, and the higher cost was passed on by astute traders to planter purchasers. Moreover, the general flow of slaves was interrupted less than would appear from the complaints of unfortunate individual traders, because the number of enemy slave ships captured by British naval ships and privateers at least offset those lost to enemy cruisers.[11]

In sum, it will never be possible to calculate with certainty the total profits of the English slave trade over the entire period of its operation; yet it should now be possible to estimate more accurately than ever before the level of profit expected by a successful trader before 1789, working from the structure of the balance sheet of 1788 but employing rather more objectivity than those who constructed it for the digestion of Parliament.

	£	*s.*	£	*s.*
Cost of 150-ton ship (the average for the trade in its middle years) fully out-fitted for African trade	2625			
Cargo for 450 Negroes (presuming normal crowding at 3 per ton) at cost allowing for gross profit ratio of 3:1, with insurances out and return	6152	5		
Agent and captain's commissions, surgeon and mate's privileges and surgeon's head money, at same rates	2284	13		
Wages of crew (50s. per month for 8 months outwards for 30, 4 months homewards for 15 — remainder having died or been paid off) and ship's "disbursements" in West Indies	900		11961	18
Gross sales of 405 Negroes (presuming realistic mortality on favourable voyage of 10 per cent) at £34	13770			
Value of ship on return, at 20 per cent off	2100			
	15870			
	11961	18		
Net profit of voyage (32.7 per cent)			3908	2

Revised Balance Sheet for Slave Trading Voyage, Around 1790.

It will be noticed that one of the items omitted in this recalculation is the interest of the money advanced for outfit and cargo for the length of the voyage. For the traders to reckon as a loss the alternative employment of their capital seems a particular impertinence when at the same time they ignored the fact that they almost invariably controlled the terms by which the planters paid them for their slaves. Slave traders in effect were bankers, either on their own account or, more commonly, through the metropolitan West India merchants with whom they

were associated. Sometimes they were slave and sugar
traders and bankers all in one. Not only did they
commonly finance themselves entirely, but when
planters bought on credit, the slave traders were usually able to discount bills at rates extremely favorable
to themselves, and when the slaves were paid for in
sugar or tobacco, they fixed rates that were extremely
unlikely to show a loss. Indeed, the fact that there
was always an element of risk in carrying commodities probably explains why payment in crops was
practically superseded by bills of exchange by the
year 1700, with the canny slave traders merely looking
for return cargoes in freight, at the planters' risk. The
imbalance between seller and buyer (the perennial
bane of colonials) at the very least offset the cost
to the metropolitan traders of tying up capital on
long or even hazardous voyages. Insurance too—which
had become fairly sophisticated by 1783—seemed
bound to favor the metropolitan over the colonial,
since premiums were almost invariably fixed in England, not the colonies, and the traders were often
underwriters also. Besides this, cargoes could be in-
sured but not market prices, and while the demand
for slaves—and therefore their prices—remained steadily high, the prices of sugar and tobacco often fluctuated quite wildly.[12]

It is reasonable then to suppose that slave traders
confidently expected (at least until the last years of
the trade)—if not the huge profits described by some
writers—something like the still generous return of
32.7 percent. Unprofitable periods and misadventure,
however, determined that on the average of the entire trade this expectation was overly optimistic. Roger
Anstey in a 1972 study has even argued that the
over-all average profit for the British slave trade
from 1761 to 1808 was no more than 3 percent, with
a peak of about 15 percent profit between 1781 and
1800 offset by little or no profit during the Seven
Years' War period and serious losses in the last seven
years of the trade.[13]

The bare chance of very high profits, as well as that kind of illogical optimism that attracted diggers to the Klondike despite the failure of the majority, may have drawn adventurers into the slave trade. This, however, does not explain why the trade went increasingly out of the hands of small individual traders (who might make large profits or fail completely) into those of large concerns, whose profits were closer to the average. The reason for this trend was obviously the quest for efficiency—what economists call "economies of scale"—and Anstey himself has argued that simply by packing 10 percent more slaves in the holds, trimming outfitting costs by 10 percent, and obtaining 10 percent higher sale prices, net profits approaching 40 percent were quite possible.[14]

By the last decade of the slave trade, however, even economies of scale were failing, and abolition occurred in something of an anticlimax, with remarkably little resistance from the slave traders. The unprofitability of their ventures once "tight packing" was outlawed and costs had risen out of proportion to the prices planters were able to pay for their slaves, should not distort the picture of the earlier phases of the trade. Even if on the widest scale the level of profit of 32.7 percent predicated earlier were halved by unprofitable ventures suffering misfortunes at every stage (and the reader is welcome to make his own calculations from the basic balance sheets already given), an average profit for the whole period of the English trade of 16 percent appears quite likely. Given an average retail price of £30 for the approximately 2,500,000 slaves carried by English traders (including probably 500,000 shipped to foreign colonies at better-than-average prices), this suggests a total return between 1620 and 1807 of approximately £12,000,000, perhaps half of which accrued between 1750 and 1790. It was as much because of these profits as for the intrinsic worth of the slaves that the mercantilist Postlethwayt described the slave trade as "the first principle and foundation of all the rest, the mainspring of the machine which sets every wheel in motion."[15]

EMPLOYMENT

The business of slave trading, like most competitive commercial enterprises, was a closely guarded "mistery," learned in the unforgiving school of experience and with its expertise handed down from person to person. Yet in the business of "plantership" handbooks abounded, all giving due prominence to the management of the "nerves" or "very sinews," the slaves. Indeed, the cost of maintaining the slave work force, of caring for the slaves, and of concern for their productivity (aspects that became damagingly confused in the planters' minds) were at least as important as questions of capitalization in general, crop and animal husbandry, and market strategy in determining the profitability of plantations. Above all, it was argued in true eighteenth-century style, management should be *rational*. "He who feeds his negroes well," wrote Samuel Martin of Antigua in his "Essay upon Plantership" (1765),

> proportioneth their labour to their age, sex and strength, and treats them with kindness and good nature, will reap a much larger product, and with infinitely more ease and self-satisfaction than the most cruel Egyptian task-master.[16]

From the superficiality of the masters' concern for the slaves' welfare compared with their strong depersonalized concern for degrees of quality that determined slave prices, it is evident that slaves were regarded as units of value, their worth gauged almost solely by how well they worked and how long they lived to give useful service.[17] Once bought—in large parcels by new planters and those newly expanding their estates, or in small numbers in order to make up the annual depletions by death—new Africans were introduced into the plantation work force as quickly as possible. Only the need for the "seasoning" process of training, acclimatization, and immunization caused any delay, with large groups of new slaves kept strictly apart for several months, and single slaves farmed out to creole "monitors."[18] Some African-born slaves were found to possess skills directly useful to the plantations, such as the working of iron and other metals, or skill in woodworking, easily adaptable to plantation crafts. But the overwhelming majority were first worked as laborers in the fields and factories, where most of them lived out the remainder of their lives. Generally speaking, those positions of skill and responsibility held by craftsmen and drivers were reserved for creole slaves, so that even the limited job mobility possible on a slave estate was delayed for at least a generation. This was particularly true of the years of greater exploitation and efficiency after 1750, when planters were forced to accept an increasing proportion of slaves from the more southerly parts of West Africa, with few nonagricultural skills and with a poor reputation for educability.

The quest for efficiency coupled with a lower expectation of the work force may explain why the gang system became more rigorously standardized in nearly all plantation colonies after 1750. In the earliest years, when plantations were mainly small, black slaves, like white servants, were simply employed on an ad hoc basis, differing from ordinary farm laborers in England only in the duress under which they worked. Even in 1765 Samuel Martin, while writing of the grading of employment, said nothing of permanent gangs in Antigua. In more highly developed Barbados and Jamaica, with their larger estates, however, the system was already well rooted. "The best way I know of to prevent idleness, and to make the Negroes do their work properly," wrote the Barbadian

absentee Henry Drax in instructing his manager
Archibald Johnson in 1755,

> will be upon the change of Work, constantly to Gang
> all the Negroes in the Plantations in the Time of Plant-
> ing. All the Men Negroes into two Gangs, the ablest
> and best by themselves for holeing and the stronger
> Work, and the more ordinary Negroes in a Gang for
> Dunging, &c. The Women Negroes also in two Gangs as
> before, and the lesser Negroes into two Gangs, the least
> to be followed by some careful old Women, who must
> use them with Gentleness. Out of these six Gangs of
> Negroes must the Carters, Stillers, Curing house Ne-
> groes, Cooks, Lookers after Stock, Watchers of Provi-
> sions, &c. be drawn. Your Under-Overseer must con-
> stantly have a List of the Gang under his particular
> Care, that he may be able to give a particular Account
> of every one, whether Sick or how employed. In the
> time of grinding Canes after your Watches for your
> Mills, Boiling-House, and Cane-cutting Gangs are taken
> out, all the rest of the Negroes, except the smallest
> Gangs, must be listed into a running Gang for getting
> Home and Houseing all sorts of fuel.[19]

By the time the classic works on sugar plantation
management had been written by the Jamaicans Edward Long (1774), William Beckford (1790), and
Bryan Edwards (1793),[20] the gang system had been
refined into its final tripartite form. Males and females
were no longer separated, and women, more numerous
than in the plantations' early years, were now expected to work almost as hard and under as close a
control as the men.[21] Yet it was Thomas Roughley
who (despite some conventional romanticizing of the
blacks' lot) described the West Indian gang system
in its ultimate rigidity, significantly writing at a time
(1823) when efficiency was more important than ever
before because of the abolition of the slave trade,
rising costs, and the declining sugar prices. "Nothing
animates the planting system more than the well-
being of this admirable effective force," wrote Roughley of the First or Great Gang:

They are drilled to become veterans in the most arduous field undertakings, furnish drivers, cattlemen, mulemen, boilers and distillers. They are the very essence of an estate, its support in all weathers and necessities; the proprietor's glory, the overseer's favourite. . . . This gang, composed of a mixture of able men and women, sometimes amounting to a hundred, should always be put to the field work which requires strength and skill in the execution; such as making lime-kilns, digging cane-holes, making roads through the estate, trenching, building stone walls, planting canes and provisions, trashing heavy canes, cutting and tying canes and tops in crop time, cutting copper-wood, feeding the mill, carrying green trash from the mill to the trash-house, and repairing the public roads, when allotments are to be worked out.[22]

Despite his praise of the laborers' strength and skill, Roughley would not have entrusted all of them with even the simplest tools. Hoes, bills, knives, and axes were reserved for "those men who know how to make use of them." Nor were even the heroic members of the Great Gang to be trusted with piecework, being set to open-ended tasks throughout the hours of work, wherever possible in lines and invariably under the control of black driver and supervision of white overseer. Indeed, this system was employed throughout the plantation colonies with the sole exception of South Carolina, where setting the slaves daily tasks in the quarter-acre rectangles into which the rice fields were divided was regarded as rather more efficient.[23]

Although some differentiation was made between men and women, one of the criticisms of the piecework on the Rice Coast was that the tasks tended to be graded to the speed of the slower workers. In the tobacco and sugar colonies this difficulty was avoided by placing the weaker slaves in the two subordinate gangs. The Second Gang, wrote Roughley,

should be composed of people who are thought to be of rather weakly habits, mothers of sucking children, youths drafted from the children's gang, from twelve to eighteen years of age, and elderly people that are sufficiently strong for field-work. . . . Their strength and abilities should be ascertained and assimilated to field-work of the second order, such as cleaning and banking young canes, turning trash on ratoon pieces, threshing light canes, chopping and heaping manure, planting corn, cleaning grass pieces, carrying dry trash in crop-time to the stokeholes, and such work, requiring no great strength.[24]

The Third, or Weeding, Gang comprised mainly the children aged six to twelve, the "lesser Negroes," described by Henry Drax. At the height of the slave trade, when it was "cheaper to import than to breed" and slaves under 20 years of age were rarely carried, this group was small and economically unimportant. But as the proportion of creoles increased, so did the children, and their importance soared suddenly when the trade was ended in 1807 and slaves born in the colonies were the only labor replenishment the planters could expect. Roughley accordingly employed some of his most hyperbolic prose to describe their management. "This corps," he wrote, formed

the rising generation, from which, in progress of time, all the vacancies occurring in the different branches of slave population are filled up. . . . They are drivers, cattlemen, mulemen, carpenters, coopers, and masons, as it were in embryo. Their genius and strength rises and ripens with their years, as they are made emulous by proper treatment. It argues them what that kind of treatment should be, to promote with success so good a design. . . . The owner and the overseer of those valuable shoots should act the part of a parent, fosterer, and protector, looking on them as the future prop and support of the property.[25]

Such a wise foster parent, claimed Roughley, would regard it as "an unquestionable evil" to leave healthy blacks unemployed once they reached the age of six, since this would allow them to "imbibe . . . a tendency to idle, pernicious habits." Consequently,

> when they can be any way useful, it is best to send them with those of their own age, to associate together in industrious habits; not to overact any part with them, but by degrees to conform them to the minor field work. . . . An experienced negro woman in all manner of field-work, should be selected to superintend, instruct and govern this gang of pupils, armed with a pliant, serviceable twig, more to create dread than inflict chastisement.[26]

The Third Gang in Roughley's glamorized account (and Wackford Squeers could not have done better) was no less than a school for life. On closer examination, however, it appears that the only subjects taught the young slaves were the skills of cutting grass with small knives, weeding cane rows with specially made toy hoes, and carrying dung in baskets on their heads to dump into holes ahead of the adults planting canes, "which they can do expertly," concluded Roughley, "and by this they will be taught to observe the mode of planting."

The constant concern of the slave-owning planters was to maximize the efficiency of their work force, increasing productivity and cutting costs where they could. Yet, as innumerable commentators both in the emancipist period and more recently have pointed out, this was a losing game. Slavery was basically inefficient and, from the point of view of the planters if not of the British Empire as a whole, ultimately not even profitable. It also faced the planters with serious problems of social control.

The planters' dilemma (scarcely acknowledged by their critics) was that, though inefficient and socially explosive, slavery was an unfortunate necessity in such a labor-intensive economy as the plantations. For social as well as financial reasons, voluntary wage labor was out of the question; but labor under duress was never very productive. Costs—of the slaves them-

selves, of provisions and other plantation supplies—
were almost completely out of the planters' control,
and steadily rising. Even when costs were relatively
low and produce prices high during the plantations'
golden and silver eras, unfortunate, improvident, or
undercapitalized planters failed to make a profitable
return on their investment. As margins dwindled with
increased competition and greater production, only
the most exploitative managers continued to make
steadily high profits, and in these times slavery was
regarded as more, not less, essential as the only way of
preserving a large, cheap labor force.[27]

Most planters realized that overuse of the whip was
counterproductive, but instead of searching for effective rewards (which were regarded as impractical,
too expensive, or demeaning), they looked for greater
productivity in long working hours. These had the additional "benefit" of keeping the slaves from dangerous idleness. Even out of crop time, slaves were summoned before dawn and worked throughout the hours
of daylight with just two breaks for breakfast and
dinner, generally six days a week and 309 days a
year. Sundays were generally free of gang work, but
all "free" time was expected to be devoted to the
slaves' own provision grounds. Toward the end of
slavery some masters "gave" their slaves half or even
the whole of Saturday as well to work the "Negro
grounds," but on this day they were usually supervised
just as in the fields.[28] Moreover, during the five-month
frenzy at the crop, workers on a sugar plantation were
commonly at their masters' beck and call for eighteen
hours a day, sometimes denied even their Sunday
rest. Quite naturally, the overextended and unin-
volved slaves subtly dragged their heels at each stage
of every task, sullenly resistant to improvements
aimed at increasing their speed or efficiency, innocent
of pride of achievement and immune to charges of
indolence. As the stereotype of the ignorant, sluggish,
and lazy black took root among the frustrated plant-

ers, the standard of work expected tended to gravitate to an ever-lower level. On the best-run estates, normal productivity was abysmal. Recent researchers have shown, for example, that slaves on one Jamaican estate in the 1790s may have cut as little as one fifth the weight of canes per man per day harvested by modern wage-earning cane cutters using essentially the same laborious methods.[29]

Among the severest problems encountered in the management of sugar plantations were the periodicity of the work required, the variations in tempo, and the wide range between skilled and unskilled work. Between January and June, while the cane was harvested and processed, an extremely large work force working hard for long hours was needed; yet out of crop time it was difficult to find enough steady work to keep all the workers from "idle, pernicious habits." Today it is difficult to decide whether it was the necessity of cutting costs with such an inefficient work force or the likelihood that labor-saving devices would speed up operations in the off-season and provide the slaves with dangerous leisure, which made the planters notoriously reluctant to introduce such simple innovations as the plow into the West Indies. Official reasons given, such as that plows were not really suitable for West Indian soils, and that slaves could not be taught to use them, were obviously exaggerated.[30]

One way of avoiding seasonal underemployment might have been hiring slaves from "jobbers" when needed. But although hiring often occurred, planters could not obtain enough labor when they needed it most or pay sufficiently high prices to make slave jobbing a regular feature of the plantation economy.[31] In 1787, for example, Edward Long stated that normally planters rarely considered themselves able to pay the jobbers more than 3½d. per head per day, providing food in addition. On an annual basis this amounted to only £4.13s. sterling, which was dou-

bled when the cost of food was added. Since, as Long
pointed out, the insurance on a slave at 10 percent
alone might well cost £5, with clothing an additional
£1, medical attention 3s.6d., and the poll tax 1s.6d.,
it was extremely difficult to turn a profit in hiring out
slaves, even if no allowance were made for interest on
capital and depreciation.[32] Consequently, slaves were
only hired out by those few owners without plantations or by planters out of crop time, when work was
hard to come by. Even at 7d. a day or £9.6s. sterling a year, it was obviously cheaper to maintain an
underemployed force of slaves, including the annual
cost of making up numbers, as long as morality and
the price of replacements did not rise too high.

At the same time as Edward Long wrote, raw but
healthy African slaves were selling in Jamaica at £38
to £46 sterling, with unskilled creole slaves costing
about 50 percent more. Slaves with special skills such
as coopers, masons, boilermen, and distillers, however,
could command prices from £77 to £200 sterling
apiece[33]; and these prices (up to five times the cost
of a new African) were a fair indication of their
value to the colonial economy, as well as their growing importance in colonial society. While a businesslike owner would try to appreciate the value of his
slaves by giving them skills, he would be reluctant to
increase the need for craftsmen by making his operation more sophisticated, in case he had to buy. These
factors help to explain why the management of slave
plantations, in the social as well as the economic or
technical spheres, became increasingly archaic as the
battle for profitability was gradually lost.

Although the same constraints against hiring slaves
and refining techniques applied to some degree, the
alternating crises of over- and underemployment do
not seem to have been so prevalent in the American
mainland colonies; nor does there appear to have
been such a critical gulf between the value and status

of skilled and unskilled slaves, or even between field and factory slaves. In Virginia, for example, tobacco husbandry was much less labor-intensive than sugar; or rather, the work of preparing the soil, planting, harvesting, and processing the crop was much more evenly spread out through the year.[34] Besides this, tobacco (and rice, cotton, and coffee too) do not deteriorate immediately on harvesting like sugar, so that field slaves could also be employed in processing. Moreover, in contrast to the almost absolute monoculture of sugar plantations (where it was said that enough sugar could be produced from one acre to pay for the provisions grown on five), tobacco plantations were commonly diversified, many of them growing corn for sale as well as for feeding the plantation's population. The cycle of corn cultivation dovetailed with that of tobacco, so that the praedial slaves were kept employed at a great variety of simple tasks in the fields in all but the most wintry weather, and a much smaller proportion of time was spent in "making work" on roads, ditches, and building than in the West Indies. The only diverse employment open to field slaves in the sugar plantations was stock husbandry, but this being year-round work, it was reserved for specialized slaves, as indeed it was in all plantation colonies.[35]

Steady employment, at a hard but rarely intolerable level, may have been as much responsible as the more temperate and seasoned climate for the lower mortality among American compared with West Indian slaves, which itself was an important factor in the relative profitability of slave plantations in each area. Slave owners in all colonies, however, suffered from the problem of having to support unproductive slaves. Disease took an immeasurable toll, by debilitation as much as by making work impossible. In the West Indies in particular, where tropical African complaints lingered and indigenous afflictions caused additional havoc, the effectiveness of the work force may have been halved. The mainland colonies were generally healthier and suffered perhaps only a 25 percent loss in efficiency through disease. But epidemics that affected temperate as well as tropical climates, such as smallpox, measles, and respiratory infections, often took toll, and an unknown proportion of slaves in all areas suffered from such handicaps as intestinal parasites and diet deficiencies.[36]

Disease could affect half a plantation's population and actually carry off 10 percent a year over long periods in the worst affected areas; but ironically it was the healthier plantations that built up the largest body of permanently unproductive slaves, in the persons of the superannuated and the very young. Great efforts were made to squeeze useful work from these slaves, by employing the aged as watchmen, "nurses," and cooks once gang labor was no longer possible, and by setting the youngsters fairly strenuous tasks at an age almost before they would be sent to school today.[37] Costs were also pared by severely reducing the rations of food and clothing to the elderly, and by providing mothers with only small extra allowances for their infants. Yet the degree to which slave owners could neglect their unproductive slaves was usually legislated against by the colonial assemblies. Quite naturally, these bodies did not want the responsibility of caring for the aged and sick as well as the criminals, runaways, and masterless, much as the English central government, not wanting responsibility for indigent, aged, and sick (and these included by 1772 several thousand blacks too), delegated their care to the local authorities. Colonial planters, not satisfied that the assemblies actually reimbursed them for slaves lost by murder, war, or insurrection, constantly complained at the disbursements they were forced to make, just as English landowners yelped at the Poor Law.

Left to their own devices, callous planters might well have allowed at least their aged wards to perish for want of subsistence. On the other hand, provident planters from the earliest days saw that aiding the survival of the very young would be a good investment in saving the annual cost of importing adult replacements. Yet infant mortality (of all races) was so high that survival was a loaded lottery, and for most of the eighteenth century it was regarded as more profitable to buy than to encourage female slaves to give birth and then gamble on children surviving. Only when prices of new slaves rose beyond the cost of bringing up the survivors of a cohort of creole youngsters to the years of fully productive work did the planters in general change their views.[38] Once the slave trade was actually ended, however, really intensive efforts were made to encourage fertility—though with disappointing results.[39]

Other slaves who consumed more than they produced were the domestics, who, under careless management, tended to multiply alarmingly. This was particularly true of the households of those many planters whose foolish humor it was to live and entertain on the scale of English dukes; or of those managers and overseers without a vested interest in the property who made up for the lonely vigors of their employment by conspicuous consumption. Battalions of 25 domestics catering to a single Great House, or of 50 ministering to half a dozen white overseers and bookkeepers on an absentee's estate, were by no means uncommon. Pretentious planters were often attended by bewigged butlers, pages, coachmen, and postilions, while in the humbler parts of the Great House or around the overseers' quarters swarmed a slack retinue of cooks, washers, waiters, stable boys, and maids; not to mention those "brownskin gals" of no official function who kept the white men company in their beds and regularly added to the colored* population.

* Throughout this book the word "colored" is used only for persons of mixed black and white ancestry. "Mulatto" —also in the West Indian manner—is applied strictly to those with one black and one white parent.

PLANTATION CAPITALIZATION AND PROFITS

Having looked at some of the general problems facing owners and managers, perhaps we can best gain a more precise notion of the profitability of plantations and the contribution made by slaves, by examining critically a balance sheet drawn up by a planter-economist, much as the profits of the slave trade have already been assessed through a balance sheet drawn up by professional traders. The picture of profits given by most plantocratic writers tended to be one-sided since these writers ignored the benefits of plantations and slavery to the metropolis. They also concentrated too heavily on sugar plantations and gave a distorted view of the slave colonies as a whole. Yet even from the narrow viewpoint of the sugar planter, their argument was unduly pessimistic if not actively disingenuous.

Bryan Edwards was perhaps the most thorough and honest of the plantocratic profit calculators. He wrote his account of the finances of a typical Jamaican plantation in 1793,[40] when sugar was already facing a decline, and his purposes included convincing Parliament that the West Indian colonies should continue to be encouraged. Yet his accountancy was sufficiently detailed and candid that we can test his assumptions and also, by extrapolation, trace patterns from an earlier period with greater objectivity than one could ever expect from a planter arguing a case.

Bryan Edwards conceded that a return of 7¼ percent on capital might sound generous enough, particularly to English landowners, who expected no more than 3½ percent on farming land. But he hastened to add that his computation took no account of the annual decrease of the slaves, depreciation on buildings, or the cost of credit, and was predicated on resident ownership and the absence of visitations from

	£Jamaica Currency	£Stg.	£Stg.
A. CAPITAL COSTS			
Prime cost, 600 acres at £14 Currency	8400	6000	
Clearing 300 acres for canes at £12,100 acres provisions, 100 acres guinea grass at £7, enclosing at £700	5700	4071	
Total, Land	14100		10071
Watermill, Windmill + Animal Mill, or two Animal Mills	1400	1000	
Boiling House at £1000, Curing Home at £800, Distillery at £1600, two Trash Houses at £300 each	4000	2857	
Slave Hospital	300	429	
Overseer's Dwelling House	600	214	
Mule Stable, Sheds, Tradesmens's Shops, outfitted	700	500	
Total, Buildings	7000		5000
250 Slaves at £70 Currency	17500	12500	
80 Steers at £15, 60 Mules at £28	2880	2057	
Total, Stock	20380		14557
TOTAL CAPITAL	41480		29628
B. ANNUAL COSTS			
Clothing, provisions and tools for 250 slaves, misc. annual supplies and 1/5 of 5-year replacements	1190	850	
Salaries: Overseer, £200; Carpenter, £100 Distiller, £70, two Book-keepers, £60 each, with maintenance	690	493	
Medical care for Slaves, 6/-each and medicine	100	71	
Non-plantation craftsmen's bills and materials	250	179	
Colonial Taxes, public and parochial	200	143	
Annual Replacements, Steers and Mules	300	214	
Miscellaneous local costs	300	214	
TOTAL, ANNUAL COSTS	3030		
C. INCOME			
Sugar, 200 hogsheads at £21 Currency, c.i.f.	4200	3000	
Rum, 130 puncheons at £14 ditto	1820	1300	
TOTAL INCOME	6020		4300
NET ANNUAL PROFIT =7.22% on Capital	2990		2136

Capitalization of Typical Jamaican Estate, Around 1793.

the Almighty in the form of hurricane, drought, or war. Given the quite normal need to replace 2 percent of the slaves each year, the profit would be decreased by £250 sterling; if the buildings were annually depreciated by 5 percent this could account for £250 more; and if the owner, like so many West Indian planters, was an absentee, 6 percent of the gross income, or £258, would be further deducted as commission for the estate's managing attorney. These three additional charges would have reduced the profit in Edwards' example from £2,136 sterling to £1,378, or from over 7 percent to under 5 percent.

It is difficult to argue with Bryan Edwards' annual contingency charges, but it should be noticed that his capital costs were based on setting up a new estate in 1793 and were therefore far higher than for the average long-established estate. They therefore represent the "replacement cost" or a "wealth estimate" rather than true capitalization. Edwards' hypothetical estate consisted of nine hundred acres, but he did not charge for the three hundred acres of woodland, on the principles that in islands flatter and more completely developed than Jamaica such land did not often occur, and that it was of little worth in any case. Yet even charging an average of £10 sterling an acre for the six hundred acres of canes, provisions, and pasture was unrealistic, since a large proportion of "native" planters had originally obtained their lands virtually free by patent grants, inheritance, or marriage, valuing them only in order to provide security for borrowed money. It was only latecomers who suffered, as they constantly complained, by having to buy land at high prices often from established planters whose speculative forebears had engrossed far more than they could ever develop.[41] Therefore, in assessing the profits of plantations in the earliest years, the capital cost of land is of comparatively little account, and even as late as 1750 it is unlikely that the average cost of land was as much as half the amounts used by Bryan Edwards in 1793.

Similarly, Bryan Edwards almost certainly over-stated the average capital outlay on plantation build-ings. Although many West Indian estates possessed splendid buildings, this was more evidence of the availability of capital than of the need for it. Costs that could not be cut were those of the imported "millwork" and "utensils" for the factory, which always represented at least 10 percent of capital costs.[42] A well-ordered estate, however, employed its own crafts-men in the actual building, and used many local materials. Therefore, much of the cost of building, like the cost of originally clearing the land, should be in-cluded in the cost of the slaves (and in earlier days, white indentured servants) who performed the actual work. Yet slaves too were somewhat overcharged for in Edwards' accounts. As we have seen, slaves cost much less in the earlier days than the average of £50 sterling calculated in 1793. Moreover, once bought, slaves had merely to be augmented to make up for natural decrease, and it was a very rare planter even in 1793 who had had to pay current prices for all his slaves. The average plantation had bought its original slaves at perhaps £25 each, paying the gradu-ally rising prices only for annual replacements, which should be accounted for separately.

All in all, it is evident that while Bryan Edwards might have been accurate in suggesting that £30,000 was necessary to set up a new plantation in 1793, this amount may have been double the true capitalization of the average West Indian estate. This implies the understating of profits by as much as half. Yet the very need for Bryan Edwards to account for the re-placement value of estates in assessing average capital-ization is an indication of the general burden of debt in the 1790s, not only among new planters buying in at inflated prices, but also among the old established planters borrowing on optimistically valued security. As many writers claimed, even in peacetime and with normal harvests profits could be reduced or even wiped out by the interest payable on money borrowed at 5 or 6 percent. Very few planters had borrowed all their capital, yet as early as 1774 Edward Long calculated that an average estate making £6,000 gross income paid £2,000 a year in contingent charges in London, of which one half was interest, as well as nearly £2,000 in local costs in the colony. Moreover, the merchant—who was normally chief creditor and mortgage holder as well as agent for the purchases and sales—made sure of his own income by deducting the first £5 (or roughly one third) from the value of each hogshead and puncheon.[43]

Despite Bryan Edwards' faulty accountancy, the general burden of debt may have reduced the average level of profit in 1793 to something like 7 percent again, though the profits in an earlier period before debt became so burdensome have still to be ascertained. Certainly, prospects in the period around 1750 would have been much better. Because of low prices for slaves as well as for land and buildings, and the much lower level of plantation debt, it is likely that the capital cost of the average West Indian estate was no more than half the 1793 figure, so that although gross income was proportionately lower, the expected profit may well have been as much as 12½ percent on capital in peacetime. Even in wartime, when insurance costs reached as high as 20 percent of the value of produce shipped, this was often compensated for by higher prices, and at most meant the reduction of profits by about a fifth. The most fortunate period of all, however, was in 1700 or earlier. Because contingent charges as well as capital costs were at their lowest while produce prices were relatively high, the planter could expect to make two thirds of his gross income in profit. On an estate the size of the one cited by Bryan Edwards, the annual profit would have been £1,000, or 20 percent, representing a capitalization of about £5,000, which, curiously enough, was precisely the amount that Governor Vaughan of Jamaica in 1676 said was the minimum needed by a new planter.[44]

These tentative profit figures may be tested against further considerations of production, prices, and productivity, and here again it can be seen that Edwards' accountancy is at fault, especially when viewed against the West Indies as a whole. On Edwards' estate, 250 slaves produced only 200 hogsheads of sugar and 130 puncheons of rum a year from 300 acres of canes, and the planter received only £15 a hogshead and £10 a puncheon. At first glance, this would seem far from the actual average in most respects. A reasonably efficient planter would not only expect to make more sugar and rum from 300 acres, but would also expect to receive far more in income. Most contemporary estimates of production were based upon an average of one hogshead of sugar per acre and two puncheons of rum for every three hogsheads.[45] Moreover, Edwards claimed to have used average prices over the decade 1781–91 in his calculations; but he appears to have taken the lowest possible rather than the median returns, bringing the planter less than £1 per hundredweight net. At the other end of the scale, over the same period (in figures that Edwards himself quotes), the best muscovado was bringing an average of over £4 per hundredweight, or £80 a ton, in London, of which the planter would expect to receive £40 per hogshead at least. From these and other sources it seems that Edwards underestimated average gross incomes by at least a third and maybe a half.[46]

Yet another—and compensatory—snag appears in Edwards' calculations. Looking at West Indian totals of production and population, it can be seen that the average West Indian sugar estate was actually smaller and produced less than Edwards' model but had a larger slave population. In 1793 there were approximately 500,000 slaves in the British West Indies, and yet total sugar production was only about 100,000 tons. Sugar represented something like three quarters of West Indian exports by value (down from seven eighths in 1775 because of the short-lived expansion of coffee and cotton production),[47] but even if only two thirds of the slaves actually lived on sugar estates, the per capita production was more like six hundredweight per year than the 13 hundredweight claimed for Edwards' estate. At no time do slaves on sugar plantations appear to have produced an average of more than seven hundredweight per year, and these mediocre levels of productivity would probably eradicate the increased income made by adjusting Edwards' figures. They also strengthened the planters' argument that while slaves were indispensable, they must always be cheap.

A work force that has to pay for its initial cost is always bound to be even more exploited than wage laborers, whose cost is distributed and is more easily calculable. It is therefore not surprising that the actual returns on the cost of slave labor were always disappointing to the planters. Bryan Edwards himself commented that Jamaican planters in the 1790s expected an annual profit of £10 sterling per slave, or 20 percent of their average market value at a time when the work force—by Edwards' figures—represented 43 percent of the capital outlay. This expectation became increasingly vain, and its failure contributed to the planters' growing dissatisfaction with their work force in the last days of slavery. Yet even in earlier days, when slaves were relatively cheap, their cost represented as much as 65 percent of capital; and even if the rule-of-thumb figure of £10 per slave was not of long standing, in 1793 planters probably always aimed to recoup 20 percent of total slave costs each year. This, of course, was at a time when there were practically no laws to prevent the absolute exploitation of slaves. It was therefore the slaves who suffered from the planters' impractical ambitions while at the same time they were blamed when the impossible was not achieved.

In summary, it seems that far greater profits were made than the planters acknowledged. Sugar plantations as a whole probably made about 7½ percent on capital (when realistically computed) in 1790, at least 10 percent between 1750 and 1775, and perhaps as much as 20 percent in the halcyon days before 1700. At no time before 1800—save perhaps temporarily during wartime or locally after devastating hurricanes—did annual profits represent less than 8 percent of the market value of the average plantation's slaves. It is no wonder then that even Adam Smith wrote in 1776 that "the profits of a sugar plantation in any of our West Indian colonies are generally much greater than those of any other cultivation that is known either in Europe or America."[48]

	1700	1750	1775	1790	1800
Slave population (thousands)	100	250	400	500	600
Sugar production (thousand tons)	25	50	100	100	125
Percentage of total exports represented by sugar/rum	c. 85	c. 90	89.9	74.0	c. 75
Corrected produce per slave	6.6	5.3	7.0[49]	6.0	6.2
London average sugar price (per ton)	25	40	35	65	75
Gross income, sugar/rum (£ stg millions)	0.36	1.45	2.90	5.00	7.25
Total Capitalization (£ stg millions)	1.25	5.00	10.00	20.00	31.25
Gross profit (£ stg thousands)	220	580	1000	1500	1810
Profit, percentage of capital	17.6	11.6	10.0	7.5	5.8
Profit, percentage of income	60	40	34	30	25
Profit per slave on sugar estates (£ stg)	3	3	3½	3	4
Profit per slave, percentage market value	12	10	9	8	8

Approximate Profitability of West Indian Sugar Plantations to Owners, 1700–1800[50]

As to the profitability of the nonsugar plantations of the West Indies in the eighteenth century, Bryan Edwards can again provide some guidance. All other

operations, argued Edwards, were less labor-intensive
than sugar, and land for grazing and growing cotton
and tobacco was cheaper than cane land. Profits per
slave were therefore at least potentially higher in
other types of tropical agriculture than in sugar. This
as much as the decline in the sugar market was the
reason for the moderate diversification that raised the
level of British West Indian nonsugar exports from
10 percent in 1775 to 25 percent in 1790. Though
after 1800 these other crops matched sugar in their
decline, it is thus quite reasonable to assume that
profits on all West Indian plantations were never
lower throughout the eighteenth century than the rate
of 8 to 12 percent of the market value of the slaves
deduced from sugar plantations.

COLONIAL SLAVERY AND THE METROPOLIS

In that teleological process that makes history largely
the story of the successful, the later decline of the
plantations has obscured their earlier profitability,
both to the planters and to their metropolitan creditors, much as the "failure" of slavery obscured its
indispensability. Over the entire period of slavery the
West Indian plantations alone may have brought the
planters an aggregate profit of over £150,000,000 at a
rate that averaged £1,000,000 a year throughout the
eighteenth century, out of a private profit level for all
plantations and metropolitan interests that may have
been four times as high.

Although the start provided by the Dutch with
capital and credit as well as expertise was invaluable,
and despite the fact that the planters who succeeded
earliest were those with some financial resources to
start with, West Indian capital was largely self-generating.[51] Acting as yeast, profits from the sugar plantations enabled penniless adventurers to found rich
dynasties, created a powerful class of wealthy ab-

sentees and, ultimately, provided one of the most formative transfers of capital in England's history. Yet the very process of absenteeism and transfer has obscured the question of total profitability—that three-streamed flow of profit described by Basil Davidson and referred to in Chapter 1.[52] Most commentators have made great play of the polarization of debtor planter and creditor merchant, and to a lesser degree, of absentee and resident planter, trader and manufacturer, free trader and protectionist. They therefore find it almost impossible to disentangle profit and loss, since "losses" for one were often profits for another, and vice versa. Similarly, even huge "private profits" can be made to mean a much lower level of profit or even a loss for the British Empire as a whole.[53]

Certainly the case of the British West Indies was very different from that of the plantation colonies of British North America. Close examination of the histories of planter families shows that there was never an insuperable divide between West Indian planters and English merchants. Many West Indian planters, like the Jamaican Beckfords, had close personal connections with English mercantile houses from the beginning; many planters, like the Lascelles of Barbados or the Pinneys of Nevis, moved from planting into mercantile activity; and most West Indies merchants became in course of time not only plantation mortgagees but, practically, planters too.[54] The very process of absenteeism could be seen not as the irresponsible flight of vulgar hedonists but as the attempt of wise West Indian planters to obtain better control over their own finances and wider scope for the reinvestment of their profits.[55] Typically, they bought land and entered English politics, many of them "buying" into titles by political patronage or marriage. They lived conspicuously well while profits were huge and tropical flamboyance was still first nature to them, but they gradually became more sober and responsi-

ble. Then, while constantly complaining of the loss of
protection and the decline of plantation profits, they
tended to transfer their West Indian fortunes gradually from an enterprise that might make 20 percent
one year and be wiped out by hurricane the next, into
securities at a reliable 3 or 4 percent. For some, however, the lure of adventure and high returns died
hard, and an incalculable amount of money was
shifted from West Indian plantations into the almost
equally risky enterprises of England's burgeoning in-
dustrialism. Generally speaking, though, English society tamed the West Indian absentee as it never quite
tamed the Indian "nabob," or ever had the chance to
change the planter from the American mainland
colonies.

Yet American plantations differed from West Indian
in ways more fundamental and wide-ranging than that
West Indian planters became English again and
Americans did not; and it was these differences that
helped to bring about American political independence. At the same time that American planters had
fewer ties with Britain and gained fewer benefits from
the British connection than did West Indians, Caribbean colonies were regarded as invaluable by old-
fashioned imperialists while American colonies were
considered of comparatively little worth. The basic
difference lay in the financial structure and balance of
American plantations. Although capital costs were
lower than in the sugar colonies, produce prices were
lower too, and American planters therefore had to
work on slimmer profit margins. The amount of initial
capital needed was less than in the West Indies; for
not only were tobacco, rice, and even cotton before
Eli Whitney in less need of capital plant, but land
was even cheaper. Slaves were initially expensive, but
since they increased naturally, the plantation work
force was cheaper to maintain than in the unhealthy
West Indies. Running costs in general were less than
in sugar colonies, particularly in food for the slaves,

which was either grown on the estates themselves or imported quite cheaply from other mainland colonies. Indeed, in many respects American slave plantations were economically integrated with the main continent rather than with their transatlantic motherland. Not only was the demand for new slaves met increasingly by New England traders, but shipping, insurance, and the whole machinery of plantation credit were gradually changing their locus from England to New England and the middle colonies. While this placed the planters in a debtor relationship to their fellow Americans, it was generally a handier and cheaper arrangement than transatlantic credit.

The critical areas were those in which the plantations were dependent upon the metropolis either by the arbitrary fiat of the British Parliament or by the equally inflexible laws of economics, particularly in the control of the sale of their staples and the reciprocal purchase of English manufactures. Nothing could quickly change the situation by which Americans were dependent upon trade with Europe and the West Indies; but Americans preferred this to be with England and English colonies only while profits there were highest. As long as the Old Colonial System prevented them from finding the most lucrative markets while failing to provide compensatory benefits, Americans could not be enthusiastic colonials.

Sir Charles Whitworth's famous tables demonstrated that the trade between England and the American plantation colonies in 1773 was by no means negligible, and Sir Arthur Young even went so far (in retrospect) as to say that while, "the sugar colonies added about three million a year to the wealth of Britain, the rice colonies [added] near a million, and the tobacco ones nearly as much."[56] Yet examination of Whitworth's figures shows not only that the balance of trade was relatively unfavorable to the American colonies, but also that much of the trade was of a kind that was not dependent upon the imperial con-

| | British imports from | | | British exports to | | | Totals 1714–73 | | | |
	1697	1773	% 1773	1697	1773	% 1773	Br. imports	%	Br. exports	%
Barbados	197	169		77	149		14,506		7,443	
Leewards	60	399		25	207		34,009		8,312	
Windwards		860			215		5,813		1,859	
Jamaica	70	1,287		41	683		42,260		16,845	
British West Indies general							220		7,194	
BWI TOTALS	327	2,705	24.8	143	1,254	8.6	96,868	20.5	41,653	6.2
British North American plantation cols.										
Middle cols.	240	1,132		64	737		47,192		27,561	
New England	40	238		76	1,243		7,160		37,939	
BNA Totals	280	1,370	12.5	140	1,980	16.1	54,352	11.3	65,500	9.6
Africa	7	68		13	662		2,407		15,236	

British Plantation Trade, 1697–1773 (rounded £ sterling thousands)[57] nection. As Josiah Tucker presciently noticed, the American colonies would be economically dependent upon England in certain respects long after political independence was achieved, while the imperial ties binding America to England were nothing but a burdensome expense to the mother country. Consequently, the majority of southern planters eventually sided with their secondary creditors in New England and the middle colonies in breaking the imperial bonds. English merchants and manufacturers could find far less enthusiasm for prosecuting a war to retain the Thirteen Colonies than they had often generated to preserve the British West Indies. Nonetheless, it was in the American plantation colonies that the largest proportion of Empire Loyalists was to be found, just as it was those colonies most unlike and least rivaling the metropolis that mercantilist Englishmen were most reluctant to lose.

Despite Sir Arthur Young's assessment, the trade of Jamaica alone in 1773 was worth as much as that of the entire belt of plantation colonies on the American mainland. Fifteen years after American independence was achieved, William Pitt (while making his notorious income tax proposal) reckoned that the West Indian plantations made four times as much profit for their owners as all other overseas holdings put together, and that the triangular trade produced a quarter of the profits of all overseas English trade.[58] Yet these combined profits, rather optimistically estimated at £7,000,000 a year, were still only part of the total benefits from the possession of West Indian colonies. For what made mercantilist writers from Josiah Child (1668), Dalby Thomas (1690), and Charles Davenant (1698) to Malachi Postlethwayt (1759) and Charles Whitworth (1776)[59] compete with each other to magnify the worth of West Indian plantations were also the direct or indirect benefits in profits and employment, through sugar refining and rum distilling, shipbuilding, and manufacturing for

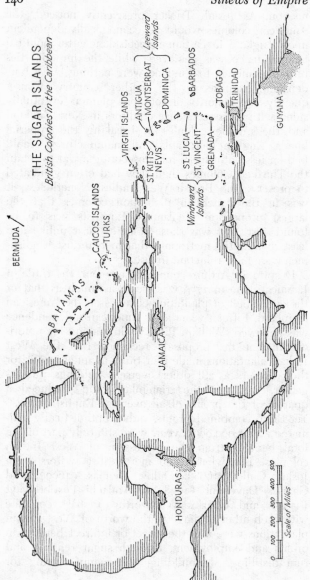

THE SUGAR ISLANDS
British Colonies in the Caribbean

BERMUDA

BAHAMAS

CAICOS ISLANDS
TURKS

JAMAICA

VIRGIN ISLANDS

ANTIGUA
MONTSERRAT
DOMINICA

} Leeward
Islands

ST. KITTS
NEVIS

BARBADOS

ST. LUCIA
ST. VINCENT
GRENADA

} Windward
Islands

TOBAGO

TRINIDAD

GUYANA

HONDURAS

0 100 200 300 400 500
Scale of Miles

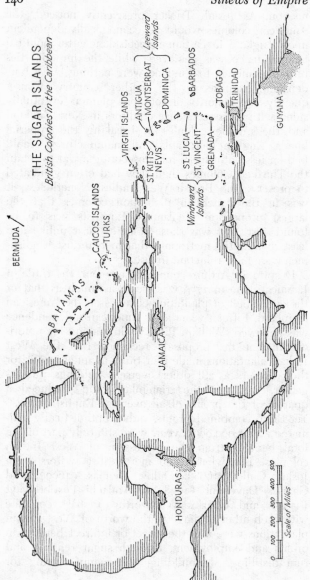

both the plantations and African trades, and the management of credit and insurance. That tireless calculator Edward Long estimated the annual private profit to Great Britain of Jamaica alone in 1773 to be £1,250,000, which he would probably have doubled to arrive at the value of the British West Indies as a whole.[60] Long's calculations were somewhat unsophisticated, but were almost certainly not understated. R. B. Sheridan has refined Long's figures to make a total of approximately £1,500,000 a year for Jamaica and £2,600,000 (or 8.4 percent on capital) for the whole of the West Indies on the eve of the American war. Of this, rather more than two thirds represented the private profit to metropolitan interests.

	£Stg. thousands
A PROFIT ON PRODUCTION	
Retained profit	250
Remittances to Great Britain	200
B PROFIT ON TRADE, CREDIT and MANUFACTURE	
Freight	419
Insurance	20
Commission and brokerage	260
Indirect remittances via America and Ireland	60
Interest on loans	35
Slave trade	125
Profit on manufacturing	130
	1499

Annual Profits of British West Indian Plantations (According to R. B. Sheridan).[61]

Of modern writers, Eric Williams in *Capitalism and Slavery* (1944) has given the most penetrating analysis of profits and tangential benefits and—more important still—has looked beyond the façade of figures into the *effects* of the sugar-slavery nexus. First, there were those areas (apparently not considered by either Edward Long or Richard Sheridan) in which the rivalry between England and New England contributed so much to the economic alienation before 1775: shipping, sugar refining, and rum distilling.[62] The skills developed in shipbuilding, and the "nursery of seamen," provided by overseas trade and the fisheries, as well as the plentiful supply of merchantmen convertible to warships, were always given as reasons for promoting the Navigation Acts. The profits generated by a pampered industry were at least as strong as personal interest among British legislators. At no time in the eighteenth century did the African and West Indian trades employ less than a tenth of English shipping, with much more English tonnage employed in the Caribbean trade than in trade with the American mainland.[63] That a large shipbuilding industry did not grow up in the British West Indies as in New England was one of the reasons why the sugar colonies remained dependent upon Great Britain and correspondingly more popular with doctrinaire imperialists.[64] Similarly, the fact that sugar could not economically be refined in the West Indies, while New England could both refine sugar and distill molasses into rum more cheaply than the metropolis, increased West Indian dependence on England while promoting greater rivalry between mother country and North American colonies. The profits of sugar refining—in which London led, followed by Bristol, Liverpool, and Glasgow—founded almost as many metropolitan fortunes as other branches of the triangular trade, but here (as will be examined again later) the interests of planter and refiner diverged, and it was the constant quest of the refiner for cheaper raw sugar that crimped the planters' prices and profits. In rum production the West Indian planter held his own save against the New Englander, for molasses did not travel easily across the Atlantic. Rum came to represent between a quarter and a third of all sugar income to the planters, and in bad periods the margin between profit and loss.

Second, there were those industries that supplied the plantation and the African trade. Included in these should be the trade in provisions and lumber, without which West Indian plantations would have been snuffed out. This is usually ignored in computations of profits, because at the time when most contemporary commentators wrote, the supply of the plantations was almost entirely in American hands and little profit accrued to the metropolis. Yet slave ships also had to be provisioned, though again this often occurred in Ireland, which was only marginally integrated into the British economic system. After 1783 and the failure of attempts to encourage Nova Scotia to fill the gap caused by American exclusion, Ireland's share of the plantation provision trade suddenly increased, and the potential profits played a large part in the campaign to bring Ireland fully into the magic circle of British protectionism. At the same time British fisheries also received a boost from the increased demand, though this was an industry in which very few fortunes were made.

Far more important throughout the slavery period were the English manufacturing industries, particularly in textiles and metallurgical products. In both, the West Indian trade was at least as important in volume and profits as the African.[65] As Eric Williams argues, it was England's traditional commitment to the woolen industry that forced the Africans and West Indian slaves to buy the type of cloth least suited to their climates. In the early days of the slave trade it was the weavers not patronized by the Royal African Company who spearheaded the woolen manufacturers' complaints against monopoly, and the freeing of the African trade doubtless helped stimulate the woolen industry in the west and north of England.[66] Yet the natural preference of tropical customers for lighter cloths made African and West

Indian traders always highly dependent on foreign linens like Osnaburgh, and gave an even greater stimulation to East Indian cotton exports. That the re-export of these cloths exempted them from English protectionism explains both the failure adequately to encourage Ireland's linen industry by bringing it under the protection of the Navigation Acts, and the power of the East India lobby. Although the woolen industry continued to expand, the share of its total exports represented by the African and West Indian trades had fallen by 1772 to 4 and 3 percent, respectively.[67] At the same time, Lancashire manufacturers were striving to copy and produce more cheaply East Indian types of cotton cloths, an effort that was only to be rewarded once dyeing and weaving processes became more sophisticated and the supply of raw cotton could be hugely increased.

The effects of the African and plantation trades upon the English metallurgical industries were rather more important because these industries were colonially more suitable and adaptable than English textiles. It has already been noted how West African trade goods such as guns and knives boosted the light-metal industries of the Midlands, but to this must be added the huge annual demands for tools for the plantations and the steady demand for heavy iron and copper machinery for the sugar factories.[68] If 10 percent of capital was the standard cost of sugar factory plant, the total exports of mill, boilinghouse, and distillery equipment must have been vast even without taking into account the quinquennial costs of replacement parts. West Indian technology was unsophisticated and notoriously unprogressive, yet these very facts probably increased the profits to the ironmaster and copper factor.

Third, Eric Williams, like most commentators, makes much of the effects of slavery and sugar on the growth of the British seaport towns, particularly Bristol and Liverpool. These changes, however, should not be exaggerated, for they were only relative and pertained more to the slave trade than to the slave-sugar nexus as a whole. London remained the predominant financial center and the most important destination for West Indian trade even after it lost primacy in the slave trade, and Bristol in turn retained great importance in the sugar trade long after Liverpool had taken over the majority of the trade in slaves. What is more important is what these switches represented. London remained England's chief West Indian port largely through the inertia of size, being the focus of the largest market and thus the most important center for sugar refining, distribution, and re-export, as well as the most important commodity market for establishing prices. Yet the creation of the West India Docks in 1803 disguised the fact that the share of London's total trade represented by the West India and African trades had fallen steadily over the previous century. The congestion of the river as well as the inconvenience of transporting industrial products to the south and east, coupled with the fact that London enjoyed no positive advantages in the slave trade, consecutively aided the development of Bristol and Liverpool. Bristol had the advantages of facing west and being easily connected by sea with the fisheries and the Irish provision ports, and overland to the centers of the earlier stages of the Industrial Revolution in Wiltshire, the Mendips, the Forest of Dean, and those parts of the Midlands served by the River Severn. Liverpool, which was assessed for the Ship Money tax in the 1630s at £20 when Bristol paid £2,000 and London £20,000, came into its own between 1700 and 1770 for much the same reasons as Bristol in an earlier period. It was able to offer great efficiency in the slave trade; a safe, uncongested waterfront; excellent facilities for ship-building; and, chief of all, easy access not only to its trading areas but also to the burgeoning industrial hinterland.

Instinct (if not post hoc logic) tells us that Britain's economy was greatly affected by the African and plantation trades, much as it informed the drunken actor who told his rowdy Liverpool audience that he had not come "to be insulted by a set of wretches, every brick in whose infernal town is cemented with an African's blood." Yet it is dangerously easy to overstate the *direct* influence of the triangular trade. The volume of demand from Africa and the plantations was never enough of itself to dominate English shipping, textiles, and metal industries or significantly to shape their development. Even when they were England's second and third ports, Bristol and Liverpool handled only a small part of her total trade; and although Liverpool went from strength to strength while Bristol gradually declined, Liverpool's greatest days came after the ending of the slave trade in 1807 and even after the final abolition of the sugar duties in 1854.

Historians should therefore look to indirect forces, working through less obvious channels, to trace the most potent influences of the slave-sugar phase of Britain's economic history. In arguments given earlier it is implied that between 1640 and 1838 private English individuals and concerns interested in slavery may have generated as much as £450 millions in profits: two thirds of it in the eighteenth century and half in the half century after 1750. If these arguments and figures are not entirely false, there was a tremendous fund of surplus capital available for redeployment. Some West Indian fortunes were squandered, most notoriously the million pounds inherited by William Beckford that were dissipated in a dozen years. Much "West Indian" money was tied up in English land, which those with commercial fortunes were bound to acquire if they aspired to gentility or real power. Yet probably even more money originating in the triangular trade was reinvested in other enterprises—either directly and obviously, or more subtly by way of the fast-developing English banking system. It therefore remains in this chapter only to assess briefly the volume and directions of flow of this reinvestment and to decide which of the economic changes that occurred in England after 1700 or 1750 were affected by it.

One of the most notable entrepreneurs who spanned both worlds was Richard Pennant (1737?–1808), the first Lord Penrhyn. The great-grandson of one of the humble "conquerors," of Jamaica, Pennant inherited a fortune based on 8,000 acres of sugar plantations and over 600 slaves, worth perhaps £3,000 a year. This fortune and a judicious marriage brought Richard Pennant a huge estate in North Wales, upon which he became famous as an improving landlord and roadbuilder. More important, Pennant developed the slate quarries on his Welsh land, which eventually employed 300 men and brought in £7,000 a year, thus, in the opinion of a local historian, bringing "to North Wales the industrial revolution."[69] Member of Parliament for Petersfield (a notoriously corrupt or "pocket" borough) as early as 1761–67, Pennant, significantly, sat for Liverpool from 1767–80 and 1784–90. A friend of William Pitt, Pennant was created Baron Penrhyn (in the Irish peerage) in 1783, becoming the most active chairman of the West India Committee of Merchants and Planters.[70]

Just as the fortunes of planters and merchants were interrelated, so was the business of merchants concerned with plantations and slavery increasingly indistinguishable from that of banker. The nature of merchants' business always involved the lending, holding, and reinvestment of money, and one of the marks of the successful merchant was the diversification of his interests. As capital multiplied, its original sources became progressively less important, while at the same time many merchants went into full-time banking or insurance. London, overwhelm-

ingly the financial center of English commerce, was
the leader in this process of transition too. Many
banks, such as Barclays and Williams Deacon's, were
originally based upon slave and West Indian business,[71] and it was to such as these that the inventors,
ironmasters, and entrepreneurs of the Industrial Revolution turned. The same process occurred on a lesser
but more intensive local scale in Bristol and Liverpool, as Eric Williams has brilliantly suggested.[72]
Boulton and Watt, the Birmingham steam engine
pioneers, for example, looked actively to West Indian
capital for expansion. At one stage during the Maritime War their whole future hinged on the successful
arrival of a West Indian fleet in which their London
bankers were deeply involved; and a few years later
the partners were looking for venture capital from
prominent West Indians such as Edward Long's
brother and "Mr. Pennant, who is a very amiable man,
with ten or twelve thousand pounds a year."[73] Similarly, the whole complex of ironworks in South Wales
based on imported ore and local coal—Merthyr Tydfil,
Cyfartha, Penydaren, Dowlais—was based on a foundation laid between 1765 and 1783 by slave and
artillery contractor Antony Bacon and his planter
partner Gilbert Francklyn, a tireless lobbyist.[74]

According to Eric Williams, the most dramatic
transfer of all involved Liverpool and the way in
which capital based on sugar and slaves was used to
fertilize the Industrial Revolution in Lancashire. "The
growth of Manchester," wrote Williams in 1944,

> was intimately associated with the growth of Liverpool,
> its outlet to the sea and the world market. The capital
> accumulated by Liverpool from the slave trade poured
> into the hinterland to fertilize the energies of Manches-
> ter; Manchester goods for Africa were taken to the
> coast in the Liverpool slave vessels. Lancashire's foreign
> market meant chiefly the West Indian plantations and
> Africa. The export trade was £14,000 in 1739; in
> 1759 it had increased nearly eight times; in 1779 it was

£ 303,000. Up to 1770 one-third of this export went to
the slave coast, one-half to the American and West
Indian colonies. It was this tremendous dependence on
the triangular trade that made Manchester.[75]

By 1788 Manchester was said to export goods to
Africa alone worth £200,000 a year, with another
£300,000 worth exported to the West Indies; these
trades providing employment for no less than 36,000
men, women, and children.[76] Moreover, as late as
1780, the West Indies provided as much as two thirds
of the 6,500,000 pounds raw cotton imported annually.[77]

Yet Williams' phrase "intimately associated with"
betrays a failure conclusively to prove causation,
just as the scattered examples mentioned earlier are
not conclusive proof that the transfer of capital was
general, or critical. Though the African trade did
stimulate some areas of manufacture, and slave trade
and slave plantation profits undoubtedly contributed
to the nascent Industrial Revolution, there is perhaps
a danger of exaggerating the "Williams Thesis." It is
well to remember that the African and West Indian
trades never represented much more than a tenth of
total British trade, and never came close to rivaling
the trade with Europe; and also that even the largest
estimates of profits from slave trade and plantations
are insufficient to account fully for the industrial
"take-off" that occurred in the later eighteenth century. The very likelihood that the chief base of the
British slave trade migrated from London and Bristol
to Liverpool—and thus closer to the heart of an industrial complex already rapidly expanding, for other
reasons—because of economies of scale in a tightening
enterprise, could take some of the force out of Eric
Williams' arguments. Even if the industrialization
of Liverpool's hinterland can be shown to have accelerated after the shift of most slave trading to the
port, *post hoc* is not necessarily *propter hoc*.

What cannot be denied, however, is the fantastic

growth of the Lancashire cotton industry, and its
subsequent results. At the time of the War of American Independence only a beginning had been made,
yet on this foundation was laid an amazing expansion
after 1800, which saw raw cotton imports and finished
exports multiply five hundred times in fifty years.
The effects were as startling and far-reaching as any
in the history of economics. The huge expansion of
production based on factories and inventions capital-
ized from all quarters besides Liverpool, required
markets for cotton goods far larger than provided by
Africa and the West Indies under the Old Colonial
System. This placed Lancastrians among the leaders
in the demand for freer world trade and for an end
to the old formal colonialism, which, incidentally,
destroyed the traditional Indian cotton industry.[78]
At the same time, the demand for raw material,
coupled with the invention of a rapid process for
cleaning cotton after picking, hugely boosted the
cotton-growing economy of the American "New
South, and this revivified slavery in the United States
just as it was dying alongside the old protective
economy in the British West Indies.

Thus Liverpool gained greatly in importance even
as the slave trade on which it was founded was
officially abolished. The city's slave-trading past, indeed, was smugly overlaid by a respectability based
on cotton, of which W. E. Gladstone, scion of a slave-
and plantation-owning family, was perhaps the most
distinguished representative.[79] Yet by a cruel irony,
slavery remained one of the bases of the wealth of
Lancashire, and of Liverpool's prosperity, which together provided such a large component of Britain's
nineteenth-century supremacy. For a further 27 years
after the slaves were nominally emancipated in the
British Empire, as for the previous two centuries, the
black slave remained the prop, and victim, of the
British economy.

Chapter 4

SLAVE SOCIETY

Caste

"Slave society" is now taken to mean not merely that part of society composed entirely of slaves, but the whole social fabric of communities based on slavery, including masters and all freedmen as well as slaves. One purpose of this modern definition is to reduce the peculiar social components of plantation polities into a more general pattern of class and function, such as the Marxist categories of aristocracy, bourgeoisie, and proletariat, and in so doing to minimize the uncomfortable fact that the helot, or proletarian, class was of a different race from that of the masters.

Yet playing down the racial element in plantation society must have greater advantages than aiding social categorization, for that in itself can be dangerously oversimplifying. After all, it was Marx himself who spoke unfeelingly of "the idiocies of the rural life," and the father of Russian Marxism, Plekhanov, who wrote, "The *muzhiks* are just like one another, and their women are just like one another, with the same uniform thoughts, costumes, with the same uniform songs, and so on."[1]

It was a plantocratic conceit that slaves constituted not only a separate race and caste, but an aggregation no more differentiated than cattle. Yet it would be ironic if ignoring the fact that the slaves were uniformly black were to perpetuate the fallacy that they were more homogeneous than whites or any body of individuals. The third and most valuable purpose of the new definition should be, in other words, to help rehumanize and individualize the slave: to see him not as slave *qua* slave or black *qua* black but, for example, as a father, lover, craftsman, artist, who merely happened to be in permanent servitude, and black.

Yet, though new definitions can reflect or even shape revised interpretations, they cannot change history itself. In ancient times slavery rarely had any connotation of race or color,[2] and in the earliest days of the British Empire "servants" could be white as well as black. But this did not last, and as soon as the need was strong enough, tendencies to equate black with slave and white with free triumphed— distinctions that have affected West Indian (and Southern American) social attitudes ever since. To say that the crucial distinction was between slave and free is to ignore the facts that no white man was ever fully a slave nor any black in the days of slavery entirely free.

Similarly, to say that white and black, slave and free in the plantations formed a single society is also to present a half truth. Masters and slaves were inexorably tied by the processes of acculturation; symbiotically interrelated by interdependence and emulation (neither as one-sided as the masters liked to maintain) and by a perverse admixture of fear, hatred, sex, grudging respect, and occasional affection. Besides, alienation often existed within the races: between ordinary slaves and the black plantation elite, between absentee masters and their peripatetic white hirelings, and between free coloreds and both races from which they had sprung.

But these were not absolute and permanent barriers; the only uncrossable lines existed between the races. The black could ape but never fully enter the ruling caste; the white could claim to understand his slaves better than they understood themselves, but never entered the most secret places of their hearts and lives. Finally, to try to see the slave as a multifaceted man, not just a piece of property, unit of value, or economic function, is all to the good. But the all-pervasive reality of his enslavement cannot be denied. Too often he was a father in a nonfamily, a clandestine and temporary lover, a craftsman only for his master's purposes, an artist only in his secret skills like carving, weaving, music, medicine, and the telling of tales.

The labor force for the first English colonies was, in fact, originally expected to be white. Once it was realized that the natives were intractable, perishable, or nonexistent, it was obvious that the proletariat would have to be imported. Naturally the earliest planters were contented with the kind of socioeconomic realities and legislation that made laborers in England then and later practically bondsmen to their masters, and they planned to transfer this system to the New World entire. This was the presumption of Richard Hakluyt's pioneer proposals for Virginia in *A Discourse of Western Planting* (1583), which suggested that sufficient artisans and craftsmen might easily be recruited in Britain and made no mention at all of black slaves. Even when the West Indian colonies showed that labor needs had been underestimated and that the work required was more onerous and unhealthy than freemen would willingly accept, it was still presumed that white "servants" would be the norm.

What was needed was a larger supply of less free laborers brought to the plantations as cheaply as possible, and in following the preference for white laborers several sources were exploited to the extent that the law was conveniently stretched. Irish rebels rounded up in Cromwell's campaigns and the ignorant peasants who flocked to Monmouth in 1685 were "Barbadoed" if they were not executed, presumably on the precept of Roman and civil law that war captives were subject to enslavement. In ancient times the same penalty was incurred by criminals, and this may have been the principle behind the invention of the sentence of transportation, which was used more frequently as overseas "opportunities" expanded. Slavery no longer existed in England, and English criminal law claimed to owe nothing to Roman law precedents; yet anyone in prison had clearly forfeited his liberty. Transportation was merely a form of overseas imprisonment, which had the additional merit of clearing England of expensive undesirables. At the height of the demand, violent abuses occurred, with contractors conniving with justices (the representatives of respectable ratepayers) to empty the jails, particularly of those arrested for being "disorderly"—the "rogues and whores" who formed the "rubidg" that Henry Whistler in 1654 claimed England had cast forth on the "dunghill" of Barbados. By the barbaric (and biblical) standards of the day even debtors were regarded as criminals who had forfeited their liberty and whose labor (with that of their dependants) might be sold.

Transportation, however, did offer some small chance of social and economic redemption for the unfortunate victims of the English penal system, as General Oglethorpe argued in founding the colony of Georgia in 1735 or as Christopher Jeaffreson, the St. Kitts planter, realistically explained half a century earlier:

> For if Newgate and Bridewell should spew out their spawn into the islands, it would meet with no less encouragement; for no gaol-bird can be so incorrigible, but there is hope of his conformity here, as well as of his preferment, which some have happily experimented; insomuch that all sorts of men are welcome to the public, as well as the private, interests of the island.[3]

A slightly better chance than in England was probably also the motive that spurred on most of those freemen who, more or less voluntarily, made the contracts called indentures for their service in the colonies for four, seven, or even more years; though the gullible were lured by contractors and ship captains with promises of sure fortunes. Some were so eager to sail for the fabulous new colonies—or so desperate—that they became "redemptioners," contracted to work without wages for up to four years simply to repay their passage money.

Life in the colonies usually provided a bitter revelation. As the planters could rarely discriminate in their choice of white laborers, all servants irrespective of origins tended to be reduced to a standard level of servitude and treated badly. Masters determined to squeeze the maximum value from white servants, who cost at least twice as much to purchase and maintain as black slaves. In Barbados the indentured whites were said to toil their lives out

> grinding at the mills and attending the furnaces, or digging in this scorching island; having nothing to feed on (not withstanding their hard labour) but potatoe roots, nor to drink, but water with such roots washed in it, besides the bread and tears of their own afflictions; being bought and sold still from one planter to another, or attached as horses and beasts for the debts of their masters, being whipt at the whipping post (as rogues) for their masters' pleasure and sleeping in sties worse than hogs in England.[4]

In early days conditions for all laborers in the colonies were almost equally harsh. Authority was derived from local laws "for the governance of slaves and servants," which were more extreme versions of the English apprentices, artificers, or masters and servants laws. Though in the West Indies "slaves" always did imply blacks and "servants" were almost invariably white men, the earliest laws made few practical distinctions between slaves and servants and none specif-

ically on account of race.[5] At much the same time
John Locke was cynically drawing up a constitution
by which white laborers in South Carolina would be
tied to the land and their masters by a form of
hereditary villeinage long eradicated in England,
while in other mainland colonies white servants were
said to be little better than chattel slaves. On the
other hand, blacks in some colonies were scarcely less
free than white servants at that time, often being
referred to as "negro servants" or plain "negars,"
rarely slaves.[6]

Colonial legislatures attempted both to keep white
servants in subjection and to keep up their numbers
by deficiency laws, which taxed masters who kept
less than a certain proportion of whites on their
estates. Yet the status of whites rose even as the
proportion of the total colonial population that they
represented fell (because the deficiency policies
everywhere failed to recruit sufficient poor whites).
The development of sugar, and to a certain degree
other plantation crops, produced a demand for a far
larger supply of cheaper laborers, which the African
trade conveniently supplied. As one contemporary
put it, "Three blacks work better and cheaper than
one white man."[7] Yet the cheapness and tractability
of Africans alone do not explain the social and legalistic gap that opened up dramatically between the
races, and that spread from the West Indies to colonies with far fewer blacks and even to nonplantation
colonies.

Today much is made of the "white slaves" of the
English plantations and their gradual emancipation,
for contrary ideological purposes. In Bermuda, for
example, visitors are likely to be told of the existence
of white slaves during the company period, with
the strong implication that white men emerged from
slavery while blacks remained enslaved through innate racial characteristics. At the other end of the
spectrum, one type of negrophile is likely to echo

the conclusion of J. S. Bassett, the North Carolina
historian, that "it was the survival of the fittest. Both
Indian slavery and white servitude were to go down
before the black man's superior endurance, docility
and labour capacity."[8] Even Eric Williams retains
more than a hint of the notion that the black was not
only regarded as more suitable for plantation labor
but actually was so. In *Capitalism and Slavery* he
quotes the saying of Herman Merivale that "in a
country where Negro slavery prevails extensively, no
white is industrious." He also writes of the "redlegs"
of Barbados, the largest surviving group of poor
whites in the West Indies, with pity masked by
contempt: "pallid, weak and depraved from in-breed-
ing, strong rum, insufficient food and abstinence from
manual labour."[9]

The question of innate racial capacities is always
riddled with fallacies, but the racialist assessments
quoted above are particularly wide of the mark since,
as Eric Williams himself points out, the whites were
never quite slaves in the senses that blacks became.
Moreover, the elevation of the whites into a master
race was aided not only by increased opportunities
but by a magnification of age-old prejudices against
the black consciously or unconsciously acquired from
predecessors in the African and plantation trades.

White servants were little better than slaves (and
were often loosely called such) during their term of
service, with only limited rights of property or litiga-
tion, forbidden to trade or plant, to move around or
marry without permission, and subject to corporal
punishment and special penalties before the courts.
Yet they suffered no legal disabilities whatsoever
once their term of service expired, a source of acute
embarrassment in the early years to the consolidating
planters, who were often sued by servants once they
were free. The unfortunate Irish captives and perhaps
some Barbadoed criminals were servants for life without indentures. But even in their case servitude did

not survive them, to be inherited by their children. Debtors might be luckier or less lucky; if they paid off their debts they became free men, but debts could be inherited and with them the obligation to repay with labor.

The only persons in perpetual bondage were chattel slaves, property, who passed on slavery through the female line. There is absolutely no evidence that whites were ever true slaves in this sense in the English colonies. It was their indentures or fixed terms of service that were sold or bequeathed, not their actual persons. If they refused to work for a new master presumbably they were sued under the English laws of contract, not any slavery law; for no English law recognized the status of hereditary slavery for Englishmen, and white inhabitants of English colonies (after some early setbacks) were able to assert their rights as English subjects. Even villeinage and its variants, despite John Locke and his aristocratic patrons, was outlawed by several colonial decisions, as in England at least a century earlier.[10]

One explanation of why the proletariat in plantation colonies became almost exclusively black is that there were sufficient supervisory and respectable jobs for nearly all the available whites, who because of their comparative freedom and freedom of choice were no longer forced into menial tasks. Yet this does not explain the growth of supremacist notions among the pockets of poor whites, or its spread to those colonies with a sizable or predominant white proletariat. In these areas it was the result of the natural struggle for the establishment and maintenance of economic and political power, a white skin often being the only claim to distinction. In eighteenth-century North America (and even in England), as in modern Britain and Australia, the cheapness of immigrant labor was a spur to native working-class racialism; though where the common enemy was the employer there was a slight change that white workers might side with the cause of black emancipation for the sake of proletarian solidarity. In the plantation colonies, with their overwhelming majorities of blacks, however, the threat posed by a cumulative increase in the population of freed blacks was much more real, and manumission was therefore made legally more difficult almost in proportion to the ratio between blacks and whites. When the threat of a general black insurrection was added, the defense mechanisms erected by the white community amounted to paranoia.

Much as social historians have recently stressed the existence of purely class tensions in American colonial society, even between the *grands blancs* and *petits blancs* of the Caribbean,[11] it must be maintained that in the British West Indies the structure of society and polity encouraged solidarity among the whites on essential issues, at least after the early presugar days in Barbados and the Leewards. If for no other reasons, the plantocrats needed the support of all white men in the colonial assemblies and militia, which, respectively, constructed the framework and provided the security of the status quo. Thus the governing class in most colonies, having established the structure of power along lines of color rather than class, vigorously excluded as long as it could all men of color, however wealthy or nearly white, for fear they might still be tainted with radical ideas.

To Eric Williams, the stereotype of black inferiority was a result, not a cause, of the nature of plantation society: "Slavery was not born of racism; rather, racism was the consequence of slavery."[12] In a sense this was true but, as has already been sketched in Chapter 1, both black slavery and the myth of black inferiority were ancient when British slavery began. There are no entirely fresh beginnings in history, and although the history of British colonies repeated the entire process whereby what was regarded as socially and economically necessary was gradually elevated to the status of positive law, superior attitudes toward blacks and a tacit acceptance of their enslavement based upon ethnocentric fallacies were common currency when British colonization began. In illustration it is interesting to compare two views of the black written almost two hundred years apart: by George Best in 1578, long before the English held plantation slaves of their own; and by Edward Long, who wrote his *History of Jamaica* in 1774 when English plantation slavery was at its height. Though he cloaked his prejudices in an array of pseudoscience, Long was by far the more negrophobic of the two, for he was himself a third-generation planter who had personally witnessed the horrific "Coromantine" rebellion and subsequent massacre in Clarendon, Jamaica, in 1760. Yet in its very naïveté, Best's account provides an accurate view of the ideas with which Englishmen came armed into the plantation and slavery businesses.

George Best, who had sailed with Frobisher and whose *Discourse* was incorporated in Hakluyt's *Voyages*,[13] set out to discover what it was that made the blacks "cole blacke, and their hair like wooll curled short." Common opinion ascribed these characteristics to the heat of the sun, but as Best pointed out, this was clearly an error, since the inhabitants of equatorial regions other than Africa were often "tawny" in complexion and straight-haired. "Ethiopians," moreover, were found as far south as the Cape of Good Hope in latitudes as distant from the equator as "Sicilia, Morea or Candie, where all be of very good complexions." Likewise, Best recounted (with a significant absence of moralizing comment on miscegenation as such)

> I my selfe have seene an Ethiopian as blacke as a cole brought into England, who taking a faire English woman to wife, begat a sonne in all respects as blacke as the father was, although England were his native

countrey, and an English woman his mother: whereby it seemeth this blackness proceedeth rather of some natural infection of that man, which was so strong, that neither the nature of the Clime, neither the good complexion of the mother concurring, coulde any thing alter.

To unravel this wonder George Best looked to the Scriptures and found his solution in the story of Noah and its apocryphal embellishments. According to this version, a somewhat puritanical Noah had ordered that his sons "should use continencie, and abstain from carnall copulation with their wives" while in the Ark. Cham disobeyed, in order that his offspring would obtain the first-born's portion when dry land reappeared. "For the which wicked and detestable fact," proclaimed Best,

> as an example for contempt of Almightie God, and disobedience of parents, God would a sonne should bee borne whose name was Chus, who not onely it selfe, but all his posteritie after him should bee so blacke and lothsome, that it might remaine a spectacle of disobedience to all the worlde. And of this blacke and cursed Chus came all these blacke Moores which are in Africa, for after the water was vanished from off the face of the earth, and that the lande was dry, Sem chose that part of the land to inhabite in which nowe is called Asia, and Japhet had that which is now called Europa, wherein wee dwell, and Africa remained for Cham and his blacke sonne Chus, and was called Chamesis after the fathers name, being perhaps a cursed, dry, sandy, and unfruitfull ground, fit for such a generation to inhabite in.[14]

In its way, Edward Long's description of blacks, their origins and destiny, would be equally quaint were it not so disingenuously warped.[15] Long too pointed out that the blacks' blackness was inherent, and behind this, as in Best, there was the eurocentric presumption that black in human beings was the reverse of beautiful. Long's description of other alleged negroid characteristics was even more calculated to arouse distaste in his readers. The blacks' hair was not just woolly but "like the bestial fleece." Then there was the "bestial or fetid smell" which blacks were said to possess in inverse proportion to their intelligence,

> the roundness of their eyes, the figure of their ears, tumid nostrils, flat noses, invariable thick lips, and the general large size of the female nipples, as if adapted by nature to the peculiar conformation of their children's mouths.

Even blacks' black body lice were claimed to be different from the white (and presumably superior) lice of white men.

Edward Long's caricature blacks were as unpromising in intellectual attainments and character as they were unpleasing in appearance. "In general, they are void of genius," he asserted of Africans with sweeping inaccuracy (and with an unconscious irony delineating many of the gross characteristics attributed to plantation whites by unbiased observers)

> incapable of making any progress in civility or science. They have no plan or system of morality among them . . . no taste but for women, gormandising, and drinking to excess; no wish but to be idle . . . they are represented by all authors as the vilest of the human kind, to which they have little more pretension of resemblance than what arises from their exterior form.

In Edward Long's view, most Africans remained irredeemable savages even on plantations, "marked with the same bestial manners, stupidity and vices, which debase their brethren on the continent." If caught early enough and "habituated to cloathing and a regular discipline of life," they had some small prospect of improvement. But at best, the blacks' highest achievement was to "ape" their betters, performing their work "in a very bungling and slovenly manner, perhaps not better than an *oran-outang* might, with a little pains, be brought to do."

Like George Best, Edward Long presented a myth of the blacks' origins provided with a spurious religious mandate. As befitted a writer in the Age of Reason obsessed with the blacks' "animal" nature, he chose the pre-Darwinian theory of the chain of being, in which blacks were farther from white men than white men were from the angels, and correspondingly closer to the apes. "We observe," wrote Long (modifying Buffon where it suited him)

> gradations of the intellectual faculty, from the first rudiments perceived in the monkey kind, to the more advanced stages of it in apes, in the *oran-outang*, that type of man [the Hottentots], and the Guiney Negroe; and ascending from the varieties of this class to the lighter casts, until we mark its utmost limit of perfection in the pure white. Let us not then doubt, but that every member of the creation is wisely fitted and adapted to the certain uses, and confined within the certain bounds, to which it was ordained by the Divine Fabricator. The measure of the several orders and varities of these Blacks may be as compleat as that of any other race of mortals; filling up that space, or degree, beyond which they are not destined to pass; and discriminating them from the rest of men, not in *kind*, but in *species*.

Ugly, ignorant, ineducable to the degree that they appeared a separate human species, Long's blacks were clearly unfitted for grafting onto "polite" society. They would remain, if Long's viewpoint prevailed, slaves forever, condemned by science and a "rational" God as surely as by the curse of Noah's God.

ATTITUDES AND THE LAW

Fittingly, Edward Long—planter and grandson of the most active of the early Speakers of the Jamaican Assembly—was the most outspoken of the admirers of the system by which the planters shaped the colonial constitutions to their own socio-economic purposes. The founding English settlers, like ancient Greek colonists, assumed that colonies were miniature replicas of the homeland. English colonists carried with them the social and political system with which they were familiar, which, of course, included the peculiarly English notion that the law was the mandate of society and rationalization of its needs, rather than derivative of some abstract natural law. Against them was ranged the "imperialist" or "Roman" concept that colonies were complementary and subordinate to the motherland in every respect. The "colonialist" position was reinforced by the "bourgeois revolution" against the Stuart prerogative, which in England established that government should be more firmly in the hands of a parliament representing those with a stake or interest in the country. This constitutional struggle had to be refought separately in practically each colony, but it led to a situation in which not only were the colonial assemblies in local affairs more nearly omnipotent than Parliament in England, but were much more "democratic," in the sense that they represented "all free-born free-holders"; that is, in plantation colony practice, all white males.

This is by no means to suggest that conflict between colonial magnates and poor whites was entirely absent, or that the interests of colonial assemblies invariably prevailed if they conflicted with the metropolitan government when concerned with imperial affairs. The power of large planters relative to smallholders and landless freemen was maintained in most colonies by the magnates' monopoly of the legislative councils, much as the House of Lords balanced the Commons in England. The imperial government always maintained the right to review all colonial laws and, through the governors and their executive councils, to convene, prorogue, and dissolve assemblies and even initiate local legislation, as a function of the "royal" prerogative. There was also the ill-defined but growing area in which the British Parliament sat as an imperial Parliament when dealing with the Empire as a whole. Yet, as has been argued already, there was a large measure of concurrence between all whites in the colonies, and for most of the eighteenth century either no conflict of interest occurred between assemblies in the plantation colonies and the imperial government, or there was an actual indifference on the part of the latter to the interests of the former.

Thus the colonial assemblies were able to pass laws that followed closely their special socio-economic needs concerning the status of slaves and free blacks (and the sustaining myth of black inferiority) despite the absence of similar laws in England. The preamble to a typical colonial slave law, the Bermudian Act of 1730 reducing the penalty to whites for murdering slaves to a simple fine, provides a telling illustration:

WHEREAS Negroes Indians Mulattoes and other Slaves are very Numerous within these Islands, and that the wilfull killing of any such Slave as aforesaid (by the Strict Laws of England) comes within the penalty of Murder, the Judgement whereof is forfeiture of Life and Estate, And whereas the Priviledges of England are So universally Extensive as not to admitt of the least thing called Slavery, occasioned the making of such Laws for the preservation of every Individual Subject in his or their Lives, Estates, and Indisputable Rights and properties; But here in his Majesties Colonies and plantations in America the Cases and Circumstances of things are wonderfully altered, for the very kindred nay sometimes even the Parents of these unfortunate Creatures (upon the Coasts of Affrica) Expose their own Issue to perpetual Bondage and Slavery by selling them unto your Majesties Subjects trading there and from thence are brought to these and other your Majesties Settlements in America and consequently purchased by the Inhabitants thereof, they be-

ing for the Brutishness of their nature no otherwise
valued or Esteemed amongst us than as our goods and
Chattels or other personal Estates; therefore our pru-
dent neighbours in America as Barbadoes &c have
thought fitt (in Case of Killing any Such Negro or
Slave) to make Laws to prevent the penalty and for-
feitures aforesaid.

That such transparent self-interest with no visible
means of support in logic should pass muster in London says much for the responsiveness of the imperial
legal system to different needs. In reviewing colonial
laws, the law officers of the Crown were not so much
looking for their congruence with English law as
making sure that they were not "repugnant"—that is,
did not promote a conflict of interests between one
set of English subjects and another. Even after the
anomalies of allowing slavery in the colonies but not
in England were pointed out by the emancipists, the
special slave laws of the plantations were regarded
at most as *supplemental* to metropolitan laws.[16]

At least the principle of approval by the Crown
helped to reduce the anomalies in the slave laws
among the plantation colonies themselves.[17] In fact,
it did as much as simple emulation among colonies
to standardize the laws. Pragmatic flexibility (and
human fallibility) still determined, however, that the
British colonial slave laws fell short of a code comparable to the French *Code Noir* or the Spanish slavery laws. Yet this failing also decided that there was
generally a narrower gap between the law as promulgated and its modification by custom in the British
than in either the French or Spanish colonies.[18]

In drawing up a précis of British colonial slave laws
for the benefit of the Committees of Inquiry in 1788–
89, the legal expert consulted, John Reeves, made the
following percipient summary:

the leading Idea in the Negro System of Jurisprudence
is that which was the first in the Minds of those most
interested in its Formation; namely, that Negroes were

Property, and a species of Property that needed a rigorous and vigilant Regulation.

The numerous Laws passed in the different Islands immediately upon their first Settlement, and for a considerable time after, with all their multifarious and repeated Provisions, had uniformly this for their Object. To secure the Right of Owners and maintain the Subordination of Negroes, seem to have most occupied the Attention and executed the Solicitude of the different Legislatures; what regarded the Interests of the Negroes themselves appears not to have sufficiently attracted their Nature.[19]

Slave laws can thus be divided into four types, of which the first was basic but the second and third easily the most common: laws defining property in slaves; "policing" laws; laws to maintain the social order, extending to free blacks as well as slaves; and laws to protect the slaves.

When bought in Africa, blacks had, of course, no indentures or fixed terms of service. Therefore it was easy for colonial legislatures to decree that they served *durante vita,* particularly since some masters were in the habit of setting their blacks free once they had passed the years of useful work, so that they were likely to become a burden on the public. Once it had been established that masters were permanently responsible for the sustenance of the blacks they had bought, it became more than ever obvious that it was not just their service that had been purchased, but their persons too. Purchasers were thus encouraged to regard slaves as chattel property, permanently owned along with their increase, like so many cattle bought at a fair.[20]

Moreover, a legal basis for this assumption was ready to hand: the blacks were not English. They were therefore more subject than Englishmen to precepts of the "Law of Nations" (i.e., Europe), which recognized permanent slavery for captives, criminals, and even persistent infidels (alias "brutish victims of unreason"). For long it was scarcely necessary to assert these legal fictions because the slaves were not in a position to challenge their enslavement in the courts, and had few allies. Yet the argument that all slaves purchased in Africa had originally been captured in war or sentenced for crimes was increasingly used once slavery was challenged, until it became an article of faith among slaveowners. Another loophole proved more difficult to close. As has already been noted, there was a real doubt in those foreign colonies where Canon Law prevailed whether a black who had seen the light of Christianity could still be enslaved. Britons eschewed Canon Law where it suited them, yet in certain English colonies freedom from enslavement had been extended (along with other privileges) to "all Christians," in order to include non-English European settlers.[21] There were even cases of captured Indians being released when it was proved that they had been baptized, albeit in popish realms. Baptism was thus apparently tantamount to manumission, a presumption which, as Handlin notes, "as labor rose in value . . . dissipated the zeal of masters for proselytizing"[22] their slaves. To resolve the danger (not, it seems, in order to spread the Gospel more widely), a series of Virginian laws between 1667 and 1671 stated clearly that conversion of itself did not free a slave. In the West Indies, however, sufficient doubt remained to ensure that preaching to the slaves hardly ever occurred—on the principle that since Christians possibly could not be slaves, slaves should not be encouraged to be Christians.

By about 1700, then, in nearly all English colonies, blacks were presumed to be slaves and everywhere, including England itself, laws recognized that slaves, unlike servants, were chattels.[23] British slaves therefore tended to suffer the worst of two legal systems. Denied the protection of the antislavery bias of the English common law because they were not English, they were also cut off from much of the protection provided for slaves under Roman law—and its offshoots the Spanish *Siete Partidas* and the French *Code Noir*—because they were decreed as property, the peaceful enjoyment of which was a right even more sacred to Englishmen than personal liberty. As property, black slaves became trammeled in the web and mystique of English property law. Bought as simple merchandise, slaves could be resold, used in payment of debts once other assets were exhausted, and even, in some islands, sold in case of intestacy. In other respects they were regarded as real estate. When sold within a colony they were conveyed in proper legal form (the surviving paperwork providing a valuable historical source). Slaves were regarded in probate law as freehold inheritance, bequeathed in wills with widows' dower rights and the rights of orphans protected. They could be entailed to estates and mortgaged, either with estates or separately.

Since the protection of property was a cornerstone of the English constitution, a colossal irony determined that the black's enslavement was based upon one of the Englishman's dearest rights. To free the slaves was to dispossess the master of his "liberty." Thus, when emancipation was finally decreed, the owners gained handsome compensation from a British Parliament dedicated to property rights on much the same principle that in some colonies masters had been so protected in their property that assemblies reimbursed them when their slaves were killed in war, murdered, or permanently ran away.

Yet, however superbly the masters rationalized their property rights in slaves, resolutely refusing to pass laws dealing with slave marriages, families, education, or religious conversion, they could never entirely obscure the fact that slaves were persons rather than things. The very prevalence and severity of police laws attested to the slaves' personality, if in negative ways. Similarly, the ways in which the majority of slave laws—even those that were claimed to protect slaves' minimal rights—were designed to preserve the socio-economic system, testified to the real and imaginary threats posed by the slaves to white supremacy and to the ways in which custom and human nature constantly triumphed over the reduction of the black from person to legal abstraction. As usual, it was Bryan Edwards who produced the most candid analysis of the realities of plantation society:

> In countries where slavery is established, the leading principle on which the government is supported is fear: or a sense of that absolute coercive necessity which, leaving no choice of action, supersedes all questions of right. It is vain to deny that such actually is, and necessarily must be, the case in all countries where slavery is allowed.[24]

Even Edwards, however, only implied the corollary. Slavery engendered fear, both of violence and social dislocation; these fears reactively provoked counter-violence and social dispossession in due proportion.

Although the very earliest British colonial slave laws, those promulgated in Barbados in the 1640s and 1650s, have been lost, references to them imply that they reflected the need of the white planters completely to subjugate the blacks who were so rapidly outnumbering them. For convenience colonies developing later tended initially to adopt slave laws evolved elsewhere, whether or not the old and the new colonies' circumstances matched. The comprehensive Jamaican slave law of 1667, for example, was almost a copy of the earliest Barbadian law still extant, that of 1664. Subsequently, the Jamaican law was closely copied both by Antigua and by South Carolina. Yet, in time slave laws were modified to a significant degree. Generally, the severity of penal laws was an index of the threat the blacks were thought to pose to white control, which normally related to the proportion of the total population that they represented. Thus the penal laws of Jamaica, where blacks outnumbered whites by twelve to one over-all (and thirty to one on estates) were much harsher than those of New York, where the race ratio was reversed, with Virginia coming somewhere in between in both respects.

But these indices might be modified by several factors. For example, Antigua, with its limited flat area highly developed with plantations and its population never rapidly augmented once the colony was developed, possessed a black code noticeably milder than that of Jamaica, with its rapid and incomplete expansion, continuing large influx of Africans, innumerable hiding places, intransigent Maroons, and the growing threat of "infection" from St. Domingue. Barbados, on the other hand, though an island more similar in geography and development to Antigua than Jamaica, retained a notoriously severe penal code from its pioneer sugar days. This was not just through legislative inertia but because the black population of Barbados was thought by the legislators to be excessive in numbers and dangerously underworked, while the comparatively numerous poor white population suffered from an extreme case of "siege mentality." Similar effects can be traced in the plantation colonies of the American mainland, particularly the Carolinas and Maryland before 1750.

It should be emphasized, however, that the absence of harsh laws did not necessarily mean easy treatment; rather the absence of a need for legislation, real or imagined. Likewise, harsh laws sometimes stayed in the statute books long after they were needed or normally applied, as an increasingly empty menace.

In all colonies the most savage laws tended to be passed as the immediate result of black rebellions, as in Jamaica during the First Maroon War or after the 1760 uprising, or in Antigua after the rebellion of 1736, or in South Carolina after the insurrection of 1740. Even in tranquil Bermuda (where whites outnumbered blacks by two to one), the law quoted earlier, along with several others, was the reaction of the assembly to the bloody and unexpected black revolt earlier in the same year.

Rebellion indeed was the ultimate threat and therefore the worst crime in the slavery code, retributively punished not just by death but death in barbaric forms, accompanied by torture and mutilation.[25] Any activity that could possibly be construed as conducive to rebellion was drastically countered: the congregation of slaves without supervision; moving around without passes or after dark; possession of firearms or other weapons; the blowing of conch shells or beating of drums, which were said to convey secret messages. Likewise, the recovery of runaways always mobilized the entire machinery of social control, though in small islands in placid times this was less from fear of encouraging rebellion than because of the loss of the slaves' services and the threat of social disorder short of rebellion in the towns.[26]

The punishment for ordinary crimes was predictably flexible, and in some cases superficially milder than in England at that time. Yet penalties were so determined by socio-economic factors that their relationship to normal canons of crime and punishment were dangerously obscured. Murder is an excellent case in point. As has already been seen, murder of a slave by a white man was normally punishable merely by a fine.[27] Yet the fine was highest when the slave belonged to another; and when a white person's own slave died as the result of overwork or "deserved Correction or punishment,"[28] no fine was levied at all. At the other end of the scale, however, the murder of a white by a slave was the most heinous of all individual crimes and was punished with medieval barbarity. In some colonies at some times even a threat by a slave to a white was punishable by death.[29] If a black murdered another black, the penalties varied from savage whipping to execution, with the master doubly recompensed, for murderer as well as victim.

The laws against theft showed similar flexibility, varying from theft from another black, through praedial larceny to theft from whites other than the slave's master, though the death penalty—which deprived a master of his property—was imposed far less often in the colonies than in England, where Tyburn Tree was as effective as the plague or transportation for weeding out undesirables. In sex crimes there was not so much a flexibility as a completely double standard. In the almost unthinkable case of a sexual assault by a black man on a white woman, the punishment was similar to that for murder, if indeed the slave lived long enough to be brought to trial (far more concern being caused by sexual relations actually encouraged by the women).[30] Yet over the far commoner cases of white men's transgressions against black women, the law was as silent as in the case of sex crimes between black and black; though in the first case it was the turning of a blind eye, and in the second, sheer indifference. In general, only in cases in which the crime amounted to an abuse of an owner's property or where the status quo was threatened, did the law come into operation.

In most colonies for most of the slavery period, masters had almost absolute control over their slaves and did not bother the courts with slavery matters. Scales of domestic punishment for slaves were usually laid down by law, but these were as severe as the penalties to masters for overstepping the line into sadism were mild. The restrictive clauses were in any event almost a dead letter, since it was almost impossible to convict a master for crimes against his own slaves. In the period before amelioration the rare laws passed to lay down minimal standards for slaves' conditions were similarly nugatory, if not actually ambiguous, like the laws compelling masters to support their superannuated slaves. Generally speaking, all such legislation was as much concerned with cutting down public expense and embarrassment and with creating a colonial standard, as with improving conditions for the slaves. For example, all West Indian colonies passed laws at different times (often during wars) to compel the growing of "Negro provisions," but these were aimed more at reducing dependence on outside supplies and cutting down the problem of slave thefts than in improving slaves' diet. Similarly, the regulation about the provision of clothing for slaves laid down in some colonies were as much concerned with standardizing slave dress and forbidding the wearing of finery by slaves as to ensure that they were at least minimally clothed. Fixed holidays were also decreed in most colonies; but this had the purpose of determining that slaves were all free together at times known by everyone. Penalties were prescribed for giving too many, or irregular, as well as too few, holidays, and provisions were usually made for declaring martial law on days of general holiday.

In a "well-ordered" colony there was no call for masters to be summoned to court over their slaves or for slaves to appear in court themselves at all. When slaves were arraigned on criminal charges this was almost invariably before special courts, either with a justice giving summary judgment or, at most, a jury of three white men. In theory, slaves could not appear in normal courts on their own behalf, especially in civil cases; for chattels could hardly litigate or even own property themselves. In fact, it was well known from the earliest times that slaves did own property and money, and they did appear in court on their own behalf (if with sponsors), though their evidence was never accepted save against another black.

The degree of practical freedom enjoyed by slaves can be deduced from the need to legislate against conditions that were nominally illegal, or illogical. This was particularly true in islands like the Leewards, Bermuda, and the Bahamas, with comparatively large populations of urban and seafaring slaves. From the laws to control such activities, it is evident that slaves grew provisions and fished on their own account and sold their produce for their own benefit,[31] privately served as ferrymen or chair-men, worked as tailors, carpenters, coopers, or masons in their own time, took in laundry or sewing, and even hired themselves out for labor, giving their masters only a portion of their wages. Slaves acting as seamen, despite provisions that seagoing ships should be manned by at least one white, were practically as free as slaves ever became—and rarely in such vile servitude as the ordinary white seamen on English merchant and naval vessels at that time.

Legal manumission, however, was extremely difficult to obtain until the very last days of slavery, because of both the jealous retention of the slaves' services by the masters individually and the obduracy of the laws in general. No custom of buying freedom on the installment plan at the slaves' own initiative had grown up in the British colonies like the *coartacion* of the Spanish. Manumission in the British Empire could never be obtained save on the initiative of the masters or the master class. Except in the rare cases in which assemblies decreed freedom for certain blacks for special services, masters had to lodge heavy security with parish authorities and could not fully surrender responsibility during their own lifetimes or those of their ex-slaves. Consequently, free blacks were only a minor component of slave society before 1800, amounting to 3.7 percent of the population of Jamaica in 1787, 3.0 percent in Antigua, and 2.6 percent in Barbados, with no more than fifteen thousand for the British West Indies as a whole.[32] They consisted, moreover, almost entirely of the most assimilated blacks: faithful domestics or gangmen toward the end of their lives, or the bastard offspring of white fathers and black slave mothers.

Without overstating the case, it is perhaps true to say that manumission was additionally retarded by a lack of will or incentive on the part of the slaves most likely to be freed. The great majority of slaves surely craved their freedom; yet the machinery of manumission was not designed for them, but for those most closely attuned to slavery's rules, who enjoyed the greatest degree of practical freedom already. Manumission itself brought few practical benefits, while it deprived the ex-slaves of their masters' full legal responsibility for their welfare and protection. A similar dependence in a world inimical to the poor and masterless helps to explain the anomaly that thousands of blacks continued in a state of more or less voluntary servitude in England long after Lord Mansfield's judgment in 1772; just as English lawyers a century earlier had been forced to recognize villeinage as a voluntary condition long after its continuance by constraint had been declared illegal. In the colonies there was the additional discouragement that the legal status of free blacks was only gradually raised after manumission and never reached the same level as that enjoyed by persons recognized as whites.

Indeed, the discrimination practiced almost everywhere against blacks once nominally freed is the best proof that colonial laws were racial was well as socioeconomic in inspiration. Almost as much care was taken in framing laws against freed blacks as against the slaves, with restrictions actually tending to tighten with the increase in the numbers of those freed. In Jamaica, for example, at different times at least four categories of free men of color were distinguished, each differing in its relative freedom: those decreed their freedom by the state, those obtaining manumission in the normal form, those who were the sons of freemen, and those who were so light in complexion as to be recognized as whites. In early days certain slaves decreed free by the Crown were granted practically all the rights of freeborn Englishmen. The most famous example was that of the "Spanish Negro" Juan de Bolas and his followers, in 1661. Those of their descendants who became the Jamaican Maroons, living in inaccessible areas, were able to retain their practical freedom and even negotiate special privileges after a successful war of resistance. Yet such of these free blacks as tried to assimilate fully (at a time when colonial assemblies were gaining independence from the Crown and becoming more bigoted) soon lost all their privileges save that of jury trial, and like all other free blacks were denied the right to be justices, jurors, members of the assembly, vestrymen, officers of the militia, or militia cavalrymen.

Of the remainder of free blacks, those who had been personally manumitted were at first carefully distinguished from those who were the children of free blacks. The former were treated very little better than slaves, being subject to practically the same criminal law, denied jury trial and the right to serve in the militia. In court cases their evidence could only be used against slaves or their own kind, not against the sons of free men, just as no evidence of any black could be used against a white man until the very last days of slavery.

Elsewhere, the codes of legislation against free blacks were less complex and comprehensive than in Jamaica; but this generally meant less freedom for the average rather than more freedom for some. In Barbados, toward the other end of the spectrum, there was no rank order of color among freedmen decreed by law and no special privilege legislation for freedmen. Freedmen played only a minor role in the militia, and when ameliorating legislation was generally introduced toward the end of slavery.

It seems clear that for the freed blacks—as for the slaves—their legal and actual situation was largely a function of their relative numbers, which in turn reflected the demographic composition of each colony. Jamaica had a comparatively large free black population because of the overwhelming ratio of blacks to whites and the shortage of white women on the plantations: The colony was forced into a complex but marginally and selectively more liberal freedman's code because of the indispensable role that some freedmen performed in the society. Barbados, on the other hand, with its long-established population and large minority of poor whites, had little need or tolerance for a free black population, and legislated accordingly. In this respect the island came closest to the American mainland situation in which, as Arnold Sio has stated, "there was simply no place" for the black freedman.[33] From Elsa Goveia's description it seems that the situation among the black freedmen in the Leewards came somewhere in between that of Jamaica and of Barbados.[34] The attitude of the ruling whites in Bermuda, however, seems to have been yet more antagonistic toward the black freedmen than that of the mainlanders. With the whites almost as numerous as the blacks and thus having a higher proportion of poor whites than any other island colony, the Bermudian legislators even attempted to pass a law in 1730 to "extirpate" all free blacks from the island within six months of their manumission.

Even in Jamaica, the distinction between different types of free black tended to disappear around the middle of the eighteenth century, but this (as with the Anglo-Saxons after 1066 and subjugated blacks throughout Africa) seems to have resulted less in an elevation of the lowliest free blacks than in a general reduction in the status of all. In all colonies the burden of proof of freedom lay with the black, the presumption being that an itinerant black was a runaway slave. In Jamaica by a law of 1717 all free blacks even had to wear a distinguishing mark, a blue cross sewed on their clothing. Those freed in their own lifetime, of course, carried the additional stigma of the brand in their flesh. Nearly all criminal laws distinguished carefully between blacks and whites, particularly those that dealt with violence between persons, and theft. Black companies continued to form a valuable part of colonial militias, but other

civil rights were not extended, and the right to vote—
originally granted indiscriminately to a freedmen—
was increasingly restricted. These restrictions on civil
rights were generally achieved by property qualifications rather than by overt racial discrimination,
though at the same time the rights of free blacks to
hold property were being curtailed. At first there was
a propensity to allow all free men to own as much as
they could, but in every colony there were increasing
attempts to qualify this when it was noticed that the
lands and goods of the free coloreds, like their offspring, tended to multiply more rapidly than those of
the poorer whites. In Jamaica an act of 1761 even
forbade anyone to bequeath to a black property
worth more than £2,000, on the blatantly expressed
principle that such generosity might tend to

> destroy the destinction requisite and absolutely neces-
> sary to be kept up in this island between white persons
> and Negroes, their issue and offspring, and which may
> in progress of time be the means of decreasing the
> number of white inhabitants.[35]

Nearly everywhere free blacks were discriminated
against in trade, particularly in those colonies where
the whites felt themselves most embattled economically. Bermuda, for example, having failed to implement its hopelessly unrealistic Extirpation Act of 1730,
consistently legislated against the invasion of trade by
blacks, however free, a tradition that has unhappily
lingered—though not in law—until the present day.[36]

By legislating against free men of color on the
grounds of racial "purity," the colonial whites risked
the loss of potential allies and ran the risk of aligning
all blacks against all whites. This was because self-
interest decreed the paradox that it was in colonies
with the largest proportion of whites—and thus, generally speaking, the mildest penal laws against the
slaves—that blacks once manumitted were most dis-

criminated against. Rather curiously, only in Jamaica
was there an attempt to widen the base of the ruling
class, though even there it was done simply by broad-
ening the definition of white. By an act of 1781 all
coloreds "three degrees removed from the Negro an-
cestor exclusive" were classed as whites and were regarded as naturally free even if their mothers were
slaves. Thus the distinctions among the four degrees
of color for blacks—Negro, Mulatto, Quadroon, Mustee—assumed a socially dangerous importance in
Jamaica and other British West Indian islands, though
not to the absurd lengths of the French West Indies,
where the *Code Noir* distinguished theoretical degrees of color. This was in a society in which, despite
ostensible social disapproval, wholesale miscegenation
between white men and black women occurred, without legal let or hindrance save the law that decreed
that the offspring normally took the status of the
mother rather than of the father.[37]

In Virginia and other mainland plantation colonies,
on the other hand, not only was anyone of black
ancestry regarded as a person of color, but laws were
actually passed against miscegenation, such as the
Virginia Act of 1705 for

> the prevention of that abominable mixture and spurious
> issue which hereafter may increase in his Majesty's
> colony by English and other white men and women
> intermarrying with Negroes and Mulattoes, or by their
> unlawful coition.[38]

The civil rights of colored free men in the mainland
colonies were also reduced as their numbers increased.
For example, in Virginia until an act of 1723 all free
men owning property voted irrespective of color, even
though unpropertied white men were denied the franchise. Thereafter, all men of color were deprived of
the right to vote until after the Civil War. "This, I con-
fess," wrote Lieutenant-Governor Gooch, defending
the act, to the Lords Commissioners of trade in 1735,

. . . may seem to carry an air of severity to such as are unacquainted with the nature of negroes, and the pride of a manumitted slave, who looks on himself immediately on his acquiring his freedom to be as good a man as the best of his neighbours, but especially if he is descended of a white father or mother, let them be of what mean condition soever; and as most of them are the bastards of some of the worst of our imported servants, and the convicts, it seemes no ways impolitick, as well for discouraging that kind of copulation, as to preserve a decent destinction between them and their betters, to leave this mark on them until time and education has changed the indication of their spurious extraction, and made some alteration in their morals. After all, the number of free negros and mulattos entitled to the privilege of voting at elections is so inconsiderable, that 'tis scarce worth while to take notice of them in this particular since by other Acts of the Assembly now subsisting they are disabled from being either jurymen or witnesses in any case whatsoever, and so are as much excluded from being good and lawful men, as villains were of old by the laws of England.[39]

Thus were the laws of England borrowed, or rather "wonderfully altered," to suit the political, social, and economic needs of the dominant class in the plantation colonies.

SLAVE CONDITIONS

Since the colonial slave laws were chiefly concerned with preserving the socio-economic equilibrium, they provide less information about normal conditions than about situations of stress. As has already been sketched, they were most strident in those times and areas in which the status quo was most threatened; that is, when and where slaves were practically free and free blacks were economically potent. These conditions applied most to colonies with considerable black populations but comparatively few plantations and, in purely plantation colonies, to the towns and nonplantation holdings. Planter-legislators came to regard other colonies, towns, and even non-sugar "pens" as storm centers of radical ideas, racial mixing, and rapid change. They therefore strove to prevent such influences infecting the private domain of their plantations, or plantation slaves gaining much familiarity with the outside world. Their interest was to make plantation society as closed, as standard, and as unchanging as possible.[40]

Life in plantations was largely unruffled by the external events or even laws that shaped the lives of nonplantation slaves. Yet, though events and laws and the colorful life of the towns furnish the gist of most colonial chronicles, it was the plantations that provided the basis and standard for slave society. Even today the West Indies, with its seething cities, is predominantly a rural society; in 1775 no less than 95 percent of its slave population lived outside the towns (as many as 75 percent on sugar estates), and the proportion in the plantation colonies of the American mainland was little lower. The life of slaves on plantations was therefore the most important, though not always the most obvious, aspect of slave society.

In every society the quality of life is determined chiefly by material conditions and psychological factors arising from personal interrelationships. To separate the two completely is artificial if not impossible. Human nature is not so neatly constrained. For example, people will often unresistingly accept psychological insult when material conditions are only moderately satisfactory though stable, but fret at milder restraints when conditions and expectations improve. Yet for simplicity's sake, it is best first to look at conditions of housing, clothing, diet, health, mortality, and fertility, before assessing the ways in which these influenced or were influenced by less tangible social determinants.

Slave housing was generally so rudimentary that,

as has been shown earlier, no expenditure on it was allowed for in the capitalization of estates. Slaves were expected to build their own houses and consequently constructed them as they would in Africa, of wattle and daub, with thatch of guinea grass, cane tops or palmetto, the "poor man's shingle." Absolutely vulnerable to fire, flood, and hurricane, unlike the stone-built sugar factories and the more substantial Great Houses, they have left no traces behind. Old prints and maps, however, show that they were generally situated close to the estate factory (with its sickening stench of the final sugar waste product called "dunder") and within sight of the overseer's house, and were either clustered together like a collection of beehives or laid out in rows. Sometimes the huts of the headmen, denoting their occupiers' status, were somewhat larger and stood slightly apart, significantly closer to the plank-built houses of the managerial whites.

A Jamaica act of 1744 aimed at apprehending runaways decreed that the houses of blacks near towns should have no more than one door and that groups of huts should be surrounded by a seven-foot fence with a single gate. This provision (the probable origin of the house-crammed "yard" in modern West Indian towns) was not common on estates where security was tighter, slave huts often being quite widely spaced and separated by vegetable plots, coconut palms and, rather later, breadfruit trees. At a distance a group of "Negro houses" often appeared picturesque and exotic, but closer inspection showed that they were squalid and noisome hovels. Rarely larger than twelve feet square, they were generally divided into two rooms, without floors or windows, "sometimes suffocating with heat and smoke; at others, when the fire subsides, especially at night, admitting the cold damp air through innumerable crevices and holes.[41]

Most houses of blacks were furnished more poorly than Amerindian huts, since slaves usually slept on

the floor rather than in hammocks. "A few wooden
bowls and calabashes, a water-jug, a wooden mortar
for pounding their Indian corn, and an iron pot for
boiling the farrago of vegetable ingredients which
composed their daily meal, composed almost all their
furniture," wrote Phillippo retrospectively in 1843. For
safety, cooking was often done in a separate lean-to
in the yard, close by the crudest of earth privies. If
they were lucky, the slaves lived near a river where
they could draw water and wash their clothes and
themselves. More commonly, water came from a
nearby pond, which in times of drought might be
little better than a mudhole. Even Edward Long admitted that the slaves were cleanly when they had the
chance.[42]

As with housing, so with clothing and food the
estates took no more than minimal responsibility.
The gradual improvements that occurred were mainly
results of the slaves' own enterprise, ingenuity, and
self-respect. In most colonies laws ordained that
slaves be annually issued with suits of clothing, but
the requirements were generally rudimentary. A
Barbados law of 1688, for example, specified simply
Drawers and Caps for the Men, and Petticoats and
Caps for the Women, on Pain of forfeiting 5s. for each
Slave not so cloathed.[43] Even when clothing provisions became more elaborate and fines nominally
multiplied, most estates merely issued coarse cloths
such as Osnaburgh linen, as well as blanketing and
hats, and expected the slave women to make up the
cloth into clothes. Leslie in 1740 reported that while
the white servants generally wore "a coarse *Osnabrig*
Frock, which buttons at the Neck and Hands, long
Trowsers of the same, a speckled Shirt and no
Stockings," the blacks usually went naked save for
those domestics who were uncomfortably clad in their
masters' livery.[44]   Later writers described the town
blacks as being decently clothed though invariably
barefoot; the women with dresses and kerchiefs, the

men in trousers, shirts, neckerchiefs, and hats. Contemporary prints of estate blacks scarcely less well dressed were, however, probably glamorized or posed. Although ameliorating acts were passed such as that of Grenada in 1788,

> to allow Annually to every Man Slave above Fifteen Years old, a suit of Cloaths, consisting of a Hat, Jacket, Shirt (or in lieu of a Jacket an additional Shirt), trowsers, and Blankets; to every Female Slave above Thirteen Years old, a Suit of Cloaths, consisting of a Hat, Jacket, Shift (or in lieu of a Jacket an additional Shift) Petticoat, and Blanket; and to every Child above Eight Years old, a Hat, Shift, or Shirt.[45]

visitors described field and factory men slaves toiling simply in a "breech-cloth," and even the women with little to shield their nakedness. Only when they appeared in their Sunday or holiday finery were the plantation slaves really well dressed. These clothes, of course, they had mainly bought and made for themselves.[46]

The bulk of the slave diet—the yams, cocos, eddoes, cassava, sweet potatoes, and plantains that were so similar to the diet of many West Africans—were grown by the slaves themselves, except on those estates with insufficient provision grounds, which were forced to provide a supplement of imported Indian corn. Fortunate slaves enjoyed poultry or even pork, which they raised themselves, on special occasions. Others were occasionally able to go fishing or to trap agouti, iguanas, wild birds, or even cane piece rats for food. The great majority, however, depended on the estates for their proteins, which consisted almost entirely of a monotonous allocation of pickled herring or salted cod. Being imported only once or twice a year, these provisions often turned putrid, a fact of life that Edward Long rationalized by claiming that the slaves actually preferred their fish "stinking, fly-blown and rotten . . . and the more it stinks the more dainty."[47] Most estates also imported considerable quantities of

salt, beef and pork, tongue, butter, cheese, wheaten
flour, porter, and wine; but these were almost exclusively for the white households and, on the better
estates, to supplement the diet of slaves who were
seriously ill. On some estates an old steer was slaugh-
tered once or twice a year at Christmas and "cropover" to provide a special treat for the slaves. Besides, slaves on sugar estates were regularly issued
sugar, cane juice, or molasses, and rum whenever the
weather was foul or the work particularly hard. At
best—where masters were comparatively generous
with issues and slaves were given sufficient time and
ground to grow their own provisions—the slave diet
was barely adequate; monotonous, starch-heavy, and
deficient in protein and vitamins. At its worst—on
constricted or severely managed estates and when
foreign supplies were cut off—the slave diet was totally inadequate. In times of war, hurricane, or exceptional drought, actual starvation was not unknown.

A meager and ill-balanced diet contributed as much
as poor working and living conditions to the low general level of the slaves' health. Diet-related illnesses
such as tuberculosis, rickets, and scurvy were lamentably familiar on slave plantations, though probably no
more so than in European slums or on the lower decks
of oceangoing ships. Much is made by some writers of
the effects of physical cruelty in maiming slaves and
encouraging infection by lowering resistance; but
overt cruelty was a less general influence than being
compelled to work hard for long hours while exposed
to extreme weather. Setting off for work in the chill-
ing predawn mists, the field slaves were alternately
broiled and soaked with tropical sun and rain, with
no protection save their hats of felt or straw or the
flimsy shelters erected at the edge of the fields. Factory slaves were shielded from the rain, but the hell-
ish heat and stink of the boiling, curing, and distilling
houses were scarcely more healthy than the fields. In
all phases of work, pulmonary infections and fevers

had ideal conditions in which to flourish and spread. At night slaves were exposed to infection with diseases such as malaria, dengue, and yellow fever, which were known by bitter experience to be associated with swamps and stagnant ponds, though not with the ever-present mosquitoes against which they had no protection. Likewise, the slaves had few defenses against the innumerable viruses, bacteria, and parasites that flourished in the crowded and insanitary conditions of their huts and compounds. Yet the worst scourges of plantation slaves were those diseases that came and spread in the same pattern of contagious infection and low immunity associated with the Middle Passage: yaws, elephantiasis, "coco bays," ophthalmia, smallpox, measles, the common cold, pneumonia. These, indeed, were most destructive among large groups of new Africans, or where small numbers of new arrivals reinfected the seasoned slaves.

Although pioneer work in the detection of measles and inoculation against smallpox was carried out in the West Indian slave plantations, preventive medicine was cruelly deficient. It was well known that by quarantining fresh Africans until they were seasoned, mortality could be reduced; but since full seasoning took three years, this was an expense that few estates could afford. Instead they concentrated, as far as they considered it economical, on treatment. Virtually every plantation had a slave "hot house" or hospital, and employed a more or less qualified white doctor, either permanently on salary, or part-time on a per capita basis. Although eighteenth-century qualifications would rarely pass scrutiny today, Jamaica had over 200 professional doctors in 1790, more than it had in 1970 for a population five times as large. Slaves suffering from contagious diseases were placed in the hospital under the care of unqualified nurses, fed comparatively well, and treated with a wide variety of the cheaper medicines then known, as long as there was a chance of their return to work and full

usefulness. The fate of those mortally ill or irreversi-
bly sick was far worse. For example, on some badly
affected estates there was a separate "yaws house"
where the hopeless sufferers from this hideous disease
were allowed to wither away in isolation.

The high mortality and low fertility of slaves was,
of course, directly related to the generally poor state
of the population's health. But it was also affected by
purely demographic factors, particularly the high proportion of epidemiologically unseasoned slaves and
the superabundance of males. Thus the steady decrease in mortality and increase in the birthrate, on
particular estates as in the slave population at large,
was due not only to the amelioration of material conditions, but also to the rise in the proportion of creoles
and the equalization of the sex ratio. Nonetheless,
though in the American mainland colonies the slave
birthrate exceeded the deathrate from the beginning,
mortality in the West Indian plantations was always
too high and fertility too low to maintain the population naturally throughout the slavery period. There
always remained a need for a regular influx of slaves
merely to "top up" the population, so that between the
compulsory ending of the slave trade in 1807 and full
emancipation in 1838, the slave population actually
declined.

Several writers estimated from personal experience
that one third of fresh Africans died during the first
three years, and that the African-born always suffered
a higher mortality rate than colony-born slaves.[48]
Accordingly, those estates, or colonies, expanding rapidly with large influxes of new slaves suffered mortality rates approaching 10 percent per year, with the
rate remaining high so long as the African-born slaves
predominated. These figures are well borne out in
the case of Worthy Park, where the sudden increase
in the slave population by 31 percent with the importation of 225 new slaves by Rose Price beween
1792 and 1796 resulted in the sudden rise in the over-

all deathrate from 31 per thousand to 57 per thousand, which indicated a rate as high as 120 per thousand among the fresh Africans, compared with roughly 67 per thousand for all African-born and 35 per thousand for creoles.[49] Averaging islands as a whole, in Barbados around 1670 it was reckoned that an annual importation of 6 percent of the slave population was necessary to keep numbers up, which suggests a mortality rate in excess of 70 per thousand. This rate was almost matched by Jamaica as a whole down to about 1710.

As estates and colonies became established, the proportion of noncreoles in the total slave population fell, and with it the mortality rate. In 1788 Edward Long, though campaigning for a continuation of the slave trade, argued from importation figures that the annual average net decrease for Jamaica was down to about 2 percent, which indicated a deathrate of under 40 per thousand. This was at a time when the proportion of African-born in Jamaica's slave population was down to about two thirds from a level of over 90 percent in 1710. In 1788 it would be a rare estate on which more than 5 percent of the slaves would be Africans in their first three years.

Edward Long did point out, however, that the mortality rate varied greatly from estate to estate and area to area, apparently in relation to altitude, local climate, type of work, and size of plantation. Least healthy of all were large sugar estates on the marshy plains; most healthy, small coffee plantations in the mountains. The reasons suggested were plausible but incomplete: the prevalence of disease near marshes, the comparative arduousness of the work, and the overcrowding on sugar estates. Edward Long's figures were not complete enough to suggest the further relationship between the proportion of Africans and the prevalence of epidemics; and he naturally dismissed the charge of the emancipists that high mortality (and low fertility), related to the cruelty of the planters, attorneys and overseers. There may well have been some truth in the emancipists' opinion, but they were certainly wrong in believing that mortality would be highest on small estates since small groups of slaves would be driven more cruelly than large. Hard-driven or not, slaves on small estates almost invariably seemed to live longer on the average.

By 1807, when approximately 50 percent of the slaves were creoles, the Jamaican slave deathrate had fallen to a level of about 30 per thousand, which was much lower than the rate among the urban population in England at that time. The fertility rate, however, was still no more than 25 per thousand, so that a "natural decrease" persisted. Slave fertility and in-

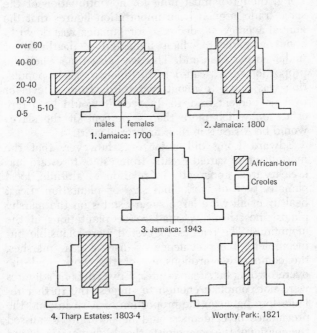

Jamaican Population Pyramids, 1700-1943
(largely hypothetical)

fant survival rates were always abysmally low. These were due chiefly to the low ratio of nubile women in the population and the generally poor standard of health among mothers and the very young; but less obvious factors more directly related to the condition of slavery also had a damaging effect.

For much of the period of the British slave trade it was usual for slave cargoes to consist of proportions of three males to each two females, and in the very earliest days the ratio may have been even higher. Thus the higher the proportion of African-born in the population the lower would have been the proportion of women and, consequently, the fertility potential. The live birthrate for Jamaica around 1700, for example, when females represented no more than 40 percent of the population, was probably less than 15 per thousand per year for the total slave population. It was not until about 1815, eight years after the ending of the slave trade, that the ratio of females to males reached a demographically normal fifty-fifty, and since slave women tended to live slightly longer than men, it was even longer before the proportion of nubile females reached normal levels.

Yet, even taking into account the disparity between the numbers of males and females, the fertility of slave women was always disastrously low. Although sure data are lacking through the reticence or sheer ignorance of contemporary commentators, this was probably the combined result of a low rate of sexual intercourse due to the effects of dislocation and subjugation, a low rate of conception due to disease, contraception, and the absence of stable partnerships, and the high rate of abortion, still-births, or even infanticide. When the horrifying susceptibility of slave infants to diseases such as tetanus, and the tragic mortality of all young children—white as well as black—in tropical areas are also considered, it is not surprising that most masters preferred purchasing new adult Africans to gambling on the fertility of

their female slaves and the survival of those born.
There is absolutely no evidence in the British colonies
of the slave breeding that is said by some writers
to have occurred in parts of the United States after
1800. Some planters, however, did encourage slave
women who successfully reared children, with gifts
of cloth or even money, especially after the ending
of the slave trade. During the amelioration period
laws were passed to excuse the mothers of 6 children
from manual work; but those who qualified were
sadly few. On Green Park estate in Jamaica in 1823,

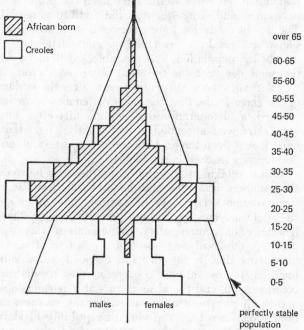

HYPOTHETICAL POPULATION PYRAMID
FOR BRITISH WEST INDIAN SLAVE POPULATION circa 1750

(Predicating birth rate, 1.5%; death rate, 5.0%; African-born 75%;
males among African-born, 62%; males among Creoles, 50%)

for example, there were only 4 such mothers-of-6 out of a slave population of 490.

As long as slavery lasted, West Indian slave society was demographically not self-sufficient, though the gap between deathrate and birthrate gradually narrowed and was finally closed shortly after emancipation. Until 1807 the slave trade disguised the chronic deficiency, but the trade itself exacerbated the situation. British slave society during its heyday, in fact, presented an almost classic example of a demographically unstable population. Not only did males outnumber females, but there was also a disproportionate "bulge" in the middle age ranges in most British slave populations, factors that surely contributed as much as purely material conditions to the shaping of slaves' lives.

THE CREOLE WHITES

Material conditions, though they gradually improved, were generally harsh for plantation slaves; yet the less tangible social determinants were at least as important, particularly those concerning human relationships. Besides the preponderance of slave men and the unnaturally small proportion of children already touched upon, the quality of life on plantations was determined by whether the owner was resident or absentee, by the proportion of whites in the population, by the ratio of Africans to creoles among the slaves, and by the degree of social mobility associated with employment and miscegenation. As with material conditions, these factors were sufficiently standard from colony to colony and period to period for generalizations to possess reasonable validity, whether derived from contemporary observers or from those few estates for which adequate records survive.

The presence of the owner in the Great House, or his absence in England or the colonial capital, was regarded as extremely important during the slavery period itself and has assumed even greater importance to present-day social analysts. Wherever they actually lived on their plantations, the owners sought to reproduce the semifeudal paternalism of the landed gentry in England, whether in the form of the caricature squirearchy of Barbados and Jamaica (more Squire Weston than Squire Allworthy) or in the grand manner of the Virginian patriarchs, with their mansions scarcely less elegant than Fonthill or Stowe. Most resident planters affected a style up to and often beyond their means, furnishing their houses ostentatiously, sporting a fine coach, stable to match, and even a pack of hounds, and keeping a splendid table and cellarful of imported wines. By common account they overate, overdrank, and spent too much of their time and substance in horse racing, gambling, and other entertainments—particularly during the "season" in the colonial capital. Yet the season coincided with the meetings of the Assembly, councils, and courts, and the annual review by the governor of the colonial militia. Since nearly all considerable landowners served their time as assemblymen, and the largest magnates made up the councils, and all landowners served in the militia as officers with ranks in proportion to their holdings, much business was thus combined with pleasure. All these activities were also planned to avoid the crop times on the plantations, for the waltzing legislators and fancy-dress officers were farmers too, and it was a rare owner who was so dissolute that he totally dissipated the source of his wealth and power. To Edward Long, indeed, the resident planters were the props of colonial society. By his account, not only did they maintain the best estates, but also served zealously as parish vestrymen and local justices of the peace— all activities that have left sadly few traces among the surviving records. To Long, of course, it did not seem anomalous that the landowners should legislate and act as justices too, for this was a hallowed English tradition. Pelf ruled.

Yet, though planters exploited land and slaves and used legislatures, vestries, and courts to perpetuate their power, it is almost certain that while they actually lived on their estates these compartmentalized segments of slave society were relatively stable. In an age when it was not thought absurd to feel affectionate respect for any source of wealth, and children were regarded as a form of investment and often cruelly exploited, the planters' feelings of stern proprietorship over their slaves were not incompatibly tinged with sentiments amounting to paternal affection. For their part, the slaves possessed the tenuous security of three principles, instinctively felt: that a profitmaker does not abuse the source of his profit; that mastery itself can be as sweet as profit (or even a substitute for it); that an owner of individuals finds it harder to be cruel in person than indirectly from across the ocean.

Unfortunately, absenteeism had become the rule for West Indian estates by the middle of the eighteenth century. Even the few planters remaining in the islands often owned several estates and solved the dilemma of choosing which one to reside at by living in town or in a Great House separately built, and conveniently placed to visit all estates. At best, the politest society in the West Indies was a pale and philistine imitation of life in the metropolis, and those who could afford to choose preferred to live in England. Typically, the first generation of West Indian planters did not enjoy sufficient wealth to revisit their homeland, but sent their sons for an education that would equip them for their plantocratic duties. The third generation stayed in England, further retarding the chances of developing an indigenous master-culture in the British West Indies. Thereafter, the plantations were in the hands of overseers and attorneys, the most mediocre members of the imperial middle

class. Elder sons of absentee planters would sometimes serve a three-year apprenticeship on the West
Indian estate, never to return once the choice was
theirs.[50] Even less frequently an Englishman like
Matthew "Monk" Lewis, coming unexpectedly into
a West Indian inheritance, would visit his property
curiously and briefly, bringing a gust of naïve idealism and *noblesse oblige*. The sycophantic joy of the
plantation blacks at Massa Bukra's coming and the
equal consternation of the malpracticing overseer
shine convincingly through the charming artlessness
of Lewis's account (1817).[51]

In the mainland colonies such experiences were
rare, for owners were rarely absentees. As has been
suggested earlier this was partly because the planters
were not rich enough but mostly because they had
little dislike for the colonial climate and much distaste
for the climate of opinion in the motherland. American colonial society thus became more rounded than
that of the British West Indies and, at the upper
levels, much less philistinely derivative. It was not
even necessary for American planters to send their
sons to England for their education, for adequate
schools and colleges existed in the mainland colonies,
with a very respectable intellectual output. At the
level of the plantations, because resident ownership
was the norm, the close paternalistic relationship between master and slaves was much more common in
the American mainland colonies than in the West
Indies. To some commentators, of whom U. B. Phillips was the most distinguished, this made for a cozy
society in which the masters were civilized gentlemen
and the slaves idyllically contented and secure. Curiously, present-day Marxist historians of the school
of Genovese have resurrected Phillips as being more
accurate than false. Because American profit margins were slim and southern aristocrats were more
concerned with maintaining their "civilization" than
with questions of profitability, they argue, American

plantation society provides a classic, if anachronistic, example of a pre- (or extra-) industrial, prebourgeois, precapitalist society.

This interpretation may well be plausible for the nineteenth century, when the United States divided fatally into the industrialized North and reactionary South, yet it is less convincing for the colonial period, when all colonies were basically agricultural with a commercial fringe. Despite the differences already considered, the plantation economy of the American mainland still took most of its cues from the British West Indies, where the majority of estates were under the control of exploitative managers, and profit margins were decisively more important than the maintenance of an indigenous culture. Even as residents, it is easier to picture the early Virginian and Carolinian planters as profit-oriented managers than as makers of a civilization. The myth of southern culture that flowered in the mid-nineteenth century was probably the creation of a society beset by declining profits and external criticism, much as the West Indian planters became bitterly defensive in the years of sugar's decline and emancipist campaigning.

One clinching argument for the Marxist interpretation is said to be that in the American Civil War the planters of the Confederacy were prepared to die for the way of life that included plantation slavery, profitable or not. But it is extremely doubtful whether a colonial American planter any more than a West Indian would have risked his life for such an abstraction. If he dressed up in the militia and made martial noises before the governor once a year, it was his property, not abstract principles, that he was preparing to defend; indeed, to defend himself *against* his property, if need be. On the few occasions when the rickety West Indian militia went to war it was to defend the islands against foreign invasion or internal rebellion. Similarly, the mainland militia fought with scarcely greater distinction in the French and Indian wars. Such threats receded after 1763, and when other Americans felt sufficiently threatened to declare their independence in 1776, southern planters and their militia were severely confused. Not equally sharing the same interests, they were not able to concur in the ideological propaganda of their northern neighbors, and were torn between fears of republican egalitarianism and the insensitivity of an imperial government that could allow the blundering Lord Dunmore to free the Virginia slaves.[52] Individual decisions, however, were made on the grounds of personal interest, not abstract principle.

An interest in defending the plantation system extended to the poorer whites, and this ensured that slave society divided on racial rather than purely class lines. "The poorest white person," wrote Bryan Edwards in 1793,

> seems to consider himself nearly on a level with the richest, and, emboldened by this idea approaches his employer with extended hand, and a freedom, which, in the countries of Europe, is seldom displayed by men in the lower orders of life towards their superiors. It is not difficult to trace the origin of this principle. It arises without doubt, from the pre-eminence and distinction which are necessarily attached even to the complexion of a White Man, in a country when the complexion, generally speaking, distinguishes freedom from slavery.[53]

Yet this apparent egalitarianism, and the gulf between the races, should not disguise the artificialities and anomalies of plantation life. The latter arose chiefly because of the decline in the proportion of whites and the prevalence of absentee ownership. "Such is the nature of Slaves," wrote Governor Edward Trelawny of Jamaica as early as 1747,

> the presence of the Master is all in all. . . . I would ask any of these absentees whether, suppose a Plantation of 320 Negroes, he doth not in his conscience think

that the Master with 10 Servants is more likely to keep these Negroes quiet than 16 Servants without the Master.[54]

The old-style planter whom Trelawny visualized would have ruled impartially and maintained the tradition that set owners apart from white servants and poor white smallholders in the early days. Indeed, it must have been one of the attractions of absenteeism that in England it was inconceivable that a landowner would mingle socially with foremen, accountants, and tenants any more than with farmhands. Certainly, between 1747 and 1793 the number of West Indian absentee owners trebled, while a ratio of one white to every 20 or even 30 or more blacks on estates became increasingly difficult to maintain. Many absentees continued to write paternalistic letters of instruction, but these were no substitute for personal supervision.

Profit making became ever more important, for absenteeism was expensive on both sides of the Atlantic. The owners' agents were the attorneys who, being paid a commission on gross sales, had an interest in higher productivity but, generally having several and often many estates to manage, were little better than absentees themselves. The estates in effect were run by overseers and a handful of white bookkeepers who had nothing but their color and a rudimentary ability to write accounts to distinguish them from the most assimilated of the creole blacks. They were an embattled, embittered class with few inner resources to resist the temptations of petty tyranny or the trauma of alienation from work or work places to which they had little personal attachment. Their salaries were insufficient to keep a decent family and provided no incentive to raise production, and their isolated lives had only the solaces and perquisites of surrogate master and the constant dream of better things.

Many plantation whites sank into a hopeless moral torpor, eating, drinking, and fornicating themselves

into an early grave. Some of those kept on estates
"to save the deficiency" were so base that even Edward Long had to record that they were heartily despised by what he called the "better sort" of slaves.[55]
But others rose slowly up the socio-economic ladder,
partly at the expense of their employers and partly
by fighting off the competition posed by the black
majority, slave and free. An energetic, able, or un-
scrupulous bookkeeper might become an overseer,
a successful overseer an attorney, and an attorney a
planter and plantocrat. En route he might painfully
acquire capital by selling vegetables, poultry, and
pigs in the towns, buying up and hiring out slaves
and, too often, cheating on his employers. Graduating
from the acre of provision ground granted as a perquisite on the estate, he might acquire a few acres of
wasteland nearby leased from the Crown for a nominal quit-rent, a decaying mountain pen to be turned
into coffee production, and finally, the pinnacle of a
factory sugar estate.

Yet the actual number of poor whites who achieved
upward mobility is at present largely hypothetical.
Even in the "democratic" mainland colonies, A. E.
Smith and Richard Hofstadter reckoned that no more
than 20 percent of indentured servants became farmers, overseers, or prosperous artisans, though "redemptioners" did rather better. The unsuccessful 80
percent, however, included those who died or returned to England, as well as those who drifted into
the ranks of the rural and urban poor. For the West
Indian colonies the "dropout rate" by death was far
higher (perhaps 40 percent in the first three years
alone), but the chances for survivors much better.[56]

Thus, a doubtful but potentially open-ended social
mobility was the chief reward for the poorer whites,
a characteristic they defended against the free coloreds with all the power their whiteness bought them.
As a class they were rootless and almost peripatetic,
the best through ambition, the worst through unreliable shiftlessness. For example, no fewer than eighty-

five white men lived on Worthy Park estate, Jamaica, between 1783 and 1796, but never more than 10 at one time, compared with over five hundred slaves. In the six years after 1785 there were five different overseers. Similarly, Benjamin M'Mahon, who wrote from personal experience in the 1830s one of the most lurid descriptions of the ignorance and sadism of the Jamaican plantation whites, was able to describe more than a dozen estates on which he had been employed as a bookkeeper in less than four years. Migration, however, did not bring him success, and he eventually resorted to authorship in the emancipist cause, though without much sensitivity.[57]

It was a deranged mixture of brutishness, rootlessness, and spurious claims to racial superiority that prevented the poorer whites from identifying with their black fellow victims of the socio-economic system or even acknowledging the ways in which they copied them. For most the aspiration toward the norms of the class of property and power was an alienating delusion. Paradoxically, the creole blacks had deeper roots in the individual estates, which were their homes, birthplaces, and the burial places of their kin. Even the slave elite of drivers and craftsmen had a greater interest in the maintenance and well-being of estates and thus an instinctive rapport with the absentee owners. The run of resident whites, in contrast, had little more commitment than the mass of unassimilated slaves.

CREOLIZATION OF THE SLAVES

Some writers have seen the plantation slaves as living in a tragic social limbo,

> Wandering between two worlds, one dead,
> The other powerless to be born.

Yet to see plantation society simply as poised hopelessly between Africa and Europe is to miss the point.

	ages	colour	African or creole	male or female	salary (for whites) or approx. value (£stg.)
A. Whites (10-11)					
Owner (absent in England)					
Attorney (resident in Kingston)					2,000-4,000
Overseer	42	white			200
Overseer's wife	40	white			
Head bookkeeper	38	white			100
3 Under bookkeepers	20-30	white			50-80
Head boiler	40	white			100
Head distiller	42	white			100
Doctor	47	white			6s. 8d. slave
Settler & wife "to save deficiency"					
B. Negro elite (13)					
3 Drivers & 1 Driveress	40-60	black	2A 2c	3m 1f	120-150
Head housekeeper	35	sambo	c	f	75
Head cooper	35	mulatto	c	m	200
Head mason	50	mustee	c	m	175
Head carpenter/sawyer	65	black	A	m	175
Head blacksmith	50	black	A	m	180
Head cattleman	35	black	A	m	120
Head muleman	45	black	c	m	120
Head wainsman	40	mulatto	c	m	150
Head watchman	50	mulatto	c	m	80
C. Special workers or lower elite (53)					
2 Waiting boys	15,16	mulatto	c	m	60-80
Groom	35	sambo	c	m	80
Seamstress	15	quadroon	c	f	75
Washerwoman	41	mulatto	c	f	60
Cook	35	black	c	f	60
Midwife	60	black	A	f	150
Hothouse nurse	30	black	c	ff	90
Yaws nurse	35	black	A	f	70
Black doctor	49	black	A	m	140
3 coopers	25-50	2 b., 1 sam.	1A 2c	3m	120-175
3 carpenters	25-55	1 b., 2 mul.	1A 2c	3m	140-150
Sawyer	32	black	A	m	100
Mason	22	mulatto	c	m	150
Blacksmith	31	black	c	m	150
6 Boilers	40-50	black	6c	6m	140-200
2 Distillers	30,45	1 b., 1 mul.	2c	2m	150-250
2 Potters	40,50	black	1A 1c	2m	120-170

The Population of a Typical Jamaican Sugar Estate, Around 1780-90 (Total Acreage 1,000; 300 Acres Cane, 388 Slaves).

	ages	colour	African or creole	male or female	salary (for whites) or approx. value (£stg.)
2 Home wainsmen	25, 40	black	1A 1c	2 m	90-120
4 Road wainsmen	20-40	black	4 c	4 m	90-120
8 Mulemen	20-35	black	4 A 4 c	8 m	90-120
Hog tender	40	mulatto	c	m	80
2 Poultry tenders	55, 60	black	1A 1c	2 f	50-60
2 New Negro tenders	30, 60	black	2 c	1 m 1 f	50-80
4 Cattlemen & boys	15-60	2 b., 2 sam.	2 A 2 c	½ m	80-120
Ratcatcher	21	mulatto	c	m	100
D. Gangs (229)					
121 Great, or First, Gang	26-50	black	75% African	60% female	50-125
43 Second Gang	16-25	black	70% African	64% female	50-100
45 Third Gang	12-15	black	60% creole	55% female	50-80
12 Grass, or Weeding, Gang	5-11	black	99% creole	60% female	50-60
8 Vagabond Gang	18-40	black	60% creole	60% female	50-100
30 Pen Negroes (mountain pen)	18-45	black	75% African	50% female	50-75
E. Marginally productive or unproductive					
15 Watchmen	35-70	black	12 A 3 c	15 m	30-70
2 Grass gatherers	60, 65	black	1 A 1 c	2 f	60
2 Child watchers	60, 70	black	1 A 1 c	2 f	50
Pad mender	65	black	A	f	80
3 Women with six children	30-55	black	1 A 2 c	3 f	50-80
11 Hopeless invalids	15-50	9 b., 2 mul.	7 A 4 c	6 m 5 f	5
2 Superannuated	75, 85	black	2 A	2 f	5-10
27 Infants	0-5	23 b., 4 mul.	27 c	13 m 14 f	10-60

NOTES

1. The amount of clothing (and rum) issued appears to have been a fairly accurate gauge of status.
2. The attorney's high salary was the result of managing 5-6 estates. Some managed 15-20 and may have made £8-10,000 a year.
3. When the owner was in residence, the nominal Great House staff of two may have been raised as high as 25.
4. Prices of new African slaves ranged £50-70 for males, £50-60 for females. For seasoned slaves, the ranges were £80-125 and £70-110.
5. The Vagabond Gang consisted of persistent runaways and other miscreants.
6. Most Jamaican estates included related "pens," which served as way stations on journeys to the coast, for breeding animals, growing provisions and seasoning new Negroes.
7. Material derived from Worthy Park, Longville, Good Hope, Braco, Retreat, Jerusalem Estates.

It is true that the masters decreed the eradication of African influences, yet drew a line beyond which assimilation should not go; but in both respects their success was limited. Slaves quickly realized that a degree of acceptance was necessary for the sake of rewards or an easy life; yet they lived ambivalently. They did not so much exist wavering between two worlds, as being in the energetic process of creating a third, in which the masters were unconscious allies. Plantations then were social crucibles. Their society (on which modern West Indian society is largely based) was an alloy, a creolization, a product of acculturation rather than the assimilation of the weaker by the stronger.

Once plantations were firmly established, almost invariably Africans were drafted into the First Gang on arrival and remained regarded as the *Lumpenproletariat* of plantation society for life. The custom of looking for craftsmen among new Africans almost died out, not so much because the later arrivals were less skilled, or skilled in crafts less adaptable to plantation uses, but because the special plantation crafts and the training for them were monopolized by creole slaves. Fieldwork, moreover, was by no means totally unskilled, and the fact that most Africans were practiced agriculturalists made them particularly suitable for work in the fields or cattle pens. Indeed, their special skills may have helped to shape plantation husbandry. Africans were generally hoe farmers used to "slash-and-burn" techniques, and this may at least partially account for the preference for the hoe over the plow in the West Indies and the readiness with which the newcomers learned to wield the "cutlass" for weeding and cutting cane. That many Africans were also skilled in cattle husbandry when they arrived may explain why so many were drafted into the cattle pens, and may even help to account for the comparative preference for steers over mules in West Indian plantations. Besides, plantation Africans

have too often been judged through the masters' eyes
by their sluggish and sullen performance in the masters' fields. A better indication is the cheerful and
energetic way in which they cultivated their own
provision grounds using a type of agriculture practically indistinguishable from that with which they
were familiar in West Africa, including the long journeys to and from the fields described by William
Beckford and Mungo Park alike.

Similarly, the all too rare accounts of life in the
slave cantonments and during the rare days of fes-
tivity provide glimpses into a life little different from
that in an African village. Here in their circumscribed
private world the blacks assumed an individuality unrelated to and unrecognized by the estates. Besides
the hierarchy, which owed its authority largely to the
estate, were such respected figures as the *obi*-man,
with his skill in bush medicine and arcane charms,
and, rather more often acknowledged by the estates,
the old women skilled in the respected arts of mid-
wifery, nursing, and laying out the dead. Then there
were the musicians, much in demand to provide en-
tertainment and pass on their skills in the making and
playing of drums, lutes, and flutes; the carvers and
weavers; and the creators and weavers of stories, varying from heroic epics to comic parables and lyrical
nostalgia. In some areas there were even literate
Moslems—Mandingos or Fulani for the most part—
who met to recite, discuss, and pass on the sacred
teachings of the Koran. Presumably, in most slave
groupings there were also the equivalents of the village reprobates: drunkards, harlots, whoremongers,
and buffoons.

Africans from different areas, however, were mixed
as much as possible so that tribal identity or common
language would not constitute a rallying point, and
the teaching of "creole" English by way of the various forms of "pidgin" like the *ticky-tacky* of Surinam
would facilitate assimilation. So jumbled were the

Africans by successive stages in their acquisition that
each plantation's population was likely to be as varied
in appearance and as confusingly polyglot as the slave
population at large. The 198 Africans listed on Good
Hope estate, Jamaica, in 1804, for example, came
from at least 12 major tribal groupings originating
thousands of miles apart. Yet even on Good Hope
estate, 88 "Ibos," 27 "Coromantines," and 21 "Chamba"
constituted sizable subcultural groups, which doubtless retained much of their identity and heritage in
language, customs, law, and religion beyond the ken
or comprehension of the masters, passing them on for
generations. Indeed, each new wave of Africans revived the link with the motherland, and this rather
than the desire for domestic quasislaves may account
for the eagerness of creoles to take in fresh Africans,
as described by Sir William Young. The percipient
Bryan Edwards guessed as much. "Many . . . proposed each of them to adopt one of their young
country-folks in the room of the children they had lost
by death, or had been deprived of in Africa," he
wrote in 1793,

> others, because they wished, like the patriarchs of old,
> to see their sons take to themselves wives from their
> own nation and kindred; and all of them, I presume,
> because, among other considerations, they expected to
> revive and retrace in the conversation of their new
> visitors, the remembrance and ideas of past pleasures
> and scenes of their youth.[58]

Modern scholarship, spearheaded by Melville J. Herskovits and his disciples, has shown the degree to
which the masters deluded themselves as to the per-
suasiveness of their brand of culture in eradicating
Africanisms. Yet there is perhaps a danger of overstating the case. The very fact that the most persistent
traces linger in those areas where tribes were least
split up, where the blacks arrived latest and were
least incorporated into plantation society, argues for
a more limited view. Slaves, like all human beings,

constantly sought identity with their fellows. Where possible, the ties were those of family, kin, tribe, or language. Where not or where these faded, the identity came from common experience, be it the Middle Passage or the life of the estate. If slavery called forth any latent virtues, said Bryan Edwards,

> they are those of sympathy and compassion towards persons in the same conditions of life; and accordingly we find that the negroes in general are strongly attached to their countrymen, but above all to such of their companions as came in the same ship with them from Africa. This is a striking circumstance: the term *shipmate* is understood among than as signifying a relationship of the most enduring nature.[59]

Stanley Elkins' description of the Middle Passage as "almost too protracted and stupefying to be called mere 'shock'" would seem to be wide of the mark.[60] On the other hand, it would probably be too facile to trace a similarity to the curious emotions felt by most Americans (including those whose forebears came later and in far worse circumstances) for the Pilgrim Fathers and their *Mayflower*. A far more obvious parallel lies in the emotions that must have been felt by soldiers and sailors for the regiments and ships in which they suffered a bestial but common fate—to the degree that they showed perverse loyalty when it came to fighting other men's wars.

Africans were often sundered from their wives and children in the process of sale, and all came into the plantations bereft of wordly goods. To the extent that they remained human draft animals, these conditions persisted. Outnumbering the women (who were in any case often pre-empted by the more privileged males), few African men enjoyed the prospect of stable sexual relationships any more than they were able to acquire more than the most pitiful scraps of personal property. At the inscrutable will of their masters, all slaves could be stripped of whatever they had, resold, or shifted from property to property; men and women could be forbidden to cohabit permanently and children separated from their mothers as easily as cattle.

Such deprivation and dislocation, however, were known to be dangerous and may have been both rarer and—where they occurred—less the result of a calculated policy on the part of the planters than some commentators have imagined. Consider, for example, the question of the incidence of stable sexual relationships among the slaves. Nothing in the law encouraged permanent cohabitation, since blacks were given the status of their mothers; yet the fact that estate lists only recorded mothers (and thus make it impossible to trace patrilineal descent) means that it will never be known with certainty how cohesive family patterns were in slavery days.

Moreover, there is no evidence of a consistent policy on the part of the planters to discourage cohabitation, and in the absence of such a policy it seems likely that the slaves would follow familiar African patterns, as far as estate conditions allowed. The persistence of matrifocal families, impermanent liaisons, and a high rate of "illegitimacy" in the modern West Indies is commonly attributed to the institution of plantation slavery; but it seems evident that at least equally relevant are the incidence of such characteristics in pre-Christian West African society and in present-day peasant societies without a slavery legacy.

Barry Higman has recently adduced considerable evidence that in the black cantonments the "nuclear" family—man, woman and their children—was much more common than described by most writers, and that this applied to Africans as well as creoles. At Montpelier Estate, Jamaica, in 1825, for example, Higman has found that at least a third of the slaves lived in nuclear family groups, and even that close relatives tended to live in clusters of huts approximating to modern West Indian "yards."[61] The late date of this and other examples, however, suggests that the tendency towards nucleation may have been the result of Christian influences, or of amelioration in the provision by the masters of a standard two-room hut. Another reason may have been the natural operation of incest taboos in a small and relatively closed population. Moreover, it has not yet been possible to demonstrate that what was true of any given time was not changed over a longer period, through a tendency to "serial monogamy" or the constant aim of males to be "polygamous" if possible.

Certainly, it seems clear that the vast majority of slaves lived out their lives on a single estate, achieving a locational stability that dampened tensions. Indeed, as generation succeeded generation and estates were more commonly sold with the slaves upon them included, slaves often achieved more permanency than the owners or the transient white staff. In the course of time very many slaves built new families without the sanction of marriage, put together furniture, utensils, poultry, stock, and small sums of money despite the laws, and even gained a customary right to the huts they lived in and the plots of land they worked for themselves. "He has his own house," wrote Rose Price of the Jamaican slave toward the end of slavery,

> which is as much his own, as any building erected on a leasehold estate in England, *which goes to whom he pleases at his death, with his other property,* which I firmly believe, was never deviated from, *when no law existed to secure it to him.* . . . [Furthermore,] a negro and his family generally cultivate annually a new piece of ground in provisions, of about 40 laces or poles, besides having about three times that quantity of ruinate provision ground, which require no further care, (the cultivation of former years) to produce, him food, in all about an acre to a family, *which is as much his own property as a freehold estate can be.*[62]

Kindly (or wise) masters accommodated the natural processes of custom and creolization to a degree, but the need to keep their slaves in subordination and dependence was basically incompatible with the slaves' human craving for status. Friction was inevitable, as a result of frustrated expectation if not of downright repression. Slaves' names suggest a simple but important illustration.[63] In estate records African slaves were generally known by their native names, but Creoles acquired English names. At Worthy Park, for example, 62 percent were known by recognizably African names in 1730; but by 1780 65 percent had acquired English names—roughly the proportion of those born on the estate. This change denoted a form of assimilation but not necessarily a rise in status; for the new names were often degrading nicknames, and the lists of slaves were difficult to differentiate from the cattle, often given similar names and listed on adjacent pages in the records. Status was related to the acquisition of surnames, grudgingly recorded in plantation lists. Doubtless slaves called themselves by two names long before slave records acknowledged the change, just as slaves probably used familiar African names among themselves long after the estates had renamed them for the estates' own purposes. At Worthy Park the first surnames listed, around 1811, belonged to the chief members of the slave elite, though by 1834 nearly all slaves had surnames tacked to their long-held first names. Derived from practically every white man who had ever served on the estate, these surnames (where no more than 10 percent of the slaves were of mixed blood) seem to indicate aspiration toward the white man's status rather than belated recognition of wholesale miscegenation.

Whether or not surnames represented true patronymics, their acquisition related to the development of European family concepts among the slaves. They also provide evidence of the growing influence of Christianity. As Livingstone was to find, Christianity made very slow inroads into Africa; but it satisfied deep-seated needs among the creolized Africans of the slave plantations. Slaves were attracted to Christianity not only by spiritual craving in a brutalized world and the escapism served by the gospel of redemption, but also by the status brought by belonging to a church. Baptism provided a name and membership in a society extrinsic to the plantation, which in turn brought a glimmer of education and even a chance of leadership. It was for these reasons that the masters and the established Church of England (the ministers of which were often planters themselves, as well as being described in 1740 as "generally the most finished of our Debauchees"[64] were at first as adamantly opposed to proselytizing the slaves as to providing them with a literate education.

Gradually, however, some masters encouraged the baptism of their slaves into the Established Church, even before this was positively encouraged by the imperial government. At Worthy Park, for instance, a church was endowed in the black village in place of the owner's private chapel around 1820, and baptisms (and even a few marriages) occurred soon after. The motives for such innovations, however, were rarely spiritual enlightenment so much as social calculation. Baptism into the Established Church could forestall the sectaries who were the first and most active preachers to the slaves, providing the slaves with the illusory sense of belonging to a master church, and the masters with the chance of shaping the Church of England into an arm of plantation society. Certainly, Anglican ministers in the colonies, emulating in every respect their English brethren, were even more likely than Baptists and Methodists to promote the message of passive and cheerful obedience inherent in such texts as Paul's letter to Philemon concerning the slave Onesimus,[65] or such improving hymns as that which begins:

> Awake my soul! and with the sun,
> Thy daily course of Duty run.
> Shake off dull sloth, and joyful rise
> To make thy morning sacrifice.[66]

One motive for belatedly converting the slaves may have been to encourage stable sexual relationships, since the sacrament of baptism might quite naturally lead to that of marriage. Certainly, the promotion of marriage, among the freed blacks after 1838 as well as among slaves, became the concern of Christian philanthropists in England, though their zeal in this respect does not seem to have been shared equally by the planters.

Another motive for encouraging Christianity among the slaves was undoubtedly the prevalence of *Obeah*, despite innumerable attempts to suppress it by legislation.[67] To the masters *Obeah* was simply witchcraft, detested both for its secrecy and its alleged skills in the poisoning of enemies. Even to blacks once assimilated, *Obeah* assumed a sinister aura because of its association with the casting of spells to cause harm as well as good. To the unassimilated, on the other hand, *Obeah* was both a genuine religion and a potent source of medicine. *Obeah* (like the Haitian *Voodoo*, or the Jamaican variant, *Myalism,* or Trinidadian *Shango*) sought ritualistic links with the spirit world beyond the shadows and the sacred trees, providing a mystical sense of continuity between the living, the dead, and those yet to be born. *Obeah's* rituals and fetishes, moreover, were regarded as powerful specifics against human ailments, and the successful *obi*-man combined his command of "mumbo jumbo" with an impressive knowledge of bush medicines. These links with Africa, though they have undergone infinite mutations, are by no means eradicated even today.

What was called *Obeah* was itself syncretic, and this may account both for its persistence and for its power to infuse Christianity in creating a truly creole religion. Like Haitian *Voodoo*, it may well have been basically the intermingling of two main streams, the Rada rite of Dahomey and the Congo rite of the equatorial forests farther south, constantly colored and changed by other influences.[68] "Many of these religions," claims one persuasive writer on Haiti,

> had become inextricably tangled by foreign influences long before they were thrown into the same alembic and melted into one religion by the fire of a common evil. Faint rings of sound from Luxor and Athens and Bethlehem and Mecca had crossed the empty wildernesses, and their remote messages had become garbled and woven into the animism of the forests. Neighbouring tribes left inevitable deposits of belief and practice, and it was already an amalgam of complexities that, as they united and merged into a single faith, was exposed to its last great influence, the factor that was to provide its final and definitive twist: the teaching of Christianity.[69]

Obeah is by no means as dominant as *Voodoo*, but it is probably not an oversimplification to say that it is those Christian sects that have been most able to assimilate aspects of African religion that have become the most effective types of creole Christianity.[70] It was probably because the Anglican Church was the least willing and later least successful in adapting to African religion that it combined a paranoid opposition to *Obeah* practices with its condemnation of Baptist and Methodist sectaries. In 1832, for example, it was seriously suggested by Anglicans that the Baptist membership tickets were regarded as fetishes by converts, and thus were encouragements to rebellion.[71]

A similar degree of ambivalence has characterized the development of creole music. African music was extraordinarily rich, and the slaves showed great ingenuity in adapting West Indian materials to the making of familiar sounds. Hans Sloane in 1707 wrote of instruments

> made of small Gourds fitted with Necks, strung with horse hairs, or the peeled stalks of climbing Plants or Withs. These instruments are sometimes made of hol-

lowed Timber covered with Parchment or other skin
wetted, having for its Neck the strings ty'd or shorter,
so as to alter the sounds.[72]

These were obviously types of the stringed *banjil*
mentioned by Leslie, the gourd *chac-chacs* of Trinidad and the ubiquitous *goombay* drums with their
goatskin membranes and serrated edges scraped with
a sharpened stick. Beckford in 1793 spoke with positive admiration of the "Coromantee flute" fashioned
from the tubular branches of the trumpet tree and
the *bender,* a musical bow producing a peculiarly
haunting note, and even Edward Long admired the
grace and drama of certain African dances.[73]

Singing and rhythmic drumming were an ineradi-
cable feature of slave life, not only during the legitimate catharsis of holidays, but also in helping to relieve the daily drudgery of plantation tasks. Most
masters, however, continued to regard purely African
music as discordant and barbaric, and too much drumming and dancing as potentially dangerous. Innumerable ordinances were passed against the types of
drumming that were known sometimes to work slaves
into a frenzy and were thought also to be used to
communicate between slave groups. For much the
same reason, the sound of the cowhorn *abeng,* used by
the Maroons to rally their forces, instilled something
like dread in the Jamaican planters. Yet gradually
African instruments and styles were adapted to the
European. As early as 1770 John Wesley praised the
psalm and hymn singing of blacks and encouraged
music as a powerful force in Christianizing the slaves.
By 1800 black fiddlers and trumpeters were common,
and slaves were as likely to be singing hymns and
extempore creole "calypsos" as African songs. "Negro"
music became respectable and slave musicians important figures throughout slave society, though the music
they produced was essentially a hybrid. Even such an
"African" manifestation as the *Kumina* cult of Jamaica
incorporated a version of the European quadrille in its

ceremonies. Conversely, when the planters relaxed at Christmastime they sometimes danced with their slaves in almost African style—in a circle with rhythmic hand-clapping, drumming, and shouting.

The stability and efficiency of plantations depended more than the masters could ever afford to admit upon the slave elite of drivers, craftsmen, and domestics. In certain respects the "headmen" were the most important men on estates, and accordingly they enjoyed considerable privilege and real power. Yet the very degree of their privilege made their role equivocal and, paradoxically, their practical power could be frustrating because it stopped short at the plantation's bounds. The colored domestics had wider social expectations, yet their indissoluble dependence upon the dominant section of society was even more traumatizing than the relationship of those who gained practical power through cooperation with the masters but retained their racial integrity.

Drivers and "driveresses"—the slaves' "worst domestic tyrants," as they were often called—served as essential liaisons and buffers between masters and workers; without them work would almost cease and social order be in danger of breaking down. Head craftsmen, as guardians of the most critical skills, were at least as important; without their expertise and control, efficiency and profitability would have declined disastrously. From the earliest days it was found that only blacks made satisfactory drivers; but as long as they could, plantations tried to reserve the most skilled craftsmen's posts for whites. By the third quarter of the eighteenth century, however, this was generally impossible, and the trustier blacks rapidly filled the vacancies produced by the shortage of white men prepared to toil in such onerous and unremitting tasks. Indeed, this quite sudden expansion of the black elite was one of the most important social developments in the later period of slavery, being accompanied by considerable racial friction during the transitional period, when head craftsmen might be either the most assimilated blacks or the poorer whites.

Drivers and other headmen were rewarded with the largest allowances of clothing and food, the best houses, the most fertile plots of land, and in some cases, for exceptional service, the ultimate crown of manumission in their old age. At work their authority was symbolized by the whip they carried as a permanent threat, often cracked, and sometimes applied. During out-of-work hours and almost beyond the custody of the overseer, they lived in the black hutments like very African tyrants, able to command their slaves to work for them in provision grounds and household and, apparently, able to take the women whom they chose. Yet here lay the alienating paradox, which few whites were ever able to grasp: The power of slave headmen was based on their ability to command their fellows, but it was dependent on nominally absolute acceptance of the rules of the dominant class. Like the appointed African chiefs of the later British Empire, they never quite knew which world they belonged to. Nonetheless, the masters (in Africa as in the plantations) were often deluded by the readiness with which volunteers came forward to fill the places of trust and the apparent relish with which they fulfilled their duties, into thinking that unqualified success had been achieved.

This delusion is tellingly illustrated by the story told by Edward Long of one of Sir Charles Price's slaves. Noticing the man's haughty demeanor and discovering that he had been a chief in Africa, Price offered him repatriation, which he declined. Instead, he was given manumission and the slave girl of his choice, and settled down to work for Sir Charles on the margin of one of the Price estates. According to Edward Long, in gratitude to his benefactor this ex-chief, ex-slave was instrumental in preventing the spread of the 1760 rebellion to Sir Charles Price's slaves, both by his powers of persuasion and by his voluntary intelligence work. The romanticized tale even claimed that Price and his freed slave called each other friend. Yet to Long and his readers the relationship was far from one of equality: The implication was clear that this black was the white man's creature, who knew his place and duty. The only good black was a grateful one.[74]

According to one account Sir Charles Price freed one of his most faithful slaves each year as an encouragement to the others. Certainly in his will (1772) he granted manumission and an annuity of £10 to "a Mulatto woman named Margaret . . . and her two Elder children" living on one of his estates,[75] and the colonial record offices discreetly guard innumerable similar pieces of evidence of the pattern of miscegenation. Naturally, Edward Long said nothing of the mulatto Margarets and their children in his encomiums on Sir Charles Price and his kind; for believing that the black was tantamount to an animal, he would thereby be accusing his fellow planters of bestiality. Instead it was the black whom Long, like nearly every stereotypist then and since, accused of "promiscuity." He, and they, totally ignored the obvious facts that not only were the planters the authors of conditions that made promiscuity inevitable, but also that the whites of all degrees themselves were the most callously libidinous of mortals. The charge of promiscuity was common to all, or meaningless.

The sexual life of plantations tended towards anarchy, and its most degrading aspect was the hypocritical double standard applied by the whites. Yet sex was a racial solvent, and sexual anarchy and miscegenation alike helped to shape creole society. Marriage was rare in slaves but just as infrequent among the white managerial staff, who were rarely employed if they had the encumbrance and expense of a wife.[76] Miscegenation was so common and, covertly, so condoned that even respectably married men were not disgraced if they were known to have produced illegitimate offspring in their youth. The harems of mulatto girls around the overseers' houses on plantations were taken for granted, and a white bookkeeper who did not cohabit with one slave woman or more was regarded as less than a man.[77]

Sadly, this often quite casual coupling was connived at by the women through social ambition (not often through love), to the undoubted alienation of the blacks deprived of their sexual attentions. For such relations provided not only the least onerous life available to plantation slaves (a very high proportion of the colored population of both sexes being employed as domestic servants), but also the best chance of manumission for descendants, either through the indulgence of a wealthy father or through being able in the fourth generation of such demoralizing existences to "pass for white." Besides this, black women understandably often exploited as far as they could the power that their sexual attractions held over all men, black as well as white. "Monk" Lewis, for example, described with positive admiration the slave girl Mary Wiggins on one of his estates, haughtily independent, and rich from her many admirers, of every shade and degree. Sexual rivalry helps to explain not only the ambivalence of white men in regard to the sexual characteristics of blacks, but also how black women in plantation societies were able to reinforce the African tendency toward matriachy. It is pleasing to speculate that the laws passed in slave colonies to decree that colored children took the status of their mothers (aimed as much at increasing the hold of white men over colored women as at cutting down the volume of instant manumissions through miscegenation), may have been as hotly debated in the legislators' bedrooms as in the legislation chambers.

Affection between white men and colored women was stifled by prejudices and convention on the one hand and calculation on the other, but it was by no means unknown. In a pre-Freudian age white men were often not ashamed of the sentiments they felt for the aged domestics who had been their wet nurses in infancy or their playfellows in budding youth. Besides, few persons are capable of complete lack of feeling for those who have regularly shared their beds. Who knows but that Edward Long's negrophobia may have been the overcompensatory product of an unfortunate liaison. In startling contrast, the ever-candid Bryan Edwards wrote and printed an absolute paean to African womanhood (albeit somewhat cloaked in conventional conceits).

ODE TO THE SABLE VENUS

Sweet is the beam of morning bright,
Yet sweet the sober shade of night;
　　On rich Angola's shores,
While beauty clad in sable dye,
Enchanting fires the wond'ring eye,
　　Farewell, ye Paphian bowers.

When thou, this large domain to view,
Jamaica's isle, thy conquest new,
　　First left thy native shore,
Bright was the moon, and soft the breeze,
With wanton joy the curling seas
　　The beauteous burden bore.

Her skin excell'd the raven plume,
Her breath the fragrant orange bloom,
　　Her eye the tropic beam:
Soft was her lip as silken down,
And mild her look as ev'ning sun
　　That gilds the Cobre stream.

The loveliest limbs her form compose,
Such as her sister *Venus* chose,
　　In *Florence*, where she's seen;
Both just alike, except the white,
No difference, no—none at night,
　　The beauteous dames between. . . .

> Do thou in gentle *Phibba* smile,
> In artful *Benneba* beguile,
>   In wanton *Mimba* pout;
> In sprightly *Cuba's* eyes look gay
>   Or grave in sober *Quashiba*,
>   I still shall find thee out.
>
> Gay Goddess of the sable smile!
> Propitious still, this gracious isle
>   With thy protection bless!
> Here fix, secure, thy constant throne;
> Where all, adoring thee, do ONE,
>   ONE deity confess.[78]

ALIENATION AND ACCOMMODATION

The success of a society can be judged by the incidence within it of alienation, tension, and revolt. By
these criteria the record of British slave society was
lamentable. Yet serious controversy does remain over
the nature and extent, and thus the causes, of slave
resistance, and some attempt must be made to resolve
the clash of interpretations. Most interest has naturally
centered on actual slave rebellions, but by playing with
definitions and either failing to differentiate or over-
differentiating, commentators with polarized view-
points have been able to derive contradictory conclusions. Herbert Aptheker, for example, detected no
less that 250 revolts and conspiracies in the history of
American slavery, and H. O. Patterson claimed that
Jamaica suffered almost continuously from intensive
servile revolts[79]—forms of resistance that were the
reactive antithesis of the masters' violent abusage.
These assessments run counter to the bland assumptions of U. B. Phillips and his school that black slaves
were generally contented because they were well
treated and that it was the nature of blacks to accept
servility if conditions were easy. They also clash with
the line of argument developed by Stanley Elkins and
others that the black slaves were passive and docile,

as all human beings would have been, not because they were well treated or were naturally servile, but because of the elements of control that cowed and brainwashed them like the inmates of concentration camps.[80] The view that violent revolt (whether or not as a response to the severity of the master class) was endemic is probably exaggerated. Yet, conversely, it is simplistic to see organized and armed rebellion as the only manifestation of slave resistance. The various forms of escapism and more or less passive resistance must also be considered before final conclusions are attempted.

In assessing American slave revolts Aptheker weakens his case by using a definition that reduces the outbreaks more to the level of localized mutinies than of authentic rebellions. His impressive total is arrived at by taking all revolts and conspiracies involving 10 or more slaves, and since the largest he can find—the famous revolt led by Nat Turner in 1831—involved only 70 slaves, Aptheker almost proves the argument that genuine slave rebellions in America were rare. The reasons for the low level of organized and widespread revolt are, however, more debatable. Nat Turner's rebellion is a case in point.[81] It is difficult to decide with certainty whether it occurred as a reaction to the harshness of slave rule or as a result of the weakness of control. This rebellion can also be discounted as atypical of the colonial period, since its leader was of a type of ambitious, frustrated, semiliterate, largely assimilated black peculiarly a product of the later stages of plantation slavery. Earlier slave uprisings in the mainland colonies were sporadic and localized, probably as the result of the comparatively small groupings of slaves and the overwhelming strength of the forces of control. They seem to have been more frequent and serious, however, in the period before 1750, when the proportion of unassimilated Africans in the slave population was at its highest.[82]

In analyzing Jamaican slave revolts, Orlando Patterson falls into pitfalls similar to those that trip American commentators. Although several West Indian outbreaks involved upward of one thousand blacks, under his generic heading Patterson includes at least three disparate types of conflict between blacks and whites. The first was the Maroon wars of the 1730s and 1790s. These bore little relation to true slave rebellions, being closer akin to the almost inevitable conflict (with its equally inexorable outcome) between settlers and indigenous inhabitants, such as the "wars" between the United States and the red Indians. It is true that the Spanish blacks who formed the nucleus of the Jamaican Maroons were constantly reinforced, at least down to 1739, with "English" slave runaways, and that the first war was fought as much to destroy the runaways' sanctuary as to remove the menace to settlements in outlying areas. By the treaties signed with Cudjoe and Quao in 1739, however, the plantocratic government gained the Maroons as nominal allies in the recapture of runaways, in return for practical independence. The second war eventually broke out in 1795 basically through friction between two sovereign powers, with victory going to the more sophisticated and powerful of the two.

The second type of Jamaican rebellion was epitomized by the serious outbreak of 1760, in which large numbers of Coromantine slaves took advantage of wartime—which combined harsh living conditions with the preoccupation of the forces of control—to concert a rebellion in the south of the island that lasted from April to September and resulted in the deaths of 60 whites, 1,000 slaves, and the loss to the planters "in ruined buildings, cane pieces, cattle, slaves and disbursements" of at least £100,000.[83] Yet this rebellion, which was almost as traumatic to the Jamaican planters as the Indian Mutiny was to be to the rulers of India, was clearly distinct from the equally serious outbreak that occurred at Christmas 1831. This later rebellion, like those in Barbados in 1816 and Demerara in 1823, occurred not during a period of particular repression but after a considerable degree of amelioration had been achieved; and it was led not by intransigent Africans but by some of the most assimilated of the slaves.

It seems possible then to distinguish—if not entirely to separate—four situations conducive to slave rebellion, which may have relevance in assessment of other types of slave resistance as well: conditions of extreme repression; the presence of unassimilable elements; the weakening of the forces of control; and the frustration of slave expectations.

Many rebellions do seem to have been led by unacculturated Africans, particularly in the early years. Yet Patterson's belief that fierce resistance was peculiarly African is probably as exaggerated as Edward Brathwaite's assertion that African slaves possessed peculiar qualities of endurance. In any slave society the least assimilated were those likely to be most severely regimented and thus to have the most reason to rebel. At the same time the masters' vigilance provided fewer chances for resistance than with other slaves, and outbreaks were as likely to be caused by a failure of control as by any special qualities in the tyrannized slaves. It could indeed be argued that the planters' policy of meeting danger with repressive force was remarkably successful, that the most downtrodden were usually the most docile. Some would hold the converse to be truer: that the Ibos, for example, were downtrodden simply because they were placid, whereas the fierce Coromantines were often humored. In response, the Coromantines often rebelled, the Ibos rarely. Were these results then brought about by the degree of severity or lenity on the part of the masters or by slave characteristics?

African-led rebellions grew less frequent as time went on, not only because the number of Africans became fewer and the impress of Africa less strong, but also because the influences of slavery and creolization became more pervasive. The repression and dehumanization of slavery were cumulative in their effects. In the first generation the more obdurate might rebel, but the inevitability of bloody retribution coupled with a conscious policy of depersonalization and deculturation subdued the majority into the syndrome of unheroic adaptation-for-survival traced in prisoners at Dachau and Buchenwald (from personal experience) by Bruno Bettelheim.[84] These conditions were not necessarily irreversible: Jews who survived Hitler's extermination camps were no less Jews after the war. Yet even Jews who lived ten generations in East European ghettos were less deculturated than black slaves, in successive generations forcibly detribalized, de-Africanized, and partially assimilated. Even the strongest of cultures could not have retained its integrity sufficiently unimpaired to provide a focus for revolt.

It was then possible to supersede the repression of the concentration camp with a more subtle tactic, making it clear that the price of easier conditions of bondage was acceptance of the masters' view of society. There is a traditional Jamaican saying that is often quoted to argue that a wise master gratified his slaves: "Good Massa, good Negro."[85] Yet this old saw, like so many such, is ambiguous. It could indeed mean that blacks of their own free will respected kind masters; but also that the kindness of masters was dependent on the slaves remaining good. Good Sir Charles Price's faithful Coromantine died a good Negro, but the fate of the Coromantines who rebelled in 1760 was horrifically different.

The inevitability of such retribution compared with the comparative ease that grew from apparent acceptance explains the relatively small number of open slave revolts in completely developed, densely populated, and strongly controlled islands such as Barbados, or any West Indian colony in the last quarter of the eighteenth century, even during the period of the American, Haitian, and French revolutionary wars.[86] Yet even the degree of acceptance that deluded masters into placing great trust and responsibility in their slave elite, was to prove reversible if control were loosened, if change were too rapid, or if steady progress were suddenly blocked. Many of the later outbreaks, then, had something of "the revolution of rising expectations" about them. To the consternation of the whites, they were often led not by the recalcitrant and downtrodden but by the plantation elite, such as the "drivers, tradesmen, and other most sensible slaves on the estates" who were prominent in the 1808 rebellion in Guyana.[87] In a sense it could be said that ambition was a white man's gift; yet in the last days of slavery it was likely to be most frustrated even while it was most encouraged. Some masters, beset by economic recession or deploring the latitude allowed to slaves by their fellow planters through indifference, complacency, or "misplaced" philanthropy, sought in vain to tighten the bonds on their own estates. Many of the most assimilated slaves, finding their progress suddenly balked, turned to the ultimate resort of rebellion, a desperate expedient that was often accompanied by a conscious reversion to African norms that was now as much a motion of the head as of the heart and blood.

The role of Christianity, especially sectarian forms, in these later rebellions was highly significant. The process of socialization was designed by the master class to establish a slave personality that accepted its own lack of worth and attached exaggerated kudos to the whites. The policy of inculcating the establishment brand of religion was, somewhat reluctantly, adopted with the aim of entrenching the social order. Yet the Baptist, Methodist, and even evangelical Anglican preachers of the missionary societies placed much emphasis upon redemption and "conversion," processes that essentially changed the personality structure of the slaves. Immediately the planters sensed the danger and condemned the "enthusiasm" that the missionaries generated as being dangerous to social order, even though the ministers universally claimed—and sincerely believed—that they encouraged greater obedience in the slaves.

Christianity proved to be a two-edged sword. The "enthusiasm" that missionaries blithely encouraged made the slave believe he was a new man, a regenerate worthwhile in his own if not in other mens' eyes. As Robert Moore has perceptively pointed out, the diary of John Smith (the Baptist missionary whom the Guyanese planters largely blamed for the 1823 rebellion) illustrates the honest delusion under which the missionaries labored. The diary refers constantly to the black slaves' testimony that they were miserable sinners craving change, and yet "it seems," says Moore,

> that their sense of sin was rather a sense of social worthlessness or inferiority than the concept of personal depravity in which the missionaries believed. Services in slave chapels usually followed the pattern of people weeping for their sins, people crying out loudly for their guilt, and then coming away refreshed by a new confidence, almost a new personality, but no longer feeling the peculiar mixture of guilt and unworthiness which characterized the typical Creole slave. Even if the experience of conversion was not followed by baptism or a particularly close adherence to the church the effect seems to have been to change the Creole slave not necessarily into an outwardly less obedient slave but inwardly into a less accepting one.[88]

The slave elite became the leaders among the new converts not so much because the chapel was the projection of slave society but because the new kind of leadership provided the security of self-esteem and opportunities of vocal self-expression denied by the positions of qualified authority granted by the estates. Indeed, the change in their drivers and headmen once converted was deprecated by many masters; for it made the privileged slaves far less brutal. Telemachus, one of the 1823 rebel leaders, for example, had been a notoriously sadistic driver before his conversion but became so kindly that his master, after trying in vain to whip him back into severity, sacked him from his post. Thus, those who were not attracted into "alternative society" were driven into it by insensitive or beleaguered masters.

Despite the frequency of actual revolts and conspiracies spread over the British colonies as a whole, an "average" plantation would probably not experience an outbreak throughout its entire history. But this did not mean that the stability of any slave population was ever perfected. Perhaps the most general and obvious evidence was the extremely high incidence of running away. From the vestry returns it is clear that it was a rare estate that had no runaways at any given time, and a study of estate records discloses that a remarkably high proportion of slaves had absented themselves at least once during their lives.[89] Some, such as the degradingly named Whore and Strumpet of Worthy Park, were listed as "persistent runaways." Running away, however, was not a simple phenomenon either in causes or effects. Obviously, most slaves ran away if they could; but a distinction should be made between those who escaped into the wilds because the life of an outlaw was preferable to the intolerable harshness of plantation life, and that large and increasing proportion that simply absconded to the towns because lax security on the estates made it physically possible and the attractions of tenuous and temporary freedom outweighed the punishments inflicted after the almost inevitable return. Of the two types of runaway, the first was naturally regarded by the whites as the more dangerous, since the slaves' running away represented a total rejection of slave society. Such desperate, and often armed, men were hunted down by Indian or Maroon trackers with guns and dogs. Those who "pulled foot" to the towns, on the other hand, were rebels *within* the system, impelled by a rebellion tinged with ambition. These were punished by the masters, like all simple miscreants, merely with the lash or with a spell in the "Vagabond Gang."[90]

Predictably, those who fled to the mountains and woods were commonly Africans (those, indeed, most able to sustain themselves in the wild), while the most persistent of the town runaways were those over whom security was most lax: domestics, or those like wainmen with some occupational freedom of movement outside the estates in the first place. Precise motives for running away must, however, have varied with every runaway, and much remains in the realm of speculation. What, for example, is one to imply from the cases of Whore and Strumpet? It would be extremely interesting to know whether they ran away because of the degradation they experienced on the estate, or because of the opportunities for profit offered in the towns for certain proclivities that they possessed. A third possibility is that they were named as a form of punishment for running away, after the trade that they were forced to follow in order to sustain themselves while away.

Unlike naval captains, plantation overseers were rarely compelled to keep lists of punishments, and so evidence in estate records of resistance to slavery short of rebellion or running away must be inferred indirectly from details of productivity or obliquely in comments made about individual slaves. Much resistance, moreover, was not recorded because it was manifested either in forms that the masters came to accept as inevitable, or in guises that they failed to recognize.

Slaves had subtle ways of disguising their low productivity and of compelling the masters to accept this as a fact of plantation life. The occasional slave of whom it was recorded that he was "lazy and good for nothing" had achieved a quite exceptional (and un-necessarily uncomfortable) degree of resistance. Simi-larly, the even rarer slave who committed suicide or went mad—probably no more commonly than in train-ing regiments during British National Service—was as much a "misfit" as his counterpart in nonslave society. The generality, or "normal" majority, of slaves were much better adjusted. They produced only as much as was necessary to forestall punishment, alternating between sullen obduracy when worked hard and manic cheerfulness when the load was lightened. Yet it is a psychological commonplace that such trucu-lence is no more indicative per se of harsh conditions than explosions of gaiety are of general contentment. Rather, both were part of the mechanism of adjust-ment, designed to confuse and bewilder the master class.

Slaves were encouraged to sing at their work as in Africa, though even Edward Long recognized that many of the "digging songs" were satires at the "Obisha's" or "Buckra's" expense.[91] There was also a large degree of disguised insolence in ordinary slave conversation, taking the forms of exaggerated defer-ence, "puttin' on ole massa" in a manner that was only superficially jocular, and the use of derogatory slang and nicknames, such as "cockroach" as a synonym for white man. The true nature of conversation between plantation whites and blacks was only apparent to visitors, the local whites having come to accept it through long usage, deluding themselves that what was in fact their weakness was the product of good humor and good management. In much the same way slaves got away with a fair amount of petty crime, particularly praedial larceny. Around the plantation houses, for example, the whites turned the blind eye on a level of pilferage that almost became an ac-cepted perquisite of domestic slaves. If pressed, the whites could always claim that such customs were an inevitable product of "African" traits in their slaves.

In a sense, the very stereotyping of the black as lazy, shiftless, childishly dependent, manic-depressive, and a thief, was a psychological adjustment on the masters' part, citing as evidence of black inferiority qualities which, even if they were real, were the product of deficiencies in the system of slavery or in themselves. The need to stereotype and the form the stereotyping took can actually be seen as something of a victory of the slaves over their masters, though degrading and permanently damaging nonetheless. As we can see from unbiased accounts of African tribes, of the Jamaican Maroons during slavery days, or of the peasant blacks of the West Indies after 1838, blacks diverged from the stereotype almost in the degree of their freedom from plantation slavery. Yet the case should not be overstated. Not only did slavery reinforce the white man's prejudices but, over the generations, blacks tended to fulfill the roles wished upon them. Regarded long enough as "Quashie," some blacks undoubtedly slipped into that "Quashie mentality" of lethargic unreliability that Patterson describes and deplores.[92]

An unjust and evil social system such as slave society degrades and demoralizes all those involved in it; not only the obvious victims but also those apparently most adjusted to it and those with apparent dominance. In slave society, obviously the slaves themselves suffered most, by being placed under the ultimate control of another race, by being regarded not as persons but as things and property. In a racially dominated socio-economic system even manumission offered them only a limited escape, and even after slavery ended, scars remained. Yet though sympathy for those with almost absolute power is naturally qualified, the master class was also alienated by the system of slavery in ways that were nonetheless severe for being unrecognized. All elements in slave society were involved in the evolution of modern creole society. Yet in one sense at least the slaves were more fortunate than the masters. Accommodation was facilitated for the slaves because they had no choice, and in course of time creolization with freedom seemed to them the best of conditions. The white masters, on the other hand, at least in the West Indies, constantly resisted their fate, regarding themselves always as exiles, never quite natives. During slavery days the proprietors tended toward absenteeism, the managers and bookkeepers toward a peripatetic restlessness. Later, all whites saw themselves as progressively less rather than more integrated in the society that evolved from slavery—not European or even African, but creole. Thus, it might be argued that the combination of rootlessness, fear, hypocrisy, and delusion inherent in their role, corrupted and demoralized the masters even more than the slaves. It was not the sins of the white fathers but rather their delusions that were to be visited upon their descendants.

Chapter 5

MOUNTING ATTACK AND REARGUARD ACTION

OUTLINE OF THE DEBATE

When the Treaty of Utrecht was signed in 1713, the attainment of the Spanish *asiento* was regarded throughout England as an unequivocal triumph. Even in 1783, when the War of American Independence ended and sympathy for slaves was already widespread, the remaining plantation colonies were generally considered of paramount importance within the British Empire, and slavery as essential as empire itself. Yet, within a further fifty years, new colonies and new policies had radically shifted the emphasis of empire, and from being the chief slave-trading and slave-holding power, Britain became the leader in the movements first to end the slave trade and then to free the slaves.

These dramatic changes can be attributed to four broad elements, each of which could be argued to have been chief in importance: the economic decline of plantations manned by slaves; the concomitant political decline of the West India interest; the growing power of the philanthropic movement; and the double switch in imperial focus—from West to East and from protectionism to *laissez faire*. At one end of the scale it has been argued by such as Coupland and

Mellor that abolition and emancipation were victories
for disinterested philanthropy, and by others that
plantation colonies declined chiefly because the slaves
were freed. At the opposite pole Eric Williams has
eloquently maintained that philanthropy was never
disinterested and that the slave trade and slavery were
abolished only because they were no longer economic.[1]
In re-examining the evidence, it is hoped to show that
both interpretations are partly, but only partly, true:
that philanthropy gained its "great victories" not only
because of its own strength but because of the weakening of the opposition, at a time of fundamental
changes in the course of empire.

The ending of the Seven Years' War in 1763 saw
the beginning of that gradual process of institutional
reform that brought the branches of the imperial executive under more centralized control and increased
their efficiency, while the executive for its part was
gradually made more responsible and responsive to
the British Parliament. This was a radical change,
but it proceeded so slowly that it was not completed
even by the time of the first great reform of Parliament itself in 1832. Eventually the scope of debate
was widened, and slavery and mercantilism in general
were thrown open to Adam Smith's query as to
whether the private profit accruing outweighed the
public cost. Yet for a generation the effect was not
only to place more power in metropolitan hands (this
would last) but also actually to increase the power of
the mercantilist and slavery lobbies.

In the early part of the eighteenth century, when
colonial or economic matters were scarcely ever the
subjects of debate in Parliament, the London West
Indians and the African Merchants formed but two of
the dozen or more "Meetings or Clubs of particular
Merchants, either fix'd or occasional" described by a
writer in 1734,[2] which gathered together to discuss
policy and draw up plans for parliamentary action
and petitions to present to ministers and department

heads. The "Africans" never grew more formal as a separate lobby, but in the period of sugar's ascendancy between the Treaty of Paris and the outbreak of the American War, the West India interest emerged as perhaps the most numerous and influential lobby that the unreformed Parliament was ever to see. The West India Merchants and Planters Club, although still not a permanent body, took on a much more formal aspect, with regular meetings, and minutes that are still extant from 1769 onward.

Yet, in a sense, actual lobbying was of less importance than it was to become later when the power of the slavery nexus was on the wane. Throughout the age of the elder Pitt (when Alderman Beckford could summon all the important men in England to one of his City banquets), the presence in Parliament itself of 50 to 60 MPs with West Indian or slave-trading affiliations[3] was more than enough to ensure that their interests swayed debates and influenced the minister informally. The West India Committee's minutes dealing with policy decisions have a confidently imperative ring to them during the 1770s—almost as if they were already government ordinances.[4]

A telling, and ironic, example of the dominance of the sugar-slavery nexus in the imperial government can be traced in the fate of the Virginians' attempts to limit slave importations in the 1770s. It is also of interest because it showed ways in which American colonial attitudes foreshadowed those of the imperial Parliament itself a generation later. In many ways the Virginian House of Burgesses was more democratic than the British House of Commons, and despite the opposition of some local planters and slave traders, a majority voted to place a tax of 25 percent on slaves in order to discourage importations. Speakers in the debate made conventional references to the evils of slavery, but the bill undoubtedly passed the legislature because the majority felt that there were already too many blacks in the colony and that continuing imports would increase the problems of security.[5] Unfortunately, none of these arguments, idealistic or practical, moved the imperial government. The Virginian law was arbitrarily disallowed by the Privy Council after memorials had been received from the merchants of Bristol, Liverpool, and Lancaster that the slave trade should not be hampered by colonial duties.[6] Although Thomas Jefferson's assertion that Britain's enforcement of the slave trade was a crime against humanity was deleted from the Declaration of Independence in deference to the planters of the Carolinas and Georgia, in 1788 George Mason of Virginia claimed that the disallowance of 1772 had been "one of the great causes of our separation from Great Britain."[7]

Although the secession of the Thirteen Colonies reflected a preference on the part of British imperialists for plantation colonies and mercantilist patterns of trade, it accelerated the process of reform and reassessment in imperial government. The key figures in this transitional phase, respectively in political theory and practical politics, were Edmund Burke and William Pitt the younger. Burke combined an enthusiasm for administrative and parliamentary reform, sympathy for the Americans, and opposition to unbridled interest, with the development of the philosophy of imperial trusteeship. In 1792 he published a *Sketch of a Negro Code,* which he claimed to have drawn up as early as 1780, setting out to reform and humanize both slavery and the slave trade. Burke's caution and conservatism were too ingrained, however, to make him an outright abolitionist; he was merely among the first to argue that if slave traders and colonial assemblies could be encouraged to improve conditions, slavery would naturally die.[8] William Pitt was even more equivocal. In many ways an imitator of his imperialistic father, he claimed at the same time to be a disciple of the radical reformer

Adam Smith. A close friend of William Beckford and Lord Penrhyn, the leaders of the West India interest, he was equally intimate with William Wilberforce and Thomas Clarkson, the apostles of abolitionism. These apparent paradoxes can only be resolved if William Pitt the younger is seen as the last great minister who saw his destiny as simply to rule. Sensor not censor, he avoided a doctrinaire party line by a masterly technique of listening to both sides. Constantly he disturbed the diehard conservatives by the way he allowed the radicals to call him their champion, but in actual fact he pursued reform only when he thought it was the will of the majority in power.[9]

Largely because of the impact of the French and Haitian Revolutions, nothing of great importance in the way of reform was achieved during Burke's lifetime, and it could almost be maintained that William Pitt had to die before even the slave trade was abolished. Yet from the time of the War of American Independence, the relative power of the West Indians and Africans insensibly declined. Significantly, even the temporary reinforcement of doctrinaire mercantilism that followed the victory of Lord Sheffield's views over those of Lord Shelburne in the peace treaty debate of 1782–83 was a partial setback for the West Indians[10]; for by declaring the Americans aliens in the fullest sense, the imperial government made it impossible to obtain cheap provisions in the West Indies, thereby effectively laying an additional charge of at least 5 percent on West Indian plantations. At the same time, the reform of the customs service and the Vice Admiralty courts (coupled with the zeal of the young Horatio Nelson) made evasions more difficult, so that by the later 1780s West Indians began to complain of "imperial tyranny" in language scarcely less severe than that employed by the Americans before 1775.[11] The situation was exacerbated once the imperial legislature, while abrogating more power, showed little inclination to increase the protection af-

forded West Indian sugar and showed an increasing
propensity equally to favor sugar and other competing
produce coming from nonslave, or even non-British,
areas.

Far more serious causes of the decline of the West
Indian plantations were almost beyond the reach of
legislation: the increasing burden of plantation debts
and the unavailability of new capital. In a depressed
market, the general level of planters' indebtedness—
initiated in more expansive times or extended in the
hope of their return, and made worse by absenteeism
—was bound to rise. Besides, it was against nature to
expect a national economy accustomed for nearly a
century to the inward capital flow of high profits from
slave trade and plantations to reverse the tide and
provide anew that type of pump-priming that had
started the plantations in the first place. From 1783
onward marginal plantations began to collapse or,
with quickly eroded optimism, looked to diversification. Bryan Edwards estimated in 1793 that the number of sugar plantations in Jamaica had already fallen
to 767 from a peak of 1,061 in 1780, that a third had
changed hands in the previous 20 years, and that one
in eight were in the often reluctant (and certainly exploitative) hands of their mortgagees.[12]

Even a rise in prices, such as the destruction of
rival plantations by the Haitian Revolution or a
general European war seemed to offer, would not
save established plantations. For what capital there
was available was not attracted to estates that were
often worked out and inefficient; investors preferred
(if they favored plantations at all) the undeveloped
areas brought within the Empire such as Trinidad
and Guyana, or beyond imperial surveillance in Cuba,
Brazil, or even the southern United States. Sugar production in the original British West Indian colonies
reached a peak in 1805 that it was not to top until
1945. But the 70 percent increase between 1783 and
1805 was not indicative of great profitability, rather
the reverse: it represented an attempt to restore

		1739	1768	1780	1800	1833	1875	1900
JAMAICA	Sugar estates	419	651	1,061	800	600	244	140
	Production (thousand tons)	12	35	50[13]	60	70	35	20
	Slaves	100	180	210	285	310	—	—
GUYANA (British)	Production				10	50	110	80
	Slaves				65	55	—	—
CUBA	Production			12	35	75	500	1,000
	Slaves			50	130	280	325	—
HAITI	Production	42	63	60[14]	—	—		
	Slaves	117	257	250	—	—		

Table 17. The Rise and Fall of West Indian Sugar: Jamaica, British Guyana, Cuba, and Haiti, 1739–1900.[15]

profits by increased production, with inflationary results. Similarly, the crescendo in the British slave
trade to the West Indies that occurred after 1783
(which all but made up for the loss of the American
market for slaves) did not indicate a period of burgeoning prosperity, but rather the only moderately
successful attempts of Liverpool traders to increase
profits by greater efficiency and an increase in the
flow of (usually inferior) slaves, to foreign as well as
British colonial markets, old and new.[16] By this means
the slave traders naturally focused even more public
attention on themselves, just as the public in the
face of increasing sugar imports, yet continuing protection and high consumer prices, became skeptical
of pleas of declining profits.

As recognizable parties formed from factions, and
debates on colonies, trade and reform became more
common, the declining value of West Indian plantations and the slave trade was reflected in the decreasing power of West Indian and African representation in Parliament. The number of MPs chiefly
engaged in West Indian trade and with a predominance of West Indian holdings may actually have
risen slightly; but their relative power declined with
the growth of the East Indian and industrial lobbies
and the decrease in the number of merchant and
banker MPs with minor West Indian interests.[17]
At the same time the first indications occurred that
public opinion at large was sufficiently important to
influence Parliament on major issues.

Yet decreasing representation in Parliament and
the growth of contrary sentiments among the general
public could be at least partially offset by intensified
lobbying, particularly by gaining direct access to ministers, as well as by carrying the campaign into the
country at large. Through the correspondence committees of the colonial assemblies, the colonial agents,
the West India Committee itself, and the agents of
the Liverpool and Bristol merchants, increasing pressure was applied behind the scenes. At the same time

journalists and lecturers were employed to restate for the consumption of the general public the old arguments for maintaining slavery and protection. Right up until the final defeat in 1833, the West India Committee could always gather large numbers of interested persons at public meetings, put out propaganda almost to match the opposition's, arouse sympathy for the rights of property in Lords and Commons and, at the last resort, go directly to the Cabinet, which, being faced with ultimate decision making, always tended to be at least as conservative as the parliamentary majority.

Indeed, it could be maintained that the efficiency and stridency of the campaigning carried on by the West Indians and Africans were in reverse proportion to their declining power, as well as being an accurate index of the opposition with which they were confronted. The process began in the 1780s when, in response to the mounting tempo of attacks upon both protection and slavery, the West India Committee first became a permanent body with a professional staff. Yet even this was not enough to counter the increasing concentration of the opposition on the issue of the slave trade, and on February 7, 1788, a standing subcommittee was formed expressly to conduct the fight against the abolitionists, whose own new Society for the Abolition of the Slave Trade had been constituted just eight months earlier.[18]

Issue had now been fully joined in the first of the great reform campaigns, outside as well as inside Parliament. For the slavery lobby it was the concentration of a narrowing circle of beleaguered special interests; for the abolitionists, the mobilization of a widening medley of disparate allies.

THE ROOTS OF OPPOSITION

Many but by no means all of those campaigning against slavery were idealists. The most extreme were motivated by religious revivalism; others by the secular Enlightenment, particularly by the movements for legal and economic reform.

To a degree, opposition to slavery on religious grounds was almost as old as slavery itself, yet the general effects of this opposition were slight until the third quarter of the eighteenth century. The pioneers at each stage were the Quakers, whose attitudes and actions toward slavery accurately foreshadowed those of other religious denominations. By no means averse to commerce, Quakers owned slaves in both the West Indies and Pennsylvania, yet as early as 1671 George Fox enjoined slave-owning Friends in Barbados to treat their slaves humanely, to teach them Christianity, and to free them after a period of servitude.[19] In 1727 the central Society of Friends went further and condemned both the slave trade and slave holding, and in 1761 all who engaged in slave trading were excluded from membership. Actual slave owning by Quakers lingered longer, but between 1774 and 1776 the Pennsylvania Society passed resolutions declaring that those who held slaves could not be members.

Quakers also led the opposition to slavery on religious grounds as it spread to non-Quakers. It was a Pennsylvania Quaker, Anthony Benezet, who, through his *Historical Account of Guinea* (1766), converted Thomas Clarkson and many others to abolitionism, as well as powerfully influencing John Wesley and Granville Sharp, who began his philanthropic legal work with the rescue of the slave Jonathan Strong in 1767. Besides, Quakers opened the active phase of English abolitionism by presenting the first important petition to Parliament in 1783, and in the following year by circulating twelve thousand free copies of a pamphlet entitled *The Case of Our Fellow-creatures, the oppressed African, respectfully recommended to the serious Consideration of the Legislature of Great Britain by the people called Quakers*. When the Society for the Abolition of the Slave Trade was founded in

1787, its committee of 12 included no less than nine Quakers.

Abolitionism would not have prospered, however, without its spread into the religious mainstream. Largely through John Wesley, who experienced slavery in practice in the Carolinas and whose *Thoughts Upon Slavery* (1774) was the first really penetrating attack upon the system, opposition to slavery became inextricably tied up with the religious revivalism that swept through all classes of Englishmen after 1770. Revivalism carried hundreds of thousands outside the established Church of England, but in due course it influenced more and more Anglicans as well. That spiritual worthiness would be attained by all men even in the face of the blight of industrial urbanization, explains why first Wesleyanism and then Anglican evangelicalism achieved such remarkable success among the English proletariat. It also explains why the Englishman's new sense of self-discovery was accompanied by an awareness of the even more miserable lot of the black slave. The combination of proletarian revivalism with abolitionism made inevitable the bitterness with which Wesleyanism was attacked by most sections of the English establishment, at least until the movement spread back into the Established Church by way of the evangelical "saints" of the Clapham Sect, when the opposition became simply a virulent and interested minority.

One of the features of eighteenth-century revivalism was that conversion occurred as suddenly as to Paul on the road to Damascus. Spiritual rebirth was accompanied by a flooding love of all men and by a sense of mission, so that converts either became abolitionists in the selfsame instant, or became converted to abolitionism with a subsequent flash of revelation similar to the experience of religious conversion. In either case, religion and philanthropy were permanently annealed, philanthropy being given a mandate through the power of revelation,

while religion was given greater validity by the prosecution of good works. In this light, it is interesting
to compare the autobiographical accounts of conversion given by prominent abolitionists, such as Clarkson's experience at Wade's Mill on the way from
Cambridge in 1785, and Wilberforce's under the
Holwood oak in 1787. The experience of John Newton
(1727–1807) was more gradual, but in a sense even
more telling. At the time of his first religious conversion he was a slave trader. The conversion did not immediately lead him to forsake his calling, but merely
to treat his slaves well and to conduct daily services
upon deck from the Anglican *Prayer Book*. Around
1780, however, he became quite suddenly converted
both to evangelicalism and abolitionism, dedicating
the rest of his life to both causes as rector of St. Mary
Woolnoth in the City of London. Thus, the career of
one key figure can symbolize the crucial transition
among the majority of English Christians during the
later eighteenth century; from a position that since
slavery was so necessary and valuable it was obviously
God's will it be accepted, to a certitude that it was
God's will it be eradicated at all costs.

Though much of abolitionism's fervor stemmed from
religious revivalism, its philosophical and practical
bases were mainly secular. Indeed, the origins of
philosophical objections to slavery were at least as
ancient as the purely religious, despite the fact that
during most of the eighteenth century slavery continued and even grew in power because expediency
was philosophically respectable and practically more
potent than idealism. The two main strands of abolitionism converged in the 1780s, when in the cause of
philanthropy religious devotees campaigned alongside
ardent freethinkers; yet victory was not won until the
institution of slavery was discredited on utilitarian as
well as idealistic grounds.

At one level the secular abolitionists opposed slave

trading as an "ungentlemanly" pursuit, and slavery as an affront to Europe's claim to be civilized. "Slavery is so vile and miserable an Estate of Man, and so directly opposite to the generous Temper and Courage of our Nation," wrote the insular John Locke in 1689, "that tis hardly to be conceived that an *Englishman,* much less a *Gentleman,* should plead for it." At another level, philanthropy fed on the anomaly that while men were increasingly believed to hold certain inalienable rights, these rights were notoriously withheld from subject races, particularly the black. The black, asserted the *Encyclopedia* in 1765,

> cannot under any condition divest himself of his natural rights; he carries them everywhere with him, and has the right to demand that others allow him to enjoy those rights. Therefore, it is a clear case of inhumanity on the part of the judges in those free countries to which the slave is shipped, not to free the slave instantly by legal declaration, since he is their brother, having a soul like theirs.[20]

The philosophic bedrock was provided by the optimistic belief, revived with fresh force by the Enlightenment, that men were not only basically equal, but, in an aboriginal state, naturally good. All these ideas, however, remained in the realm of sentimental impracticality until the notion gained ground that physical constraint could not possibly be economic. Slavery was doomed only when it was seen as inutile as well as uncivilized and unjust, a position that was best comprehended, in due course, by Bentham's definition of utility as "the greatest happiness of the greatest number."

One of the most significant adoptions of the secular Enlightenment was the myth of the Noble Savage: the assumption that the closer a man lived to the state of nature, the nearer he was to the perfect life.[21] Its earliest manifestation in English was the novel *Oroonoko* written in 1688 by the enigmatic Mrs. Aphra Behn. This tale, which the author claimed to

be based on personal experience in Surinam, was the
forerunner of a whole genre in France as well as
England. The noble Coromantine Oroonoko mouthed
sentiments echoed by Rasselas, the creation of the
Tory humanist Samuel Johnson (1759); and Oroonoko's sufferings after leading an abortive rebellion
might well have been the model for the unfortunate
slaves encountered by Voltaire's Candide (1759) and
Rousseau's Héloise (1761) or depicted by William
Blake in the illustrations to Stedman's account of
the revolt in Surinam (1796).[22] Dramatized in a
slightly watered-down version by Thomas Southerne
in 1696, *Oroonoko* was an almost annual production
on the London stage throughout the eighteenth century.

Yet admiration for the aboriginal or sympathy for
the oppressed slave were by no means abolitionism in
themselves. For a start, they generally rested on a
cultural contradiction. Apparently, even the most enlightened of eighteenth-century thinkers could believe both that man was aboriginally noble, and that,
since Western European culture was the summit of
human civilization, its attainment was man's highest
aim. Consequently the Noble Savage was generally
considered as a European *philosophe* in blackface.
Oroonoko and his lover Imoinda, though black as
"perfect Ebony or polished Jet," had the figures and
features of Europeans. Similarly, William Blake por-
trayed the tormented Surinam blacks as tinted Europeans, as well as being capable of the ingenuous
lines:

> My mother bore me in the southern wild,
> And I am black, but O! my soul is white.[23]

If based upon such eurocentric misconceptions, the
myth of the Noble Savage was easily shown to be
absurd in fact. For every optimistic (or audience-
conscious) traveler who reported the discovery of
noble savages, tales could be told with equal plausi-

bility of African barbarity. At the same time, negrophobes could mock the pretensions of those semi-
assimilated blacks such as Ignatius Sancho, Ottobah
Cuguano, Oloudah Equiano, Francis Williams, and
Phyllis Wheatley, who were paraded by abolitionists
to "prove" the African's perfectibility.[24] Moreover,
the unfortunate discovery of what Edward Long
called orangutans (actually gorillas or chimpanzees)
in the blacks' homeland around 1765 even encouraged
arguments that, far from living in an idyllic state, the
black was lower than the European on the scale of
being.

Even if the black were believed to be intrinsically
equal, his evidently backward condition could be
used to justify enslavement as a stage in that gradual
betterment that it was the duty of civilized men to
bring about. If, on the other hand, the black were
intrinsically inferior (as, for example, David Hume
and Thomas Jefferson believed), the rights of man
were not even applicable in his case. God, or the
Prime Mover, had ordained the variety of mankind.
Certain people were fitted by Nature to be slaves. It
was simply the Duty of enlightened masters to treat
them as well as was consistent with Reason and
enlightened Self-Interest.

These confusions and paradoxes are nowhere better
illustrated than in the work of Daniel Defoe (1661–
1731). In *The Reformation of Manners* Defoe condemned slavery as uncivilized, and in *Colonel Jack*
he implied that, though it was inevitable, it should
be humanized. His most famous hero, Robinson Crusoe, is described without moralizing comment as a
slave trader, the trade by implication being justified
as an economic necessity. Yet Crusoe's companion
and friend is Man Friday, who though pointedly not
an African black and often sounding like an enlightened Englishman, is the most celebrated Noble Savage of all.

Robinson Crusoe is remarkable to us in that Defoe

was apparently able both to view blacks sentimentally and yet to accept their enslavement if interest decreed. It is, however, an excellent example of the operation of the eighteenth-century principle that natural rights could be outweighed by utility. The Enlightenment had to demonstrate that slavery was not indispensable before idealism could come closer to success. Even Montesquieu, who attacked black slavery and the arguments used to sustain it with savage irony, was essentially ambivalent. He argued that law was not only the reflection of the higher law of reason, but also of the variety of humankind and its divergent needs. To his mind slavery no longer served a rational purpose in Europe; but observation made it seem equally true that under despotic regimes (such as those in Africa) bondage was preferable to death, and in tropical countries, sloth was so natural that coercive force was the only way to encourage heavy work.

The paradoxes apparent to Montesquieu were deeply imbedded in English law. The antislavery arguments of the French writer (whose *Esprit des Lois* was translated into English by, among others, Edmund Burke) influenced William Blackstone to incorporate them into the first edition of his definitive *Commentaries* in 1761, but with such confusing results that they were dropped from the third and subsequent editions. Indeed, no aspect of English law was more confused than that which related to slavery. The concept of bondage for Englishmen had gradually been eradicated centuries before, yet the possession of slaves in the colonies had always been upheld by specific colonial laws. Moreover, the trade in slaves as chattels had been legalized by most of the charters to trading companies, and all the relevant Acts of Trade, particularly after a 1677 judgment cast slaves as commodities under the provisions of the Navigation Acts.[25] Even the possession of slaves in the mother country was sustained by the laws of property and contract, if not also by the vague general percepts that ordained the forfeiture of liberty for crime, debt, and capture. In particular, a decision by the Law Officers of the Crown in 1729 had decreed that neither coming to England nor baptism freed a slave, and that slaves might be forcibly returned to the plantations.[26] This was the decision that Granville Sharp attempted to overthrow in the famous case of the slave James Somerset in 1772. As James Walvin has cogently shown, Sharp's victory was far from complete, for Lord Chief Justice Mansfield (who was subtly misquoted in all the printed accounts of the case, including Howell's prestigious State Trials series) was at pains to uphold the slavery laws wherever they applied, and merely decreed that a slave could not be forcibly returned from practical freedom into slavery against his will.[27] As late as 1827 it was possible for Lord Stowell to decree that a certain slave called Grace should be retained by her mistress in Antigua since a period of residence in England did not itself make a slave free.[28]

The Somerset case nonetheless was of crucial importance. Not only did the majority of Englishmen ignore Lord Mansfield's sophistry and believe that the fifteen thousand slaves in England were free if they wished; the case also highlighted the absurd anomalies that while Britons never could be slaves, they might quite easily enslave others, and having done so, might quite legally treat them in the colonies in ways increasingly regarded as barbaric in metropolitan law. The anomalies were not finally removed until British slavery itself was abolished; yet Granville Sharp was a pioneer among those legal reformers and philanthropists who included in Parliament Burke, Romilly, and Brougham and, behind the scenes in the Colonial Office, the father and son called James Stephen, who combined a passion for legal and administrative reform with evangelical zeal as members of the Clapham Sect.

The legal reformers gained increasing support from economists as they, in turn, were increasingly supported by practical men. From the mid-eighteenth century onward, French physiocrats maintained that since law reflected the dictates of necessity as well as a more abstract natural law, rational utility could be used as an argument against slavery as long as slavery could be shown to be uneconomic. Physiocratic ideas were brilliantly developed by the Scottish economist Adam Smith (who had been feted by Turgot and his circle on a visit to France in the 1760s) in the form of arguments for the unimpeded operation of the principle of enlightened self-interest.

Although Adam Smith and his followers believed that the proper operation of enlightened self-interest and the removal of narrow protectionism would result in moral as well as material improvement, their attack upon slavery was concentrated on its uneconomic aspects. The expense of slave labor placed it beyond the means of the producers of any but the most lucrative crops, so slavery encouraged the tendency to monocultural plantations in high-profit crops such as sugar, which nonetheless required protection to sustain their advantage. Moreover, slavery had disappeared from Europe (save Russia) because it was found more economic to provide workers with the incentive of a share in the produce. The continued existence of slavery in a nondespotic empire that protected property, meant that the masters' self-interest in subduing the slaves was tolerated although it was in conflict with the self-interest of the slaves not to work. Enlightened self-interest could only work to the public good if it were to the advantage of employers and employed alike that the workers advance in intelligence, usefulness, and the ownership of property. This could only be achieved by emancipation and the consequent decline of plantations based on slavery. Yet by condemning the old plantation system, emancipation might destroy the justification for mercantilist protection and release such energies that all sections in due course would be bound to benefit.

Adam Smith's arguments, particularly that which maintained that slavery was so manifestly inefficient that it was only sustained by the slave owners' lust for power, naturally never convinced slave traders or West Indian planters. But his arguments were deeply attractive to a growing body of practical men with countervailing interests. Chief among them were those whose interest it was to import sugar into England as cheaply as possible in order to satisfy the seemingly illimitable demand at home and in the rest of Europe. Sugar refiners, retailers, and re-exporters therefore argued for the removal of duties designed to protect the West Indian colonies, and the tapping of sugar plantations in the unprotected East or even outside the formal British Empire. The freeing of the sources of sugar, they claimed, would not only bring cheaper sugar to the masses but would have the additional merits of dooming slavery on British plantations while distributing sugar produced not by slaves but by "free" laborers. Accordingly, in setting afoot a campaign for "free sugar," disinterested abolitionists worked with capitalists who were far from altruistic, and together they had considerable success in convincing the ordinary people that in opting for unprotected sugar they would not only aid the slaves but also, in course of time, pay less. Apparently, philanthropy, *laissez faire,* and enlightened self-interest were neatly blended, at every level.

Although their campaign did not reach so wide an audience, the other "Easterners" who attacked the East India Company's monopoly in the hope of expanding Asian trade, and all those manufacturers who followed Adam Smith in believing that the Old Colo-

nial System stifled their growing export potential,
abetted the free sugar advocates. Among the East
India Company's most cherished privileges was the
re-exportation of Indian cottons to West Africa duty-
free, while the expansion of the Lancashire cotton industry was hampered by duties designed to protect
British Empire producers, including the few slave cotton plantations in the West Indies. The removal of
these forms of protection would serve the purposes
of encouraging English textile manufacturers and
raw cotton importers, while discouraging the slave
trade that had stimulated the old re-export trade and
helped to supply the sugar plantations. It was acknowledged that the inefficient Indian cottage cotton
industry might suffer as well as the slave traders, but
it was argued that Indian raw cotton producers would
benefit from increased demand, while Indians as a
whole would benefit from the importation of cheaper
English textiles. At the same time English workers
would benefit from wider employment. As the free
trade net spread to even wider areas and to other industries, so similar benefits would be brought to the
people of the world, consumers and producers as well
as capitalist entrepreneurs. The general good—to re-
vert to Adam Smith's theme—would far outweigh the
loss to the narrow interests dependent on slavery and
protection.

These trends were not merely speculative; they
were already discernible in British import and export
figures in the last years of the eighteenth century,
despite the prevalence of mercantilist policies. While
sugar imports from the British West Indies between
1772 and 1807 barely doubled, the imports of raw cotton from all parts of the world went up by 1,000 percent. Over the same period the value of exported
English cotton goods rose from an average of £240,-
000 a year in the five years after 1772, to £8,740,-
000 a year between 1802 and 1806. It is true that the
proportion of British trade represented by the West

Indies remained high until the ending of the slave trade, exports to the Antilles remaining roughly around 10 percent of the British total and imports around 20 percent from 1772 to 1793, and both actually rising during the subsequent war years to about 15 percent and 30 percent, respectively. Yet the very imbalance between exports and imports provided grist for the free traders, who maintained that drawing sugar and other West Indian products from a wider area while actively expanding exports would lead to Britain's general profit. Moreover, the wartime expansion of British West Indian trade was the result of the destruction or takeover of French, Dutch, and Spanish colonies, which as far as the colonists of the old-established British plantations were concerned, was tantamount to free trade anyway.[29]

Certainly, the upsetting of the Caribbean and Latin American balance of power did much to promote the benefits of freer trade once the last French war was over, and this was highlighted by the adamant opposition to expansionism as well as by any move on the part of the embattled West India interest that undermined the Old Colonial System. Between the ending of the slave trade in 1807 and the ending of slavery itself in 1834, the index of British industrial output rose by 125 percent and total British exports by 133 percent; yet the amount of trade with the British West Indies (including new colonies) stayed practically stationary, and the percentage of total British exports destined for the West Indies fell from 15.1 to 4.8. The figures for capital investment in West Indian enterprises, if they were obtainable, would almost certainly show a similar relative if not absolute decline. Long before 1830 it should have been obvious that the increase in volume and the shifts of trade had already made the British sugar plantations based on slavery obsolete. Philanthropy was now a luxury that could be enjoyed by almost all.

To Eric Williams and his most ardent disciples, the

degree to which the abolitionists and emancipists
claiming to be motivated by religion or the rights of
man subscribed to economic reform or were engaged
in nonplantation trade made them no more philanthropic than the slave traders and slave holders
themselves. This is almost certainly to understate the
perverse power of disinterested idealism, as well as
the value of engaging in good causes for dubious
reasons, though not so absurd as to maintain that the
philanthropists could ever have carried the day
against unweakened vested interests. A more balanced summary might state that abolition and emancipation, while inevitable in the long run, occurred
when they did because of a fortunate concatenation
of interests, ideas, and extraneous events. To a certain extent the reforms were based upon misappre-
hensions. It was not long before it was apparent that
unprotected sugar and cotton were by no means
"freely" produced, coming in their largest quantities
from the American slave states and slave-based Cuba
and Brazil. Having destroyed Indian cotton manufacturing, free trade debilitated Indian raw cotton
production as well. To some observers it was also
ironically apparent that conditions for ex-slaves in
the West Indies and English workers in textile and
other "dark, satanic mills" alike, were in some ways
worse than those for plantation slaves. Yet by that
time the strange alliance, or *mésalliance*, of free
traders and philanthropists had done its work.

ABOLITION—THE PARLIAMENTARY CAMPAIGN

By 1787 it had become impossible for Parliament to
continue ignoring the slave trade and the conditions
under which slaves labored on the plantations. The
publicity given the *Zong* insurance case in 1783, when
Lord Mansfield (despite pious expressions of distaste)
felt compelled to find for the owners of 132 live

slaves thrown overboard on the way to Jamaica, aroused a storm of public concern.[30] In place of the sterile shuttlecock of biblical quote and counterquote, and the battledore of arguments without proof, such as whether the Middle Passage was horrific or benign or whether African conditions were better or worse than West Indian, two writers outstandingly provided facts from personal observation or research. In 1784 James Ramsay, who had been a parson in St. Kitts for 19 years, published a devastatingly circumstantial account of plantation slavery, assaulting the pride of planter and nonplanter alike by condemning British slavery as worse than French.[31] Shortly afterward Thomas Clarkson began the painstaking (and dangerous) compilation of data that showed for the first time the horrors of the Middle Passage, for whites as well as blacks, in statistical detail, among other things effectively challenging the myth that the slave trade was a "nursery" (rather than graveyard) for British seamen.[32] Finally, in response to demands from all sides, Parliament was impelled to uncover all the available facts of the complex dispute. In 1788, working mainly behind the scenes with the King's ministers, William Wilberforce was able to initiate the series of pioneer inquiries before the Privy Council and select committees of Commons and Lords, which brought something like the truth of slave trade and plantation slavery out into the open between 1789 and 1791.[33]

Some results occurred almost immediately, but the majority of Parliament regarded the help given to ship indigent blacks off to Sierra Leone and the passage of Sir William Dolben's act (1789)[34] to regulate the overcrowding on slave ships as quite adequate. Wilberforce's first motion to bring in an abolition bill was decisively defeated in the Commons in April 1791 by 163 votes to 88.[35] Accordingly, the abolitionists redoubled their campaign in the country, with the help of pamphlets abstracting the evidence given before the parliamentary commissions. At the same time Josiah Wedgwood's famous medallion of the kneeling slave in chains inscribed "Am I Not a Man and a Brother?" sold 200,000 copies and became the equivalent of a modern campaign button. While the enthusiasm for the revolution in France (which seemed likely not only to end the French slave trade but French slavery itself) was still widespread in England, a wave of over 500 petitions from regional abolition committees and correspondence societies swept into Westminster. A second rejection of the principle of abolition by Parliament would clearly spell political trouble at large. William Pitt rose to the occasion, and in what some regarded as his most brilliant speech, in April 1792 carried both Houses toward a motion for gradual, not immediate, abolition, which passed in the Commons by 235 votes to 85.[36] It is almost certain, moreover, that a fair number of nonphilanthropic MPs were swayed to vote for abolition in the belief that ending the British slave trade would actually damage the French colonies more than the British; for it was commonly held that not only were St. Domingue, Martinique, and Guadeloupe expanding rapidly but were also heavily dependent on slaves carried in British ships.[37]

After further debate the date for the ending of the British slave trade was fixed for January 1, 1796; but pretty soon it was apparent that the tactics of the antiabolitionists in forestalling immediate abolition served their cause extremely well. The Jacobin Terror and the war with France in 1793 discredited the correspondence societies and made such overtures as Thomas Clarkson's visit to the French abolitionists seem treasonable as well as futile. Burke, Fox, and Pitt ceased to pay more than lip service to abolitionism, while the internal disruption of the French colonies in the Caribbean and the British invasion of St. Domingue in 1794 invalidated the argument that abolition would be a blow for the French. Thus, 1796 passed without abolition being effected, and even the efforts of Wilberforce and Thornton to abolish the slave trade to the foreign West Indies or to restrict it to part of West Africa, failed almost equally decisively.[38]

The revelation of the conditions imposed upon slaves by West Indian slave society had, however, not failed to make a mark on Parliament. Even most of those who believed that ending the trade would be economically and politically inopportune considered that some degree of slave amelioration would be wise, while moderate abolitionists argued that by amelioration the slave trade would be gradually rendered unnecessary. Only the extremists on both sides were adamantly opposed: the ultra-abolitionists because amelioration was not enough; the most reactionary slave owners because any concession was dangerous.[39] Parliament passed some minor legislation concerning the sale of slaves for debts and the further improvement of conditions on slave ships,[40] and after a "Humble Address to the Crown" from the Commons in 1797, Lord Portland sent two circulars to colonial governors in the spring of 1798, instructing them to urge reforms upon the colonial assemblies. The results, however, were merely token legislation in some colonies, and in others nothing at all.[41]

Meanwhile the slave trade to the captured colonies flourished, and this provided the abolitionists with another hopeful tactic. As Wilberforce said of the planters of the old-established colonies,

> they have not the assurance to pretend to be influenced by any principles of justice, (this is literally true) but merely by a sense of interest. The soil of Demerara, Berbice, and Surinam is so fertile that an acre will produce as much as those (generally speaking) in our old islands. There is also in them an inexhaustible store of untilled land, fit for sugar. Consequently the proprietors of estates [in the old colonies], knowing that the demand for sugar is not even now greater than the

supply, are afraid lest they should be in the situation
of the owners of an old and deep mine, who are ruined
by the discovery of some other where the ore can be
obtained almost on the surface.[42]

Abolitionists and old-established planters actually negotiated with each other in 1804 for the suspension of
the slave trade for two to three years, but at the last
moment West Indian opinion hardened, with the fear
that, once suspended, the trade might never be revived.[43] The rift between the old and new planters,
however, was never to be completely healed.

Despite the West Indians' opposition, an abolition
bill passed three readings in the Commons in 1804
with the help of the Irish MPs, though it was decided
not to press in the Lords so late in the session. The
following year, however, brought one more setback.
An Order-in-Council abolishing the slave trade to the
conquered colonies, agreed to by Pitt in 1804, was
finally announced by Castlereagh in September 1805;
but now that their chief rivals were denied fresh
slaves, the old planters redoubled their efforts, and
the motion for general abolition was defeated for the
last time by 77 votes to 70.[44]

William Pitt died in January 1806, with the slave
trade still in being, though probably only flourishing
in the shipment of slaves to foreign colonies such as
Cuba and Brazil. Even this branch of the trade was
stifled, however, when in May 1806 the Grenville-Fox
government obtained the passage of an act incorporat-
ing the 1805 Order-in-Council, which also forbade the
shipping of slaves to foreign colonies.[45] Deprived of
the only markets which, they claimed, were still lucrative, the slave traders had nothing left to fight for;
and with the West Indian planters divided and with
few allies, the passing of a comprehensive abolition
bill became virtually inevitable. In something of an
anticlimax, the motion for a bill swept through the
Commons, and the bill itself passed the Lords by 100
votes to 36 and the Commons by the incredible mar-

gin of 283 to 16, receiving the King's assent on March 25, 1807.[46]

By the Abolition Act no ships could clear out from Britain for Africa to trade in slaves after May 1, 1807, and from March 1, 1808, the British slave trade was "utterly abolished, prohibited and declared to be unlawful," with large fines levied for transgressions. Slaves rescued from illegal ships were to be "apprenticed" for up to 14 years, and their rescuers paid bounties as high as £40 per head. In 1811, moreover, slave trading was made a felony liable to the penalty of transportation for foreigners trading in British dominions, as well as for Britons everywhere. In 1824 slave trading on the high seas was declared piracy, though the death penalty was removed in 1837 in favor, once more, of transportation.[47]

Although the abolitionists had never entirely ceased their agitation and continued to issue and reissue pamphlets in large numbers from 1792 to 1807, the preoccupation with the French war naturally weakened their support in the country, while it made the war-strengthened executive less susceptible to popular pressures. Therefore, the arrival of abolition with such remarkable suddenness and completeness in 1807 can hardly be claimed as an unequivocal triumph for the abolitionists, or even as the result of long attrition. Rather, it should be seen as the long-delayed victory of a principle accepted by all humane opinion for 20 years, once the humanity of Britain's legislators ceased to be overridden by specific considerations of profit and political expedience.

Only to a tiny proportion of Parliament in 1807 was the slave trade still regarded as indispensable; yet British slavery itself was far more deeply entrenched, and it was to be a further 31 years before it was finally uprooted. The earnest belief of all abolitionists was that the ending of the slave trade would make the slave owners so concerned about the natural increase of their slaves that material conditions would greatly

improve, and that with an expanding black population the very need for slaves would eventually pass.[48]
Besides this, it was believed that missionary activity
would help toward the moral improvement of the degraded slaves. As time went on, however, these hopes
evaporated. After a dozen years it was discovered
with horror that the over-all slave population was
actually declining, while material and moral improvements, in the face of the planters' indifference or opposition, fell far below the philanthropists' expectations. Clearly the plantocracy was incorrigible, and
the whole system so baneful that the only solution was
legislated emancipation, even if imposed on slave society by the imperial government. Convincing the
majority of Englishmen that slavery was evil, and a
majority of British legislators that it brought no imperial benefits, were comparatively easy tasks, convincing those who mattered that legislated reforms,
such as emancipation, which involved private property, were not only compatible with *laissez faire*
principles, but politically expedient, was far more difficult.

FROM ABOLITION TO EMANCIPATION

What must be stressed before looking at the period
between abolition and emancipation is that the slave
plantations were already in a state of flux. The ready
availability for the first time of accurate statistics and
disinterested firsthand accounts confused emancipists
and has led historians since to fail to recognize
changes that had occurred since 1808. First, and perhaps most important, the very ending of the trade
had certain unexpected demographic effects, some of
which passed completely unnoticed. The outlawing
of slave imports meant that it was impossible to "top
up" populations, and the tendency to natural decrease, though it was down below five per thousand

per year on the average, was thrown into high relief —a cause for concern for planters and philanthropists alike. With the trade's ending, optimists expected that the slaves' general health would improve, and that by cutting off the influx of adult Africans with a preponderance of males, the increasing proportion of creoles and females would lead to a rapid rise in the over-all birthrate. The results shown in the first returns of the registration censuses—started in 1815— were therefore disappointing to all.

Yet, despite the alarmism of such as T. F. Buxton, who claimed in 1830 that the British West Indian slave population had absolutely declined by one hundred thousand in 23 years,[49] it was not the continuation of slavery in itself that prevented the blacks from increasing naturally. Not only was it not realized how serious the demographic imbalance had been in earlier times, but the demographic effects to be expected from a change merely from an annual importation of 2 percent of the total population to zero, were overestimated. Moreover, what was not acknowledged was the "ageing and wasting effect" that meant that until the African-born (who had been imported for the most part after they had begun to be capable of reproducing themselves and thus gave an unbalanced look to the colonial slave population "pyramids") actually died out, the transition to a normal demographic balance with tolerable birthrates and deathrates was bound to be slow.

Nonetheless, it seems that in certain islands like Barbados (and on individual plantations elsewhere), with well-established and thus healthy populations, natural increase had been achieved by 1807, and it is almost certain that by then the creole slaves were increasing naturally in every colony. Moreover, projections can be made to show that the population would have been increasing naturally in Jamaica by 1845, and rather later in Trinidad and Guyana, had slavery never been abolished—though it could always be argued that had slavery been abolished with the slave trade in 1807, this might have occurred even earlier than it did.[50]

Colonies and mother country alike were affected by many other changes and accelerations after 1807 that influenced the progress toward emancipation. For the planters it was a period of mounting economic and social crisis approaching panic conditions. The steady decline in sugar prices was speeded up by the ending of the war, the increase in world production, and the spread of British protection to the newly acquired colonies; and falling sugar prices sped the decline of plantations.[51] In the long-established colonies marginal estates collapsed, while the survivors found their attempts at raising efficiency by consolidation and technical improvements blocked by the preference of capital for more profitable areas. Among these were the new Crown colonies of Trinidad and Guyana (Berbice, Demerara, Essequibo), which were continued sources of jealousy and fear on the part of planters committed elsewhere. Development of the new colonies was also hampered, however, by the shortage of labor due to the ending of the slave trade between the colonies as well as with Africa itself.

In any case, the slave laborers suffered. Ironically, the period of the amelioration laws was one in which, for economic reasons, the lot of many or most slaves deteriorated.[52] In the old plantations it became increasingly necessary to work the slaves hard in order to raise production and maintain profits; for the planters in new areas the shortage of slaves in a period of expanding cultivation had a similar result. At the same time, however, planters realized that if they worked their slaves to death there were no adult replacements. More than ever before it was vital to steer a precise course between enforcement and inducement, while simultaneously trying to reduce the odds determined by nature, the climate, and the plantation system against high birthrates and infant survival rates.

The slaves throughout the plantation colonies were, in fact, caught between the effects of the planters' need for greater productivity and their own rising expectations. The creolization of slave society rapidly accelerated after the direct links with Africa were practically severed in 1807. As has already been suggested in Chapter 4, merely to know a system is to make it less constricting; to be involved in it for generations is to begin to shape it to one's own character and needs. Even without the passage of ameliorating laws, the slaves insensibly increased their economic power and social mobility. Practically the owners of their tenements and plots in most colonies, they made money by trading their produce to the point where a fortunate few were able to purchase their own manumission. At the same time, continuing miscegenation made it statistically inevitable that the number of slaves rising socially through the "lightening of the skin" increased steadily.

With rising expectations grew a sense of worth and self-respect, all of which were served by the rapid, but dangerously uneven, spread of sectarian missions, which followed the foundation of the London, Baptist, and Church Missionary societies between 1792 and 1800. As has already been traced, the slaves' own churches provided not only spiritual relief from the plantations' hardships but some education, self-expression, and a real sense of belonging to an alternative society outside the planters' control. It is small wonder that the planters generally resisted the spread of missions just as they opposed any recognition in law of the slaves' advances in social mobility, material well-being, and legal rights—regarding all such changes as emanating from the inimical philanthropists in London and their faceless allies in the Colonial Office. Indeed, the planters visualized themselves as existing in a state of siege, beset by rising tides of economic misfortune and popular pressure, both of which were encouraged by an increasingly unsympathetic imperial Parliament. Their response was that of the impotent and doomed: desperate obstructionism.

While the last French war lasted, Parliament was preoccupied, and it was to be eight years after the Battle of Waterloo before public concern reached the intensity of the early abolitionist period once more. As early as 1809 Wilberforce was expressing disappointment with the effects of abolition on slave conditions,[53] and in 1811 the publicizing by Brougham and others of the Huggins and Hodge cruelty cases in Nevis and Tortola[54] indicated serious attempts to rearouse the public. Yet during this period the most significant progress was made behind the scenes by James Stephen, the Colonial Office lawyer. Stephen's strategy was to persuade the Cabinet—through the Colonial Secretary—to use the Crown colonies as laboratories for gradual slave reforms. Imposed upon the assemblyless Crown colonies by orders-in-council, these reforms could then be urged upon the older colonies through their governors, with the assemblies encouraged to pass their own acts for fear of dictation from the imperial Parliament at Westminster.[55]

In 1812 James Stephen received approval from the inner circle of emancipists to press for slave registration. This moderate reform, it was argued, would serve four purposes: to ascertain whether illegal slave importations were still occurring despite the abolition acts, to provide accurate statistics concerning slave mortality and fertility (by so doing further to publicize slave conditions), and thus to provoke further reforms. Without pressure from Parliament, however, the Cabinet proved extremely cautious in the face of well-organized West Indian resistance. It was not until 1815 and a parliamentary campaign that Stephen's principal, Lord Bathurst, and his colleagues were persuaded to approve the first Order-in-Council and bring the initial pressure to bear on colonial governors. Resisted by the planters even in Trinidad, implementation was delayed in the Guyanas, and in Jamaica it was categorically rejected. Only over the subsequent five years were the self-legislating colonies, one by one, induced to pass the necessary acts. In the case of Jamaica, a definite undertaking had to be made that as a reward for compliance the principle of colonial legislative autonomy was permanently guaranteed. It was not until January 1, 1820, when an imperial act setting up a central Slave Registry came into effect,[56] that a workable uniform system of registration existed, with only Bermuda not having passed its own registration act.

In fact, no less than 22,000 slaves were shipped between British West Indian colonies more or less legally between 1808 and 1830, largely under the system of licenses permitted by the Act of 59 Geo. III, c. 49. Demerara alone received some 7,600 and Trinidad 7,000, with about 2,000 apiece going to St. Vincent and Jamaica. About 3,700 came from Berbice, 3,400 from Dominica, and 3,100 from the Bahamas. This covert trade, however, was effectively curtailed by the Slave Laws Consolidation Act of 1824 (5 Geo. IV, c. 113), after considerable philanthropic agitation led by Dr. Stephen Lushington.[57] By this time considerably more publicity had been given to West Indian conditions through the work of Stephen, Brougham, and Samuel Romilly. If anything, the Hatchard case in 1818, in which it was decreed that it was a libel to maintain that West Indian grand juries were not disposed to render justice for maltreated slaves, whetted rather than dampened public curiosity. Considerable anger was generated, for example, in the same year by Romilly's revelation of the case of Congo Jack in St. Kitts, in which the Reverend Henry Rawlins' flogging to death of a runaway was declared by a local coroner's jury, with unintended irony "a visitation of God.[58]

With the easing of the postwar economic depression and of the consequent domestic turmoil in England, many more people were disposed to consider the plight of the slaves. Accordingly, a fresh wave of fervor was generated, beginning with the formation of the Liverpool Anti-Slavery Society in 1821 by James Cropper, a Quaker philanthropist who significantly combined his emancipism with a heavy involvement in the East Indian sugar trade. During the following two years, the central Anti-Slavery Society was constituted under Quaker impetus and the leadership of Zachary Macaulay, ex-plantation bookkeeper, evangelical "Saint," East Indies Company stockholder, and pioneer of Sierra Leone. At the same time a "Secret Cabinet Council" was set up to press action in Parliament, in which the mantle of leadership passed from the opium-addicted Wilberforce to the businesslike brewer T. F. Buxton, with Viscount Suffield to carry the fight into the Lords. The warfare of the printed word revived, with a fusillade of pamphlets on both sides culminating in the devastating broadside of James Stephen, Jr.'s, *Slavery Delineated*.[59] Besides this, newspapers and journals took a large part for the first time. On the emancipist side the *Edinburgh Review* was joined by the *Christian Observer* and the *Anti-Slavery Reporter*, edited by the tireless Macaulay. The slavery lobby could be heard in the *Quarterly Review* and *Westminster Review* until both changed sides in the later 1820s. After this the fighting retreat was carried on in many of the leading newspapers, *Blackwood's Magazine* and the scurrilous *John Bull*, which in its personal attacks on the morals and special interests of prominent emancipists anticipated some of the arguments of Eric Williams, in parody form.[60]

The campaign of the emancipists in 1823 centered on a plan to achieve legislated amelioration in the colonies in much the same way as with (though more rapidly than) registration. Wilberforce's contribution was practically limited to the introduction into Parliament in March 1823 of a Quaker petition similar to that which he had introduced 40 years earlier to initiate abolition. The real battle was joined two months later with Buxton's forthright motion that all blacks henceforth born in the West Indies should be freed, and that the conditions for the rest should be drastically ameliorated. After an acrimonious debate, in which the West Indian case was ably presented by Charles Ellis, the much more moderate resolutions of George Canning (performing the same role as had Pitt and Dundas in 1792) were carried by a large majority on May 15, 1823:

1. That it is expedient to adopt effectual and decisive measures for ameliorating the condition of the slave population of his Majesty's colonies.

2. That through a determined and vigorous, but at the same time judicious and temperate, enforcement of such measures, this House looks forward to a progressive improvement in the character of the slave population, such as may prepare them for a participation in those civil rights and privileges which are enjoyed by other classes of his Majesty's subjects.

3. That this House is anxious for the accomplishment of these purposes at the earliest period that may be, consistently with the welfare of the slaves themselves, the well-being of the colonies, and a fair and equitable consideration of the state of property therein.[61]

Almost immediately Lord Bathurst—whose tendency hitherto had been to compromise and call for further information—sent out copies of Canning's summary speech and two dispatches, informing the governors of Crown colonies of forthcoming amelioration decrees, and strongly advising the other governors to press for specific local amelioration measures. These consisted of the encouragement of religious instruction, the observation of the Sabbath by the abolition of Sunday markets, the ending of the flogging of female slaves and the regulation of punishments for males, the outlawing of the breakup of slave families at the time of sale, the facilitation of savings and slave-purchased manumission, and the allowing of slave evidence in the general law courts under certain conditions.[62] Some colonies considered these suggestions sufficiently moderate, close enough to the facts of slave life as it was already, or easy enough to evade in practice, that they thought it judicious to legislate immediately. The Barbadian Assembly, on the other hand, was politely intransigent and the white Jamaicans outraged. In the context of a slave rebellion scare—a minor outbreak being suppressed with savage force—the Jamaican Assembly in December 1823 passed a positively insolent series of resolutions against what it called "the machinations of a powerful and interested party" in the imperial Parliament.[63] The Trinidad Order-in-Council was nonetheless promulgated in March 1824, and the Guyana Order slightly later, the Barbadians and Jamaicans being forced into an increasingly bitter rearguard action that had hardly produced the required legislation before the next round in the campaign opened in 1830.

In fact, during the middle and later 1820s the impetus of emancipism slowed once more. The emancipist leadership dissipated its forces, turning equal attention to the questions of "free sugar," the illicit slave trade to Mauritius (which increased rapidly after the island's sugar industry was placed on the same protected footing as that of the West Indies in 1825),[64] and the fate of the Cape Hottentots. The Demerara slave rebellion of 1823 and constant reminders of the Haitian revolution had disposed many to await more patiently the results of the official government policy of gradual amelioration. More concern was shown about the fates of the Baptist missionary John Smith in Guyana and the Methodist William Shrewsbury in Barbados than those of the revolted slaves. It might almost be said that even philanthropists were more concerned with the religious and moral than the material improvement of the slaves' lot, and that the parliamentary majority was in favor of any kind of improvement only if it lessened the chances of social unrest. For those in Parliament it was, indeed, a disquieting period, at home even more than abroad, in which popular unrest and demands for reform increasingly focused on the unrepresentative nature of Parliament itself.

Certainly the patience of Parliament over slavery was not matched in the country, and emancipism gained immeasurable popular support from the general agitation for reform. It was at about the time of the campaign for Catholic emancipation, for example, that a certain J. H. Flooks wrote a famous letter from Wiltshire to the Secretary of the West India Committee:

> In this neighbourhood we have anit-slavery clubs, and anti-slavery needle parties, and anti-slavery tea-parties and anti-slavery in so many shapes and ways that even if your enemies do not in the end destroy you by assault, those that side with you must give you up for very weariness of the subject and resentment of your supineness.[65]

Regional antislavery committees indeed proliferated and public meetings grew in frequency, size, and ardor. This can best be gauged by reading the description of a meeting of the London Anti-Slavery Society held at Exeter Hall in May 1830, given by Sir George Stephen, James Stephen's son. After Buxton had attacked slavery unequivocally enough, the fiery Henry Pownal said that the time for temporizing had ended and that the meeting should assert boldly its determination that British slavery should exist no longer. "It was a spark to the mine!" wrote Stephen a quarter century later.

> The shouts, the tumult of applause were such as I never heard before and never shall hear again. Cheers innumerable thundered from every bench, hats and handkerchiefs were waved in every hand. Buxton deprecated, Brougham interposed, Wilberforce waved his

hand for silence, but all was pantomime and dumb show . . . We would allow no silence and no appeals. At the first subsidence of the tempest we began again, reserving our lungs till others were tired. We soon became the fuglemen of the mighty host, nor did we rest, or allow others to rest, till Wilberforce rose to put the amendment, which was carried with a burst of exulting triumph that would have made the Falls of Niagara inaudible at equal distance.[66]

Wise statesmen began, perhaps, to consider that the encouragement of emancipism might be one means of directing the people's ardor away from domestic issues. Certainly the government, encouraged by the decision of the Law Officers that the passage of an imperial bill to rectify omissions in Jamaican legislation concerning slave testimony would not be *ultra vires*, sent out fresh orders-in-council concerning amelioration in February 1830. In the general election, which lost the proslavery Lord Wellington 50 seats and brought Lord Grey's Whigs to power in December 1830, slavery was a crucial issue in many constituencies.[67] A series of debates was held in Parliament in 1831, as a result of which a third set of orders-in-council, amounting almost to a comprehensive slave code for the Crown colonies, was sent out by Whig Colonial Secretary Lord Goderich in November 1831, closely followed by the now-traditional injunction to the governors of the self-legislating colonies.[68]

At this juncture occurred the serious rebellion of the slaves in western Jamaica at Christmas 1831. To the most reactionary of the planters this was ample justification of their policy on obstructing legislation and hampering the work of the missionaries, and an all-out campaign was pursued to convince the Ministry to call a halt to reform. In contrast to 1823, however, it was clear to the emancipists and their allies, even before clinching evidence arrived, that this rebellion was provoked not by too rapid an advance in the slaves' expectations but by the repressions of the local planters. Far from accepting a slowing down of progress, the antislavery forces called for an immediate acceleration of emancipation. Rather prematurely, Buxton divided the Commons on a resolution for immediate emancipation in May 1832, and was defeated by 162 votes to 90. The only immediate result was the setting up of a Commission of Inquiry under Sir James Graham, which was universally seen as an attempt at procrastination. Yet, as Lord Althorp remarked to T. B. Macaulay, if Buxton could get such support when he was tactically wrong, the complete success of the emancipists was only a matter of time.[69]

Already in the middle of 1831 an activist Agency Committee of the Anti-Slavery Society had been set up under George Stephen, two Quaker brothers called Cooper, and another Quaker, Joseph Sturge. While the country already seethed with the later stages of the campaign for parliamentary reform, lecturers were sent around on systematic tours, and in a single year the number of local antislavery societies and committees rose from 300 to 1,300. During the general election, which followed the passage of the Great Reform Act in June 1832, practically all the tactics familiar to modern electioneering were employed. Tons of pamphlets were distributed, the streets were placarded, rival meetings were broken up, and virtually all parliamentary candidates were compelled to pledge their "soundness" on the slavery issue.[70]

Once again, firsthand accounts of the conditions of slave society proved the most potent propaganda. No pamphlet had more impact than Henry Whitely's *Three Months in Jamaica,* produced in huge quantities in 1833. But perhaps the crucial event in the last stages of the emancipist campaign was the arrival in England from Jamaica late in 1832 of the dynamic Baptist missionary, William Knibb, who was immediately made the star attraction on the speaking circuit and introduced to key members of the Cabinet. The picture that Knibb painted of the crisis in the plantations was a revelation to many, concentrating as he did upon the lawless and violent behavior of the whites. Although conditions in Jamaica were more critical than elsewhere, a clearer picture emerged of a society polarized more than ever before. Public audiences, already disillusioned by the reactionary behavior of the Anglican hierarchy during the Reform Bill campaign, were incensed by accounts of the attacks upon sectarian chapels such as Knibb's by white Jamaican mobs under the aegis of the Anglican Colonial Church Union. At the same time percipient observers were even more dismayed by the disclosures that not only were the black elite among the most disgruntled of the slaves, but also that the intransigence of the whites had driven the increasing body of free coloreds—who might otherwise have been conservatives—over to support the cause of the slaves. In Jamaica this phenomenon of racial solidarity was largely achieved through the medium of the radical newspaper *The Watchman*, edited by the mulatto Edward Jordon.

When the new Parliament met at Westminster early in 1833, it was inundated with petitions, signed in all by more than 1,500,000 people. Yet, despite the unique popular sound and fury of the reform campaigns, neither was the new Parliament so different from the old nor the Whig Ministry as totally committed on the slavery issue as the radical emancipists imagined. Emancipation was now inevitable, but the Cabinet still preferred to engineer some form of cooperation with the West Indians rather than to resort to absolute coercion.[71] Angered by the absence of any reference to emancipation in the King's speech in February, Buxton gave notice for a motion involving unconditional emancipation. A two-month delay was negotiated by the government, while a special committee of the Cabinet met almost daily. Meanwhile, Downing Street was besieged by swarms of antislavery delegates and visited, more discreetly, by West Indian "lobbyists." At first the planters' representatives made no concessions, demanding promises on continuing protection, high compensation, and a system of compelled work that was tantamount to slavery continued. But when the dynamic E. G. S. Stanley (who had just succeeded the pusillanimous Goderich as Colonial Secretary in a Cabinet shuffle) published a comparatively moderate but definite plan for emancipation in *The Times* on May 11, the West Indians changed tack and mobilized themselves to obtain the best possible terms through parliamentary debate.[72]

The final debates in Parliament opened on May 14, with Stanley outlining a modified plan in which the slave owners were to be compensated by a loan of £15,000,000. This was said to amount to ten years' profits, or one quarter of the value of the slaves' labor for 12 years. Accordingly, the slaves once freed were to be compelled to work as apprentices for their former masters for a dozen years, for three quarters of normal working hours. Slaves under the age of six at the Act's passing were to be immediately free. In the course of protracted exchanges Buxton and his fellow campaigners were able to reduce the terms of apprenticeship to six years for praedial slaves and four years for domestics (working a 45-hour week) and to introduce the motion that the provisions of apprenticeship would be supervised by stipendiary magistrates rather than local justices of the peace. A Parliament now almost totally dedicated to free trade ideas was unable to make any commitment over continued protection for the sugar plantations. But the defenders of property rights, such as the landed magnates who still largely made up both houses of Parliament (not to mention those MPs and Lords who themselves held equity in slaves) were able to increase the scale of compensation to an outright grant of £20,000,000. This, though only an average of some £25 per slave, was by far the largest such sum Parliament had ever considered raising.[73]

These then were essentially the terms incorporated into the Emancipation Bill that finally passed the Commons by a wide margin after minor amendments in the Lords, on July 31, 1833, just four weeks after the death of William Wilberforce. The Act was, of course, only a model for the colonies, and India, Ceylon, and St. Helena were specifically excluded from its provisions.[74] But a parallel order was sent to the other Crown colonies early in 1834, and since receipt of compensation was dependent of echoing legislation being passed, the colonial assemblies competed with each other to comply. Ironically, the first colony to complete its legislation was Jamaica.

At midnight on July 31, 1834, some 776,000 slaves in the British plantation colonies became technically free. Naturally such a dramatic transition was awaited by the plantocracy with considerable trepidation. Yet, except for joyful scenes in many chapels, the occasion passed with remarkable restraint. The reasons may have been the general ignorance and cowed apathy of the mass of slaves. But a more plausible explanation is that there was a general mood of doubt and uncertainty, not only about the nature and working of apprenticeship, but also about the future in freedom. The majority of the newly emancipated were too realistic to imagine that the action of the distant imperial parliament and that all-too-familiar local assembly, were designed for their unequivocal benefit, any more than they could (or we can) believe that the motives of the legislators were wholly disinterested.

APPRENTICESHIP, 1834–38

Public campaigns need clear-cut issues, and one of the last times that the plantation colonies presented the English people with the evident confrontation of right and wrong was over the question of apprentice-

ship. The certitude with which the abolitionists after
1835 maintained that apprenticeship was but slavery
cloaked was, however, by no means general in the
government. It was in fact a period of transition in
British politics, in which free trade had not yet
polarized the parties, crossvoting was common on
many issues, and Lord Melbourne's Whigs were sustained in power as much by the opportunist Irish
MPs as by the ever-fading myth that they were the
party of reform. The planters' sympathizers were still
numerous in Parliament, and on the apprenticeship
issue they found common cause with the growing
number of adherents of *laissez faire* who believed
that the colonies should be left to their own devices.
The Colonial Office, moreover, was reluctant to dis-
own a scheme that it had so painfully produced and,
like many parliamentarians, had to be convinced
not so much that apprenticeship was oppressive or
unjust, but that it would not work.

The chief intentions of the designers of apprenticeship were fairly transparent: to determine that the
transition to liberty should not be accompanied by
social license, and to ensure the continuity of labor
on estates. In the first case it proved unnecessary,
and in the second it promised to be ineffectual. Contrary to the planters' fears, nowhere were the apprentices rebellious and scarcely anywhere insolent;
yet it was soon apparent that only where they had to
would they continue to work on the plantations. In
some colonies the blacks had no option; in others they
could not be constrained. In neither case could the
continuation of apprenticeship be justified, and when
it was revealed that in Jamaica at least its enforcement had been accompanied by serious abuses, public
clamor in England brought it to a premature conclusion.

Antigua and Bermuda had nicely assessed the situation in 1833 and waived apprenticeship altogether.
In both colonies there were more blacks than were

needed for the available work, and too little unadopted land to provide the freedmen with alternative opportunities. There were also what were regarded by the whites as quite adequate laws already
on the statute books to control freed blacks. Similar
conditions applied in all the islands of the Lesser
Antilles save Trinidad, so that although their ruling
classes had opted for apprenticeship, they did not
feel the need to fight hard for its retention. In Barbados and St. Kitts, large black populations, sugar
monoculture, the lack of spare lands, and dependence
on imported food meant that blacks even when free
would be forced to work for wages in order to sustain
themselves. In the other small islands there was less
dependence on the purchase of imported foodstuffs,
but at the same time the smaller number of plantations meant that the labor supply easily outran the
demand.

Conditions were crucially different in Mauritius,
Trinidad, Guyana, and Jamaica, though even in these
colonies apprenticeship proved of dubious value. The
first three had been acquired by Britain since the
slave trade ended, yet they possessed tremendous
potential for the expansion of sugar cultivation.
Guyana had already progressed far while under Dutch
control, containing twice as many slaves and producing twice the tonnage of sugar of Trinidad and Mauritius combined. But Guyana also contained large areas
suitable for cultivation by those who did not wish to
work on the estates, as well as a long tradition of
independent settlements, such as those of the "bush
Negroes" in neighboring Surinam.

The situation in Jamaica was worst of all. There
was a large slave population, but although many estates had already fallen into disuse, the labor force
was regarded as insufficient to work the remainder
efficiently. The chief problem was that there was far
too much undeveloped land, unsuitable for sugar but
ideal for peasant cultivation. As has already been
seen, there was a well-rooted tradition in Jamaica of

working provision grounds on estate margins, and the period of apprenticeship provided plentiful evidence that the blacks far preferred working these lands and selling produce in the local markets to toiling on the estates. In a period of desperately declining profit margins it was essential for Jamaican planters to produce more efficiently than ever before. Yet with outmoded methods, antique plant, and sugar lands that had been overworked for a century, they had none of the advantages of the new planters of Trinidad, Guyana, or Mauritius. Consequently the Jamaican planters tended to extract the maximum from their apprentices, and tension and grievances inevitably occurred.

At first, though, even the emancipists were satisfied. "Everything . . . going on marvellously well in the West Indies," wrote T. F. Buxton euphorically in March 1835. "The Negroes quiet, dutiful and diligent. It is quite amazing, it is contrary to reason, it cannot be accounted for, but so it is."[75] Pretty soon, however, a less favorable picture emerged. As early as June 1835, the indomitable Rev. William Knibb was calling apprenticeship (particularly the workhouses in his parish), "thrice accursed . . . nothing but blood, murderous cells and chains."[76] Reports sent back by stipendiary magistrates such as R. R. Madden, who resigned in November 1835 to write a book about his experiences,[77] while less lurid, provided ample grist for the alarming editorials in the *Anti-Slavery Reporter, Patriot,* and new *British Emancipator.*

In 1836 Buxton, urged on by the Birmingham radicals and Quakers, successfully called for a parliamentary inquiry. Its bland report was unsatisfactory to the emancipists, and at least four of them set out for the West Indies in October 1836 to judge conditions for themselves. The most influential result was *The West Indies in 1837* by Joseph Sturge and Thomas Harvey, though almost equally effective was the Governor of Jamaica Lord Sligo's own account,

Jamaica under the Apprenticeship System, published at the same time. These books described not only such abuses as the employment of treadmills in the workhouses and the flogging of women, but also the dubious quality of the stipendiary magistrates—overworked, undertrained, and too often partial to the plantation whites.

Meanwhile the last great emancipist campaign was raging in England. "Slavery has not been abolished," thundered the *Emancipator* in December 1837, "the Demon has but changed its name and, under its assumed disguise, it still revels in its wonted recklessness of Crime."[78] Speakers such as Sturge and Brougham spoke to huge audiences throughout the country, while the Anti-Slavery Society circulated thousands of posters and pamphlets and organized hundreds of petitions. After a second parliamentary inquiry late in 1837, Brougham carried the campaign into Parliament with a famous speech in the Lords on February 20, 1838. The parliamentary debate was accompanied and spurred on by a great public series held in nearby Exeter Hall.

An Abolition Amendment Act became law in April 1838,[79] though a further amendment proposed by Strickland was narrowly defeated as the result of a brilliant speech by W. E. Gladstone and the abstention of Irish MPs, who were unwilling to bring down the government. A second attempt made by Sir John Wilmot on May 22 was successful by the margin of ninety-six votes to ninety-three. Although the government hesitated to implement the change by law, orders went out immediately from the Colonial Office to the Crown colonies, and all the self-legislating colonies quickly passed enabling laws. In the case of Jamaica, where the law was signed only two weeks before coming into effect, the legislation was passed in an atmosphere of disgusted resignation sped only by the fear of the consequences of refusing to follow suit.

Chapter 6

AFTERMATH AND LEGACIES
THE FADING IMPULSE OF PHILANTHROPY

Whether it were believed that slavery was abolished because it was no longer economical or, alternatively, that plantations finally collapsed because the slaves were freed, it would come as no surprise to find that after emancipation the fate of the West Indian plantations and ex-slaves alike aroused progressively less concern in Britain. It was, after all, the age of official *laissez faire*. The triumph of free trade was not complete until the last sugar duties were removed in 1854; yet by that time the West Indies had become an imperial backwater, with the focus of interest on richer areas of formal empire such as India or the huge new fields of informal influence. After the premature ending of apprenticeship in 1838, philanthropy itself turned to different areas and fresh causes.

Indeed, the impulse of philanthropy gradually faded even as the fallacies of Social Darwinism gained ground. Disappointment with the achievements of the missionaries and the progress of the free peasantry in the West Indies was succeeded by the shocks of the Indian sepoy mutiny in 1857 and the Jamaican rebellion in 1865. As the will to rule revived with the onset of a new imperialism, so did attitudes of racial superiority, which found their most splenetic spokesman in Thomas Carlyle.

By 1900 the population of the British West Indies had multiplied four times since emancipation, and the total of sugar production had fallen from 40 percent of world production to 2 percent. Yet, though a consciousness of creole identity was insensibly developing, no significant political progress had been granted and no permanent substitute for the plantation economy had emerged. Indeed, the importation of 410,000 Indians and 50,000 Chinese in a vain attempt to bolster the sugar industry had both increased population pressures and added to the turbulence of the genetic pool.

The First World War brought few changes to the British West Indies (to which it was almost entirely irrelevant); but the Second hugely sped the processes of democratization, self-government, education, and the search for economic diversification—the processes, significantly, beginning at a sugar estate, Frome, Jamaica, in 1938. To a remarkable degree, however, the sugar industry also revived, reaching a volume of production in 1970 that was 10 times the level of 1935 and 20 times that of 1900. Despite tourism, bauxite, oil, and alternative agricultural produce, sugar threatened to re-establish monoculture at least in parts of the British Caribbean. Many commentators have gone much farther and said that the phoenix-like sugar plantation is symbolic both of a neocolonialist conspiracy to restrict the Third World Caribbean to the role of primary production under external exploitation, and also of an even more subtle tendency to perpetuate the sociopolitical patterns of slavery days.

Clearly then, the legacies of the sugar-slavery nexus are extremely important to the development of a creole society ten times as numerous as and far more complex than that which emerged from slavery in 1838—in mythology if not in fact. Comparing the oft-criticized effects of slavery and the plantation economy of the West Indies with the Empire's legacies to that area which once provided the slaves, modern West Africa, presents an ironic contrast. It also challenges the notion that the separate nations of the alleged Third World can ever join common cause.

Until the plantation slaves had achieved their full freedom on August 1, 1838, the fervor of the philanthropists had remained unabated and their tactics unchanged. Yet already their interests had greatly widened to extend the abolition of slave trading beyond the confines of British law, and to better the lot and bring the missionary light to others besides the British slaves. Decisive victory in the great Napoleonic war, moreover, had made it seem natural to many that the philanthropic will of the victors be generally imposed, and to others the prospect of an extensive British antislavery naval patrol was more attractive than complete peacetime demobilization.

At the time of British abolition, the government had been led to pledge that at the end of the war it would organize an international convention to promote general abolition.[1] On Napoleon's defeat, eight years later, the British government came under great pressure from the public actually to incorporate abolition in the peace settlements. In the month of July 1814, 772 petitions along these lines, containing nearly 1,000,000 signatures, were delivered to the House of Commons. Accordingly, Lord Castlereagh went to Vienna instructed to press for immediate universal abolition, an international right of search, and heavy penalties for illegal slave trading.[2]

The results were disappointing to the British abolitionists. The majority of delegates at Vienna, as at the subsequent congresses at Aix-la-Chapelle (1818) and Verona (1822), had far less interest than the British in ending the trade. Russia, Prussia, and Austria, having no overseas colonies, were concerned only with European matters, while Spain, Portugal, and France (not to mention the Americans, who were not represented at the European congresses) had an active interest in continuing or reinstating the trade. France was particularly skeptical of Britain's aims, seeing them as motivated by a desire to prevent the revival of French colonies. Talleyrand and other French diplomats therefore played upon the susceptibilities of the minor colonial and maritime powers, pointing out that Britain had nothing to lose and everything to gain from universal abolition, and that a general right of search would make Britain predominant since she had ended the war with her Royal Navy supreme.

Consequently, the slave trade clause in the final Act of Vienna, signed on June 9, 1815, was couched in the vaguest terms.[3] Although a quintuple treaty over the slave trade between the great powers of Britain, France, Russia, Prussia, and Austria was eventually signed in 1842, no general agreement proved possible while plantation slavery lasted anywhere. Britain was forced to pursue universal abolition piecemeal by bilateral treaties, repeatedly having to overcome vested interests and skepticism by a mixture of bribery and coercion, while at the same time asserting her own disinterestedness and disavowing the unilateral application of naval power. The 1,529 volumes in the British Foreign Office records dealing solely with the suppression of the slave trade[4] bear overwhelming testimony not only to the complexity and drawn-out nature of the campaign, but also to its very qualified success.

In diplomacy, power and interest reign. The slave trading treaties and conventions signed by Britain with more than 30 substantial powers down to 1877,[5] varied chiefly according to each party's interest in the trade and its suppression and the naval power available to back its interest. The Anglo-Spanish treaty signed in Madrid on September 23, 1817, for example, reflected the facts that Spain had never been heavily engaged in the slave trade even with her own colonies, possessed negligible naval power, and was eager for a British loan.[6] Accordingly, Spain agreed to immediate abolition north of the equator and complete abolition after May 30, 1820, in return for an "indemnity" of £400,000. Besides, she promised the immediate amelioration of trading conditions and regulation by means of a system of passports. Enforcement was to be aided by the granting of mutual rights of search and the setting up of Courts of Mixed Commission.[7]

By 1840 a web of treaties had been constructed, but the problems of enforcement were still not solved. Up to 35 British warships, a sixth of the strength of the Royal Navy,[8] patrolled the slave trading lanes, capturing 137 slavers in the years 1839–41 alone. Cases were adjudicated in the Vice Admiralty or Mixed Commission courts established at Sierra Leone, Loanda, St. Helena, Cape Town, Havana, Barbados, Surinam, and Rio de Janeiro.[9] Yet diplomatic squabbles over the right of search continued, and the subterfuges of the slave traders in concealing evidence made prosecution a chancy, protracted, and sometimes costly business. The insertion of "equipment clauses" in the treaty with Spain in 1835, specifying what constituted a reasonable presumption of guilt, finally drove the Spanish out of the trade, but the change did not quickly become general. Of those who continued most to trade, the Portuguese were least able to resist the often Palmerstonian action of Royal Navy captains in stopping, searching, and seizing. But at the same time the Portuguese showed great ingenuity in concealment, the carrying of false papers, and the judicious switching of flags. American slavers were the most brazen of all, being able to prevent search by any but U. S. Navy ships (of which there were rarely more than three on the African coast), but if not, to outsail or even outfight any would-be detainer. W. E. B. DuBois even claimed that in the last years of Atlantic slavery the trade "came to be carried on principally by United States capital, in U.S. ships, officered by U.S. citizens, and under the U.S. flag."[10]

Nearly 30 Royal Navy vessels continued to be stationed in West Africa and at the Cape until 1852, when the slave trade to Brazil was quite suddenly terminated by the action of the Brazilian government. Yet it is unlikely that the British squadron ever saved more than 15 percent of the slaves shipped in any one year either before or after 1852. Indeed, it seems certain that the volume of the slave trade to Brazil, Cuba, and the United States was far greater during the period of the Anti-Slavery Squadron than before 1807.[11] Those who measure the intention of a policy by its results are therefore inclined to argue that British philanthropy was not only ineffectual, but also hypocritical.

The detailed evidence presents a much more complex situation. For one thing, some philanthropists were opposed to the Anti-Slavery Squadron, for blameless if misguided reasons. The official policy of the British and Foreign Anti-Slavery Society formed by Joseph Sturge in 1839, for example, was unremitting pacifism. Many members of Buxton's much larger Society for the Extinction of the Slave Trade (SEST), founded in the same year, were also "noncoercionists," preferring rather to work for the "civilizing" of Africa by means of trade and Christian missions. All their ventures, however, proved disastrous, and after the failure of a third expedition to the Niger in 1841, SEST itself collapsed.[12]

In the crucial parliamentary debate over the continuation of the Anti-Slavery Squadron in March 1850,[13] the noncoercionists were strangely allied with the pacifist disciples of *laissez faire* and retrenchment such as Cobden, Bright, and Gladstone, as well as the negrophobes of the Carlyle school who held that black slavery was not an evil in any case. That the Squadron was continued (the crucial vote being defeated by 232 to 154) was due as much to the inertial imperialism of Russell and Palmerston, the lingering opinion that suppression would damage imperial competition, and the feeling that the Squadron was necessary to protect the "free" black settlements of Sierra Leone, Liberia, and Libreville, as to pure philanthropy.

The West African Squadron gradually declined as the need for it grew less and the activities of the Royal Navy became more diffuse; but it could never claim to have been the chief cause of the decline of Atlantic slave trading. By 1865, when slavery in the United States was ended by the Civil War, the number of ships stationed in West Africa had fallen below 20, though all were now steamers, with much greater range and effectiveness. By no coincidence, almost equal focus had already shifted to East Africa, where it was discovered with revived horror that a slave trade little less in volume than that of the Atlantic, and at least as deleterious in its effects, had been flourishing for centuries. By 1871, when even the Cuban slave trade had almost ceased, there were as many Royal Navy warships patrolling East as West Africa, but their combined total represented no more than a twelfth of the Navy's total forces now carrying the *Pax Britannica* to even more distant parts of the globe.

In sum, it seems evident that slaves ceased to cross the Atlantic neither because of the activities of the antislavery patrol nor through the influence of British philanthropists, but rather because the need for slave labor in the Americas had passed. This is not in itself to condemn British philanthropy. Yet philanthropic activism and the activities of the Royal Navy during the "free trade era" did have some curious results. If the slave trade left as unwanted legacies those West African forts that later were to form the basis of the Gold Coast and Gambia colonies, its suppression led to the establishment of the nucleus of other colonies.

Sierra Leone, intended as a home for liberated slaves where they could govern themselves, was taken over as a Crown colony as early as 1808. Lagos, the foothold that expanded into Nigeria, was annexed in 1862, largely as the result of the frustration of less direct methods of ending the slave trade of the Niger Delta.[14] Much the same was to happen 28 years later to Zanzibar, which was acknowledged by Bismarck as a British protectorate in 1890. Ironically, it was in the same year that the Brussels Convention completed the work of the Vienna Congress of 75 years earlier and "finally" outlawed African slavery.[15] British imperialism moved in mysterious ways and not often along predictable or intentional lines.

Indeed, it is only in recent years that it has been acknowledged that the "free trade era" was an age of expansionism differing only in degree from the period of "classic" imperialism between 1870 and 1919. The British free traders failed to recognize the ways in which their economic theory was a luxury based upon industrial, commercial, and maritime predominance. This blindness had other effects, particularly the assumptions that material success was based upon moral superiority, and that both materialistic and moralistic notions should be exported, along with trade goods, under the Union Jack. Although Africa, Asia, and the Pacific were not partitioned until after 1870, the British free trade culture had been actively diffused throughout the globe during the preceding 40 years. Moreover, though their policy was officially nonimperial and pacifist, complacency led British statesmen into gunboat adventures and even the acquisition of colonies wherever their concept of progress seemed unjustly blocked.

The diffusion of British philanthropic, missionary, and economic activity should therefore be regarded as related imperial phenomena. One very important transition was the emergence of an active trusteeship policy as the result of the work of the parliamentary

Aborigines Committee, which sat between 1835 and 1837.[16] During this period T. F. Buxton formed the British and Foreign Aborigines' Protection Society, which was "to be governed in all its measures by the fact that the complete Civilization and the real Happiness of Man can never be secured by anything less than the diffusion of Christian Principles."[17] It has already been seen how Buxton's parallel attempts to bring "civilization" through Christianity and trade to darkest Africa received a crude setback on the Niger in 1841. Other fields proved much more promising. The successful conclusion of the Treaty of Waitangi with the New Zealand Maoris in 1840, for example, more than compensated for Lander's failure to negotiate similar treaties with the Sultans of Kano and Timbuktu. Before the tide of missionary activity returned to tropical Africa, important progress was achieved with the "aborigines" of South Africa, British North America, and Australia as well as New Zealand.[18]

At the same time, even greater efforts were made to "civilize" British India. It was not until 1813 that Governor General Lord Minto had allowed missionaries freely into India, as part of that same movement that led to the abolition of the East India Company's monopoly in the cause of free trade. In 1835, however, T. B. Macaulay's notorious Education Minute signified the adoption of the principle that British policy should be the assimilation by Indians of British culture. For a generation, philanthropic trusteeship principles, Christianity, Westernization, the "benefits" of free trade, and a forward military policy were all heterogeneously, and ingenuously, combined.

THE COLONIAL FREEDMEN: OPTIMISM, 1838–46

With the whole world opening up to British trade and missionary activity, it is not surprising that the

old plantation colonies—no longer economically profitable and with the slaves freed and nominally Chris-
tianized—should have become relatively unimportant,
to private interests, bureaucrats, and philanthropists
alike. To Eric Williams and others, the switch of
attention is prima facie evidence that emancipation
was based upon economic interest, and philanthropy
nothing but the covering propaganda.[19] Yet, even
more than with the theory that ascribes slavery itself
purely to economic needs, the case should not be over-
simplified. Pure philanthropy (if indeed such an abstraction ever existed) was dead by 1840, but considerable ambivalence remained, at every level. For
example, apprenticeship collapsed, yet to say that
the British government callously threw the plantation colonies and their black freedmen immediately
on their own devices is to ignore the evidence. What
has to be determined is not whether a policy was
promulgated but whether the policy was applicable.
This in turn depended on the degree to which the
imperial plans were shaped, or distorted, by the action
of colonials, white and black, and conditioned by the
passage of events beyond the control or prediction
of imperial government, white oligarchs, and freed
blacks alike.

In a sequence of events by now long established,
the Colonial Secretary, Lord Glenelg, under the guidance and urging of the Permanent Under Secretary,
James Stephen, sent an outline of government policy
in a circular letter to the governors of the Crown
colonies in September 1838, accompanied or closely
followed by a set of orders-in-council.[20] Copies were
sent to the self-legislating colonies in the pious wish
that they would follow suit. The matters dealt with
amounted almost to a code, dealing comprehensively
with master-servant relationships, vagrancy, the militia and police, marriage, the poor, and the problem of
the squatters. The intention of the imperial government was to continue to facilitate the transition of the

slave to the status of free laborer. This was to be achieved by making colonial laws as comfortable as possible both to the changed conditions and current metropolitan norms, while at the same time taking into account the peculiar problems of plantation colonies. It was a hopeless ideal.

The labor laws, while they specified workers' rights and masters' duties, were, like those in Britain, far more concerned with guaranteeing the masters' regular labor than with protecting the servants from abuse. Terms of oral and written contracts and apprenticeships were laid down, yet the penalties decreed for nonfulfillment by the workers consisted of an immediate fine of up to a month's wages or 14 days in prison, but for the masters simply of an order for redress in the first instance followed by a distraint order for nonpayment, with imprisonment only in the last resort.

Largely to arbitrate in master-servant cases, the stipendiary magistrates appointed to oversee the apprenticeship system were permanently established, the cost of their upkeep being the largest continuing expenditure undertaken by the imperial government. However, because of the nature of the laws they adjudicated, the stipendiary magistrates were hardly champions of the workers' rights against their employers. Moreover, they were never numerous enough to supplant the justices of the peace entirely, and as time went on, the system whereby the ruling class enforced its own rules in the local courts became if anything more deeply entrenched. The freed black now had readier access to the law, yet it was a law still largely determined by the old regime.

As befitted the trend toward *laissez faire*, even less attempt was made to legislate fair and standard wage scales than during the apprenticeship period. This threw the "free" workers who had to work for wages disastrously upon the law of labor supply and demand, so that there were damaging variations from colony to colony, season to season, and year to year. In colonies like Trinidad, while the needs of the expanding plantations outran the labor supply, masters were compelled to pay wages that they claimed were ruinous (though few if any were, in fact, ruined by their wage bills) and that gave regular workers the prospect of a modest living. Yet in less fortunate islands, workers with no alternative were forced to compete with each other and were consequently paid wages only a fraction of the Trinidad levels. In some cases free laborers worked for board and subsistence alone.[21]

Equally unsatisfactory was the periodicity of wage labor caused by the nature of sugar husbandry, a blight that has continued to the present day. Sugar estates required as much as four times the work force during the five months of the crop than during the *tempo moto,* or intercrop period, and after slavery ended, planters were not compelled to maintain their entire labor force throughout the year. In practice they were often forced to provide more continuity of employment than was minimally necessary in order to ensure labor when most needed, and detailed work on wage bills in the years after 1838 may show that there was far less of a general exodus from the estates than is described by many writers.[22] But in years of poor prices and profits, or as the sugar industry gradually declined, it was always the wage bills that were cut back first and the laborers who suffered most. Naturally, for these reasons alone, the free blacks were reluctant to continue working on the estates, though they were almost always therefore castigated by the planters as unreliable and lazy.

"Free labor" in practice meant the freedom of the planters to employ labor only when they wished. The cruel dilemma is admirably illustrated by an exchange that occurred between a planter and one of the committeemen in the parliamentary inquiry presided over by Lord Bentinck in 1848. It was suggested that the lack of continuous labor was the fault not of the blacks but of the planters. This was hotly challenged.

> PLANTER: I think that the Negroes having set the example in the matter of not having given continuous labour, it is very possible that the planters may not have given them continuous work, but all the estates which are actually at work, I have reason to believe, would give as much continuous employment as they possibly could.
>
> COMMITTEEMAN: What you want is this, that at any moment when it suits your convenience you may be able to put your hand on the labourer?
>
> PLANTER: Undoubtedly. You could not have better expressed my meaning.
>
> COMMITTEEMAN: Can you expect to do that, unless you give continuous employment at continuous wages?
>
> PLANTER: Certainly not; there are duties on the one side and the other.[23]

One of the most debated issues was the way in which planters tried to tie their workers by the need for accommodation or the reluctance to move. In the very last days of apprenticeship, for example, Governor Smith of Jamaica visited twelve parishes, pointedly telling the blacks that they held no freehold on their huts and grounds and that henceforward they might be expected to pay rent. Emancipation threatened to be followed by a wave of evictions comparable only to the Scottish Highland clearances of much the same period. Turning the freedmen out of the houses they had lived in and off the lands they had worked in some cases for generations, and away from the sacred burial places of their kin, would be a traumatic shock almost as severe as the Middle Passage in the description of Stanley Elkins. Consequently, a very large proportion elected to stay, thus providing the estates with at least a potential continuously resident work force. The extraction of rent (for the short period in which this proved possible) provided an additional incentive for the freedmen to work for wages, while also helping to reduce the estates' wage bills.

Differing interpretations of vagrancy also led to serious conflicts between the imperial government and the self-legislating colonies. Islands like Jamaica wished to use an extremely flexible definition in order both to keep the blacks in continuous employment and to continue the elements of social control by legislation from slavery days. The orders-in-council of 1838 defined vagrants carefully to include all such social undesirables as prostitutes, beggars, gamblers, fortune tellers, those guilty of "indecency" and those found with housebreaking tools or weapons. But also included were those "persons wilfully refusing to support themselves and their families." Many of the bad old laws limiting the activities of freed blacks had been repealed during the amelioration period, but the less enlightened colonies continued to pass laws giving wide definitions of disorderly conduct and riotous assembly. Even if these were refused imperial assent, the magistrates commonly indulged in their own definitions of right and wrong. Besides this, all the self-legislating colonies attempted to raise the official qualifications for membership of the assembly and grand juries and for the franchise, while at the same time, practice usually decreed that these requirements continued to be waived in the case of whites.

The question of the militia also opened up a snakes' nest of problems. In slavery days the militia had been regarded as indispensable for defense, both against outside attack and internal rebellion. In a system that dates back as far as Harrington's *Oceana* (1656), the militia had always been the military arm of the propertied classes. As a mark of the assimilation of the free coloreds, it had, with considerable reluctance, been extended to include them before 1838. Yet when all blacks became free, it was considered socially dangerous (and in the light of the militia's social role, socially nonsensical) to allow ex-slaves eligibility, even with more stringent property qualifications. The colonial militia thus began to discriminate even more on the basis of color, and as this failed to keep out colored persons, the militia forces themselves gradually faded—hastened into extinction by the realistic argument that in the age of free trade and universal peace they were no longer needed for defense.

In the militia's place, however, a colonial police force was created almost from the very moment of emancipation. This had much to commend itself to imperialists and white oligarchs alike. To enlightened men at Westminster the existence of a neutral force would help to suppress crime and possible violence, while taking these duties ostensibly out of the hands of such men as had organized the counterviolent Colonial Church Union in Jamaica in 1832. The presence of a permanent professional police force—in the British West Indies traditionally of a quasimilitary nature and often recruited solely from outside each island—working closely with the magistracy was also reassuring to the local ruling classes. The fact that the colonial police forces gained and never lost a reputation for impartiality and moderation, reflecting the developments in the police forces of the metropolis on which they were based, was a triumph for all responsible.

The weak attempts to transplant British conceptions of social legislation were far less successful. The law to facilitate marriage by giving all ministers the right to publish banns and perform weddings, had the salutary effect of helping to break the stultifying monopoly of the Established Church. Yet the narrow philanthropic origins of the changes, which were based on an assumption that a British-style marriage on Christian precepts was the only way to achieve social stability at the family level, became in itself a cramping influence. The insistence on the formalization, and thus the expense, of weddings, and the reluctance to accept the validity of common-law unions or those based upon non-Christian rites, exacerbated the very problems they were intended to resolve. Matrifocal families and technical illegitimacy remained the norms, regarded as stigmas only by the small aspiring middle class of the most assimilated. The ultimate absurdity was that as they became established in the plantation colonies, even the East Indians, though they resolutely refused to be assimilated, began to follow similar patterns of family disruption and "illegitimacy." This was partly because, like the original slaves, they had a dangerous preponderance of males, but also because the civil authorities refused to accept their ethnic marriage customs as legitimate.[24]

The colonial poor law was similarly ill-conceived, though its principles were no worse than those of the British Poor Law Amendment Act of 1834, with its insistence that the poor should not be an expense on the government, its implication that poverty was not a misfortune but a crime, and its emphasis on workhouses that were much like prisons. "The principle on which the workhouse system rests is simple and intelligible," an overbearing Colonial Office official wrote in 1839:

> It consists in this, that the relief afforded to the destitute, at the expense of the community, should be afforded in such a manner as to render the condition of those who receive it less desirable than that of the independent labourer, or those who, by their previous industry, or the aid of their friends, have the means of self-support.[25]

As to education, the Colonial Office was scarcely more enlightened. Under philanthropic pressure a pitifully small annual grant of £30,000 had been made for the education of the ex-slaves, but, significantly, it was to be administered by the four chief missionary societies, with the help of the charity founded by the eccentric Lady Mico in 1690. So entrenched had the notion become that the state should not meddle in such a delicate matter as education that the crucial circulars of 1838 paid no heed to the educational needs of the colonies, and as the principles of *laissez faire* became yet more firmly rooted at Westminster, the colonial education grant was gradually reduced from 1841 onward, and in 1846 it was abolished altogether.[26] Thereafter for at least 50 years, colonial education was left to colonial authorities themselves. While this was a splendid chance for the development of an indigenous education system, in practice it meant that nothing was done in the way of support or regulation. What education there was remained the privilege of the at least moderately wealthy and continued to be riddled with racism, class consciousness, and sectarianism. Moreover, the type of education was disastrously unsuited to either practical affairs or the development of a creole consciousness.

A far more serious concern for both the Colonial Office and the plantocracy was the occupation by the freed blacks of lands to which they held no legal title, an activity disparagingly called "squatting." To the officials and planters it was a dangerous tendency, though from the point of view of the blacks the unencouraged creation of a free peasantry of which squatting was a part was one of the proudest chapters in the whole history of the colonial period.

The interest of the planters in being able to "put their hand on" their work force whenever needed has already been touched upon. This selfish concern received fortuitous support, however, in the doctrine of the "sufficient price" for land evolved by Edward Gibbon Wakefield, which was gradually gaining ascendancy in imperial policy. Wakefield argued that agriculture in the colonies could only prosper if impecunious laborers were kept from possessing their own lands by placing a sufficiently high price on unadopted Crown lands. Unable to acquire lands until they had accumulated savings, the working class would therefore work diligently for wages. Besides this, the money collected from Crown lands sales could be used to encourage immigration, which would fill the gaps caused by the emergence of the laborers into a modest landowning class.[27]

Wakefield's self-generating labor plan was beguilingly logical, but of dubious applicability even in colonies of white settlement such as Australia, New Zealand, and Canada during the age of wholesale European emigration. As to the tropical plantation colonies, it was almost certainly unworkable, though Wakefield saw it as a universal panacea. "It was the cheapness of land that brought African slaves to Antigua and Barbadoes," he wrote in 1849,

> and it is a comparative dearness of land, arising from the increase of population in those small islands, which has made them an exception from the general rule of West Indian impoverishment in consequence of the abolition of slavery before land was made dear.[28]

The chief flaw in this argument was that it was not the high price of land that made squatting rare in Antigua and Barbados, but its unavailability. The example of other colonies showed that where much undeveloped land existed, nothing could prevent its development by free peasants, whether they paid for it or not. The plantation colonies were also to demonstrate that the tendency of a "free labor" system is inevitably to press wages down to, and below, the level needed for subsistence.

The situation varied subtly between the Crown colonies and the self-legislating colonies, and between those with large areas of undeveloped Crown land and those with much of the land already patented. Trinidad was especially subject both to imperial regulation and to squatting. Of nearly a million fertile acres only 208,000 were in private ownership in 1838, of which a mere 43,000 were cultivated. The order-in-council of October 6, 1838, laid down a minimum price of £1 per acre for Crown lands, with a minimum lot of 340 acres (soon raised to 680 acres), which made it virtually impossible for the freed blacks to purchase a holding. Wholesale squatting occurred, not only on the fringes of settlements where work on estates was still possible, but also on the east coast and deep in the interior, free from government interference but without the opportunity of wage labor. In 1847 Governor Lord Harris removed the limit on the size of holdings and granted a liberal amnesty for squatters (charging as little as 6s. per acre for lands worked before December 1838), but at the same time the minimum price for Crown land newly acquired was raised to £2 per acre.[29] Although over a thousand squatters filed for their freeholds, in fact the number who completed their purchase was less than 300 and the problem of Trinidad in squatting remained unsolved.

In Guyana the area of "waste" Crown land was almost illimitable, but most of it was of dubious quality or unworkable by peasant farmers. The most attractive lands were on the margins of estates or on ruinate sugar land still privately owned. In order to keep the labor force close to the estates, or at least regain some of their capital, the planter-proprietors therefore competed with the Crown lands commissioners in offering their unwanted lands very cheaply. The result was that already by 1844 there were at least 19,000 ex-slaves living in their own cottages on freehold lands that they had purchased since 1838, many of them in villages where the land was jointly owned. By 1848 their numbers had at least doubled.[30]

In the remaining colonies, nearly all the land was already under plantocratic ownership even where it was not suitable for plantations. Squatting was therefore quite easily controlled, and in most colonies it only occurred on a large scale once the plantations had finally decayed. By that time the landowners had neither the need for labor nor the will to make evictions, while at the same time the blacks had not the money to purchase freeholds or even pay rent, and needed land simply to avoid starvation.

Jamaica was exceptional. An island more than twice the size of Trinidad, though with little more really fertile land, it had been remarkably heavily patented in the days of its expansion by selfish individuals aiming to forestall competition. It was also broken country. What Crown land there was, was difficult to supervise, and even on the wooded and hilly margins of working estates squatters could farm undetected for years. In 1838 probably no more than half the cultivable land had ever been put to use, and perhaps a quarter of the sugar lands had already fallen out of cultivation. For all these reasons Jamaica was almost the ideal country for the development of a free peasantry.

Few of the freed slaves in Jamaica seem to have bothered to take out patents for uncleared Crown lands at Wakefieldian prices, yet what analysis has been made of the subdivision of lands already in private hands demonstrates a revolutionary transition. Between 1840 and 1845 alone the number of holdings over 1,000 acres fell from at least 755 to about 650, while at the same time the small holdings of under 10 acres increased from about 900 to well over 20,000. By 1846 it was reported that in the eight years since emancipation the freed blacks had acquired 100,000 acres by purchase alone and had built nearly 200 free villages. The amount of land under cultivation by squatters in addition can only be guessed at, though by 1854, when only 330 sugar estates remained, as many as 300,000 Jamaicans were being supported by peasant farming.[31]

Missionaries such as William Knibb and James Phillippo, who had helped to found free villages, wrote glowingly of the progress made by the freedmen. Although he suffered from the optimist's habit of describing the best as typical, Phillippo in 1843 pictured life in the free villages as little short of idyllic. The oblong plots were spaciously laid out on intersecting streets with ample room at the back of the

	Under 10 acres	10–20	20–50	50–250	250+
Surrey[32]					
1840	219	192	206	275	383
1845	2,890	318	226	274	346
Middlesex[33]					
1840	364	309	434	713	900
1845	12,811	1,017	667	633	816
Cornwall					
1840	1,013	237	369	481	633
1845	5,023	777	539	472	570
Jamaica Total					
1840	883	938	1,009	1,469	1,916
1845	20,724	2,112	1,432	1,378	1,732

Table 22. Jamaica: Redistribution of Land Holdings, 1840–45[34]

houses for keeping fowls and pigs and growing vegetables and fruits, and the small space in the front sometimes "cultivated in the style of a European garden, displaying rose-bushes, and other flowering shrubs, among the choicer vegetable productions . . . and fruits of the country heterogeneously intermixed. . . ."

In contrast to the miserable cabins of the slave plantations (or the squalid barracks later given to the Indian "coolies"), the cottages were neat and positively cozy. Built of whitewashed wood or even stone and roofed with shingle or thatch, they often had ornamented porticoes in front and if not glass in their windows, jalousies and shutters. Inside, said Phillippo,

there is usually a sleeping apartment at each end and a sitting room in the centre. The floors are in most instances terraced, although boarded ones for sleeping-rooms are becoming common. Many of the latter contain good mahogany bedsteads, a washing-stand, a looking-glass and chairs. The middle apartment is usually furnished with a sideboard, displaying sundry articles of crockery ware, some decent-looking chairs, and not infrequently with a few broadsheets of the Tract Society hung around the walls in neat frames of cedar.[35]

Phillippo's free settlers were proud, ambitious, respectable: veritable "petty bourgeois." The true squatters lived a less settled, less orderly life, yet at the same time were even more self-reliant and not necessarily less prosperous. Maps drawn up later in the century by the Crown surveyors show that they lived in small scattered houses close to the lands they cultivated, often in forest clearings or on irregularly shaped pockets of fertile soil deep or high in the hills. Lacking security of tenure and often shifting their cultivation, they rarely built substantially. A typical squatter's shack was built of unpainted boards, raised above running rainwater on stones, and roofed with palmetto thatch. Some were only lived in during certain seasons, and many squatters lived an almost nomadic life, being particularly eager to fade away on the rare appearance of surveyor, tax collector, or agent of an alleged patentee. Yet with fewer needs and without the expense and responsibility of freehold lands or elaborate houses and furniture, the squatters were not only less tied to a single location, but were also far less subject than the village freeholders to serious fluctuations in the general economic situation. While produce prices remained reasonably high and fertile land was abundant, the squatter came closest to the ideal of the truly independent peasant.

THE COLONIAL FREEDMEN: DECLINE, 1846–1945

Throughout the plantation colonies the period between 1838 and 1846 was one of expansion and optimism for the freed blacks, if not to the same degree for the planters. The large-scale purchase of freeholds, the establishment of free villages and markets, the immediate diversification of the farming economy, and the sudden expansion of the cash economy were magnificent achievements. At the same time the steady increase in savings, the export of crops grown on small holdings rather than on large estates, and even the revelation in the returns of the first official colonial census in 1844 that the population was naturally increasing for the first time, pointed to continuing improvement. Even the sugar industry, despite its monotonous complaints of the scarcity and high cost of labor, recovered in 1842 from the steady slide of the 1830s and seemed to have stabilized itself.

In 1846, however, a twin disaster struck the plantation colonies, with an inimical imperial policy exacerbating the effects of an economic collapse beyond human regulation. In 1846 the great economic debate reached a climax in an overwhelming victory for the free traders. Within a year the imperial Parliament voted to end the selfish protectionism of the English landed class by repealing the Corn Laws and to remove the preferential sugar duties, which still provided protection to colonial planters equivalent to about 10 percent of production costs in a normal year. Unfortunately, the Irish potato blight, which accelerated the repeal of the Corn Laws, was part of a European malaise, and famine formed the background for a worldwide economic slump. While faced with the loss of any protective advantage through the repeal of the sugar duties, the planters were confronted with a disastrous collapse in sugar prices through the inability of distressed European consumers to buy, and with the total evaporation of credit as the result of the collapse of many businesses involved in plantation trade.

For their part, the freed blacks and their complacent philanthropic allies discovered with dismay that they were not so independent of the general plantation economy as they had thought. The sugar economy proved still to be more a determinant than a mere indicator of colonial prosperity. Relative prosperity for sugar meant a good flow of wages, a reliable market for "ground provisions" not only in the towns but also on the estates too dedicated to monoculture to grow their own, a plentiful supply of cash, and easy local credit. Moreover, the relative independence of the freed blacks since 1838 had been based on the assumption that plantation employment was still available when needed. Now, as sugar prices fell below the cost of production, planters for the first time were genuinely unable to afford the wages that were needed to "prime the pump" of the colonial economy.

Between 1846 and 1849, the debate that was to determine the fate of the plantation colonies sputtered on in Parliament, where the "philanthropic" lobby became not only numerically weaker but ideologically confused. Just as Sir Robert Peel and his disciple W. E. Gladstone (their family fortunes based, respectively, on Manchester and Liverpool) changed gradually from protectionism and the defense of the sugar-slavery interest to a doctrinaire belief in free trade and *laissez faire*, so the rearguard of philanthropists at Westminster switched from implacable opposition to the planters to a selective defense of protectionism and of the planters' interest, whereby it was hoped that the gains made by the freed slaves would be preserved. The blacks' friends were sustained by the fact that the sugar that the free traders wished to bring cheaply into England (like the cotton from the United States) was grown with slave labor, in Cuba, Brazil, and Louisiana. By an ironic and confusing twist, the "free" sugar, which in the 1820s depended on free trade and the ending of West Indian protection, now required the continuation of the sugar duties and the arrest of free trade.[36]

A painstaking parliamentary Select Committee

under Lord Bentinck in 1847–48 exposed conditions in the plantation colonies and vindicated the philanthropists' arguments irrefutably.[37] Yet the tide of free trade was inexorable. All that was achieved was the postponement of the final removal of the sugar duties from 1851 to 1854, and the passage in 1854 of the West Indian Encumbered Estates Act, aimed at aiding West Indian planters in the dissolution of their properties—largely on behalf of metropolitan creditors.[38]

Imperial cynicism had triumphed in the names of free trade, *laissez faire,* and retrenchment, winning over the Colonial Office as well as Parliament. In the same year as the ending of the preferential sugar duties and the passage of the Encumbered Estates Act, a separate Cabinet post of Colonial Secretary was created. Yet this effectively placed colonial policy more firmly in parliamentary hands and made it progressively more difficult for enlightened professional officials such as James Stephen to swim against the tide. Although there were periods of slight recovery in the sugar industry, and consequently in the plantation colonies as a whole at roughly ten-year intervals, these were the result of fortuitous fluctuations in the freed world economy and not of changes in official British policy. Generally speaking, after 1846 the diversification of the economy in the plantation colonies was no longer a cause for optimism on behalf of the freed blacks, but rather a desperate necessity for sheer subsistence.

Moreover, on the rare occasions when the imperial government aroused itself to consider the plantation colonies, it was almost invariably on behalf of the planters. This is well illustrated by the sporadic encouragement given to schemes to import cheap labor. It was the .age of general European emigration, in which nearly two million left Ireland alone. But the ideas of the "colonial reformers" of encouraging all forms of emigration were as inapplicable to the planta-

tion colonies as the Wakefieldian notion of the sufficient price for land.

All sources were scoured for labor, not only on behalf of those colonies such as Trinidad, Guyana, and
Mauritius, where the shortage of labor was demon-
strably one of the chief reasons for the stagnation of
the sugar plantations, but also on behalf of those in
which the planter could not "put his hand on" the
"lazy and intransigent" blacks. The basis had already
been laid by 1850. After successive failures to recruit
large numbers of freed blacks from overpopulated
islands, American blacks (unattracted by the prospects
of "freedom" in the West Indies), unassimilated
Africans, distressed British and continental laborers,
and Madeiran Portuguese, the West Indian plantations followed the example of Mauritius and turned
to Asia, particularly British India.[39]

Between 1834 and 1849 Mauritius imported no less
than 116,000 coolie laborers from India, ostensibly to
fill the gaps caused by the unwillingness of the blacks
to work for estates after emancipation, but making it
impossible, after the collapse of 1847, for the blacks
to return in any case. In 1846 it was reported of the
Mauritian blacks that

> they have disappeared from agricultural labour, from
> the precincts of the plantations, from any contact with
> the whites; that they are left to make their own way
> in this world, and to another world.[40]

The numbers of the Mauritian blacks may in fact have
declined by a third in the decade after emancipation.[41]

For reasons of distance alone the East Indians were
unlikely to supplant the blacks so suddenly, drastically, and completely in the West Indies as in Mauritius. Yet, beginning with the arrival of the first batch
of indentured coolies in Guyana in 1838, the West
Indies began that spasmodic influx of fresh laborers
that lasted until 1917, and that produced in due

course an almost equal ethnic balance between black and East Indian in both Guyana and Trinidad.[42] Generally cheerful workers and frugal livers, the East Indians were encouraged to remain after their indentures had expired so that over the whole period of their immigration only about one in four returned to India. Imported in periods of comparative prosperity and thus of both labor shortage and the availability of capital for immigration loans, the newcomers were particularly resented during the intervening periods of slump.

Altogether, between 1838 and 1917 no less than 238,000 East Indians were brought to Guyana and 145,000 to Trinidad, of whom 383,000 only 95,000 returned to India. East Indians as well as Chinese were also imported in considerable numbers into those colonies like Jamaica without a strict labor need for them, and in which the natural increase in population by far outran any measurable increase in labor needs. This superfluous influx resulted only partly from the freed blacks' unwillingness to work on plantations on the masters' terms. It was as much the result of the planters' search for a labor force more tightly tied to them, and the imperial government's misguided gratification of this selfish wish.

The fate of the different sugar colonies during the period of *laissez faire* and coolie immigration was clearly uneven. Conditions were relatively better in those "low density" colonies like Trinidad and Guyana that enjoyed advantages leading to cheaper production once the labor problem had been solved. To a certain extent this can be traced by comparing the scale of sugar production. Between 1814 and 1866, the annual total of sugar produced in Guyana multiplied three times, while the production of Jamaica declined to a third. Production in the Leewards remained roughly stationary and that of the Windwards fell by about 35 percent. The only apparent anomaly was Barbados—with the highest population density and intensity of cultivation—where production rose from an annual average of 11,622 tons between 1814 and 1823, to 36,367 tons between 1857 and 1866. W. A. Green has attributed this increase—as well as Barbados' marginally greater degree of prosperity—to the island's "orderliness."[43] Within this term, Green includes the continuing presence of resident planters and the lack of labor mobility, the low number of abandoned estates, paternalism, and a readiness on the part of the laborers to accept low wages in the face of a relatively low cost of living and the lack of viable alternatives.

The advantages accruing from greater production were, however, severely limited when the world price of sugar fell toward, and occasionally below, the cost of production, and in these periods—more common as the nineteenth century progressed—the social problems occasioned by the importation of coolie laborers were cruelly exacerbated.

	1815	1828	1882	1894
Jamaica	79,660	72,198	32,638	19,934
Barbados	8,837	16,942	48,325	50,958
Leewards	20,264	19,074	31,648	31,084
Trinidad	7,682	13,285	55,327	19,934
Guyana	16,520	40,115	124,102	102,502
Total B.W.I.	168,077	202,396	315,138	260,211
Cuba	39,961	72,635	595,000	1,054,214

British West Indies Sugar Production, 1814–66 (in Thousands of Tons).[44]

There is a crucial difference between those who chose to go to the plantations and then chose to stay, and those who had no choice in either respect; yet although the East Indians were much slower than the Africans to adapt to creole culture, the lot of both races became increasingly common in adversity. It was only in contrast to conditions in India that the lot of the East Indian coolies was tolerable, or even much better than formal slavery. Moreover, once the Indians' indentures had expired, black and Indian proletarians alike began to suffer (as to a certain extent, they still suffer) the ordeal of labor competition in a so-called "free labor" system. Social problems, however, were worse in those colonies, notably Jamaica, where they were not accompanied by economic expansion but by regression.

The Jamaican affair of 1865–66 was a sad symptom of the cynicism of the official imperial mind during the heyday of *laissez faire* and provided ample evidence of the decay of philanthropic feeling that had occurred since emancipation. By 1865 Jamaica was tinder dry. From the beginning of the decade a modest economic recovery had been set back by a further slump in produce prices, accompanied by an exaggerated war scare and the desperate hysteria of the Baptist revival of 1860–61. The arrival of an intemperate and short-sighted governor, Edward Eyre, exacerbated the political dissatisfactions of the emergent colored middle class, while he failed to remedy or even investigate growing popular unrest. Short-term disasters of flood followed by drought and disease in the midst of the economic slump were met with the sublime fatuity of the so-called Queen's Advice in June 1865, signed by Colonial Secretary Edward Cardwell but originally drafted by Permanent Under Secretary Henry Taylor:

> I request that you will inform the Petitioners that their Petition has been laid before the Queen, and that I have received Her Majesty's command to inform them that the prosperity of the Labouring Classes, as well as of all other Classes, depends, in Jamaica, as in other Countries, upon their working for Wages, not uncertainly or capriciously, but steadily and continuously, at the times when their labour is wanted, and for so long

as it is wanted; and that if they would use this industry, and thereby render the Plantations productive, they would enable the Planters to pay them higher Wages for the same hours of work than are received by the best Field Labourers in the Country; and as the cost of the necessaries of life is much less in Jamaica than it is here, they would be enabled, by adding prudence to industry, to lay by an ample provision for seasons of drought and dearth; and they may be assured that it is from their own industry and prudence, in availing themselves of the means of prospering that are before them, and not from any such schemes as have been suggested to them, that they must look for an improvement in their condition; and that Her Majesty will regard with interest and satisfaction their advancement through their own merits and efforts.[45]

Local grievances, concerned chiefly with the administration of justice by corrupt officials in one of the most depressed parishes, led to the conflagration at Morant Bay in October 1865. The killing of 22, the wounding of 34, and the burning of 5 buildings by the rioters was immediately followed by savage countermeasures, in the retributive style familiar from rebellions in slavery days. Martial law was declared, nearly 100 persons were shot or hanged without trial, 354 were judicially murdered, 600 men and women were flogged, and nearly 1,000 dwellings were destroyed.

When the news of Morant Bay reached England there was a furor that split the country. Exeter Hall once more became the scene of a fervent campaign against colonial brutality, reminiscent of the 1780s and 1830s. A Jamaica Committee was formed—which consisted largely of elderly nonconformist ministers and such men as the sons of T. F. Buxton—with the intention of prosecuting Governor Eyre and his "accomplices." The most distinguished adherents of the Jamaica Committee were the liberal philosopher John Stuart Mill and the brilliant scientist Thomas H. Huxley. Huxley's mentor, Charles Darwin, whose *Origin of Species* had been published in 1859, lent the weight of his name. On the opposite side were ranged such literary lions as Kingsley and Froude (both of whom were later to write negrophobic accounts of the West Indies), Ruskin, Tennyson, and Dickens—all following the lead of Thomas Carlyle, who had produced his shameful *Occasional Discourse on the Nigger Question* at the time of the sugar duties debate in 1849. Broadly speaking, these latter people were Tories, who ascribed the troubles in India and Jamaica alike to the weaknesses of liberal theorists and the gullibility of Christian missionaries toward races that were obviously destined to be ruled. It was for these that Disraeli was to speak in his famous Crystal Palace speech in 1872.

At one level, it is therefore possible to see the Governor Eyre controversy as being posed between, on the one hand, liberal philanthropists and scientific Darwinists who believed in the blacks' evolutionary perfectibility, and, on the other, those who for different reasons believed in the inherent and immutable superiority of the Anglo-Saxon race and its destiny to rule, who were to find their dogma in Herbert Spencer's popular distortion of Darwin's idea of "the survival of the fittest." This, however, would be to oversimplify. Also subscribing to the Jamaica Committee were certain Comtian positivists who were certainly not democrats or opposed to imperial ideas. Frederic Harrison, for example, attacked Eyre not because Eyre was undemocratic and racist but on the principle that if British rule was to prevail (as prevail it should), it should be just. "The precise issue we raise is this," wrote Harrison,

> that through our empire the British rule shall be the rule of law; that every British citizen, white, brown, or black in skin, shall be subject to definite, and not to indefinite powers. . . . Come what may, our colonial rule shall not be bolstered up by useful excess or irresponsible force. . . . The terrible Indian rebellion has sown evil seeds enough in the military as well as in the

civil system. It called out the tiger in our race. . . .
That wild beast must be tamed.[46]

This was the principle of trusteeship, but imperialism
nonetheless. The division in the Eyre controversy was
therefore not so much between imperialism and anti-
imperialism as between two types of imperialism. That
which was to prevail was the neomandarinism of the
British raj in India—inflexible justice accompanied by
apartheid and the slowing down not only of forcible
Westernization but also of constitutional advance.
However, in the West Indies this basic attitude was to
be accompanied by an indifference amounting to contempt.

A parliamentary inquiry praised Eyre's prompt and
forthright action, though it criticized some of its
effects. Eyre himself was allowed to retire, and after
the failure of the attempt to prosecute him, he was
eventually reimbursed for his expenses in the prosecution case, not by the Tory government that he had
served but by the Liberal government of W. E. Gladstone, which had succeeded it in 1868. The campaign
against Eyre, moreover, gained only limited popular
support. In June 1868, the liberal *Spectator* reckoned that nine tenths of the country was already
following the lead of its economic superiors:

> The upper and middle class of the English people,
> *especially* the latter . . . are positively enraged at the
> demand of Negroes for equal consideration with Irish-
> men, Scotsmen and Englishmen . . . proceedings which
> would have cost the most well-meaning of weak-judg-
> ing men his head if they had taken place in the United
> Kingdom—which would have been received with shouts
> of execration if they had taken place in France or
> Austria—are heartily admired as examples of "strong
> government" when they take place in the British West
> Indies.[47]

The direct effects of the Jamaican rebellion of 1865
on the plantation colonies and their people were few,
and none for the better. Jamaica lost her ridiculously

unrepresentative Assembly in 1866, as in due course did all the self-legislating colonies save Barbados, the Bahamas, and Bermuda. But the Jamaican Assembly voted its own dissolution on the well-founded assumption of its oligarchic members that they would thereby retain practical power through appointment to the executive and legislative councils. For the ordinary people the hope of truly representative government faded into the distant future. Indeed, it was during the period of Crown colony rule that the mass of the people suffered most from local harassment as well as from the effects of the prolonged general depression and increasing population pressure. In most colonies the poor were taxed inordinately, harried by the magistrates for petty offenses, and discriminated against in trade. In Jamaica, for example, the "higglers" of peasant-grown vegetables were prosecuted if they had not bought a license, while many unofficial markets were closed down in the course of regulation. At the same time waves of squatter evictions occurred, either when an owner wished to "improve" his land by turning it into cattle runs, or to sell it with uncluttered tenure, or when the Crown Lands Office was occupied by a surveyor nagged by that Victorian devil, efficiency. An untold number of evictions occurred in Jamaica because of the Crown Land Law of 1867, which was merely aimed at the regulation of government leaseholds but led to the repossession of 275,000 acres of alienated lands. Even the Small Holdings Law of 1895, ostensibly aimed at making it easy for peasants to acquire small freeholds, in many cases had opposite effects from those intended, many estate owners taking the opportunity to regularize tenancies loosely held, for fear they would be alienated forever.[48]

For a whole century after 1846 the freed blacks had need of powers of endurance nearly equal to those that had helped them to survive slavery. A description of the lot of the common Jamaican people given before the Parliamentary Commission of 1897—one of those massive nineteenth-century exercises in futility that simply provided maps of oblivion—can serve both as the epitaph of the hopes of August 1, 1838 and as a description of the black man's fate for a further 50 years. The Reverend Henry Clarke, one of the few humanitarian members of the governors' councils, was asked how the condition of the people had changed in the 50 years he had served them. "There is no general improvement as far as the people are concerned," he replied. "They are not any better off in their houses or in their moral conditions than when I first came to the country [in 1846]."

The people, asserted Clarke, worked with a will when wages were fair, but understandably were not willing to work on the shilling a day that was the normal wage when work was available because this was sufficient to support their families. With a population over double what it was in slavery days, though cultivation was down to a quarter, the planters could not reasonably complain of a lack of labor; yet they had several times persuaded the government to increase the island's debt by granting loans to import Indian and Chinese coolies, with the express intention of reducing wage levels still farther.

At the same time peasant proprietorship was still discouraged. The number of freeholds under five acres had risen from 15,000 to 72,000, yet only 181,000 acres in all were filled, while 1,250,000 acres of "ruinate" land remained in private hands and an additional 750,000 acres of Crown lands were unassigned.

While almost nothing had been done in the way of education, road-building, sanitation, and health services for the rural areas, the brunt of taxation fell upon the mass of the peasants. Unlike Britain, Jamaica had no income tax, and the majority of the colony's revenue came from indirect taxes (which, for example, made bread twice as dear as in England), from a house tax, and from a tax on land that charged those with one acre five shillings, those with more than 1,000 a farthing an acre, and those over 10,000 nothing.

Henry Clarke pointed out that the 700,000 inhabitants of Jamaica lived in 82,500 houses, an average of 8½ to each where (despite Phillippo's description in 1843) few houses had more than one bedroom. Besides being drastically unhealthy, such overcrowding was obviously demoralizing. Asked what possible concern the regulation of the morals of blacks could be of the imperial government, Henry Clarke replied, "The Government ought to know how to manage the country. . . . It is the function of the Government to see after the welfare of the people."

"Does any Government do this?" he was angrily asked. "Do you want a new sort of Government?"

"It would simply be the Government observing the Ten Commandments," replied the unrepentant Clarke.[49]

The imperial government was to prove sadly resistant to such a simple yet radical conversion as the Reverend Henry Clarke suggested. Conditions in the plantation colonies were to be radically changed only when the will to rule was eroded by two world wars and, as a result of the Great Depression of the 1930s, the workers began to organize themselves into trade unions to confront their employers, and political parties to push for rapid constitutional change.

LINGERING TRACES

A stranger with some knowledge of slavery visiting the West Indies today is likely to detect a remarkable number of parallels, despite the passage of more than 130 years since emancipation, the achievement of political independence, and the relative decline of the plantation economy. Yet in distinguishing parallels from true effects these "flashes of recognition" can as easily mislead as enlighten. In summarizing the legacies and influences of plantation slavery it is necessary to exclude those effects that date from slavery days or earlier but were not necessarily related to slavery or the plantation system, those that were purely a product of the plantation economy and thus outlasted slavery, those that are products of modernization and modern poverty, and finally most of those social and economic phenomena attributed to slavery for political or ideological purposes and for the allocation of retroactive blame.

Even the most casual visitor becomes familiar with West Indian music, though too often in its most crassly commercialized forms. Behind the denatured yodeling of "calypso" groups at hotel poolsides or such artificial stimuli for off-peak tourism as the Bahamas "Goombay Summer," linger a vigorous tradition of extempore satirical folksong and a carnival tradition rich in folklore nuances. Both have a long history of syncretic development in which slavery was but one stage and post- and preslavery influences at least as important. The media have greatly widened the modern calypsonian's net, bringing him both a larger audience and a richer array of those characters who are the satirist's perennial butts: politicians, preachers, in-laws, hypocrites, snobs, deviants, cuckolds, the over- and the undersexed. His function and even his idioms, however, remain similar to those of the creator of digging, dancing, and ring songs on the plantation, and comparable to the weaver of musical stories common in Africa. But for the difficulties of understanding West Indian creole in Africa and African dialects of English in the Caribbean, there would doubtless be as easy an interchange of songs with stories as there is with new rhythmic variants, like the African High Life, which enjoyed a West Indian vogue in the 1950s and the Jamaican "Reggae" beat, which spread to much of the English-speaking world at the close of the 1960s.[50]

The pre-Lenten Carnival in Trinidad provides another obvious example of the consistent and indiscriminate development of Caribbean folk music. Many aspects—the contemporary relevance of the uniforms of the groups, the ubiquitous clangor of music coaxed from cut-down oil drums, the participation of East Indians—clearly date from postslavery days. Study of the nineteenth-century Carnival also shows that it was originally associated with the masked balls held by the élite around the time of the governor's review of the militia, and that it amalgamated with the *Cannes Brulées* (or Canboulay) celebration of emancipation, transferred from August 1. Its very timing, moreover, suggests a Christian rather than pagan origin. But so many similarities remain to the Christmas, Easter, cropover, and secret Yam Festival celebrations of the slave plantations of other islands—the finery, the masks, the reversal of roles, the hilarious parodies of well-known plantation characters—that it would be foolish not to carry the origins of Carnival back at least to slavery days.[51] Yet if to slavery days, why not beyond? As many writers have noted, such seasonal explosions as the "John Canoe" parades of Jamaica and other islands can easily be traced back to preslavery Africa, and forward again to variants in modern Africa. The very existence of different bands in the parades may owe its origins to the different tribes represented in plantation societies,[52] and the prevalence of masks and parody figures to the activities of West African secret societies.[53] The following quotation (taken from West Africa in the 1920s) might almost equally be an account of West Indian or West African carnival activity at any period from the sixteenth to the twentieth century. Following a feast of yams with drinking and dancing in honor of the dead, the procession began with masked novices in the lead. More practiced entertainers followed,

> headed by the barbaric noise of amateur musicians [who] move slowly amid the whistle and shouts and cheer of the hoarse admiring crowds. Buffoons with

weapons of bladder or cow-tail clear the way for the
dancers in their motley, shaking rattles. There follow
mimics and tumblers, contortionists and merry-an-
drews who gyrate about the road and lead an ever-
increasing crowd of riotous youth from the villages,
who sing and clap and try to help in the fun by attempts to copy the agile antics of the professionals.
Some of these latter have reputations that cause their
services to be very expensive. . . . The improvised
masks seen in this section are often native caricatures of
European Officials.[54]

Similar effects can be traced in West Indian religion,
especially when it is married to music. The fervor and
emotionalism of West Indian church services and
funerals still tend to be treated by whites with condescension as primitive. Sadly, until quite recently
such esoteric observances as those of the "Jumper"
sects of New Providence were treated as tourist
spectacles. What the gaping visitors did not recognize was that these rituals, with their brass band ac-
companiment, were as much musical as religious, and
as much European and Christian as purely African.
Secular music, however, is accepted more readily, the
"Afro" rhythms that make even Englishmen into
dancers in a year or two proving absolutely contagious. Music—the rhythm in the blood—and dancing—
the ritual prelude to or dramatic surrogate for sexual
coupling—have proved as much as sexuality itself to
be the racial solvents of West Indian society.[55] The
relation of music and religion to race and the creolization of culture are obvious; their relation to the
institution of slavery is far less clear.

Close to modern plantations the apparent links and
traces are clearer, particularly on sugar estates still
owned by local families and not by faceless foreign
corporations. Yet the question remains: Can effects
still be termed legacies when they are separated from
their alleged source by a length of time as long as the
period of slavery itself? Perhaps they should be re-

lated rather to the economic phenomenon of the plantation and the lingering effects of racial differences than to slavery strictly defined.

A foreign visitor staying on a sugar estate is likely to be shocked awake by the chattering sounds of the field workers trudging to work in the predawn mists, as if they were the ghosts of their slave predecessors. Even the crack of the whip can still be heard, though for controlling cattle rather than gangs of slaves. Only the sound of the blown conch shell is missing. Many of the workers still toil at much the same tasks of digging, banking, weeding, cutting, and carrying, working indeed harder, or more efficiently than slaves kept to an invariable daily round. Yet despite unionization and modest industrial benefits it is possible to come across gangs such as the groups of old women still used for weeding tasks, who seem much as described by Edwards or Roughley, squatting and singing and joshing the forewoman as they work.

Only the core of permanent laborers now live on the estates, and the crowded villages and scattered small plots that provide the far larger work forces needed during crop periods have only a limited number of connective links with the barracoon life of the old slave quarters. Writers like R. T. Smith, M. G. Smith, and Edith Clarke have shown that a wide range of subcultural patterns have grown up within free peasant society throughout the British Caribbean.[56] Yet within the incredibly wide radius that a man or woman can walk or cover on a donkey much dependence on the sugar estates remains—for casual wages, for tenancies, for a factory to process "farmer"-grown canes. In many areas, including whole islands like Nevis, it is therefore difficult to decide whether the predominant social type among the ordinary people is that of peasant or proletarian.[57]

For the regular workers changes have occurred, but imperceptibly. In an age of overpopulation, regular employment itself is often only achieved by dogged fidelity. The laborers most valued by employers are those who work hardest and cause least trouble, which in many places means East Indians rather than blacks. Yet everywhere under the influence of modernization—with its drift to the towns and away from crushing manual labor—there is a tendency for the mass of the estate workers to be the illiterate and unambitious if not also the middle-aged and elderly. The lowest stratum of plantation society thus tends toward perpetuation or even regression: weak, ignorant, and black.

Estate elites have also tended to survive with their functions and attitudes almost intact, the most obvious change being that the role of the *petits blancs* has largely been assumed by middle-class *petits bruns*. In return for their skills and their acceptance of the system, the class of craftsmen, foremen, office workers, and junior managers—collectively called "staff"— is rewarded with only moderate salaries but considerable prestige and valued perquisites such as good housing, large gardens, cheap food in the staff shop, and membership in a staff sports and social club. Status, as ever, acts as a conforming agent.

It is perhaps the planter class that has changed least of all. Predominantly white in black independent countries, it still retains considerable political influence through disproportionate economic power and ability to combine in such organizations as the Jamaican Sugar Manufacturers' Association. Moreover, as a class, modern planters show a remarkable tendency to identify with their eighteenth-century counterparts, even if they themselves are descended from latecomers into plantation ownership. For example, an Englishwoman who had married into a plantocratic family that had shifted from the poor white managerial to the owner class only after 1846, was horrified at the suggestion that the island of her residence now belonged to the blacks as well as to the members of that class she had adopted. "Who

brought them here in the first place then?" she asked
in a tone that declared the question closed.

Such ingenuous atavism is still lamentably common. The more insensitive members of plantation
families will discuss the failings of domestics or blacks
in general as if their own servants were deaf as well
as mute. An embarrassed outsider is likely to be
regaled with complaints that the servants are unreliable, larcenous, and stupid in almost the same breath
as accounts are proudly given of the expenditure of
the amount of a domestic's annual wage in a single
senseless purchase.[58] "I could see the signs coming,"
said one employer, describing the sacking of one of
his houseboys. "The week previous he had used
his wages to buy a transistor radio and a pair of dark
glasses." "You should do what I do with our boy Jack,"
consoled another. "Save most of his wages for him
and make sure he only gets money for sensible buys."

The positive side of such dominance is the affectionate paternalism that often accompanies it. In
both the above cases, the boys concerned had been
taken on as a favor to their mothers, long-trusted
domestics themselves. Many whites still acknowledge
black nannies who were once their surrogate mothers,
who are looked after in respectable comfort for the
rest of their days. Miscegenation also retains the disturbing attractions of an irrational taboo. "Black
women are only fit for one thing," claims a young
white in his cups, before discreetly driving off to
pledge his affections to his black mistress with an
extravagance denied his wife. Far more engaging
are those occasions such as anniversaries, "cropovers,"
or special public holidays, when the estate societies
unconsciously re-enact the "Planters' Christmas" of
the eighteenth century. At some stage of the evening
the white men will dance without self-consciousness
with the black plantation women, and their white
women be unaffectedly competed for as dancing
partners by the boldest of the respectable blacks. At

such times it is difficult to stereotype the whites as oppressors or the blacks as modern Quashies.

Similarly, the positive side of the anti-intellectual hedonism and conspicuous consumption of the planter class is the tradition of *noblesse oblige*, which keeps open house for fellow whites and a large number of unofficial black retainers dependent on "make work" or plain largess. Besides this, although some plantation whites still regard England as "home" and plan to retire there (or anywhere but their own island), and nearly all look abroad for their children's education, a high proportion feel an intense pride in their lands and in their country too, fearful and resentful only when they feel that the blacks now in power do not understand the peculiar institution of the plantation.

At a deeper level, misunderstandings on both sides about "Negro" customs and characteristics and their dubious attribution to slavery may help to worsen relations. One clear example is the debate over the continuing failure to create what is regarded by the European-oriented as a stable family structure.

Over the origins of the modern West Indian family, controversy continues to rage without final resolution. In the 1940s, M. J. Herskovits picked up the threads of many eighteenth-century commentators and suggested that the pattern of sequential matings and the consequent dominance of the mother and grandmother in family patterns noticed in slave society and modern New World black societies alike were derivative from West African polygamy:

> As for the father, he continued to play for the nuclear group the institutionally remote, somewhat secondary role that in Africa was his as the parent shared with the children of other mothers than one's own, a role that was transmuted into the more or less transitory position he holds in so many of the poorer families of New World societies. . . . This also explains the importance of the household in the rearing and training of

children. In essence, this is based on the retention . . . of the nucleus of African kinship structures which . . . consists of a mother and her children living in a hut within her husband's compound, also inhabited by her co-wives and their children. That this nuclear unit has evolved into such a household as the one headed by the elderly woman . . . where her grown daughters are still more or less under her direction and some of their children entirely given over to her care, merely represents in one respect the logical development of this African institution.[59]

Herskovits' analysis was criticized on two grounds: that slavery was so traumatic and pervasive that African links were severed, and that slavery itself conditioned family life. According to these views, African sexual taboos and restraints were submerged by the plantation system. On plantations slaves were treated as instruments of production and subjected to forms of social control to the degree that sexual relationships were dehumanized. The dissociation of coupling from human sentiments was said to be exacerbated by the constant buying and selling of slaves and their shifting from plantation to plantation, which made permanent or strong attachments unlikely. Within this world (though the causal relationship is never made quite clear) it was well known that the mother "held a strategic position and played a dominant role in family groupings. The tie between the mother and her younger children had to be respected not only because of the dependence of the child upon her for survival but often because of her fierce attachment to her brood."[60] So strong were the traditions engendered by slavery, these interpreters maintain, that the effects have lasted in black societies until the present day.

A third interpretation, however, maintains that informal or impermanent families, the consequent prevalence of technical illegitimacy, and the dependence upon mothers rather than fathers, are effects of postslavery society in the Caribbean in particular and of modernization and the "culture of poverty" in general. Certainly, the shifting and scattered nature of peasant agriculture, the discontinuity of estate labor, and the constant migration of male workers have contributed to the fact that the male is rarely a permanent provider—or even permanent—in Caribbean families. Tasks performed by the females, such as keeping the provision plots going, selling crops in the local markets, laundering, needlework, and other handicrafts, on the other hand, are not only necessary for subsistence but also more continuous than the occupations of many males. Added to this are the dislocating effects of towns common to all rural countries in the process of modernization. Males and the young migrate temporarily for work or a chance of work, leaving the older women and the very young behind in the rural areas.[61] Casual relationships develop in the overcrowded slum areas of the towns, with illegitimate offspring returned to the maternal grandmothers. Even more widespread are the effects of poverty in making marriage, and particularly weddings, irrelevant or impossible expenses in a life dedicated primarily to bare subsistence. It is only the moderately well-to-do who can afford respectability, only the very wealthy who can afford to emerge from respectability into elegant vice.

In the assessment of creole family patterns, ideologues are placed in a difficult position on several counts. If serial monogamy and matrifocalism are thought to be derived either from the slavery system or the subsequent history of poverty and deprivation, they are obviously to be deprecated. Yet once it is well established that it is the middle class of the most assimilated that has always provided the most enthusiastic advocates of marriage and the regular family as status symbols, good socialists are likely to regard such bourgeoisation as anathema, particularly as it has traditionally been such agents of assimilation to European norms as missionaries and well-wishing governors (and their wives) who have encouraged permanent marriage ties and the patri-focal family. Black socialists, on the other hand, are unable wholeheartedly to subscribe to the notion that serial monogamy and matriarchy derived from Africa, or that they are wholly good, because of the corollary, which would devalue the deleterious influence of slavery and postslavery deprivation.

The solution to this dilemma is, clearly, to conclude that present-day marriage, family, and kinship pat-terns in the Caribbean are, like all social functions, complex products of syncretization. Herskovits' sum-mary is perhaps still the best and least value-loaded. The nuclear matrifocal family, he claimed, merely represents the logical development of African insti-tutions "under the influence of slavery and of the particular socio-economic position of the Negroes after slavery was abolished."[62]

PRESENT AND FUTURE

Slavery, the plantation economy, and colonialism arouse an exaggerated animus today among radicals, black nationalists, and promoters of black conscious-ness, verging on the mythopoeic. This evil trinity, it is proclaimed, were not merely the origins of most modern ills; they have never been exorcised. Stripped of its political and racist rhetoric, this belief contains strong elements of plausibility, especially in the eco-nomic sphere. But the past, though it can be dis-torted or ignored, cannot be eliminated. Justice de-crees greater democracy, the spread of social benefits and, at the national level, economic independence— changes that may amount to, or require, a revolution. Yet solutions, to be effective as well as truly just, should take into account that ex-colonial society is not only made up of ex-slaves, and that neither the plantation economy in some form nor some dependence on outside help can be quickly dispensed with.

"The Jamaican worker loathes and hates the sugar estate and rightly so," wrote Orlando Patterson in 1969:

> It is my contention that it is immoral and perverse for anyone not to sympathise with and understand this dislike on the part of the rural working class. For if members of the rural upper classes and the urban middle classes have forgotten slavery and the horrible association of the sugar estates with that cruel and ghastly institution, the Jamaican countryman has not.[63]

It is, of course, not the poor countryman but the intellectual who has the longest memory, and the bitterest tongue. Not all radicals advocate sugar's extirpation; most favor the nationalization of the factories, the expropriation of the cane land, and its subdivision among peasant proprietors. Such an idyllic populist solution, however, is almost certainly unworkable. Apart from the mechanical difficulties of running nationalized sugar factories, it would be extremely difficult to keep them supplied with cane. The peasant farmer would probably opt not to plant cane, not through his memory of slavery but because of the difficulties of getting help in the cutting, the low prices, and the far more attractive prospect of growing provision crops for market. If the growing of canes were enforced by law, efficiency as well as the natural unevenness in skill, energy, and ambition would ensure that certain "peasants" would consolidate their holdings and become large exploitative cane farmers instead. Such a man was Fidel Castro's father in early twentieth-century Cuba. Already in Jamaica the All Island Cane Farmers' Association includes men with three and men with 3,000 acres.[64]

The sugar industry no longer has an absolute stranglehold on the West Indian economy, yet its history and present operation can be used to illustrate the type of exploitation that is still too general. In a perceptive article in 1968 Lloyd Best put forward a "Model of Pure Plantation Economy" to demonstrate unchanged elements.[65] What he called the *muscovado bias* (the system by which sugar was shipped in its raw form and not even as semiprocessed "clayed" sugar) can be seen as symbolic of the continuing status of ex-colonial countries as raw material producers, allowed only simple extractive industries and denied the opportunity of processing their own produce, let alone developing any more sophisticated forms of manufacture.

To the *muscovado bias* Lloyd Best added three elements that originally gave an unfair advantage to the imperial metropolis and that have been perpetrated either by the original imperial power or by some other "neo-imperial" outside source of capital: the *navigation provision,* giving the monopoly of the carrying trade to metropolitan ships; the *metropolitan exchange standard,* tying the colonial economy to the metropolitan banking system; and *imperial preference,* providing special economic terms for transactions between colony and metropolis.

To these four elements the addition of three others is implied by Best and other contemporary commentators. The first is what might be called the *saltfish habit*—the tendency originally induced by monoculture to import provisions and other goods that could easily be produced at home. But saltfish, far from being hated for its slavery associations, is a modern West Indian delicacy, or "soul food." In much the same way, imported goods retain a spurious glamor out of all proportion to their value.

The second additional phenomenon is that of foreign ownership, which might be termed the *absentee syndrome.* Just as the eighteenth-century proprietor preferred to exploit the West Indies from a metropolitan base, so a very high proportion of the profits

of all modern extractive or primary industries in the
Caribbean continue to be expatriated. Perhaps this
aspect was not strongly emphasized in Best's analysis because although such giants as Tate and Lyle and
Booker are foreign-owned they are not necessarily
more "exploitative" than the smaller sugar operations
still in West Indian ownership.

Finally, a common theme running through the
writings of Patterson, Best, and most modern black
radicals is that the colonialist system was, and the
neocolonialist system is, based upon the "exploitation
of black people by foreign white capitalists"⁶⁶ in a
manner quite analogous to slavery. Moreover, claims
Mazisi Kunene, a South African commentator on the
Martinique writers Aimé Cesaire and Frantz Fanon,

> The colonization of the black people cannot . . . be
> classed simply as the temporary occupation of the weak
> man's territory by the physically strong. The jungle
> law has gone deeper—it has stated that that which I
> have retained by my will must express my will. It must
> become an object to fulfil my desires and wishes. . . .
> My body is given back to me sprawled out, distorted,
> recoloured, clad in mourning. . . . The Negro is an
> animal, the Negro is ugly.⁶⁷

For blacks everywhere, negritude, "black power," and
an almost mystical feeling of community between all
the "black" countries of the underdeveloped Third
World have been natural reactions to this sense of
exploitation and degradation. For all those who feel
victims of a black diaspora there has also been an
intermittent "Back to Africa" movement.

In the poetry of Aimé Cesaire or Edward Brathwaite these feelings reach the heights of a sublime
ideal:

Heia for the royal Kailcedrate!
Heia for those who have never invented anything
those who never explored anything
those who never tamed anything

those who give themselves up to the essence of all things
ignorant of surfaces but struck by the movement of all
   things
free of the desire to tame but familiar with the play of the
   world

truly the eldest sons of the world. . . .[68]

Yet on a practical plane, black people can no more be
one than any race. Separate national identities, different conditions, different needs, divide like oceans.
Pure idealists are bound to re-enact the tragic heroism
of the Jamaican Ras Tafari, craving for an Africa
that they can never reach or regain, not only because
Africa rejects them, but because the Africa they vis-
ualize is past, or perhaps never existed save in their
ganja dreams.

Even the memory of slavery divides the blacks as
much as it binds. Unlike the West Indies, West Africa
harbors little sense of trauma, and few traces remain.
Many of the trading forts can still be seen, either as
neglected ruins or, like Cape Coast Castle, tenderly
transmuted to government offices and museums. There
are also the Efik slave traders' houses at Calabar.
Yet, despite the writings of romantic travelers, around
none howl the specters of crime and guilt or the
ghosts of black men and women in chains.

Modern West Africans play down the slave trade
and slavery itself. This may be, as Basil Davidson
suggested, because of a sense of inferiority resulting
from such easy exploitation by the Europeans, or
from guilt at having participated in the trade.[69] More
likely it is because their perspectives are entirely
different from those of West Indians or Europeans.
After all, most West Indians are descended from
slaves, and many Europeans unconsciously retain the
lingering ethos of a slavemaster race. For the West
Africans, on the other hand, it is almost as if the
Atlantic slaves and their descendants no longer exist.
Survivors do not become obsessed with the fate they

escaped, and the West Africans are descended from those who resisted or escaped enslavement, if not from the caboceers and Kings who grew rich and powerful on the trade.

West African scholarship when dealing with the Atlantic trade has never felt compelled to indulge in the expressions of outrage common in the Americas. From the West African viewpoint the Atlantic slave trade was but a phase, the effects of which can too easily be exaggerated. True, it took from West Africa millions of farmers and craftsmen, bringing as a result of the flood of cheap European goods, gunpowder, and liquor the decay of native crafts and industries and a decline in the quality of life close to the coast. Yet at the cost of the trade in human cargoes, West Africa began the process of modernization without undergoing direct colonization. The pace of political change sped, but West African essential nature did not change until the end of the nineteenth century. Then proud nations arose, the history of which is of much more moment to modern West African scholars than the Atlantic slave trade: Dahomey and Ashanti, closely related though they were to the coastal trade, and the Fulani Empire of the interior, product of a great indigenous revival. Moreover, the Atlantic trade itself was reciprocal. Largely through the importation of new staple crops from the New World, West Africa grew demographically healthier, so that its population did not actually decline over the entire period of transatlantic slavery. Sierra Leone and Liberia, based on populations of repatriated slaves, also provided models for a new type of state-building once the colonial period was over. West Africans, in sum, see the Atlantic slave trade simply as a dynamic phase, not necessarily even deleterious in the long run, in the process of modernization and national emergence, still actively under way.

The countries that were formerly not only colonies but also slave colonies are in the same process, but there the roots of colonialism are deeper, the peoples and problems more diverse. "Given its past history," writes Eric Williams toward the end of his magisterial *Columbus to Castro,*

> the future of the Caribbean can only be meaningfully discussed in terms of the possibilities for the emergence of an identity for the region and its peoples. The whole history of the Caribbean so far can be viewed as a conspiracy to block the emergence of a Caribbean identity—in politics, in institutions, in economics, in culture and in values. Viewed in historical perspective, the future way forward for the peoples of the Caribbean must be one which would impel them to start making their own history, to stop being the playthings of other people.[70]

True independence, in other words, requires both the ending of economic dependence and a psychological change. "In the last analysis," writes Williams,

> dependence is a state of mind. A too-long history of colonialism seems to have crippled Caribbean self-confidence and Caribbean self-reliance, and a vicious circle has been set up: psychological dependence leads to an ever-growing dependence on the outside world. Fragmentation is intensified in the process. And the greater degree of dependence and fragmentation further reduces local self-confidence.[71]

"History is built around achievement and creation," wrote V. S. Naipaul in 1962, "and nothing was created in the West Indies."[72] Here the Trinidadian expatriate novelist was disastrously wrong, as a heartening number of West Indians have hastened to point out. What has been in the process of creation in the British West Indies at least since 1838, and must surely continue vigorously to be pushed toward completion, is a creole society, a creole culture, a creole identity. For only when the Jamaican motto—Out of Many One People—becomes a fact of life for the entire galaxy of islands, and not just a dream, will the era of British slavery properly end.

NOTES

Chapter 1

1. Richard Hakluyt, *The Principal Navigations, Voyages, Traffiques & Discoveries of the English Nation . . .* (1582, etc.), Dent, Everyman edition, 7 vols. (1926), VII, p. 5.

2. Carl O. Sauer, *Agricultural Origins and Dispersals,* MIT Press, 1952, pp. 20–22. Sauer's themes were developed into a general theory by Ester Boserup, *The Conditions of Agricultural Growth: The Economics of Agrarian Change under Population Pressure,* Aldine Publishing Co. and G. Allen and Unwin (1965).

3. Bernard Lewis, "Race and Colour Is Islam," *Encounter* (August 1970), pp. 18–36.

4. Charles Verlinden, *L'esclavage dans L'Europe médiévale,* Brugge (1955); *Les origines de la civilization atlantique de la Renaissance à l'age des Lumières,* Neuchâtel (1966); *The Beginnings of Modern Colonization: Eleven Essays with an Introduction,* Cornell University Press (1971); Noel Deerr, *The History of Sugar,* 2 vols., Chapman & Hall (1949–50).

5. C. R. Boxer, *The Portuguese Seaborne Empire, 1415–1825,* Hutchinson (1969), p. 19; E. W. Bovill, *The Golden Trade of the Moors,* Oxford University Press (1958).

6. Boxer, pp. 20–23.

7. J. W. Blake, *European Beginnings in West Africa, 1454–1578* (Longmans, 1937), pp. 5, 85; Elizabeth Don-

nan, *Documents illustrative of the history of the Slave Trade to America*, 4 vols. (Carnegie Institute, 1930–35), I, pp. 1–41.

8. Boxer, pp. 88–89.

9. Eric Williams, *From Columbus to Castro* (Deutsch, 1970), p. 13.

10. Adam Smith, *The Wealth of Nations* (1776) (Random House, 1937), III, pp. 7, 590.

11. Williams, p. 25.

12. See, for example, Eric Williams, *Documents of West Indian History, Vol. I, 1492–1655* (P.N.M., 1963), p. 27.

13. Gonzalo F. de Oviedo y Valdes, *Historia General de las Indias* (1535–57) (Madrid, 1851–55), quoted in Williams, *Documents*, p. 26.

14. Ibid., p. 25.

15. Ibid., pp. 27–30.

16. Basil Davidson, *Black Mother* (Gollancz, 1961), pp. 3, 61.

17. J. A. Saco, *Historia de la Esclavitud de la Raza Africana en el Nuevo Mundo* (Barcelona, 1879), pp. 89–92, quoted in Donnan I, pp. 15–16.

18. Williams, *Documents*, p. 142; but cf. *Columbus to Castro*, p. 45.

19. Williams, *Documents*, p. 199; but cf. *Columbus to Castro*, p. 62.

20. Williams, *Documents*, p. 147.

21. The charges, amounting to 37½ percent *ad valorem*, which Bernaldez vainly tried to levy for the blacks imported by John Hawkins in 1566, were probably an index of the normal surcharge to Spanish planters at that time; James A. Williamson, *Hawkins of Plymouth* (1949) (Barnes & Noble, 1969), p. 79.

22. Williams, *Documents*, p. 147.

23. Bartolomé de las Casas, *Historia de las Indias* (1559) (Madrid, 1875), quoted in Williams, *Documents*, p. 158.

24. Ibid.

25. Williams, *Columbus to Castro*, p. 44.

26. Ibid., p. 39; but cf. Williams, *Documents*, p. 36.

27. An *arroba*, as used here, is the Portuguese measure, equivalent of about thirty-two pounds, rather than the Spanish measure of about twenty-five pounds; six hundred thousand *arrobas* were therefore about ten thousand long

tons. For Brazil, see Frédéric Mauro, *Le Portugal et l'Atlantique au XVIIᵉ siècle, 1570–1670* (Paris, *Étude économique*, 1960); and Boxer, pp. 104–5. Estimate of Spanish plantations by colonies: Hispaniola, fifty; Cuba, forty; Jamaica, thirty; Mexico and Spanish Main, twenty; and Puerto Rico, ten; Williams, *Columbus to Castro*, pp. 26–29. For slave totals, Philip D. Curtin, *The Atlantic Slave Trade: A Census* (University of Wisconsin Press, 1969), p. 25.

28. Boxer, p. 105.

29. For example, *The Masters and the Slaves: A Study in the Development of Brazilian Civilization*, 2nd ed. (Knopf, 1956). C. R. Boxer, however, tends to be critical of Freyre's thesis.

30. The *peça* (*pieza* in Spanish) was a unit based on a healthy young adult male; Curtin, pp. 23, 116.

31. Willem Bosman, *A New and Accurate Description of the Coast of Guinea* (London, 1721), quoted in Boxer, p. 106.

32. Harley Papers, Welbeck Abbey mss., quoted in Donnan I, p. 125, n. 2.

33. C. Raymond Beazley and E. Prestage (eds.), *The Chronicle of the Discovery and Conquest of Guinea, by Gomes Eannes de Azurara*, 2 vols. (Hakluyt Society, 1896–97), II, xxxii–xliii; C. R. Beazley, *The Dawn of Modern Geography* (Clarendon Press, 1905–6), pp. 430–40, though cf. Blake, 3–4, Donnan, I, p. 2.

34. Blake, pp. 7–8.

35. R. J. Harrison Church, *West Africa: A Study of the Environment and Man's Use of It* (Longmans, 1957), pp. 3–84; Daryll Forde, "The Cultural Map of West Africa: Successive Adaptations to Tropical Forests and Grasslands," in S. and P. Ottenberg (eds.), *Cultures and Societies of Africa* (Random House, 1960), pp. 116–38. See also Roland Partères, "Berceaux Agricoles Primaires sur le Continent Africain," in *Journal of African History* 3 (1962), pp. 195–220, as well as critical articles by J. D. Clarke, H. G. Baker, and W. B. Morgan in the same issue.

36. J. E. Flint, *Nigeria and Ghana* (Prentice-Hall, 1966), pp. 33–70; J. D. Fage, *An Introduction to the History of West Africa*, 3rd ed. (Cambridge University Press, 1962).

37. J. D. Fage, "Slavery and the Slave Trade in the Context of West African History," in *Journal of African History* X, 3 (1969), pp. 393–404.

38. Walter Rodney, *History of the Upper Guinea Coast, 1545–1800* (Oxford University Press, 1970).

39. David Birmingham, *Trade and Conflict in Angola: The Mbundu and their Neighbours under the Influence of the Portuguese, 1483–1790* (Oxford University Press, 1966); Jan Vansina, *Kingdoms of the Savanna* (University of Wisconsin Press, 1966).

40. Fage, "Slavery," pp. 394, 397.

41. Davidson, pp. 27–50.

42. Ibid., p. 35. For Europe, Davidson interestingly cites Maitland's classic *Domesday Book and After*.

43. From the official report of the Niger Valley Exploring Party, published in New York (1861), p. 40; quoted in Davidson, p. 39.

44. B. Martin and M. Spurrell (eds.), *The Journal of a Slave Trader, 1750–1754* (Epworth Press, 1962), pp. 107–8, quoted in R. B. Sheridan, "Economic and Demographic Factors in the Rise of the British West Indies Slave Trade," conference paper unpublished in 1972.

45. Davidson, p. 42.

46. Walter Rodney, "A Reconsideration of the Mane Invasions of Sierra Leone," in *Journal of African History* VII, 2 (1967), pp. 219–46.

47. Boxer, pp. 28–29.

48. Davidson, p. 57.

49. Rodney, *Upper Guinea*, pp. 71–222.

50. Williamson, *Hawkins;* Irene A. Wright (eds.), *Spanish Documents Concerning English Voyages to the Caribbean, 1527–1568*, 2nd ser., LXII (Hakluyt Society, 1928); G. C. Smith, *Forerunners of Drake: A Study of English Trade with Spain in the Early Tudor Period* (Longmans, 1953).

51. *Calendar of State Papers* (henceforward *CSP*), Venetian I, p. 142, quoted in J. M. Sarbah, *Journal of African Studies* III, pp. 194–97; Hakluyt IV, p. 21.

52. Hakluyt IV, pp. 35–36.

53. Ibid., pp. 47–66.

54. Ibid., pp. 66–128.

55. Ibid., p. 78.

56. Ibid., p. 65; "They brought with them certaine blacke slaves, whereof some were tall and strong men, and could wel agree with our meates and drinkes. The cold and moyst aire doth somewhat offend them. Yet doubtlesse men that are borne in hot Regions may better abide colde, than men that are borne in colde Regions may abide heate."

57. Ibid., pp. 91–92.

58. Ibid., p. 101.

59. Ibid., p. 130.

60. Ibid., p. 133.

61. Evidence of William Fowler before the High Court of Admiralty (1569), quoted in Donnan I, p. 72. Fowler, who did not sail with Hawkins, was referring to the slave trade in general, not Hawkins' voyages in particular.

62. See, for example, the Instructions from the Queen in 1567, signed by William Cecil, which gave the lie to Cecil's later disavowal of the slave trade and his part in it; quoted in Williamson, p. 110; also *CSP, Domestic, 1595–97*, p. 299.

63. P. L. Hughes and J. F. Larking (eds.), *Tudor Royal Proclamations* (Yale University Press, 1969), pp. 221–22.

64. Williamson, pp. 42–158.

65. Hakluyt VII, p. 6.

66. Ibid., p. 53.

67. Rodney, *Upper Guinea*, pp. 98–100.

68. Ibid., p. 92.

69. Ibid., p. 122.

70. Curtin, pp. 116–19.

71. Davidson, p. 54.

Chapter 2

1. Winthrop Papers in Collections of the Massachusetts Historical Society, 4th ser., VI, pp. 537–9, quoted in Elizabeth Donnan, *Documents Illustrative of the History of the Slave Trade to America*, 4 vols. (Carnegie Institute, 1930–35), I, p. 125.

2. Ibid.

3. *CSP, Colonial, American and West Indian, 1574–1660*, pp. 240, 446; *1661–1668*, p. 529; *1657*, p. 1901; *1669–1674*, pp. 1101, 1249; *1677–1680*, p. 1336; Richard

B. Sheridan, *The Development of the Plantations to 1750* (Caribbean Universities Press), 1970, pp. 26–32; Richard S. Dunn, "The Barbados Census of 1680: Profile of the Richest Colony in English America," in *William and Mary Quarterly* (January 1969).

4. *CSP, Col., A. & W.I., 1661–68, 1657*. Of the twelve thousand, thirty-three hundred were said to have gone to Jamaica with Venables in 1654 and three thousand in 1666. Except for twelve hundred who had departed for New England in the 1640s, the remainder had scattered to ill-starred ventures in Trinidad, Tobago, Martinique, Guadeloupe, Marie Galante, Grenada, Curaçao, and Guyana, most to perish miserably.

5. Philip D. Curtin, *The Atlantic Slave Trade: A Census* (University of Wisconsin Press, 1969), pp. 56–64.

6. J. Harry Bennett, "Carey Helyar, Merchant and Planter of Seventeenth Century Jamaica," in *William and Mary Quarterly* (June 1969), pp. 53–76.

7. Sheridan, pp. 38–47; Curtin, pp. 56, 59; Michael Craton and James Walvin, *A Jamaican Plantation: The History of Worthy Park, 1670–1970* (W. H. Allen and University of Toronto Press, 1970), pp. 74, 156.

8. 1700–20, 68 percent; 1720–40, 74 percent; 1740–60, 67 percent; 1760–80, 88 percent; 1780–1808, 82 percent; Curtin, p. 140.

9. The "Neutral Islands" of Grenada, Dominica, and St. Vincent, acquired in 1763, were confirmed in 1783. Tobago, acquired in 1763, was restored in 1783 but reacquired in 1797. St. Lucia, captured in both the Seven Years' and Maritime wars but restored in both 1763 and 1783 was, like the Guyanas, Trinidad, and Tobago, not acquired permanently until 1815. They had all been taken over, however, at various times during the last French wars. Moreover, in several areas British planters were present before formal acquisition. In Demerara, for example, the British outnumbered the Dutch before 1793. There were even sizable British colonies in islands never formally acquired, such as Danish St. Croix and Dutch Curaçao.

10. Curtin, p. 66.

11. For the more or less legal trade in domestic slaves under licenses between West Indian colonies, see D. Eltis, "The Traffic in Slaves between the British West Indian Colonies, 1807–1833," in *Economic History Review* XXV

(February 1972), pp. 55–64, and below, Chapter 5. In all, no less than twenty-two thousand slaves were shipped between the Caribbean colonies between 1808 and 1830.

12. Donnan IV, pp. 175–234, 612–25; Curtin, pp. 73, 118, 143–44; Melville J. Heskovits, *The Myth of the Negro Past* (Harper, 1958), pp. 45–47; U. S. Bureau of Statistics, *Historical Statistics of the United States* (Washington, D.C., 1960).

13. Robert E. and B. Katherine Brown, *Virginia, 1705–1786: Democracy or Aristocracy?* (Michigan State University Press, 1964), p. 75. For the British West Indies, estimates vary because of the difficulties of defining estates and slave holdings. R. B. Sheridan, "Africa and the Caribbean in the Atlantic Slave Trade," in *American Historical Review* LXXVII (February 1972), argued for an average of 277 slaves for 1,550 sugar plantations in 1770, but has since revised this to 179 slaves for 1,800 plantations in 1774. My own estimate of 240 for Jamaica in 1790—revising Bryan Edwards' calculation of 182–is argued in "Jamaican Slavery," an MSSB Conference paper given at Rochester, New York, in March 1972, to be published by Princeton University Press in 1974.

14. Ulrich B. Phillips gave the following figures for the population of South Carolina: 1708, 3,580 whites, 4,100 slaves; 1724, 14,000 and 32,000; 1749, 25,000 and 39,000; *American Negro Slavery* (Appleton, 1918). These figures have recently been revised by Peter H. Wood to 4,080 whites, 4,100 black slaves, and 1,400 Indian slaves in 1708; 6,523 free and 11,828 slaves in 1720; 13,000 free whites and 24,000 slaves in 1730; 20,000 free whites and 39,155 slaves in 1740; "'More like a Negro Country': Demographic Patterns in Colonial South Carolina, 1700–1740," MSSB Conference paper given at Rochester, New York, in March 1972, to be published by Princeton University Press in 1974.

15. Henry C. Wilkinson, *The Adventures of Bermuda* (Oxford University Press, 1933); *Bermuda in the Old Empire* (Oxford University Press, 1949); Michael Craton, *History of the Bahamas* (Collins, 1962).

16. *CSP, Col., A. & W.I., 1574–1660*, p. 295; Arthur P. Newton, *Colonising Activities of the English Puritans* (Yale University Press, 1914).

17. James Walvin, *White and Black: A History of the Negro in England* (1555–1945) (Longmans, 1973).

18. See Tables 1–2. These are derived largely from *Historical Statistics of the United States;* J. Potter, "The Growth of Population in America, 1700–1860," in D. V. Glass and D. E. C. Eversley (eds.), *Population in History* (Aldine Publishing Co. and Edward Arnold, 1965); E. B. Greene and V. D. Harrington, *American Population before the Census of 1790* (Columbia University Press, 1932); F. W. Pitman, *The Development of the British West Indies, 1700–1763* (Yale University Press, 1917); Edward Brathwaite, *The Development of Creole Society in Jamaica, 1770–1820* (Clarendon Press, 1971); R. B. Sheridan, *Plantations to 1750;* Curtin, *Atlantic Slave Trade;* Noel Deerr, *History of Sugar;* Peter H. Wood, "More Like a Negro Country."

19. Donnan I, pp. 11, 78.

20. [A Mandingo trader] "showed unto me certain young black women who were standing by themselves . . . which he told me were slaves, brought for me to buy. I made answer, We were a people who did not deal in such commodities, neither did we buy or sell one another, or any that had our own shapes." Richard Jobson, *The Golden Trade, or a Discovery of the River Gambra and the Golden Trade of the Aethiopians,* (1623) (London: Dawson, 1968), p. 160.

21. G. F. Zook, *The Company of Royal Adventurers Trading into Africa* (Lancaster, Pennsylvania, 1919.)

22. Richard Ollard, *Man of War: Sir Robert Holmes and the Restoration Navy.*

23. Zook, *Royal Adventurers,* 62. It is an interesting coincidence that George Downing was heavily engaged in the Anglo-Dutch diplomacy of these troubled years, as English plenipotentiary at The Hague.

24. Donnan I, pp. 177–92.

25. K. G. Davies, *The Royal African Company* (Longmans, 1957), pp. 64–70.

26. Donnan II, p. 34 (1709). The annual need for slaves was then estimated at twelve thousand for the Spanish West Indies and Jamaica, four thousand for Barbados, four thousand for the Leewards, four thousand for Virginia and Maryland, and 1,000 for the Carolinas and New York.

27. For an excellent account of life in the West African forts see the extracts from John Atkins (1721) in Donnan II, pp. 267–69.

28. This pattern—which appears to have been general —is, of course, prima facie evidence not only that the trade was essentially controlled on the mainland by Africans but also that there were very real commercial benefits to African traders in keeping the Europeans at the coastline.

29. Davies, pp. 213–32.

30. For an interesting contrast, compare the pro-Company *Certain Considerations* . . . (1680) with the antagonistic *Systema Africanum* . . . (1690), both quoted in Donnan I, pp. 267–71, 377–85. Among the pamphleteers was the prolific Daniel Defoe, whose *An Essay upon the Trade to Africa* . . . (1711) argued for the continuation of the Company, once reformed.

31. For a further discussion of prices, costs, and profits, see Chapter 3.

32. Act of 9–10 William III, c. 26.

33. G. Schelle, *La Traite Négrière aux Indes de Castille*, 2 vols. (Paris, 1906); Davies, pp. 326–35.

34. Donnan II, pp. 16–21, 142–44.

35. Davies VIII, pp. 344–45.

36. The English trade to foreign colonies may account for the discrepancies between figures for slave exports from Africa according to shipping data and official figures for imports into English colonies noticed by Curtin, pp. 136–40. The total difference may have been as much as four hundred thousand between 1750 and 1800 alone. See Tables 5 and 20.

37. Richard Hofstadter, *America at 1750: A Social Portrait* (Cape, 1972), now the best short account of American colonial slavery and the American slave trade. See also Daniel Mannix and Malcolm Cowley, *Black Cargoes* (Viking Press, 1962), which Hofstadter used extensively.

38. Donnan II, p. xxxii. It was temporarily raised to £20,000 in 1744.

39. Act of 23 Geo. II, c. 31. Clause IV forbade the "Company" to trade in its corporate capacity, to issue stock, or even to borrow money; Donnan II, pp. 474–85.

40. Henry Laurens to John Laurens, August 14, 1776; Donnan IV, p. 471.

41. Curtin, pp. 265–73. One scarcely predictable effect of general Atlantic trade was the improvement in West African fertility and natural increase through improved diet, by the introduction of such American staples as maize, cassava, and yams. See Chapter 6 below.

42. Basil Davidson, *Black Mother,* especially pp. 179–248.

43. *Memoirs of the Late Captain Hugh Crow of Liverpool* . . . (Longmans, 1830); John Mathews, *A Voyage to the River Sierra Leone* . . . (London, 1791); Donnan II, pp. 264, 342, 567, 597; I, pp. 134, 199, 392.

44. John Atkins, *A Voyage to Guinea, Brasil and the West Indies* . . . (London, 1735), quoted in Donnan II, pp. 264–83.

45. Davies, pp. 165–79, 350–57.

46. Americans also sometimes shipped cargoes of provisions to West Africa in their ingenious attempts to find cheap trade goods that were regarded as valuable on the West African coast. The rum and slaves traffic of Rhode Island alone is said to have yielded £40,000 a year for remittances to England in the mid-eighteenth century; W. B. Weeden, *Economic and Social History of New England* (1890) II, cited in Hofstadter, p. 74.

47. Mathews (1791); Donnan II, pp. 567–71.

48. ". . . From this Ship we learned also, that the inland Country who had suffered by the Panyarrs of the Cobelohou and Drewin People, have lately been down, and destroyed the Towns, and the Trade is now at a stand . . . ," in John Atkins (1721); Donnan II, p. 266.

49. Cf. Kwame Arhin, "The Structure of Greater Ashanti, 1700–1824," in *Journal of African History* VIII, 1 (1967), pp. 65–85; J. D. Fage, *An Introduction to the History of West Africa* (Cambridge University Press, 1962), p. 97; or A. Norman Klein, "West African Unfree Labour Before and After the Rise of the Atlantic Slave Trade," in L. Foner and E. Genovese (eds.), *Slavery in the New World* (Prentice-Hall, 1969).

50. Barbot (1682), in Churchill (1732) V; Donnan II, 15.

51. Bryan Edwards, *The History, Civil and Commercial, of the West Indies,* 2nd ed., 2 vols. (London, 1801), II, p. 45.

52. Codrington to Board of Trade, December 30,

1701, *CSP, Col., A. & W.I.* (1701), p. 721; Donnan I, p. 398.

53. Donnan I, p. 398.

54. Portland mss., in Donnan I, pp. 134–36.

55. Donnan I, pp. 199–209.

56. In Churchill VI, pp. 173–239, and Astley II, pp. 387–416, quoted in Donnan I, pp. 392–410. Cf. Barbot, Donnan I, pp. 292–98; Bosman (1701), Donnan I, pp. 438–44.

57. *Proceedings of the American Antiquarian Society*, new ser. 39, pp. 379–465; Donnan II.

58. Gomer Williams, *History of the Privateers . . . with an account of the Liverpool Slave Trade* (London, 1897), p. 680; Donnan II. The normal price per slave in rum during the 1760s was 80–110 gallons.

59. The King also taxed each African seller's payment at something like 10 percent.

60. Quoted, complete with music, in Crow, pp. 120–28.

61. Prince Hoare, *Memoirs of Granville Sharp*, Appendix VIII, pp. xvii–xviii; Donnan II, pp. 555–57.

62. Usually 6 percent of the value of the cargo actually delivered.

63. Phillips (*Hannibal*, 1693–94); Donnan I, p. 410.

64. I.e., partridge shot, capable of wreaking terrible havoc at short range.

65. *British Sessional Papers, Commons, Accounts and Papers* (1789) XXV, p. 214.

66. Ibid.

67. The mean tonnage of Liverpool ships in the African trade was 75 tons in 1730, 180 in 1790, and 226 in 1806.

68. *British Sessional Papers, Commons, A/P, 1789* XXVI, Part Two. Proslavery witness Archibald Dalzell testified that he had sailed in the following slave ships: one of 500 tons fitted for 600 slaves; 300 tons fitted for 360; 200 for 170; and 50 for 106.

69. Sir William Young described a vessel he had seen at St. Vincent in 1792, only 3 feet, 6 inches between decks, "disagreeably offensive in smell," carrying 210 slaves but with no sick. Only 20 of the 210 slaves were youngsters; *A Tour through . . . Barbados, St. Vincent, Antigua, Tobago and Grenada* (London, 1801), p. 270.

70. *British Sessional Papers, Commons,* A/P (1789) XXV, Part Two, p. 215.

71. Donnan II, p. 406.

72. In 1789 James Penny said that while Indian corn was the staple diet of the Gold Coast and Whydaw blacks (one of the chief reasons, he claimed, that they were healthiest), those of the Windward Coast preferred rice, and those from Upper Guinea, yams; *British Sessional Papers, Commons* A/P (1789) XXVI, Part Two.

73. Donnan II, p. 407.

74. *British Sessional Papers, Commons* (1789) XXVI, Part Two. Penny, however, was arguing for a ration of two slaves per ton displacement, and against any legislation concerning treatment of slaves.

75. For a perceptive introduction to the subject see Philip D. Curtin, "Epidemiology and the Slave Trade," in *Political Science Quarterly* LXXXIII (June 2, 1968), pp. 190–216.

76. The death rate per thousand per year of British troops recruited in England serving on the Cape Coast, 1823–26, was 668.3, compared with 483 for Sierra Leone. See also K. G. Davies, "The Living and the Dead: White Mortality in West Africa, 1684–1732" (MSSB Conference paper given at Rochester, New York, March 1972, to be published by Princeton University Press, 1974), in which the author estimates a mortality among the Royal African Company's factors, officials, and soldiers stationed in West Africa at more than 50 percent in the first year, with "no certainty that more than one-tenth got back to England." With the chances of survival so desperately slim, modern man is at a loss to comprehend the conditions or motives that impelled men to sign on for a spell on the Guinea Coast, particularly since some survivors even returned for a second dice with death.

77. Especially the variety called "cocoa bays" or "Arabian leprosy" on the plantations.

78. *British Sessional Papers, Commons* (1789) XXV, p. 216. Evidence of J. Knox, op. cit.

79. Malagueta pepper, once it lost favor as a spice in England, was often carried on slave voyages as "medicine" for the slaves.

80. William Snelgrave, *A New Account of some Parts of Guinea* (London, 1734); Donnan II, pp. 352, 359.

81. Slave ship mutinies await their scholarly analyst. Lorenzo J. Greene, "Mutiny on the Slave Ships," in *Phylon* (5, 1944), pp. 346–54, gave some useful examples but dealt exclusively with the North American trade, and was not analytical.

82. Donnan II, p. 354.

83. Ibid., p. 359.

84. Ibid., p. 361.

85. Examples given by fairly credible proslavery witnesses included 59 dead of 1,060 slaves carried on three voyages (1782–84) by John Knox (18/450, 40/320, 1/290); 54 of 598 on 3 voyages by William Littleton (13/140, 38/242, 3/216); 110 of 2,576 on six voyages (1775–86) by James Penny to Bonny and Angola (27/531, 24/539, 31/560, 26/571, 1/209, 1/166); and 78 of 2,175 in 5 voyages (1769–77) by Robert Norris. The combined total for these 17 voyages was 301 slaves dead out of 6,409, or only 4.7 percent; *British Sessional Papers, Commons* (1789) XXV, pp. 73–110, 212–30; XXVI, Part Two.

86. Davidson, p. 87; Robert Rotberg, *A Political History of Tropical Africa* (Harcourt, Brace 1965), p. 149. This is not to mention the tendency of some writers to take the figures for Middle Passage mortality as being indicative for slavery in general. See Chapter 4 below. For the best discussion of losses in transit, see Curtin, *Census*, pp. 275–86.

87. C. S. Higham, *The Development of the Leeward Islands under the Restoration, 1660–88* (Cambridge University Press, 1921), p. 158.

88. I.e., 8.75 percent of 15,754 in 1791 and 17 percent of 31,554 in 1792; T. F. Buxton, *The African Slave Trade* (Philadelphia, 1839), p. 124.

89. Dieudonné Rinchon, *Le Trafic négrier, d'après les livres de commerce du capitaine gantois Pierre-Ignace-Liéven van Alstein*, Vol. 1 (Paris, 1938), pp. 248–305. In fact, the 14.33 percent given by Rinchon included losses from all causes, the deaths from disease alone amounting to 13 percent, the figure accepted by Basil Davidson. Gaston Martin calculated losses from Nantes 1715–50 at 14.9 percent; G. Martin, *Nantes au XVIIIe siècle: L'Ere des négriers* (1714–1774) (Paris, 1931).

90. T. Clarkson to Lords of Trade and Plantations, July 27, 1788, *Board of Trade Report, 1788,* Part Two; Curtin, *Atlantic Slave Trade,* p. 285.

91. Donnan I, pp. 199–209.

92. Ten had died during the eight months on the coast and eleven more were to die at Barbados. Of those who died on the passage, twelve succumbed to fluxes, six to "consumption," three to "dropsy," two each to "fever," "cramp," "convulsions," and drowning, and one starved himself to death; ibid., pp. 206–9.

93. These stratagems were described by Captain Alexander Falconbridge in 1789; *British Sessional Papers, Commons* (1789) XXVI, Part One.

94. Bryan Edwards (1793) reported that the Jamaican legislature had "of late years" outlawed the scramble on shipboard, and had even tried to avoid the breakup of families on sale, in the latter case without complete success.

95. Donnan I, p. 206.

96. Ibid. IV, pp. 300–471.

97. Ibid. IV, pp. 188–234; III, pp. 510–2.

98. Henry Laurens to John Heslin, November 19, 1764; Donnan IV, p. 407.

99. Donnan IV, pp. 389–90.

100. February 15, 1762; Donnan IV, p. 382.

101. Henry Laurens to Ross and Mill, September 2, 1768; Donnan IV, pp. 424–26.

Chapter 3

1. "Circumstantial Account of the True Causes of the Liverpool African Slave Trade by an Eye Witness" (Liverpool, 1797), in *A General and Descriptive History of the Ancient and Present State of the Town of Liverpool* (Liverpool, 1798), extracted in Donnan II, pp. 625–31; Gomer Williams, *History of the Privateers . . . with an Account of the Liverpool Slave Trade* (London, 1897); Eric Williams, *Capitalism and Slavery,* pp. 36–38; *Columbus to Castro,* p. 147 (in which the Royal African Company's export of £4,252 worth of trade goods to Africa and subsequent sale of 296 blacks in St. Kitts for £9,228 is cited as evidence of a profit of 117 percent). See also S. Dumbell, "Profits of the Guinea Trade," in *Economic History* II, pp. 254–57; James Pope-Hennessy, *Sins of the*

*Fathers: A Study of the Atlantic Slave Traders, 1441–
1807* (Weidenfeld & Nicolson, 1967), p. 145; Daniel
Mannix and Malcolm Cowley IV, pp. 69–73, *Black Cargoes.*

2. Thomas Clarkson, *Essay on the Impolicy of the
African Slave Trade* (London, 1788); Williams, *Capitalism and Slavery,* p. 38.

3. Tarleton & Backhouse (Liverpool) to Lord Hawkes-
bury, June 9, 1788, *B.M. Add. Mss.* 38416, ff. 107–9, in
Donnan II, pp. 578–81, and *British Sessional Papers,
Commons, Accounts and Papers* (1789) XXVI (June 6,
1788), pp. 21–22, 52. The document estimated that carrying one slave per ton, a two-hundred-ton ship would
lose £ 5836s., but that carrying five slaves per two tons it
would make a profit of £ 7635s.6d., or almost exactly 10
percent on the outlay, compared with roughly 3 percent
on the example given.

4. *British Sessional Papers, Commons, A/P* (1789)
XXVI, Part Four.

5. "Circumstantial Account . . ." (1797).

6. The average price for 15,872 slaves sold by the
Royal African Company in Jamaica, 1679–88, was £ 13
1s. 9d. stg.

7. Gomer Williams, p. 680.

8. Ibid., pp. 599–607; Donnan II, p. 631.

SLAVE RE-EXPORTS, 1784–91

	Jamaica	Grenada	Dominica	St. Vincent	BWI Total
1784	4,465	31	13	400	5,263
1785	4,589	90	117	91	5,018
1786	3,643	–	189	50	4,317
1787	1,780	536	2,018	660	5,366
1789	2,030	3,440	2,357	845	8,756
1790	1,970	3,143	1,690	611	7,487
1791	2,815	6,362	2,099	1,346	12,866

British Sessional Papers, Commons (1789) XXVI, Part
Four, No. 4; (1792) XCIII, p. 766.

9. Gomer Williams, pp. 599–607; Donnan II, p. 631.
These figures were drastically pared by Dumbell.

10. W. Roscoe, *A General View of the African Slave
Trade demonstrating its Injustice and Impolicy* (London,
1788), pp. 23–24; Williams, *Capitalism and Slavery,* p.
48.

11. However, R. B. Sheridan has produced figures for Jamaica between 1751 and 1787 that show slight but perceptible declines in the inflow of slaves during wartime, which he suggests were probably as much due to higher insurance premiums as to anything else: Average imports into Jamaica 1751–55 were 8,178; 1756–62 (wartime), 6,864; 1763–67, 8,540; 1771–75, 9,375; 1776–83 (wartime), 7,349; 1784–87, 9,468; R. B. Sheridan, private correspondence. But cf. Table 3, Chapter 2.

12. For a much more professional account of slave trade financing see Richard B. Sheridan, "The Commercial and Financial Organization of the British Slave Trade, 1750–1807," in *Economic History Review*, 2nd ser. XI, 2 (1958), pp. 249–63. For a brilliant introduction to the system of factorage, commission, and bills of exchange by which planters tried to dominate the terms of trade in sugar, see the Alexander Prize essay, K. G. Davies, "The Origins of the Commission System in the West India Trade," in *Transactions of the Royal Historical Society*, 5th ser. LII (1952), pp. 89–108. Three works by Richard Pares are also obligatory reading: *Merchants and Planters* (Cambridge University Press, 1960); *A West India Fortune* (Longmans, 1950); and *Yankees and Creoles* (Longmans, 1956).

13. "The Volume and Profitability of the Atlantic Slave Trade, 1761–1810," MSSB Conference paper given at Rochester, New York, in March 1972, to be published by Princeton University Press, 1974.

14. Ibid., p. 38.

15. Quoted by J. F. Rees, *Economics* (June 1925), p. 143; Williams, *Capitalism and Slavery*, p. 51.

16. *Essay upon Plantership*, p. 3.

17. For an interesting examination of the econometrics of labor maximization in a slave context, see Dave Denslow, Jr., "Economic Considerations in the Treatment of Slaves in Brazil and Cuba," MSSB Conference paper given in Rochester, New York, in March 1972. The value of Denslow's equations, however, does depend on both the degree to which average slave owners were absolute maximizers and were sophisticated in their manipulation of variables. Unfortunately the significance of variables and even the meaning of maximization do not seem clear even the econometricians. For example, Denslow is unable to resolve

whether C. Vann Woodward's dictum concerning "periods of hard times and sluggish markets" is correct or not. There is in fact plentiful evidence that the contrary was true—that leaner times led to economics of scale, which meant greater exploitation of labor in order to increase productivity while profits were low. Denslow himself also quotes Eugene Genovese to the effect that slave conditions in nineteenth-century Louisiana were relatively easy because development occurred on virgin land, where high profits were easily obtained; C. Vann Woodward, *American Counterpoint: Slavery and Racism in the North-South Dialogue* (Little, Brown, 1971), p. 98; Eugene Genovese, *In Red and Black: Marxian Explorations in Southern and Afro-American History* (Pantheon, 1971), p. 167.

18. Sir William Young, *A Tour Through . . . Barbados, St. Vincent, Antigua, Tobago and Grenada* (London: Stockdale, 1801), pp. 289–90.

19. Quoted in William Belgrove, *A Treatise upon Husbandry and Planting* (Boston, 1755), pp. 64–65.

20. Edward Long, *The History of Jamaica*, 3 vols. (Jamaica, 1774); William Beckford, *A Descriptive Account of the Island of Jamaica . . .*, 2 vols. (London: Egerton, 1790); Bryan Edwards, *The Civil and Commercial History of the British Colonies in the West Indies*, 2 vols. (London, 1793); Thomas Roughley, *The Jamaica Planter's Guide* (London, 1823).

21. One factor that commentators have so far ignored is that with the equalization of the sex ratio in plantation populations and the monopolization of crafts and factory jobs by men, women were bound to predominate in the field labor force, even the First Gang. At Worthy Park, Jamaica, for example, women made up 60 percent of the First Gang by 1793. See Chapter 4.

22. Roughley, pp. 99–100.

23. Edmund Ruffin, *Agricultural Survey of South Carolina* (Columbia, 1843), quoted in Ulrich B. Phillips, *American Negro Slavery* (New York: Appleton, 1918), pp. 240–50.

24. Roughley, p. 102.

25. Ibid., pp. 103–4.

26. Ibid., pp. 105–6.

27. For the vigorous debate over the profitability of American slavery, which reached something of a climax

at the 1967 Economic History Association convention, see
the excellent compilation by Hugh G. J. Aitken, *Did
Slavery Pay?* (Houghton Mifflin, 1971), which contains
articles by no less than twenty-one authors from the time
of U. B. Phillips to the present day. Unfortunately, all deal
with cotton plantations in the United States during the
nineteenth century and only provide guidelines for the
work yet to be done elsewhere for different crops and for
an earlier period. Moreover, despite much sophistication,
no final conclusion is reached, so that the editor has, in
his introduction, to have recourse to: "Did slavery pay?
Of course it did. And of course it did not. It paid, in cash
and other ways, those who, because they controlled the
distribution of power, were able to appropriate the surplus
produced by slave labor. And it did not pay, because it
nearly ruined the South and because it implanted in the
core of American society a source of conflict, guilt and
hate that is still with us . . . ," ibid., p. xi.

28. Edwards, *History*. As a matter of fact, Hans Sloane
nearly a century earlier had mentioned that Jamaican
slaves often had two days off a week to work the provision
grounds, but this system seems to have fallen into abey-
ance for most of the eighteenth century; *Voyage to . . .
Jamaica* (London, 1707), p. xlviii.

29. Though with better canes and on piecework;
Michael Craton and James Walvin, *A Jamaican Plantation*,
pp. 103–4.

30. Samuel Martin, however, did give the plow a fair
trial in Antigua but gave it up, probably because of the
heavy demands it made on draft animals and pastures.

31. At the time of emancipation in Jamaica, only 19,500
of the 218,500 praedials were "jobbing slaves"—that is,
one in eleven, or about one in sixteen of the total slave
population; D. G. Hall, *Free Jamaica, 1838–1865: An
Economic History* (Yale University Press, 1959).

32. Edward Long to Lord Wakingham, March 15, 1787,
B.M. Add. Mss. 12404, f. 405, quoted by F. W. Pitman,
"Slavery in British West India Plantations in the Eighteenth Century," in *Journal of Negro History* II, 1 (1926),
pp. 605–6. In the following year William Beckford mentioned slaves being hired at 1s.3d. a day, though this
was presumably in Jamaican currency, with food included,
and for short hirings; *Remarks upon the situation of the*

negroes in Jamaica (London, 1788), pp. 94–95. Long stated that in times of "drowth and scarcity," 5d. a day was the normal payment.

33. *British Sessional Papers, Commons, A/P* (1789) XXVI, Part Three, No. 26. For comparative values of slaves, see 1808 figures derived from Retreat Estate, Jamaica, Table 14, Chapter 4.

34. Though a fifteen-hour workday was quite normally expected of American mainland slaves. A Georgia law of 1755 set a maximum of sixteen hours' work and South Carolina ordained fifteen hours during spring and summer and fourteen hours during the winter; Hofstadter, p. 96. These hours, though as unenforceable as the penalties for infractions, could scarcely have been less than those exacted in the sugar colonies.

35. In mainland colonies the mule rather than the steer was the chief stock animal. Plowing was the norm, for which the mule was more suitable. Many Virginia plantations grew tobacco, corn, and clover in rotation, almost like English farming before the rhyme of "Turnip" Townshend; U. B. Phillips, pp. 230–40.

36. The curious and disturbing malady of "dirt eating" was, probably erroneously, cited as the cause of intestinal worms. Instead, it was probably the result of a craving unconsciously related to mineral deficiencies.

37. Indeed, at Worthy Park, Jamaica, between 1783 and 1838 only five slaves were specifically listed as "invalid." Robert Fogel and Stanley Engerman even mention in their 1974 book *Time on the Cross* that—in the antebellum United States South at least—there was no such thing as a truly superannuated slave, slaves being expected to pay their way up to the time of their death.

38. This seems to have been around 1783. Calculated on an annual live birthrate of 2 percent and a survival rate to age six of 25 percent, coupled with a 30 percent productivity loss in employing the survivors from six to twenty (the usual age of importees), this works out at about £75 stg. a year for a population of five hundred to produce two fresh slaves a year, between 1750 and 1790. This would have purchased three slaves at the beginning of the period, but less than two at the end. Such a plantation would normally have suffered an annual net decrease of about ten slaves.

39. See Chapter 4.

40. *History* I, Book V, iii, pp. 244–62.

41. A constant theme, particularly in midcentury Jamaica; F. W. Pitman, *The Development of the British West Indies, 1700–1763* (Yale University Press, 1917), p. 110.

42. For example, Carey Helyar's small Jamaican estate (Bybrook) was valued at £1,858 in 1672, of which £199 was for the "millwork" and no less than £1,170 for the fifty-five slaves and fourteen indentured servants; J. H. Bennett, "Carey Helyar Merchant and Planter of Seventeenth Century Jamaica," in *William and Mary Quarterly* (June 1969), pp. 53–76.

43. Long I, p. 462; Sir William Young, *A Tour Through . . . Barbados, St. Vincent, Antigua, Tobago and Grenada* (London: Stockdale, 1801). The normal rates of interest were 5 percent from the planter's factor and 6 percent outside. In 1790 Beckford reckoned that the latter was cheaper in practice, since the planter did not thereby tie up all his produce; Beckford, *Jamaica* II, p. 357; Pares, *Merchants and Planters*, p. 47, n. 69.

44. Vaughan to Secretary of State, *P.R.O.*, *C.O.* 138/3.

45. W. Barrett, "Caribbean Sugar Production Standards in the Seventeenth and Eighteenth Centuries," in J. Parker (ed.), *Merchants and Scholars* (University of Minnesota Press, 1967), pp. 147–70.

46. Edwards, *History* I, V, iii, p. 262. Between 1776 and 1796, Worthy Park Estate, Jamaica, appears to have received an average of £15.11s. a puncheon for its rum; Craton and Walvin, *A Jamaican Plantation*, p. 117.

47. *British Sessional Papers, Commons, A/P* (1789) XXVI, Part Four, No. 7.

48. *Wealth of Nations* (New York, 1937), p. 366, quoted by Eric Williams in *Capitalism and Slavery*, p. 53. For a more detached view of many of these profitability factors see the controversy between R. B. Sheridan and R. P. Thomas in *Economic History Review* XVIII (1965); XXI (1968). Contrarily, it should be pointed out that there were said to be 1,000 sugar estates in Jamaica around 1790, when sugar production totaled roughly 50,000 tons. This indicated an average production of only 62.5 hogsheads a year. Yet in making his claim that total

capitalization in the West Indies was £70 million, Edwards seems to have multiplied his figure of £30,000 for an average estate by 1,700 and then to have added £19 million for the remaining properties. A more realistic figure would be 1,700 × £12,000 plus perhaps 20 percent or £4 million for the other properties, making £24 million in all. The lower figures are quite compatible with Edward Long's statement in 1774 that estates were valued at 10 years' purchase rather than the "inventory aggregation" method (cited by Edwards in *History* II, p. 372; R. B. Sheridan, "The Wealth of Jamaica," p. 305).

49. Between 1770 and 1779, 82,000 slaves in the Leewards produced an annual average of 21,200 tons of sugar, or 5.16 cwt. each on the average. If only three fourths worked on sugar estates, the average was about 7 cwts.; Deerr II.

50. Slave population from Chapter 2; sugar production from Pitman, p. 169 and Deerr II; produce per slave calculated on three fourths of the slave population for 1700–75, two thirds for 1790–1800; sugar prices from Pitman, Williams, Craton, and Walvin; gross income at rate of 10s. per cwt. in 1700, £1 in 1750–75, 30s. in 1790, £2 in 1800, and rum at 44 percent of sugar; profit per slave worked out again on three-fourths and two-thirds totals; market value of slaves at £25 for 1700, £30 for 1750, £35 for 1775, £40 for 1790, and £50 for 1800 (see above). Figures for 1775 largely from Sheridan, "Wealth of Jamaica," corrected. In 1774 Edward Long calculated that there were 775 sugar estates in Jamaica, when annual Jamaican sugar production at 50,000 tons was half the BWI total. If there were then 1,550 sugar estates in the BWI, average production was only 80 hogsheads a year. Total capitalization (1,550 × 200 acres at £10, 80 slaves at £40, buildings £1,000, stock £500 = £7,000 per estate) was therefore no more than £10 millions for sugar estates, with perhaps £1 million over for other holdings.

51. "The profits of the plantations were the source which fed the indebtedness charged upon the plantations themselves. In this sense Adam Smith was wrong: the wealth of the British West Indies did not all proceed from the mother country; after some initial loans in the earliest period which merely primed the pump, the wealth of the West Indies was created out of the profits of West Indies

themselves, and, with some assistance from the British tax-payer, much of it found a permanent home in Great Britain"; Richard Pares, *Merchants and Planters,* p. 50, quoted by R. B. Sheridan, "Wealth of Jamaica," p. 311.

52. Chapter 1, p. 40.

53. I.e., when measured as "social profits." This, of course, was what Adam Smith's argument was all about. For a neo-Smithian viewpoint, forcibly argued, see R. P. Thomas, "Sugar Colonies," pp. 30–43.

54. ". . . it is evident that the plantation economy of Jamaica came to be controlled and directed by a group of London merchants and absentee planters, and that the great family fortunes were more nearly allied to commerce and finance than they were to tropical agriculture. . . ."— Sheridan, "Wealth of Jamaica," p. 310, citing the planter-merchant families of Beckford, Long, Fuller, Vaughan, Bayly, Hibbert, Bourke, Grant, and Morse for Jamaica. For the Beckfords, see Boyd Alexander, *England's Wealthiest Son: A Study of William Beckford* (Centaur Press, 1962); for Pinneys, Richard Pares, *A West India Fortune* (Longmans, 1950). For the notion that the assumption of responsibility for plantations by mortgagees was a reversal of the capital flow, see Chapter 5.

55. Or even as a desperate expedient to save the plantations from financial disaster, as is argued in the case of the Jamaican Price family; Craton and Walvin, pp. 71–73, 156–58.

56. Sir Charles Whitworth, *State of the Trade of Great Britain in its imports and exports progressively from the year 1697–1773* (London, 1776) II, as tabulated in Eric Williams, *Capitalism and Slavery,* pp. 225–26; Arthur Young, *Annals of Agriculture* (London, 1784) I, p. 13.

57. Adapted from Eric Williams, *Capitalism and Slavery* III, n. 16, pp. 225–26.

58. *The Parliamentary History of England to the Year 1803* (London, 1819) XXXIV, 14–18, quoted in R. B. Sheridan, "Wealth of Jamaica," p. 306.

59. Telling quotations from most of these writers are used by Eric Williams, *Capitalism and Slavery,* pp. 51–57. See also F. W. Pitman, *British West Indies.*

60. Edward Long, *Jamaica* I, p. 507.

61. R. P. Thomas, "The Sugar Colonies of the Old Empire: Profit or Loss for Great Britain," in *Economic History*

Review XXII (1968), p. 36. Thomas reduced this estimate to £870,450 (while adding up Sheridan's figures incorrectly), which Sheridan countered by raising it to £1,547,055, largely by raising the figure of retained profits; ibid., p. 56.

62. Though these areas do receive full treatment in R. B. Sheridan's *Sugar and Slavery* (Caribbean Universities Press, 1974).

63. Eric Williams, *Capitalism and Slavery*, p. 58.

64. An exception was Bermuda (not properly in the West Indies despite Colonial Office classification), the economic viability of which was largely dependent on the famous locally built sloops and schooners. That Bermuda was more closely akin and sympathetic to the mainlanders was not unrelated to this fact.

65. The amount of clothing listed as needed for the 250 blacks of Bryan Edwards' 1793 estate was approximately what was required in trade at that time for eight to ten slaves in Africa—just about the average importation each year by a 250-slave estate! Although the commodities are less comparable, metal supplies for the estate were also of roughly equivalent value; Edwards, *History*, pp. 253–54.

66. See, for example, the numerous petitions to Parliament of the weavers of Exeter, Plymouth, Totnes, Ashburton, Kidderminster, and Minehead between 1694 and 1711, and from those in Halifax, Burnley, Colne, and Kendal around 1735; Eric Williams, *Capitalism and Slavery*, pp. 66–67.

67. Ibid., p. 68, n. 90.

68. For a complete inventory of one estate's imports for one year (1789), see Craton and Walvin, *A Jamaican Plantation*, Appendix I, pp. 320–27.

69. A. H. Dodd, *The Industrial Revolution in North Wales* (University of Wales Press, 1933), p. 37.

70. Sheridan, "Wealth of Jamaica," p. 307.

71. Just as the great insurance complex of Lloyd's could never have developed without the triangular trade or perhaps, indeed, without wars as well.

72. *Capitalism and Slavery*, pp. 98–107.

73. Boulton to Watt, quoted in J. Lord, *Capital and Steam Power, 1750–1800* (P. S. King, 1923), pp. 113, 192.

74. J. H. Chapman, *The Early Railway Age, 1820–1850* (Cambridge University Press, 1930), pp. 187–88; Eric Williams, *Capitalism and Slavery,* p. 103.

75. Eric Williams, *Capitalism and Slavery,* p. 68.

76. *British Sessional Papers, Commons,* A/P (1789) XXVI, Part Four, No. 2, evidence by Mr. Samuel Taylor, March 8, 1789. Eric Williams, *Capitalism and Slavery,* p. 70, misquotes £380,000 and 180,000 for Africa alone, citing Holt and Gregson Papers (Liverpool Public Library) X, pp. 422–23; J. Wheeler, *Manchester, its Political, Social and Commercial History, Ancient and Modern* (Manchester, 1842).

77. L. J. Ragatz, *Statistics for the Study of British Caribbean History, 1763–1833* (London, n.d.), Table VI, p. 15.

78. While also helping to erode the East India Company's monopoly.

79. For a brilliant account of the fortune built by William Ewart Gladstone's father, see S. G. Checkland, *The Gladstones* (Cambridge University Press, 1971). Superficially Gladstone went against the trend, shifting his burgeoning investments from general trade into plantations and slaves (as well as home-based industry) in the last decades of slavery. The fact that his overseas investments were almost exclusively in newly acquired Guyana indicates that they were speculative consolidations in a relatively expansionist area in which an efficient manager could expect to make whatever profit was going. Much of Gladstone's new property, moreover, was acquired at knockdown prices from colonials who were already his debtors. Finally, despite being one of the largest beneficiaries of the slave compensation payment after 1834, the Gladstones did not make an over-all profit on their West Indian enterprises. For their pains they also suffered the stigma of owning properties affected by the serious slave rebellion of 1823. See Chapter 5.

Chapter 4

1. G. V. Plekhanov, *Literatura i estetika* (Moscow, 1958) II, pp. 245–46, quoted by Donald Fanger, "The Peasant in Literature," in Wayne S. Vucivich (ed.), *The Peasant in Nineteenth Century Russia* (Stanford Univer-

sity Press, 1968), p. 232. Marx, of course, despised the peasant chiefly for his "petty bourgeois" tendencies. The slave (or serf), on the other hand, is more properly "proletarian," even an "industrial proletarian."

2. Frank M. Snowden, Jr., *Blacks in Antiquity* (Belknap Press, 1970).

3. J. C. Jeaffreson (ed.), *A Young Squire of the Seventeenth Century* (London, 1878) I, p. 258; Eric Williams, *Columbus to Castro*, p. 100.

4. L. F. Stock (ed.), *Proceedings and Debates in the British Parliaments respecting North America*, 5 vols. (New York, 1924–41) I, p. 249; Eric Williams, *Capitalism and Slavery*, p. 17.

5. Such a law was one of the half dozen passed in the very first session of the Jamaican Assembly. Bermuda Acts as late as 1730 referred to "Negroes and other Slaves . . ."

6. C. A. Herrick, *White Servitude in Pennsylvania* (Philadelphia, 1926), p. 3; Eric Williams, *Capitalism and Slavery*, pp. 16–17; Oscar Handlin, *Race and Nationality in American Life* (Doubleday, 1957), pp. 10–11. For white bondsmen in mainland America, see Richard Hofstadter, *America at 1750: A Social Portrait* (Cape, 1972).

7. *Calendar of State Papers, Colonial America and the West Indies, 1675–77* IX, p. 445 (August 15, 1676).

8. J. S. Bassett, *Slavery and Servitude in the Colony of North Carolina* (Baltimore, 1896), p. 77; Eric Williams, *Capitalism and Slavery*, pp. 19–20.

9. Eric Williams, *Capitalism and Slavery*, p. 25; Herman Merivale, *Lectures on Colonization and Colonies* (Oxford University Press, 1928), p. 62.

10. Handlin, pp. 10–12.

11. This is the position argued with some plausibility, for example, by Jesse Lemisch, "Jack Tar in the Streets: Merchant Seamen in the Politics of Revolutionary America," in *William and Mary Quarterly*, 3rd ser. XXI (July 1968), pp. 371–407.

12. Eric Williams, *Capitalism and Slavery*, p. 7.

13. Richard Hakluyt, *The Principal Navigations, Voyages, Traffiques and Discoveries of the English Nation* (1582) (Maclehose, 1904), pp. 262–64, incorporated in James Walvin, *The Black Presence: A Documentary History of the Negro in England* (Orbach & Chambers, 1972), pp. 34–37.

14. Thomas Browne in his famous *Enquiries into Vulgar and Common Errors* (1646) echoed Best's dismissal of the sun as the cause of the black's complexion, but rejected the Noah myth of the black's "Second Fall." However, he was unable to present an alternative hypothesis save God's inscrutability, though to his eternal credit he ridiculed the notions that black was ugly and white beautiful per se; Walvin, *Black Presence*, pp. 37–47.

15. *History of Jamaica*, 2 vols. (London, 1774), pp. 351–83; Walvin, *Black Presence*, pp. 117–31.

16. Sir Fortunatus Dwarris, *Substance of three reports . . . into the administration of civil and criminal justice in the West Indies* (London, 1827), p. 433.

17. The quaint formula in the 1730 Bermuda Act was, "We . . . do most humbly beseech your Majesty that it may be Enacted and be it Enacted by your Majesties Lieut. Governor Council and Assembly and hereby it is Enacted and ordained by the Authority of the Same . . . from and after Publication hereof. . . ."

18. See particularly Elsa Goveia, *The West Indian Slave Laws of the Eighteenth Century* (Caribbean Universities Press, 1970).

19. "A General View of the Principles on which this System of Laws appears to have been originally founded . . . ," *British Sessional Papers, Commons, A/P* (1789) XXVI, p. 646a, Part Three. John Reeves (1752–1829), who had been Chief Justice of Newfoundland, was also, significantly, cofounder in November 1792 of the Association for the Preservation of Liberty and Property against Republicans and Levellers.

20. F. C. Innes, "The Pre-sugar era of European settlement in Barbados," in *Journal of Caribbean History* I (November 1970), pp. 1–22.

21. And perhaps to exclude Jews as well as infidels.

22. Handlin, pp. 13–14.

23. Several Navigation Laws declared slaves to be commodities, and at least two Acts specified the rights of Englishmen to hold property in slaves. The legal status of slavery *in England*, however, remained ambiguous; James Walvin, *Black and White: A Study of the Negro in England, 1555–1945* (Longmans, 1973).

24. Edwards III, p. 36, quoted in Elsa Goveia, *Slave Laws*, p. 35.

25. The legal form in Jamaica, where the 1717 law allowing mutilation was not repealed until 1787, was "death or any other punishment." See Edwards II, pp. 66–67; W. J. Gardner, *History of Jamaica* (London, 1873), pp. 177–79; Elsa Goveia, *Slave Laws*, p. 23, n. 51. Of the conspirators of 1736 in Antigua, "six were gibbeted, five broken on the wheel, and seventy-seven burned alive," F. W. Pitman, *The Development of the British West Indies, 1700–1763* (Yale University Press, 1917), pp. 59–60. See also Hans Sloane, *A voyage to the islands . . .*, 2 vols. (London, 1702); John Atkins, *A Voyage to Guinea, Brasil and the West Indies* (London, 1737).

26. Good (or horrid) examples from the mainland colonies during the early days of slavery are quoted by Richard Hofstadter: "In 1712 and again in 1714 South Carolina codified its slave controls and punishments, provided for patrols, and prescribed death for running away. . . . In North Carolina runaways were defined as outlaws liable to be killed, and a conspiracy by any three slaves was made a felony. Maryland's laws . . . provided for cropping the ears of blacks who struck whites and allowed that fugitive and resisting Negroes be 'shot, killed or destroyed'"; *America at 1750*, pp. 124–25.

27. Though several codes decreed that a second case of willful murder should be treated as such. Only Tobago decreed that willfully killing a black could count as murder at the first offense, and then not until 1775; Elsa Goveia, *Slave Laws*, p. 29.

28. The Bermuda law of 1730.

29. See, for example, the horrific fate of the South Carolina slave who had killed his overseer—suspended in a cage to die of wounds and starvation while his eyes were pecked out by scavenging birds—described by Hector St. John de Crèvecoeur, *Letters from an American Farmer* (1782), (Dent, Everyman ed., 1912), p. 173.

30. Though a New Jersey law decreeing castration for rape or even willing intercourse between black men and white women, and a Pennsylvania law ordaining castration even for attempted rape, were disallowed by the Crown as being repugnant to metropolitan law; Arthur Zilversmit, *The First Emancipation* (University of Chicago Press, 1967), pp. 9, 16.

31. The origins are still largely speculative. For Jamaica, see Sidney W. Mintz, "The Jamaican Internal Marketing Pattern," in *Social and Economic Studies* IV, i (March 1955).

32. H. A. Wyndham, *The Atlantic and Slavery* (Oxford University Press, 1935), p. 284; Edward Brathwaite, *The Development of Creole Society in Jamaica, 1770–1820* (Clarendon Press, 1971), p. 168.

33. Arnold Sio, Colgate University, in private correspondence.

34. Elsa Goveia, *Slave Society in the British Leeward Islands at the End of the Eighteenth Century* (Yale University Press, 1965), pp. 203–62.

35. Act No. 28 of 1761 I, 7, 12; Wyndham, p. 281.

36. For a brief description of the plight of the free coloreds in the American mainland colonies, see Hofstadter, pp. 114–19.

37. The sole exception being that in Jamaica the child of a mustee slave woman and white father was decreed automatically free by an act of 1781.

38. Wyndham, p. 295.

39. *P.R.O., C.O.* 5/1324, Index, 8331; Wyndham, pp. 297–98. The contemporary spelling of "villain" for "villein" was as significant as the failure to distinguish between 'Slav' and slave in describing the inhabitants of Eastern Europe.

40. The degree to which a sugar estate was even like a village is admirably shown in an eighteenth-century description quoted in W. J. Gardner, *A History of Jamaica* (London, 1873), and requoted in F. Henriques, *Family and Colour in Jamaica* (Eyre Spottiswoode, 1953), p. 18, and Douglas Hall, *Free Jamaica, 1838–1865: An Economic History* (Yale University Press, 1959), p. 208.

41. Michael Craton and James Walvin, *A Jamaican Plantation: The History of Worthy Park, 1670–1970*, p. 134, n. 43. For a splendidly detailed account of slave housing see Brathwaite, pp. 234–36.

42. Edward Long, *The History of Jamaica*, 2 vols., II (London, 1774), p. 380.

43. *British Sessional Papers, Commons*, A/P (1789) XXVI, p. 646a, Part Three, "A General View of the . . . Laws," p. 9.

44. Leslie, pp. 28–39.

45. *British Sessional Papers, Commons, A/P* (1789) p. 646a, Part Three, p. 9. The fine specified was £20, though not for each slave.

46. Ibid., Jamaica A, No. 6; Brathwaite, pp. 232–34.

47. Long II, pp. 380, 413.

48. Though the estimate of an average of "five to seven years of useful work" for the Africans after arrival given by one writer is grossly misleading. Those who survived the first three years of acclimatization could probably look forward to a further thirty years of life in 1730 and perhaps forty years after 1810; Michael Craton, "Jamaican Slave Mortality; Fresh Light from Worthy Park, Longville and the Tharp Estates," in *Journal of Caribbean History* III (November 1971), pp. 1–27.

49. Ibid., pp. 18–21.

50. A good example is provided by Rose Price, the son of the owner of Worthy Park, who spent an energetic three years in Jamaica, 1792–96; Craton and Walvin, pp. 168–79.

51. M. G. Lewis, *Journal of a West Indian Proprietor* (London, 1834). Sir William Young's tour of the Windwards (c. 1800) provides an interesting comparison, *A Tour Through . . . Barbados, St. Vincent, Antigua, Tobago and Grenada* (London, 1801).

52. Benjamin Quarles, "Lord Dunmore as Liberator," in *William and Mary Quarterly* XV (October 4, 1968), pp. 494–507.

53. Edwards II, pp. 7–8. Compare this with the following quotation from the *Pennsylvania Journal* in 1756: "The people of this province are generally of the middling sort, and at pretty much upon a level. They are chiefly industrious farmers, artificers or men in trade; they can enjoy and are fond of freedom, and the *meanest among them* thinks he has a right to civility from the greatest"; quoted by Clinton Rossiter, *Seedtime of the Republic* (Harcourt, Brace, 1953), p. 106; and Hofstadter, p. 131.

54. Trelawny to Board of Trade (October 14, 1747), *P.R.O., C.O.* 137/24; Pitman, p. 36.

55. Long, p. 289, line 15.

56. Abbot E. Smith, *Colonists in Bondage* (University of North Carolina Press, 1947); Hofstadter, p. 60.

57. *Jamaica Plantership* (London, 1839).

58. Edwards, *History* (1801 ed.) II, p. 155. "The strangers too were best pleased with his arrangement," went on Edwards, "and ever afterwards considered themselves as the adopted children of those by whom they were thus protected. . . ."

59. Ibid., p. 103.

60. Stanley Elkins, *Slavery* (University of Chicago Press, 1968), p. 100.

61. Barry Higman, "Slave Family Structure in the British West Indies, 1800–1834." American Historical Association Conference paper, 1973.

62. Rose Price, *Pledges on Colonial Slavery, to Candidates for Seats in Parliament, Rightly Considered* (Penzance: T. Vigurs, 1832), pp. 8–11. The italics are Price's own.

63. E. Brathwaite, p. 237.

64. Charles Leslie, *History of Jamaica* (London, 1840), pp. 28–39, quoted in Pitman, pp. 24–25.

65. Philemon, pp. 10–18.

66. Bishop Ken, 1692, *Hymns Ancient and Modern*, 3.

67. The word *Obeah* is used here more generically to mean African religion than perhaps it should. Modern writers such as Patterson distinguish as clearly between *Myalism* and *Obeah* as between both and the later *Pocomania*, despite the evident varieties in types of *Obeah*, the nineteenth-century use of the term *Myalism* by the whites simply to distinguish the religious element from the medicine of *Obeah*, and the fact that late in the nineteenth century *Obeah* and *Myalism* were legally identified; P. D. Curtin, *Two Jamaicas: The Role of Ideas in a Tropical Colony, 1830–65* (Harvard University Press, 1955), pp. 29–32, 158–77; H. O. Patterson, *Sociology of Slavery* (MacGibbon & Kee, 1967), pp. 185–95; Martha Beckwith, *Black Roadways: A Study of Jamaican Folklife* (University of North Carolina Press, 1929), argued that the Jamaican revivalism of the 1860s was a marriage of Baptist and *Myalist* religion, and that *Pocomania* was a synthesis of revivalism and *Obeah*. For *Shango*, see George E. Simpson, *The Shango Cult in Trinidad* (Puerto Rico, 1965).

68. For two profound accounts of *Voodoo* as an authentic religion, see James Leyburn, *The Haitian People*, rev. ed. (Yale University Press, 1966), pp. 131–65; George E.

Simpson, "The Belief System of Haitian Vodun," in *American Anthropologist* XLVII (1945), pp. 35–59.

69. Patrick Leigh Fermor, *The Traveller's Tree* (Murray, 1950), pp. 187–88.

70. ". . . we cannot believe that anything else but desire after the word of God causes them to come, some even from distant places, but when we endeavour to get personally acquainted with them and invite them to come to speaking, they make fair promises but in vain we look for them. . . . This may be owing to several reasons, but the chief among many is, we suppose, the mere system of works, depending upon the observance of an outward christianity to combine with Beliam. . . . Mount Tabor Diary (August 14, 1830), Moravian Church Records, Mount Tabor, Barbados, quoted in E. Brathwaite, pp. 252–65.

71. P. D. Curtin, *Two Jamaicas: The Role of Ideas in a Tropical Colony, 1830–1865* (1955) (Atheneum, 1970), pp. 35–37.

72. Hans Sloane, Introduction.

73. Beckford, *A Descriptive Account of the Island of Jamaica*, 2 vols. (London, 1790), pp. 216–18; Long, p. 424, both quoted by H. O. Patterson, pp. 233–36.

74. The parallel case of Job ben Solomon springs to mind. An aristocratic and well-educated Moslem Fulani, he was himself captured while slave-trading but released, sent to England, feted as a celebrity or at least a curiosity, and finally repatriated; P. D. Curtin, *Africa Remembered* (University of Wisconsin Press, 1967).

75. Jamaica Island Record Office, Wills, 40/152; Craton and Walvin, p. 94, n. 65.

76. M'Mahon, *Jamaica Plantership* (London, 1839).

77. *British Sessional Papers, Commons, A/P, 1790–91*, evidence of Henry Coor.

78. Edwards, pp. 27–33.

79. Herbert Aptheker, *American Negro Slave Revolts* (New York: Columbia University Press, 1943); H. O. Patterson, pp. 260–83. For a collection of views on American slave resistance, see J. H. Bracey, Jr., A. Meier, and E. Rudwick (eds.), *American Slavery: The Question of Resistance* (Wadsworth, 1970).

80. Elkins, pp. 104–32. For criticisms, see Earle E. Thorpe, "Chattel Slavery and Concentration Camps," in

Negro History Bulletin XXV (May 1962), pp. 171–76;
Eugene D. Genovese, "Rebellion and Docility in the Negro
Slave: A Critique of the Elkins Thesis," in *Civil War History* XIII (December 1967), pp. 293–314.

81. For a collection of readings, J. B. Duff and P. M.
Mitchell (eds.), *The Nat Turner Rebellion: The Historical
Event and the Modern Controversy* (New York: Harper
& Row, 1971).

82. Hofstadter, pp. 119–30.

83. Long, p. 462.

84. "Individual and Mass Behavior in Extreme Situations," in *Journal of Abnormal Psychology* XXXVIII (October 1943).

85. Robert Moore, "Slave Rebellions in Guyana," unpublished paper (April 1971).

86. The Second Maroon War (1795–96) was not really
an exception. It was provoked as much by the paranoia
of the Jamaican whites in the face of French and Haitian
threats as by provocative actions on the part of the Maroons. Moreover, the Maroons had almost completely lost
their empathy with the Jamaican slaves, some of whom
were even rewarded with manumission for aiding the
campaign. For a somewhat contrary view, see E. Brathwaite, pp. 248–51.

87. Eric Williams, *Columbus to Castro*, p. 321.

88. Robert Moore, pp. 12–13.

89. Brathwaite, pp. 201–2.

90. In one case at Worthy Park, the return of a runaway headman was not even followed by his demotion.

91. Long, p. 423. The absentee master, on the other
hand, was as often the hero of the work songs. This, of
course, may have been largely because he *was* an absentee. There is little evidence that resident owners were
treated any more favorably in work songs than overseers
on absentees' estates. For U.S. examples, see Gilbert
Osofsky (ed.), *Puttin' on Ole Massa* (New York: Harper &
Row, 1969), pp. 9–44; E. Brathwaite, pp. 222–25.

92. H. O. Patterson, pp. 174–81. The original Quashie
story originated in the Abbe Raynal's tale of the slave
"Quazy," who cut his own throat rather than suffer unrighteous punishment; *Histoire des deux Indes*, pp. 254–
55, though it was retold with force by James Ramsay,
An Essay in the Treatment and Conversion of African

Slaves in the British Sugar Colonies (London, 1784), pp. 212–25. Stanley Elkins and others detect a similar trait in the United States, the "Sambo" mentality; *Slavery,* pp. 82–87, 130–33, 227–29.

Chapter 5

1. Reginald Coupland, *The British Anti-Slavery Movement* (Butterworth, 1933); *Wilberforce: A Narrative* (Oxford University Press, 1923); G. R. Mellor, *British Imperial Trusteeship, 1783–1850* (Faber, 1951); Eric Williams, *Capitalism and Slavery* (Deutsch, 1964). Roger T. Anstey, in his reassessment of Eric Williams' thesis, "Capitalism and Slavery: A Critique," in *Economic History Review,* 2nd ser. XXI (1968), 2, pp. 307–20, cites C. M. MacInnes, *England and Slavery* (L. Arrowsmith, 1934) and F. J. Klingberg, *The Anti-Slavery Movement in England* (London, 1926) as prophilanthropist accounts like Coupland's, and traces this stand back to W. E. H. Lecky, *A History of European Morals,* 6th. ed. (London, 1884) II, p. 153. He cites only C. L. R. James, *Black Jacobins* (1938) as an antecedent to *Capitalism and Slavery,* despite Williams' own fulsome acknowledgment to L. J. Ragatz. The works of W. L. Mathieson are, perhaps justly, ignored.

2. *Universal Spectator and Weekly Journal* (August 1734), quoted in Dame Lilian Penson's masterly *Colonial Agents of the British West Indies* (University of London Press, 1924), p. 196.

3. The American Jasper Maudit's estimate in 1764; Penson, p. 228. G. P. Judd, *Members of Parliament, 1734–1832* (Yale University Press, 1955), Appendix 14, p. 89, gives much lower figures, but these are misleading. Judd does not give double entries and only identifies as West Indians those with unequivocal connections that he can document. He therefore almost certainly excludes those merchants and bankers (and perhaps even Nabobs and Indians) with *some* West Indian interest, as well as those with purely family ties, and the members of the Navy Interest, who were always likely to vote with the West Indians.

4. A prime example is the minutes of a meeting between West Indian and North American merchants on

March 10, 1766, *British Museum Add. Mss.*, 8/33, C, ff. 91–92, quoted by Penson, Appendix III, pp. 16, 284–85.

5. Dunmore to Hillsborough May 1772, *P.R.O., C.O.* 5/1373, f. 202.

6. G. R. Mellor, p. 345.

7. H. B. Grigsby, *History of the Virginia Federal Constitution of 1788* (1890), p. 260.

8. Edmund Burke's position on the West Indies and slavery was made somewhat equivocal by the fact that his brother William was a well-known West Indian placeman.

9. For the difficult question of Pitt's role, particularly in the Abolition campaign, see J. Holland Rose, *Life of William Pitt, 1783–1806* (Stanford University Press, 1939), pp. 211–12; J. Steven Watson, *Reign of George III* (Oxford University Press, 1969), p. 301; P. C. Lipscomb, "William Pitt and the Abolition of the Slave Trade," unpublished Ph.D. thesis (University of Texas, 1960).

10. Richard B. Morris, *The Peacemakers: The Great Powers and American Independence* (Harper, 1965); John Norris, *Shelburne and Reform* (Macmillan, 1963).

11. Michael Craton, "Caribbean Vice Admiralty Courts, 1763–1815; Indispensable Agents of an Imperial System," unpublished Ph.D. thesis (McMaster University, 1968).

12. Edwards, *The History, Civil and Commercial, of the British Colonies in the West Indies* (1793), 2 vols. (London, 1819) I, ii, pp. 312–14. See Chapter 3. The total of 1,061 is somewhat suspect, being derived from William Beckford, who was not so alarmist as Edwards.

13. A wartime year. The potential was obviously higher.

14. By 1788, St. Domingue was producing 73,000 tons of sugar as well as 30,000 tons of coffee and 2,800 tons of cotton; Eric Williams, *Columbus to Castro*, p. 237, quoting M. de Saint Mery, *Description . . . de l'isle Saint-Domingue . . .*, 2 vols. (Philadelphia, 1797–98). In 1822, Haiti produced 15,677 tons of coffee and 291 tons of sugar for export, compared with 30,424 and 102,934 in 1791: Alexander Barclay, *A Practical View of the Present State of Slavery in the West Indies . . .* (London: Smith, Elder, 1828), p. 343, quoting *Edinburgh Review*.

15. *British Sessional Papers, Commons, A/P* (1789); William Beckford, *A Descriptive Account of the Island of Jamaica*, 2 vols. (London, 1790); Edwards II, p. 466; Noel Deerr, *History of Sugar*, 2 vols. (1949–50) I, pp.

176–98; Hugh Thomas, *Cuba: The Pursuit of Freedom* (Eyre and Spottiswoode, 1971), pp. 109–27; Eric Williams, *Columbus to Castro* (Deutsch, 1970), pp. 264, 290, 361–72; Michael Craton and James Walvin, *A Jamaican Plantation: A History of Worthy Park, 1670–1970* (W. H. Allen and University of Toronto Press, 1970), pp. 74, 156, 188, 222; R. B. Sheridan, *The Development of the Plantations to 1750* (Caribbean Universities Press 1970), p. 49. Compare the figures given in D. G. Hall, *Free Jamaica, 1838–1865: An Economic History* (1959) (Caribbean Universities Press, 1969), p. 82: 1772, p. 775; 1791, p. 767; 1804, p. 859; 1834, p. 646; 1848, p. 513; 1854, p. 330.

16. See Chapters 2 and 3.

17. See Table 18.

18. On May 22, 1787.

19. Thomas Hodkin, *Life of George Fox* (Philadelphia, n.d.), cited in F. J. Klingberg, *The Anti-Slavery Movement in England* (Oxford University Press, 1926), pp. 31–32.

20. *Encyclopedie* XVI (Neuchatel, 1765), p. 532.

21. It was, of course, not a new idea. The Renaissance writer Peter Martyr, for example, described the Amerindians discovered by Columbus as "living in that golden world of which the old writers speak so much, wherein men lived simply and innocently without enforcement of laws, without quarreling, judges, and libels, content only to satisfy nature." To Peter Martyr and his contemporaries, however, the idea of aboriginal bliss was inextricably tied up with the biblical and Christian doctrine of man's Fall from Grace: Richard Eden (ed.), *The Decades of the newe worlde of West India . . . Wrytten in the Latine tongue by Peter Martyr of Angleria . . .* (London, 1555).

22. J. G. Stedman, *Narrative of a five years expedition against the revolted Negroes of Surinam,* 2 vols. (London: J. Johnson, 1796).

23. "The Little Black Boy" (1789).

24. James Walvin, *The Black Presence* (Orbach & Chambers, 1971), pp. 81–92. The Jamaican Francis Williams, for example, was ridiculed for the poor quality of his Latin verses. Apparently no one thought to defend him on the grounds that he was, after all, the best *Jamaican* Latinist, black or white!

25. *Calendar of State Papers, Col., A. & W.I., 1669–79,* p. 412.

26. Yorke-Talbot Opinion, H. T. Catterall, *Judicial Cases Concerning American Slavery and the Negro,* 5 vols. (Washington, D.C., 1930–35) I, p. 12.

27. James Walvin, "The Somerset Case, 1772," in *Black and White: The History of the Negroes in England, 1555–1945* (Longmans, 1972); *Howell's State Trials* XX, pp. 1–2.

28. *Case of the Slave Grace,* H. T. Catterall, I, 34; James Walvin, *Black and White,* though compare the case of the ex-slave rating in HMS, *Pyramus,* John Williams, whom the Admiralty lawyers in 1826 decided was free by virtue of his service; P.R.O. Adm. 1/4240, Horton to Croker (March 28, 1826).

29. W. G. Hoffman, *British Industry, 1700–1950* (Oxford University Press, 1955); A. H. Imlah, *Economic Elements in the Pax Britannica* (Harvard University Press, 1958, pp. 37–38; E. B. Schumpeter, *English Overseas Trade Statistics 1697–1808* (Oxford University Press, 1960) XV, XVII; Cesar Moreau, *State of the Trade of Great Britain with all Parts of the World* (London, 1822); G. H. Porter, *The Progress of the Nation* (Methuen, 1912); B. R. Mitchell and P. Deane, *Abstract of British Historical Statistics* (Cambridge University Press, 1962), pp. 271, 280, 289–91, 311–14.

30. Prince Hoare, *Memoirs of Granville Sharp* (London, 1828), 2 vols. I, pp. 359–61 II, pp. xxvi–xxxiii.

31. *An Essay on the Treatment and Conversion of African Slaves in the British Sugar Colonies* (Dublin, 1784).

32. Clarkson's famous prize essay, *On the Slavery and Commerce of the Human Species,* was first published in 1786, though the publication of his statistical findings came later. In 1788 first appeared John Newton's influential *Thoughts upon the African Slave Trade,* also based on personal experience, though somewhat dated.

33. Most of the minutes of evidence and papers are to be found in the *British Sessional Papers, Commons, A/P & Reports,* 1789 XXVI, pp. 626–34; XXV pp. 635–45; XXVI, pp. 646–646a; 1790 XXIX, pp. 698–99; 1790–91, XXIV pp. 745–48; 1791 IX, p. 98; 1792 XXXV, pp. 766–69. Together these represent the indispensable basis of all our knowledge of slave trade and slavery at the height of their successful operation.

34. Act of 28 Geo. III, c. 54.

35. W. Cobbett and T. C. Hansard, *Parliamentary History of England from the Earliest Period to the Year 1803* (London, 1804–7) XXIX, pp. 250–62, 335–54, 459. For the important debates of 1789–90 see *Parliamentary History* XXVII, pp. 495–506; XXVIII, pp. 41–71, 311–15.

36. *Parliamentary History* XXIX, pp. 1055–58, 1133–58. In fact, it was Pitt's alter ego, the anti-abolitionist Henry Dundas, who substituted "gradually" for "immediately" in the motion. Besides this, the Lords delayed a decision until the following session by calling for further evidence. At this time, £235,280 was raised for the Sierra Leone project by a public issue of shares, but the overwhelming majority of subscribers were committed abolitionists. Christopher Fyfe, *A History of Sierra Leone* (Oxford University Press, 1962), p. 30; C. B. Wadström, *Essay on Colonization* (London, 1793) II, Appendix.

37. For the bitter controversy on this issue, see Eric Williams, *Capitalism and Slavery*, pp. 146–50, 219; G. R. Mellor, pp. 50–60.

38. *Parliamentary History* XXX, pp. 1443–44; XXXI, pp. 469–70; XXXIV, pp. 1118–38; XXXVIII, p. 1139.

39. It is interesting to note that Wilberforce himself rejected the amelioration proposals, which were, however, quite strongly advocated by C. R. Willis (later Lord Sanford), Chairman of the Standing Committee of the West India Merchants and Planters.

40. Acts of 28 Geo. III, c. 54, c. 88; 29 Geo. III, c. 66.

41. G. R. Mellor, pp. 60–62.

42. R. I. and S. Wilberforce, *The Life of William Wilberforce* (London, 1838), 5 vols. III, p. 164.

43. Wilberforce, *Wilberforce* III, pp. 164–67.

44. William Cobbett, *Parliamentary Debates* II, pp. 543–58; III, pp. 641–74.

45. Act of Geo. III, c. 52. An Act passed slightly later (46 Geo. III, c. 119) also forbade the employment of any new ship in the slave trade whatever the destinations.

46. *Parliamentary Debates* VIII, pp. 672, 693, 978–79, 995. Among the intransigents in the Lords were the Duke of Clarence and three other members of the Royal Family, and the crusty old Earl St. Vincent, who ostentatiously walked out of the House during the debate.

47. Acts of 51 Geo. III, c. 23.

48. See for example H. Brougham, *A Concise Statement of the Question Regarding the Abolition of the Slave Trade* (London, 1804), pp. 10–11.

49. Charles Buxton (ed.), *Memoirs of Sir Thomas Fowell Buxton, Bart.* . . . , new ed. (John Murray, 1877) XV, pp. 122–26.

50. Michael Craton, "Jamaican Slave Mortality; Fresh Light from Worthy Park, Longville and the Tharp Estates," in *Journal of Caribbean History* III (November 1971), pp. 1–27. The highest mortality occurred, naturally, in Trinidad and Guyana, where in 1830 the proportion of African-born slaves was at least twice as high as in other colonies. See Chapter 4.

51. Klingberg, pp. 278–80. The English price of sugar exclusive of duty had fallen from 73s. a cwt. in 1814 to 24s. in 1831.

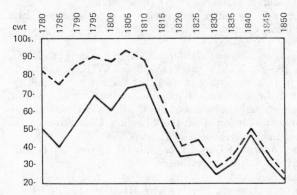

Upper and lower prices of British West Indian muscovado in London, 1780-1850

Sources: Edwards II, p. 267; Ragatz, *Statistics* IV, iii; D. G. Hall, p. 270. Note also the tendency for higher and lower prices to equalize, a sure sign that even efficient producers were facing disaster. The Parliamentary Inquiry set up in March 1807 reported that the price of sugar had fallen below the cost of production, through overconsumption; *British Sessional Papers, Commons, Reports* (1808), pp. 178, 278, 300, 318; Roger Anstey, "Capitalism and Slavery: A Critique," in *Economic History Review*, 2nd ser. XXI, 2, (1968), pp. 307–20, 313–25; Eric Williams, *Capitalism and Slavery*, pp. 149–50.

52. Gabriel Debien, the *doyen* of French Caribbeanists, has detected the same process in the last years of French rule in St. Domingue.

53. Wilberforce III, p. 481.

54. Ibid. III pp. 484–85; Stephen to Lord Liverpool (August 23, 1810), P.R.O., C.O. 152/96; *Report of the African Institution* (1812), p. 14; *Parliamentary Debates* XXXVIII (1817), pp. 304, 841; Sir George Stephen, *Antislavery Recollections . . .* (London, 1854), pp. 13–14.

55. First germinated as early as his book *The Crisis of the Sugar Colonies* (London, 1802). These ideas had insensibly developed along with Stephen's power as an *eminence grise;* D. J. Murray, *The West Indies and the Development of Colonial Government, 1801–1834* (Clarendon Press, 1965).

56. Act of 59 Geo. II, c. 120.

57. See the extremely thorough article by D. Eltis, "The Traffic in Slaves between the British West Indian Colonies, 1807–1833," in *Economic History Review* XXV (February 1972), pp. 55–64, which revises a much earlier article by Eric Williams, "The British West Indian Slave Trade after its Abolition in 1807," in *Journal of Negro History* XXVII (1942), p. 180.

58. In fact, the case was reopened and the sadistic Rawlins was sentenced to a fine of £200 and three months in jail for manslaughter; Klingberg, pp. 179–80.

59. James Stephen (Jr.), *The Slavery of the British West India Colonies Delineated*, Vol. I (London, 1824) (Vol. II, 1830).

60. See, for example, the edition of October 19, 1823: "Macaulay (who is the most active of the *set*) having made a fortune by trade in Sierra Leone, has established himself as an East India merchant, and is deeply interested in the success of the *East India* sugar trade, Stephen (another of them) sold when he could get the highest price for them, all his slaves and property in St. Kitts. . . ." Quoted in Klingberg, p. 186, n. 7.

61. *Parliamentary Debates*, 2nd ser. IX, pp. 285–86.

62. Copies of Bathurst's two circulars dated May 28 and July 9, 1823 are given in Klingberg, Appendix B, pp. 336–50. It was shortly after this that the first two Anglican

dioceses were set up in the West Indies, covering Jamaica (with the Bahamas) and the Leewards respectively.

63. Quoted from *British Sessional Papers* (1824) XXIV, 427, 2, Jamaica, 7, in Klingberg, p. 216, n. 83.

64. By the Act of 6 Geo. IV, c. 76.

65. West India Sub-Committee minutes, 1828–30, cited in G. R. Mellor, p. 97.

66. Sir George Stephen, *Antislavery Recollections*, pp. 120–22.

67. H. J. Klingberg, p. 255.

68. Ibid., pp. 256–60; *Parliamentary Debates*, 3rd ser. III, pp. 939, 1410–61; *British Sessional Papers, Commons, A/P* (1831–32) XLVI, 1, 93 ff., sections 1–121.

69. Buxton, pp. 130–42. The Report of the Graham Commission, which provided ample evidence for the emancipists' viewpoint, was published as *British Sessional Papers, Commons, Reports* (1831–32), 721 XX. Parliament, however, did vote £30,000 to relieve the damage suffered in the rebellion by the Jamaican planters; *Parliamentary Debates*, 3rd ser. XIV, pp. 1127–28.

70. For example, the Colonial Secretary, Lord Howick, who was at least partially "converted"; D. J. Murray, *Colonial Government*, p. 94. See also J. H. Hinton, *Memoir of William Knibb, Missionary in Jamaica* (London, 1847).

71. Maneuverings behind the scene are minutely recounted by D. J. Murray, *Colonial Government*, pp. 193–202. For earlier but detailed descriptions of the various plans, see W. L. Burn, *Emancipation and Apprenticeship in the British West Indies* (Cape, 1937), pp. 102–20; L. J. Ragatz, *The Fall of the Planter Class in the British Caribbean, 1763–1833* (New York, 1928), pp. 149–52.

72. Buxton, *Memoirs*, pp. 142–50; Klingberg, pp. 277–85; D. J. Murray, pp. 199–202.

73. *Parliamentary Debates*, 3rd. ser. XVII, pp. 1193–1231, 1260; XVIII, pp. 112–66, 204–36, 308–60, 458–524, 541–49, 573, 584–98, 1163–1228; XIX, pp. 1184–1270; XX, pp. 290–93, 340, 503, 587, 628, 753, 783. Buxton, pp. 151–59; Klingberg, pp. 285–302; D. J. Murray, p. 202. When the compensation accounts were finally closed in 1838, it was found that the actual total paid out was £17,669,401.

74. Act of 3 & 4 Will. IV, c. 73. St. Helena became a Crown colony in 1834, but since its former controllers, the East India Company, had arranged for gradual emancipation, this was not effected until May 1, 1836. Ceylon, a Crown colony since 1798, did not abolish slavery until an ordinance of 1844, and in India, though the legal status of slavery was abolished by an act, No. V of 1843, actual slavery lingered on much longer in the princely states; G. R. Mellor, p. 125, n. 116.

75. Buxton, pp. 354, 374.

76. Hinton, *Memoir of William Knibb, Missionary in Jamaica* (London, 1847), p. 228.

77. *A Twelve-month's Residence in the West Indies* (London, 1836).

78. Prospectus (December 27, 1837); W. L. Burn, p. 333.

79. Act of 1 Vic., c. 19. The details are given in W. L. Burn, p. 355, n. 2.

Chapter 6

1. *House of Commons Journals* LXIX, p. 231; *Parliamentary Debates* XXVII, pp. 640–42; F. J. Klingberg, *The Anti-Slavery Movement in England* (Yale University Press, 1926), p. 141.

2. C. K. Webster, *The Foreign Policy of Castlereagh, 1815–22* (G. Bell, 1925), pp. 454–66.

3. "The Powers, . . . declared in the face of Europe, that, considering the universal abolition of the Slave Trade as a measure particularly worthy of their attention, conformable to the spirit of the times and to the generous principles of their august Sovereigns, they are animated with the sincere desire of concurring in the most prompt and effectual execution of the means at their disposal, and of acting in the employment of these means with all the zeal and perseverance which is due to so great and noble a cause . . . ," quoted in R. Coupland, *The British Anti-Slavery Movement* (Butterworth, 1933), p. 155.

4. *P.R.O., F.O. 84* series. See also digests in *British Sessional Papers, 1844,* L; *1850,* IX, 406.

5. The forty treaties and conventions in effect with thirty-one powers in 1882, listed in the *Instructions for the Guidance of Officers employed in the Suppression of the*

Slave Trade, are given in Christopher Lloyd, *The Navy and the Slave Trade* (Longmans, 1949), Appendix E, p. 287. They do not include treaties with West African chiefs or earlier treaties since superseded.

6. Clearly, she also underestimated the increased demand for slaves that was soon to come from Cuba.

7. *Parliamentary Debates* XXXVII–XXXVIII; Klingberg, pp. 161–64.

8. In 1850, Hutt estimated that a quarter of the Royal Navy was employed in suppression, at a cost of £700,000 a year; *British Sessional Papers*, A/P (1847–48) LXIV, p. 51; *Hansard, House of Commons* (March 19, 1850); C. Lloyd, p. 129.

9. Of which Sierra Leone was hugely the most important; C. Lloyd, pp. 26, 77.

10. *Suppression of the African Slave Trade to the U.S.A.* (1896), p. 162.

11. For a statistical estimate of the effect of the Royal Navy's suppression activities, see Phillip LeVeen, "A Quantitative Analysis of the Impact of British Suppression Policies on the Volume of the Nineteenth Century Slave Trade," MSSB Conference paper given at Rochester, New York, in March 1972, to be published by Princeton University Press in 1974. The key section of the summary reads: "The total exports from Africa *during the suppressed trade period* . . . appears to have been the 1.5 million imports plus the number of slaves captured by the navy of 160,000, plus the mortality en route of 183,000, making a total disruption of 1,843,000. This compares with a disruption of 2.5 million exports which would have occurred without the intervention of the navy. Therefore, the policy impact on Africa was about 657,000 exports."

12. J. F. A. Ajayi (ed.), *Journals of the Rev. James Frederic Schon and Mr. Samuel Crowther who accompanied the Expedition up the Niger in 1841*, 2nd ed. (Frank Cass, 1970).

13. *Hansard, House of Commons* (March 19, 1850); C. Lloyd, pp. 104–14.

14. C. Lloyd, pp. 149–62.

15. The full text, with that of the League of Nations 1926 Slavery Convention and the United Nations Supplementary Convention of 1956, are given in C. W. W.

Greenidge, *Slavery* (Allen & Unwin, 1958), Appendices I–III, pp. 205–32.

16. *British Sessional Papers, A/P* (1836) VII, p. 538; (1837), pp. 238, 425.

17. B.F.A.P.S. *Constitution, Regulations* (1837), 7; G. R. Mellor, *British Imperial Trusteeship, 1783–1850* (Faber, 1951), p. 257.

18. G. R. Mellor, pp. 228–413.

19. Eric Williams, *Capitalism and Slavery*, p. 178.

20. *British Sessional Papers, A/P* (1839), XXXV, p. 107, Part One, 4 ff.; G. R. Mellor, pp. 128–33.

21. In Trinidad, wages as high as $0.65 per task, by which laborers could earn as much as 6s. a day were reported in 1842, though 3s.6d. may have been closer to the average. At the same time wages in Guyana were nearly as high. In Jamaica they were said to average 1s.6d. and in Barbados 9d.—both with cottages and grounds. In St. Kitts, wages were as low as 1s. with nothing found, and in Antigua and Montserrat, 9d. and 4d., respectively, where cottages and grounds were provided. In Nevis, once one of the most prosperous sugar islands, laborers were said to work simply for a roof over their heads and a small share of the produce of their labor; *British Sessional Papers, A/P* (1842) XXIX; Donald Wood, *Trinidad in Transition: The Years after Slavery* (Oxford University Press for IRR [1968]), pp. 53–55; D. G. Hall, *Free Jamaica 1838–65: An Economic History* (Caribbean Universities Press, 1969), p. 44.

22. The work force at Worthy Park during the period 1838–42, for example, seems to have been little different in total or personnel than during the apprenticeship period. Moreover, the continuity of labor out of crop time was far higher than on the same estate a century later. There were even aged workers living on the estate rent-free in 1842 still known by their single African names; Michael Craton and James Walvin, *A Jamaican Plantation: The History of Worthy Park, 1670–1970*, p. 216. Detailed analysis of the material continues.

23. *British Sessional Papers, Reports* (1848) XXXIX (March 1, 1848), pp. 4963–64; Craton and Walvin, pp. 215–16. Smith to Glenelg, No. 140 (July 11, 1838); *P.R.O., C.O.* 137/228; W. L. Burn, *Emancipation and Apprenticeship in the British West Indies* (Cape, 1937),

pp. 24, 359. At that time the governor was certain that a majority of Jamaicans would gladly work for wages.

24. See, for example, Raymond T. Smith, *British Guiana* (Oxford University Press for RIIA [1962]), pp. 128–34; *Negro Family in British Guiana* (Routledge, 1956), though the latter book has been criticized for a concentration on rural families not indicated in the title.

25. *Minute* by Sir George Shaw-Lefevre, enclosed in Glenelg circular to colonial governors (February 1, 1839), *British Sessional Papers, Commons,* (1839) XXXV, p. 107, Part One, 36; G. R. Mellor, p. 132.

26. The key documents are given in Shirley C. Gordon, *A Century of West Indian Education* (Longmans, 1963), pp. 19–42. The most dismaying document is the circular dispatch of March 18, 1841, under the signature of Colonial Secretary Lord John Russell rationalizing the progressive removal of the education grant on the grounds of the blacks' improvement since 1838; ibid., p. 38.

27. E. G. Wakefield, *A Letter from Sydney . . .* (London, 1829), pp. 68–82; *England and America* (London, 1833), p. 22.

28. E. G. Wakefield, *A View of the Art of Colonization* (London, 1849), pp. 328–29.

29. Proclamation of June 22, 1847; Wood, *Trinidad,* pp. 95–96.

30. G. R. Mellor, p. 135; J. H. Parry and P. M. Sherlock, *A Short History of the West Indies* (Macmillan, 1956), pp. 195–96.

31. Charles Buxton, "An Inquiry into the Results of Emancipation," in *Edinburgh Review* (April 1859) (quoted in *Buxton,* p. xxii); D. G. Hall, pp. 160–62; Parry and Sherlock, p. 196.

32. Excluding Portland Parish.

33. Excluding Metcalfe Parish.

34. D. G. Hall, pp. 160–62.

35. Phillippo, *Jamaica: Its Past and Present State,* quoted in C. Buxton, "An Inquiry," p. xxi.

36. For the 1820s, see Chapter 5.

37. Report of Select Committee on Sugar and Coffee Planting, and Papers, *British Sessional Papers, Commons,* A/P (1847–48) XXIII.

38. It was based on the success of a St. Lucia act of 1833; Craton and Walvin, pp. 234–38.

39. G. R. Mellor, pp. 163–227; D. Wood, pp. 59–170. See Table 23.

40. W. E. Gladstone to Governor Sir W. M. Gomm (May 13, 1846), *British Sessional Papers, Commons* (1846) XXVIII, p. 691, Part One, p. 354, No. 37; G. R. Mellor, p. 173.

41. That is, from sixty-one thousand to forty-one thousand; ibid., p. 172.

42. J. M. Cumpston, *Indians Overseas in British Territories, 1835–1865* (Oxford University Press, 1953).

43. W. A. Green, "The Abolition of Slavery and the British West India Sugar Industry: An Economic Assessment of the Great Experiment, 1834–1865," unpublished paper, 1972. For the factors involved in East Indian migration into Guyana, see Alan H. Adamson, "The Reconstruction of Plantation Labour after Emancipation: The Case of British Guiana," MSSB Conference paper given at Rochester, New York in March 1972, to be published by Princeton University Press, 1974; George W. Roberts and M. A. Johnson, "Factors involved in Immigration and Movements in the Working Force of British Guiana in the Nineteenth Century" and Lesley Key, "East Indian Immigrants and the Afro-Guyanese, 1871–1921," both conference papers given at Mona, Jamaica, in April 1972, published in the *Transactions of the Fourth Conference of Caribbean Historians,* 1972. For three papers from the same conference dealing respectively with Chinese, European, and free African immigration into Jamaica, given at the same conference, see Jacqueline Levy, "Chinese Indentured Immigration to Jamaica during the latter part of the Nineteenth Century"; Douglas Hall, "Bountied European Immigration into Jamaica, with special reference to the German settlement at Seaford Town up to 1850"; and Monica Schuler, "The Experience of African Immigrants in 19th Century Jamaica."

44. Table 21 derived from Noel Deerr, *History of Sugar,* 2 vols. I, pp. 193–203; II, p. 377; W. A. Green, "Abolition," Table Two.

45. Cardwell to Eyre (June 14, 1865), *P.R.O., C.O.,* pp. 137–391, 222.

46. *Daily News* (November–December 1866), quoted by Bernard Semmel, *Jamaican Blood and Victorian Conscience* (Houghton Mifflin, 1963), pp. 131–32.

47. *Spectator* (June 1868), quoted by Semmel, p. 171.

48. Craton and Walvin, pp. 251–54.

49. West India Royal Commission, *British Sessional Papers, Commons,* (1898) LI, pp. 1096–1104 (April 1, 1897).

50. Finding its most curious converts among the ignorant, mock-brutal, and racist English "Skinheads" and "Bovver Boys."

51. Andrew Pearse, "Carnival in Nineteenth Century Trinidad," in *Caribbean Quarterly* IV, 3–4 (1956), pp. 176–93.

52. ". . . In the towns during Christmas holidays they have several tall robust fellows dressed up in grotesque habits, and a pair of ox-horns on their head sprouting from the top of a horrid sort of vizor or mask, about which the mouth is rendered very terrific with large boar tusks. The masquerader, carrying a wooden sword in his hand is followed by a numerous crowd of drunken women, who dance at every door, bellowing out John Connu! with great vehemence. . . . *In 1769, several new masks appeared; the Ebos, the Papaws, etc. having their respective Connus, male and female, who were dressed in a very laughable style. . . . ,*" Edward Long, *History of Jamaica,* 2 vols. (London, 1774) II, pp. 424–25, quoted in H. O. Patterson, *Sociology of Slavery* (MacGibbon & Kee, 1967).

53. H. O. Patterson, pp. 244–45.

54. Butt-Thompson, *West African Secret Societies,* pp. 86–91, quoted in H. O. Patterson, pp. 245–46. The ceremony described was the Homowo Festival of the Ga.

55. It is perhaps significant that in Nassau the "native" night clubs and hangouts for prostitutes, which used to be "Over the Hill" in the black residential area and close to the "Jumper" churches, have in recent years migrated closer to the heart of the downtown area. Such is progress.

56. R. T. Smith, *Negro Family;* M. G. Smith, *West Indian Family Structure* (University of Washington Press, 1962); *The Plural Society in the British West Indies* (University of California Press, 1965); Edith Clarke, *My Mother Who Fathered Me* (Allen & Unwin, 1957).

57. See, for example, Richard Frucht, "A Caribbean Social Type: Neither 'Peasant' nor 'Proletarian,'" in *Social and Economic Studies* XIII, 3 (1967), pp. 295–300. For

a somewhat oversystematic definition of classes in West Indian plantation society, see Eric R. Wolf, "Specific Aspects of Plantation Systems in the New World: Community Sub-cultures and Social Classes," on *Social Science Monograph* VII (Washington, D.C. Pan American Union [1959]), in M. M. Horowitz (ed.), *Peoples and Cultures of the Caribbean* (Natural History Press for American Museum of Natural History, 1971).

58. Cf., for example, the almost exactly similar behaviors cited by John Shipman, *Thoughts on the Present State of Religion among the Negroes in Jamaica* (1820), Vol. 90, Wesleyan Missionary Society Archives mss., quoted by E. Brathwaite, *The Development of Creole Society in Jamaica, 1770–1820* (Clarendon Press, 1971), p. 299.

59. M. J. and F. S. Herskovits, *Trinidad Village* (Knopf, 1947), pp. 295–96, quoted in M. M. Horowitz, pp. 7–8.

60. M. M. Horowitz, p. 8, citing E. F. Frazier, *The Negro Family in the United States* (Holt, Rinehart, 1948), pp. 360–61. See also Chapter 4.

61. Or in the Bahamas, in the Out Islands.

62. Herskovits, *Trinidad Village*, p. 296.

63. "Social Aspects of the Sugar Industry," in *New World* V, 1–2; *Croptime*, 1969, pp. 47–49.

Compare Faustin Charles' poem *Sugar Cane:*

Cane is sweet sweat slain;
Cane is labour unrecognized, lost and unrecovered;
Sugar is the sweet swollen pain of the years;
Sugar is slavery's immovable stain. . . . Quoted in Andrew Salkey (ed.), *Breaklight* (Hamish Hamilton, 1971), p. 185.

64. Craton and Walvin, pp. 298–303.

65. Lloyd Best, "Outlines of a Model of Pure Plantation Economy," in *Social and Economic Studies* (September 1968). See also George Beckford, *Persistent Poverty: Underdevelopment in plantation economies of the Third World* (Oxford University Press, 1972).

66. George Beckford, review article on "A Jamaican Plantation," in *Jamaica Journal* (September 1971).

67. Mazisi Kunene, Introduction to Aimé Cesaire, *Return to my Native Land* (Penguin, 1969), pp. 10–11.

68. Aimé Cesaire, ibid., p. 75.

69. Basil Davidson, *Black Mother* (Gollancz, 1961), pp. 245–47.

70. Eric Williams, *Columbus to Castro* (Deutsch, 1970), pp. 503–4.

71. Ibid., p. 502.

72. V. S. Naipaul, *The Middle Passage* (Deutsch, 1962), pp. 28–29.

SUGGESTIONS FOR
FURTHER READING AND
RESEARCH

Assiduous readers of the notes will already have a clear notion of the chief sources for this book. Those notes should also provide an adequate guide for specialized further reading in the topical areas covered in each chapter. To avoid duplication, what follows here is therefore aimed chiefly at those who wish to pursue further research, although a short section of general works is included at pages 392–98. This is preceded by a list of guides and bibliographies, a list of printed collections of documents, and survey of the chief documentary sources.

1. Guides and Bibliographies

Those marked "°" are general books with extensive bibliographies

Andrews, C. M., *Guide to the Materials for American History to 1783 in the Public Record Office of Great Britain*, 2 vols. (Carnegie Institute, 1912–14).

Andrews, C. M. and Davenport, F. G., *Guide to the Manuscript Materials for the History of the United States to 1783, in the British Museum, in Minor London Archives, and the Libraries of Oxford and Cambridge* (Carnegie Institute, 1908).

Baker, E. C., *Guide to the Records in the Leeward Islands* (Oxford University Press for the University of the West Indies, 1965).

——, *Guide to the Windward Islands* (Oxford University Press for the University of the West Indies, 1968).

Bell, H. C. and Parker, D. W., *Guide to the British West Indian Archive Materials in London and in the Islands for the History of the United States* (Carnegie Institute, 1926).

Chandler, M. J., *A Guide to the Records in Barbados* (Oxford University Press for the University of the West Indies, 1965).

Clark, George N., *A Guide to English Commercial Statistics, 1696–1782* (Oxford University Press, 1936).

Comitas, Lambros, *Caribbeans 1900–1963: A topical bibliography* (Seattle, Washington, for the Research Institute for the Study of Man, 1968).

Foner, Eric (ed.), *America's Black Past: A Reader in Afro-American History* (Harper, 1970), pp. 557–77.*

Ford, P. and G., *A Guide to the British Parliamentary Papers* (H. M. Stationery Office, 1956).

Goveia, Elsa, *Slave Society in the British Leeward Islands at the End of the Eighteenth Century* (Yale University Press, 1965), pp. 339–51.*

Giuseppi, M. S., *A Guide to the Manuscripts Preserved in the Public Record Office*, 2 vols. (H. M. Stationery Office, 1923–24).

Greene, E. B. and Morris, R. B., *A Guide to the Principal Sources for Early American History (1600–1800) in the City of New York* (Columbia University Press, 1929).

Griffin, G. G., *Guide to Reproduced Materials from British Archives at the Library of Congress* (U. S. Government Printing Office, 1925).

Gropp, Arthur E., *Guide to Libraries and Archives in Central America and the West Indies, Panama, Bermuda, and British Guiana* (Tulane University Press, 1941).

Jordan, W. D., *White over Black: American Attitudes Toward the Negro, 1550–1812* (University of North Carolina Press, 1968), pp. 586–614.*

Mauro, Frederic, *L'Expansion Europeene, 1600–1870* (Paris: Nouvelle Clio, 1964).*

Miller, Elizabeth, *The Negro in America: A Bibliography* (Harvard University Press, 1966).

Ragatz, L. J., *A Guide for the Study of British Caribbean History 1763–1834* (American Historical Association, 1932).

——, *Check List of House of Commons Sessional Papers Relating to the British West Indies and to the West Indian Slave Trade and Slavery 1763–1834* (Bryan Edwards Press, 1923).

——, *Check List of House of Lords Sessional Papers Relating to the British West Indies and to the West Indian Slave Trade and Slavery 1763–1834* (Bryan Edwards Press, 1931).

——, *A Guide to the Official Correspondence of the Governors of the British West India Colonies with the Secretary of State 1763–1833* (Bryan Edwards Press, n.d.).

Rose, J. Holland et al. (eds.), *The Cambridge History of the British Empire: Volume I, the Old Empire from the Beginnings to 1783; Volume 2, The Growth of the New Empire 1783–1870* (Cambridge University Press, 1929, 1940).*

Sypher, W., *Guinea's Captive Kings: British Anti-Slavery Literature of the XVIIIth Century* (University of North Carolina Press, 1942).

Williams, Eric E., *From Columbus to Castro: The History of the Caribbean, 1492–1969* (Deutsch, 1970), pp. 156–58.

——, *British Historians and the West Indies* (Deutsch, 1966).

Work, M. N., *Bibliography of the Negro in Africa and America* (Wilson, 1928).

2. Documents: Printed Collections

Augier, Fitzroy R. and Gordon, Shirley C., *Sources of West Indian History* (Longmans, 1962).

Bell, K. N. and Morrell, W. P., *Select Documents on British Colonial Policy, 1831–1860* (Oxford University Press, 1928).

Catterall, H. T., *Judicial Cases concerning Negro Slavery*, 2 vols. (Carnegie Institute, 1927).

Craton, M. and Walvin, J., *Slavery, Abolition and Emancipation: A Thematic Documentary* (Longmans, 1974).

Curtin, P. D., *Africa Remembered: Narratives by West Africans from the Era of the Slave Trade* (University of Wisconsin Press, 1967).

Davenport, F. G., *European Treaties bearing on the History of the United States and its Dependencies*, 4 vols. (Carnegie Institute, 1917–37).

Davidson, Basil, *The African Past: Chronicles from Antiquity to Modern Times* (Longmans, 1964).

Donnan, Elizabeth, *Documents Illustrative of the History of the Slave Trade to America* (Carnegie Institute, 1930–31).

Encyclopaedia Britannica, *The Negro in American History*, 3 vols. (Chicago, 1969).

Fishel, L. H. and Quarles, B., *The Negro American: A Documentary History* (Scott, Foresman, 1967).

Hakluyt, Richard, *The Principal Navigations, Voyages, Traffiques & Discoveries of the English Nation . . .* (1582 etc.), 7 vols. (Dent, Everyman Edition, 1926).

Harlow, V. T. and Madden, F. W., *British Colonial Developments, 1774–1834, Select Documents* (Oxford University Press, 1953).

McCall, Daniel F., *Africa in Time-Perspective* (Boston University Press and Oxford University Press, 1964).

Navarrete, F. de, *Collección de los viajes y descubrimientos que hicieron por mar los espanoles desdes fines del siglo XV*, 5 vols. (Madrid, 1825–37); with catalogue by V. Vicente Vela (Madrid, 1946).

Oliver, Roland A. and Caroline, *Africa in the Days of Exploration* (Prentice-Hall, 1965).

Oliver, V. L., *Caribbeana: Being Miscellaneous Papers Relating to the History, Genealogy, Topography, and Antiquities of the British West Indies* (Mitchell, Hughes & Clarke, 1909–19).

Pacheco, J. F. et al., *Documentos Inéditos de America. Colección de documentos inéditos relativos al descubrimiento, conquista y colonización de las posesiones espanoles en America y Oceania, sacados de los archivos del reino, y muy especialmente del de Indias*, 42 vols. (Madrid, 1864–84); with index by Ernesto Schafer (Madrid, 1947).

Sainsbury, Noel et al., *Calendar of State Papers, Colonial, America and West Indies, 1574–1783*, 44 vols. (Longmans and H. M. Stationery Office, 1860–1969).

Stock, L. F., *Proceedings and Debates in the British Parliaments Respecting North America*, 5 vols. (Carnegie Institute, 1924–41).

Walvin, James, *The Black Presence: A Documentary History of the Negro in England* (Orbach and Chambers, 1971).

Williams, Eric E., *Documents of West Indian History, 1492–1655* (Port-of-Spain, Trinidad: P.N.P., 1963).

——, *The British West Indies at Westminster. Extracts from the Debates in the British Parliament, Part 1, 1789–1823.* (Port-of-Spain, Trinidad, for Historical Society of Trinidad and Tobago, 1954).

——, *Documents on British West Indian History, 1807–33.* (Port-of-Spain, Trinidad, for Historical Society of Trinidad and Tobago, 1962).

To this section should be added mention of the huge and invaluable collection of edited documents published by the Hakluyt Society, and to the steadily growing list of reprint titles in African, Caribbean, and general black history published by the houses of Cass, Dawson's, Kraus, Peter Smith, Arno Press (New York *Times*) Archon, Octagon, Negro Universities Press, etc.

3. Documents: General Sources

Even to summarize adequately the available documentary material is impossible in the space available here. The researcher is best advised to start with the general guides listed in Section 1, particularly those by Andrews, Andrews and Davenport, Baker, Bell and Parker, Chandler, Ford, Giuseppi, and (most valuable of all) Ragatz. Beyond this, each researcher is his own explorer, fortunate if he can balance his research satisfactorily between metropolitan and colonial archives and between printed and manuscript materials, but in any case almost certain to discover areas not yet worked on by scholars.

(a) Metropolitan Sources

Of material already printed, the British Sessional Papers are probably the most valuable. The entire run for the eighteenth and nineteenth century—an inexhaustible mine that includes in its plenitude, for example, all of the Reports of the Historical Manuscripts Commission—is now available on microcard. A large number of volumes (misleadingly numerous since they are still highly selective) have also been reprinted in handsome topical sets by the Irish University Press, including about forty volumes on the suppression of the slave trade. The Papers emanate either from the Commons or Lords, but the former are nearly always the more valuable, the latter being generally less detailed and rarely unduplicated. The chief source materials come either as "Accounts and Papers" or as "Reports," the distinction between which is not in the earlier days completely clear. The following are the most obviously valuable sources: *British Sessional Papers, House of Commons, Accounts and Papers,* XXIV–XXVI (1789), pp. 626–646a; XXIX–XXX (1790), pp. 697–99; XXXIV (1790–91), pp. 745–48; XXXV (1792), pp. 766–70; XLII (1795–96), p. 845; XLV (1797–98), pp. 931–32; XLVIII (1798–99), pp. 964–70, 987b; XLVI (1831–32), p. 93; XXIII (1848), p. 1; LXVII (1852–53), p. 2; *House of Commons, Reports,* V (1778–82), pp. 44, 47; IX (1790–92), p. 98; XX (1831–32), p. 721; XV (1836); XXXI, LI (1866); XLVI (1884); LI (1898).

Among the Sessional Papers are also found volumes of bills which, once they became laws, were periodically collected in such series as the *Statutes at Large,* 12 vols. (London, 1812). For the activities within Parliament itself, see William Cobbett (ed.), *Parliamentary History of England from the Earliest Period to the Year 1803* (London, 1804–7), continued after 1803 as the *Parliamentary Debates,* under the editorship of Cobbett, T. C. Hansard, and their successors. To this increasingly official record should be added the reports and comments provided by the *Annual Register* (founded in 1759 and originally edited by Edmund Burke) and such newspapers and periodicals as *The Times* (from 1785) and *Gentleman's Magazine* (1731).

The British Museum Library probably contains the most complete collections of contemporary books and pamphlets, especially on travels and economic theory, but the Bodleian Library at Oxford, the New York Public Library, and the Library of Congress, Washington, D.C., run close. Perhaps the best collections of printed materials on both sides of the emancipist controversy are to be found in the Goldsmiths' Library, University of London, and at Rhodes House, Oxford.

Of purely manuscript sources, the Public Record Office in London is easily the richest. The most valuable single series is probably the original correspondence to and from colonial governors in the Colonial Office archives (C.O.), though useful materials are to be found in the Board of Trade (B.T.), Treasury (T.), Privy Council (P.C.), and Admiralty (Adm.) series, in the papers of the Royal African Company, the Registrar of Slaves, and the Encumbered Estates Commissioners, and in such miscellaneous collections as the Chatham Papers (P.R.O. 30/8). Nearly all are adequately indexed.

Papers in the manuscript collections of the British Museum are far less adequately indexed, but untold riches exist in the Sloane, Egerton and Additional Manuscripts for the adventurous researcher—such as the mass of little-used material in *Egerton* 2395 and *B.M. Add. Mss.* 411 (Povey Papers), and the raw materials gathered but never used by Edward Long for the revision of his *History of Jamaica* (*B.M. Add. Mss.* 12,402–40, 18,270–75, 18,959–63, 21,931–22,639, 22,676–80).

The minutes of the various committees of West Indian Planters and Merchants, dating from 1769, lodged with the West India Committee, 18 Grosvenor Street, London, are invaluable in tracing slaveholders' strategy and tactics. The Granville Sharp Papers at Hardwicke Court, Gloucester, are among the best of the sources for the other side of the struggle. Many records from trading concerns, plantations, or local abolitionist societies can be found in English county record offices. Sources for the colonial activities of the Church of England are to be found at Fulham Palace and in the London archives of the SPG and SPCK, and important sectarian missionary records are among the London archives of the Baptist Missionary Society, Wesleyan Missionary Society, and the Moravian Church.

(b) Colonial Sources

Although notoriously the victims of damp, decay, and neglect, records in the former colonies are too numerous and various to list in any detail here. They are well listed in outline by such as Baker, Chandler, and Gropp, though lamentably many of the records listed by Bell and Parker (1926) disappeared before the spread of modern archive and preservation techniques. Printed materials usually include local laws, legislative records (generally called either Journals or Votes) and a surprisingly rich variety of newspapers. Local archives, particularly in Jamaica and Barbados, also contain a daunting wealth of estate records and maps as well as official records dating from the earliest days: land patents, deeds, wills, absentees' and minors' inventories and crop records, parish and court records, as well as the official deficiency, registration, and manumission returns.

4. General Works

Andrews, C. M., *The Colonial Period in American History*, 4 vols. (Yale University Press, 1936–38).

Ayearst, Morley, *The British West Indies: The Search for Self-Government* (New York University Press, 1960).

Barrett, W., "Caribbean Sugar Production Standards in the Seventeenth and Eighteenth Centuries," in J. Parker (ed.), *Merchants and Scholars* (University of Minnesota Press, 1967), pp. 147–70.

Beckford, G. L., *Persistent Poverty: Underdevelopment in Plantation Economies of the Third World* (Oxford University Press, 1972).

Beer, G. L., *The Old Colonial System, 1660–1754* (Smith, 1933).

Bell, Herbert C., "The West India Trade before the American Revolution," in *American Historical Review* XXII (1917), pp. 272–87.

Boorstin, D. L., *The Americans: Vol. I, The Colonial Experience* (New York, 1958).

Bosch, Juan, *De Cristobal Colon a Fidel Castro*.

Boxer, C. R., *The Dutch Seaborne Empire, 1600–1800* (Hutchinson, 1965).

———, *The Portuguese Seaborne Empire, 1415–1825* (Hutchinson, 1965).

Brathwaite, Edward, *The Development of Creole Society in Jamaica, 1770–1820* (Clarendon Press, 1971).

Bridenbaugh, Carl and Roberta, *No Peace Beyond the Line; the English in the Caribbean, 1624–1690* (Oxford University Press, 1972).

Burn, W. L., *The British West Indies* (Hutchinson, 1951).

Caines, Clement, *Letters on the Cultivation of the Otaheite Cane, the manufacture of sugar and rum . . .* (London, 1801).

Caldecott, A., *The Church in the West Indies* (London, 1898).

Chalmers, George, *Opinions on Interesting Subjects of Public Law and Commercial Policy arising from American Independence* (London, 1784).

Coke, Thomas, *A History of the West Indies, containing the Natural Civil and Ecclesiastical History of each Island . . .*, 3 vols. (Liverpool, 1808).

Craton, Michael and Walvin, James, *A Jamaican Plantation: The History of Worthy Park, 1670–1970* (W. H. Allen and University of Toronto Press, 1970).

Curtin, Philip D., *The Image of Africa* (University of Wisconsin Press, 1964).

——, *The Atlantic Slave Trade: A Census* (University of Wisconsin Press, 1969).

——, "Epidemiology and the Slave Trade," in *Political Science Quarterly* LXXXIII, 2 (June 1968), pp. 190–216.

Davidson, Basil, *Black Mother* (Gollancz, 1961).

Davies, Kenneth G., "The Origins of the Commission System in the West India Trade," in *Transactions of the Royal Historical Society*, 5th series II (1952), pp. 89–107.

Davis, David B., *The Problem of Slavery in Western Culture* (Cornell University Press, 1966).

Deerr, Noel, *The History of Sugar*, 2 vols. (Chapman & Hall, 1949–50).

Dunn, R. S., *Sugar and Slaves; the Role of the Planter Class in the English West Indies, 1624–1713* (University of North Carolina Press, 1972).

Edwards, Bryan, *The History, Civil and Commercial, of the British Colonies in the West Indies*, 2 vols. (London, 1793).

Elkins, Stanley, *Slavery: A Problem in American Institutional and Intellectual Life* (University of Chicago Press, 1959).

Fage, John D., *An Introduction to the History of West Africa* (Cambridge University Press, 1955).

Fanon, Frantz, *Black Skin, White Masks* (Paris, 1952).

Fortescue, J. W., *A History of the British Army*, 14 vols. (Macmillan, 1910–35).

Freyre, Gilberto, *The Masters and the Slaves* (Knopf, 1946).

Froude, J. A., *The English in the West Indies* (London, 1887).

Genovese, Eugene D., *The Political Economy of Slavery* (Random House, 1961).

Genovese, E. D. and Engerman, S. L. (eds.) *Race and Slavery in the Western World* (Princeton University Press, 1974).

Gipson, Lawrence, H., *The British Empire before the American Revolution*, 13 vols. (Knopf, 1946–68).

Girvan, N. and Jefferson, O. (eds.), *Readings in the Political Economy of the Caribbean* (New World Group, 1971).

Goveia, Elsa, *Slave Society in the British Leeward Islands at the End of the Eighteenth Century* (Yale University Press, 1965).

———, *The West Indian Slave Laws* (Caribbean Universities Press, 1971).

Gratus, Jack, *The Great White Lie: Slavery, Emancipation and Changing Racial Attitudes* (Hutchinson, 1973).

Guérin, Daniel, *The West Indies and their Future* (1956) (Dobson, 1961).

Guerra y Sanchez, R., *Sugar and Society in the Caribbean* (1935) (Yale University Press, 1964).

Handlin, Oscar, *Race and Nationality in American Life* (Doubleday, 1957).

Harper, Lawrence, *The English Navigation Laws* (Columbia University Press, 1939).

Herskovits, Melville J., *The Myth of the Negro Past* (Harper, 1941).

———, "On the Provenience of the New World Negroes," in *Social Forces* 12 (1933), pp. 247–62.

———, "Social History of the Negro," in *Handbook of Social Psychology* (Worcester, Massachusetts, 1935).

Hofstadter, Richard B., *American at 1750: A Social Portrait* (Cape, 1972).

Horowitz, Michael M. (ed.), *Peoples and Cultures of the Caribbean* (Natural History Press, 1971).

James, C. L. R., *Black Jacobins* (Secker and Warburg and Random House, 1963).

Kingsley, Charles, *At Last: A Christmas in the West Indies*, 2 vols. (New York and London).

Kuczynski, R. R., *Demographic Survey of the British Colonial Empire*, 4 vols. (Oxford University Press, 1948–53).

Labaree, L. W., *Royal Government in America: A Study of the British Colonial System before 1783* (Oxford University Press, 1930).

Labat, J. B., *Nouveaux Voyage aux Isles de l'Amerique*, 6 vols. (The Hague, 1724).

Lewis, Gordon K., *The Growth of the Modern West Indies* (MacGibbon & Kee, 1968).

Long, Edward, *The History of Jamaica*, 2 vols. (London, 1774).

Macpherson, David, *Annals of Commerce . . .* , 4 vols. (London, 1805).

Manning, Helen T., *British Colonial Government after the American Revolution* (Oxford University Press, 1933).

Mannix, Daniel P. and Cowley, Malcolm, *Black Cargoes: A History of the Atlantic Slave Trade, 1518–1865* (Viking Press, 1962).

Martin, Gaston, *Histoire de l'esclaves dans les colonies françaises* (Paris, 1948).

Martin, R. Montgomery, *The British Colonies: Their history, extent, condition and resources*, 6 vols. (London and New York, 1851–57).

Merivale, Herman, *Lectures on Colonization and Colonies, Delivered before the University of Oxford in 1839, 1840, 1841* (Oxford University Press, 1928).

Mintz, Sydney, *Worker in the Cane: A Puerto Rican Life History* (Yale University Press, 1960).

Neill, Stephen, *Christian Missions* (Penguin, 1964).

Newton, Arthur P., *The European Nations in the West Indies, 1493–1688* (Macmillan, 1933).

Ortiz y Fernandez, Fernando, *Contrapunteo cubano del tabaco y el azucar . . .* (Santa Clara, Cuba, 1963).

Pares, Richard, *A West India Fortune* (Longmans, 1950).

———, *Yankees and Creoles* (Longmans, 1956).

———, *Merchants and Planters* (Cambridge University Press, 1960).

Parkinson, C. Northcote, *The Trade Winds: A Study of British Overseas Trade during the French Wars, 1795–1815* (Allen & Unwin, 1948).

Parry, John H., _The Age of Reconnaissance_ (Weidenfeld and Nicolson, 1963).

———, _The Spanish Seaborne Empire_ (Hutchinson, 1966).

———, _Trade and Dominion: The European Overseas Empires in the Eighteenth Century_ (Weidenfeld and Nicolson, 1971).

———, "The Patent Offices in the British West Indies," in _English Historical Review_ (April 1945), p. 200.

Parry, John H. and Sherlock, P. M., _A Short History of the West Indies_ (Longmans, 1956).

Patterson, H. Orlando, _The Sociology of Slavery: An Analysis of the Origins, Development and Structure of a Negro Slave Society in Jamaica_ (MacGibbon & Kee, 1967).

Penson, Lilian M., _The Colonial Agents of the British West Indies_ (University of London Press, 1924).

———, "The London West India Interest in the Eighteenth Century," in _English Historical Review_ (July 1921).

Phillips, Ulrich B., _American Negro Slavery_ (Appleton, 1918).

Pitman, Frank W., _The Development of the British West Indies, 1700–1763_ (Yale University Press, 1917).

———, "Slavery on British West India Plantations in the Eighteenth Century," in _Journal of Negro History_ XI (1926), pp. 584–668.

Pope-Hennessy, James, _Sins of the Fathers: A Study of the Atlantic Slave Traders, 1441–1807_ (Weidenfeld, and Knopf, 1967).

Postlethwayt, Malachi, _The Universal Dictionary of Trade and Commerce_ (London, 1751).

Ragatz, L. J., _The Fall of the Planter Class in the British Caribbean, 1763–1833_ (American Historical Association, 1928).

———, _Absentee Landlordism in the British Caribbean, 1750–1833_ (1931). Privately reprinted from _Agricultural History_.

Raynal, G. F., _Histoire philosophique et politique des establissements et du commerce des europeans dans les deux indes_ (Geneva, 1780).

Rotberg, Robert I., _A Political History of Tropical Africa_ (Harcourt, Brace, 1965).

Rottenberg, Simon, "The Business of Slave Trading," in _South Atlantic Quarterly_ LXVI (1967), pp. 409–23.

Roughley, Thomas, *The Jamaica Planters' Guide* . . . (London, 1823).

Sauer, C. O., *Agricultural Origins and Dispersals* (American Geographical Society, 1952).

Scelle, Georges, *La Traite Négrière aux Indes de Castille*, 2 vols. (Paris, 1906).

Schuyler, R. L., *Parliament and The British Empire* (Columbia University Press, 1929).

Semmel, Bernard, *The Rise of Free Trade Imperialism: Classical Political Economy, the Empire of Free Trade and Imperialism, 1750–1850* (Cambridge University Press, 1970).

Sewell, W., *The Ordeal of Free Labour in the British West Indies* (New York, 1861).

Sheridan, Richard B., *Sugar and Slavery* (Caribbean Universities Press, 1974).

———, *The Development of the Plantations to 1750; An Era of West Indian Prosperity, 1750–1775* (Caribbean Universities Press, 1970).

———, "The Molasses Act and the Market Strategy of the British Sugar Planters," in *Journal of Economic History* XVII (1957), pp. 62–83.

———, "The Commercial and Financial Organization of the British Slave Trade, 1750–1807," in *Economic History Review*, 2nd series XI, 2 (1958), pp. 249–63.

———, "The Rise of a Colonial Gentry," in *English Historical Review* (April 1961).

———, "The Wealth of Jamaica in the Eighteenth Century," in *Economic History Review*, 2nd series XVIII, 2 (1965), pp. 292–303; with "Rejoinder" to R. P. Thomas, ibid. XXI, 8 (1968), pp. 30–61.

———, "Africa and the Caribbean in the Atlantic Slave Trade," in *American Historical Review* LXXVII, 1 (1972), pp. 15–35.

Sio, Arnold, "Society, Slavery and the Slaves," in *Social and Economic Studies* (1967).

Sloane, Hans, *A Journey to the Islands Madera, Barbados, Nieves, St. Christophers and Jamaica* . . . (London, 1707).

Smith, Adam, *The Wealth of Nations* (1776) (Random House, 1937).

Smith, Michael G., *The Plural Society in the British West Indies*.

Southey, Thomas, *Chronological History of the West Indies*, 3 vols. (London, 1827).

Tannenbaum, Frank, *Slave and Citizen: The Negro in the Americas* (Knopf, 1947).

Temperley, Howard. *British Antislavery, 1833–1870* (Allen Lane, Penguin, 1972).

Thomas, R. P., "The Sugar Colonies of the Old Empire: Profit or Loss for Great Britain?," in *Economic History Review* XXI, 1 (1968), pp. 30–45.

Thompson, H. P., *Into All Lands: The History of the Society for the Propagation of the Gospel in Foreign Parts, 1701–1950* (SPCK, 1951; Macmillan, 1952).

Trollope, Anthony, *The West Indies and the Spanish Main* (London, 1860).

Walvin, James, *Black and White: The History of the Negro in England, 1555–1945* (Longmans, 1973).

Williams, Eric E., *Capitalism and Slavery* (1944) (Deutsch, 1964).

———, *From Columbus to Castro* (Deutsch, 1970).

———, "The Negro in the West Indies," in *The Negro in the Americas* (Howard University, 1940).

———, "The Golden Age of the Slave System in Britain," in *Journal of Negro History* XXV (1940), pp. 60–106.

———, "The Historical Background of Race Relations in the Caribbean," in *Miscelanea de Estudios dedicados al Dr. Fernando Ortiz*, Vol. 3 (Havana, 1957).

Williams, Glyndwr, *The Expansion of Europe in the Eighteenth Century* (Blandford, 1966).

Wyndham, Hugh A., *The Atlantic and Slavery* (Oxford University Press, 1935).

Young, Sir William, *The West-India Common-Place Book* (London, 1807).

INDEX